1995.

Driving Down
Health Care Costs
STRATEGIES AND SOLUTIONS

1995

A PANEL PUBLICATION
ASPEN PUBLISHERS, INC.

Copyright © 1995

by
PANEL PUBLISHERS
A division of Aspen Publishers, Inc.
A Wolters Kluwer Company
36 West 44th Street
New York, NY 10036
(212) 790-2000

ISBN 1-56706-139-7

Printed in the United States of America

About Panel Publishers

Panel Publishers derives its name from a panel of business professionals who organized in 1964 to publish authoritative, timely books, information services, and journals written by specialists in the areas of human resources administration, compensation, and benefits management, and pension planning and compliance to assist business professionals, as well as owners of small to medium-sized businesses and their legal and financial advisors. Our mission is to provide practical, solution-based "how-to" information to these practitioners.

Panel's list of publications includes the following:

Managing Employee Health Benefits

Compensation & Benefits Management

Medical Benefits Newsletter

Employee Benefits Answer Book

The Americans With Disabilities Act: Revised Edition

COBRA Handbook

State by State Guide to Human Resources Law

Nonqualified Deferred Compensation Answer Book

Hiring Handbook

Flexible Benefits Answer Book

Flexible Benefits Newsletter

Executive Compensation Answer Book

The Pension Answer Book

401(k) Answer Book

Managed Care Answer Book

163, 170

PANEL PUBLISHERS
A division of Aspen Publishers, Inc.
Practical Solutions for Business Professionals

SUBSCRIPTION NOTICE

This Panel product is updated on a periodic basis with supplements to reflect important changes in the subject matter. If you purchased this product directly from Panel Publishers, we have already recorded your subscription for this update service.

If, however, you purchased this product from a bookstore and wish to receive future updates and revised or related volumes billed separately with a 30-day examination review, please contact our Customer Service Department at 1-301-698-9342 or send your name, company name (if applicable), address, and the title of the product to:

PANEL PUBLISHERS
A division of Aspen Publishers, Inc.

7201 McKinney Circle
Frederick, MD 21701

Preface

With health care premium increases running at twice the inflation rate for many companies, health care cost control remains a priority. The 1995 edition of *Driving Down Health Care Costs* provides an inside look at how leading employers have successfully implemented specific cost control initiatives. You will learn:

- How Digital Equipment Corporation is simultaneously reducing costs and improving the quality of health care provided by its HMOs.
- What health care data Mobil is analyzing to guide its health care cost control efforts.
- Why GTE decided to set up its own corporate clinic—and what cost control measures the company designed into its ambitious plan.
- How Quaker Oats involved employees in making the difficult decisions that arose while designing a flexible benefits plan.
- What actions IBM took to soften the impact of health care cost control measures—a communications strategy that has kept employee satisfaction high while reining in costs.
- Why Parker Hannifin has largely managed to avoid benefit cutbacks and cost shifting with an innovative "self-managed" plan design that has held cost increases to about half the national average.

Effective health care cost control entails far more than cutting benefits and shifting costs. As employers have learned, making the wrong cuts can actually increase bottom line health costs. *Driving Down Health Care Costs* will help you avoid plan design mistakes while pointing out the legal pitfalls in managed care, wellness, workers' compensation, and employee assistance programs. The 1995 edition will also help you understand and respond to health care reform initiatives at federal—and state—levels.

While health benefits management remains a key corporate challenge, there is good news about health care cost control efforts. Employers are reducing costs and improving employee satisfaction by focusing on quality. Finding strength in numbers, employers are banding together in cities and rural communities to control health care costs. *Driving Down Health Care Costs* provides reliable guidance for corporate benefits executives, showing what has worked, what hasn't, and why. For example:

- Thinking about a point-of-service plan—or having problems with one that's been implemented? Find out how USAir dealt with the explosion of employee complaints that accompanied its introduction of a point-of-service plan.
- What would you expect to happen when a company increases its mental health benefits? Conoco did just that and saved almost $3 million in claims.
- What's the best performing health benefits program in America? Arguably, it's one run by the federal government for its own employees. See for yourself how it works.
- Have you heard the reports that only 12 percent of companies with wellness programs can attribute health cost savings to them? Learn what successful companies already know about making wellness work.

No other source pulls together so many current reports on health care cost control efforts from such a diverse range of corporations and health benefits experts. Whether you're looking for a new perspective on utilization management, an update on benefits technology, the latest thinking on case management, tips on improving plan administration, or ways to reduce workers' compensation costs, *Driving Down Health Care Costs* offers practical, proven advice that can help you make the most effective decisions about health care benefits.

Contributors

Eugene R. Anderson is a partner in the New York, Washington, DC, Newark, New Jersey, Palo Alto, California and Philadelphia law firm of Anderson Kill Olick & Oshinsky, P.C.

Kathleen Angel has more than 20 years experience in the field of health care benefits.

Bruce Barlow is a managing consultant in Towers Perrin's general management consulting practice in Chicago.

David W. Barr is CFO and senior vice president of finance and strategic planning at PacifiCare of California in Cypress, California.

Paul M. Bernstein is an associate professor at Duquesne University, Department of Counseling, Psychology and Special Education, director of Pennsylvania Psychological Services and a forensic psychologist in Pittsburgh.

W. David Blake, MHA, is a health benefits consultant in Mission Viejo, California.

Sibyl C. Bogardus, JD, is an employee benefits attorney specializing in the area of welfare benefits and qualified plans. Her areas of expertise include Americans with Disabilities Act (ADA), COBRA, disclosure requirements under ERISA, and compliance with Internal Revenue Code requirements for favorable tax treatment of benefits. Ms. Bogardus received her undergraduate degree in history from Duke University, cum laude, and her JD from Washington University.

Shari Caudron is a freelance writer based in Denver.

Alfred C. Clapp, Jr., CLU, is president of Financial Strategies and Services Corporation. He has been a financial executive with Chase, IBM, Irving Trust and Merrill Lynch, and served as chief financial officer of three other companies. He has taught finance, chaired fund raising drives, and is a frequent speaker, seminar sponsor, newsletter publisher and author of long term care articles. He is active in the New York City and Westchester Estate Planning Councils, New York Business Group on Health Elder Task Force, Financial Executives Institute, New York Planned Giving Group and on the New York Chapter Board of the International Association for Financial Planning. He received a BA from Colby College and an MBA from New York University.

Cindy A. Cline, MPH, is manager of patient relations for the GTE Family Health Centers, and has 15 years of broad experience designing, developing, implementing and supervising preventative health care management programs. Her current responsibilities include marketing, developing, and managing communications and health education interventions for the GTE Family Health Center to all GTE business units and labor. Ms. Cline also acts as an information/advisory advocate for patients, employees, human resource representatives, providers and the public at large. Her most important charge is to bring high quality and cost efficiency to the GTE Family Health Center. Ms. Cline is actively involved with the Association for Worksite Health Promotion, a national organization dedicated to enhancing the personal and organizational health and well-being of employees and their families. She also chairs a committee for the Tobacco-Free Florida Coalition.

William S. Custer, PhD, is director of research at the Employee Benefit Research Institute (EBRI) in Washington, DC, where he conducts research related to employer health benefits and the health care delivery system. Dr. Custer has investigated a wide range of topics in health care, including the market for hospital services, hospital-physician relationships, Medicare's Prospective Payment System, and alternative physician payment mechanisms. He is currently directing studies of private health plan cost management incentives, the impact of health care reform proposals, and quality assessment in health care services. Before joining EBRI, Dr. Custer was an economist in the Center for Health Policy Research at the American Medical Association and was an assistant professor of economics at Northern Illinois University.

James A. Daddona is benefits plans & programs manager of Mobil Chemical, Fabricating Division. Prior to his current position, Mr. Daddona served as a benefits manager, senior benefits and compensation advisor, and employee relations manager. He received a BS in Industrial and Labor Relations from Cornell University.

Lisa J. Damon is an associate in Day, Berry & Howard's Boston office and practices in the area of employment litigation.

Zachary Dyckman, PhD, is executive vice president of the Center for Health Policy Studies. Dr. Dyckman has 20 years experience in health care policy research and consulting. Prior to joining the Center, he held senior level positions at the Department of Health Education and Welfare; Peat, Marwick, Mitchell & Co.; and on the President's Council on Wage and Price Stability. He has authored several studies. He received a PhD in economics from the University of Pennsylvania.

David M. Ermer is a partner in the law firm of Gordon & Barnett in Washington, D.C. His practice involves the representation of employers, insurers, Taft-Hartley trust funds and managed care organizations in the area of health benefit and government contract law. He received his BA from the University of Connecticut and his JD from George Washington University.

Rona L. Ferling is a senior associate editor at *Financial Executive*.

Glenn F. Fields is an insurance analyst at the New York, Washington D.C., Newark, New Jersey, Palo Alto, California, and Philadelphia law firm of Anderson Kill Olick & Oshinsky, P.C.

Walton Francis heads regulatory review at the Department of Health and Human Services. He is the author of *CHECKBOOK's Guide to Health Insurance Plans for Federal Employees*. The views expressed in this article are those of the author and not of the Health and Human Services Department.

Stanley D. Friedman is currently manager of personnel communications in Workforce Solutions, a unit of IBM formed to provide cost-effective human resource services to IBM divisions and outside customers. In addition to having held a wide range of other communications positions in IBM, he also held positions in IBM's marketing and development organizations.

Virginia M. Gibson is president of The MG Group Inc., a Baltimore-based consulting firm specializing in employee benefits.

William M. Glazer, MD, is associate clinical professor of psychiatry at Yale University School of Medicine. He is involved in neuropsychiatric private practice and serves as a consultant to providers, payers, and utilization review programs. Dr. Glazer received an AB from Clark University, Worcester, Massachusetts, and an MD from the University of Connecticut School of Medicine.

Judith Greenwood received her BA from the University of Michigan and her master of public health and doctorate degrees from the University of Oklahoma. Following her graduate work, she became research associate in the department of community medicine, West Virginia University, Charleston Division, where she was primary researcher and author for the study of Medical Rehabilitation Needs in West Virginia. She then assumed the position of director of human resources development with the West Virginia Department of Health, responsible for the administration of a National Institute of Mental Health Manpower Grant. In August of 1982, she joined the West Virginia Workers' Compensation Fund as director of research. Currently, she chairs the Medical Committee of the International Association of Industrial Accident Boards and Commissions and retains an academic role as associate clinical professor of Community Medicine at West

Virginia University. Ms. Greenwood authored *Physician Assistants in Primary Care*, and wrote a chapter on "The Politics of Planning and Implementing a Statewide Health Service: Medical Rehabilitation in West Virginia" and a chapter on "Socioeconomic Factors Affecting Back Pain and Compensation Systems," as well as over a dozen journal articles. Most recently, she coedited *Workers' Compensation Health Care Cost Containment* (LRP Publications).

Richard Hamer is director of the publications department at InterStudy, a private-sector health care information organization based in Bloomington, Minnesota.

John A. Haslinger is a Principal at Buck Consultants, Inc. and serves as director of Health and Welfare Administrative Consulting Services.

James A. Hayes is the president of James A. Hayes and Associates, Inc., of Placitas, New Mexico. His company provides consulting support for new product and business development for medical finance, technology assessment, and general strategic planning. Formerly, he worked for the Chicago Board of Trade and the Blue Cross & Blue Shield Association. He received a ScD from the Health Services Administration Department of the Harvard School of Public Health in 1977, where he studied medical economics.

Michael Shawn Hendryx, PhD, is an assistant professor in the graduate program in the Hospital and Health Administration and Center for Health Services Research at The University of Iowa, College of Medicine. Dr. Hendryx is the author of several published papers and a frequent speaker at presentations and seminars. He is a member of the American Psychological Association, the Association of Health Services Research and the American Public Health Association. He received a BA in psychology from the University of Nevada, and an MS and PhD from Northwestern University.

Donald G. Jones is the benefits manager for Florida Hospital in Orlando, Florida. Mr. Jones received his BA in Business Administration from Walla Walla College in 1978 and received the Certified Employee Benefits Specialist designation in 1993. He has over 15 years of experience in employee benefits and risk management.

Barbara C. Keaton is a national consultant on EAP issues and director of corporate services for Pennsylvania Services of Pittsburgh.

Martin W. G. King, who serves on NCQA's accreditation staff, is a journalist with a background in life and health insurance issues and international public health. He is the former editor of the newspaper *International Health News*.

Marie Klinkmueller is product marketing specialist, Sun Life of Canada's excess risk and group life products. She is a graduate of Wellesley College.

Donald R. Levy is a New York corporate benefits attorney and author who has designed and administered many health care programs for businesses of all sizes. He served as vice president-director of benefits and human resources for United States Tobacco Company and has been a senior technical consultant for Johnson & Higgins, Mercer Meidinger, and now for Panel Publishers, in the health care and pension benefits areas. He is the author of the *Pension Handbook* (Prentice Hall). Mr. Levy is a graduate of Harvard Law School.

Richard A. Levy, PhD, is vice president for scientific affairs at the National Pharmaceutical Council (NPC), an association of twenty-nine multinational research-based pharmaceutical companies. Dr. Levy is responsible for coordination of research, staff direction, policy analysis, development of informational materials, and the design of programs to communicate industry perspectives to professional audiences. He is the author of over fifty publications in pharmacology and public policy. Dr. Levy has spent over twenty years teaching, writing, and conducting research in universities and private industry. His current interests at NPC include tracking, analyzing, and communicating trends affecting pharmaceutical innovation; developing information on management of medications by individuals and organizations; and assessing pharmaceutical reimbursement policies of insurers and managed care providers. Dr. Levy has previously taught and conducted research in neuropharmacology at the University of Illinois College of Medicine. He received his BS from the City College of New York and a PhD from the University of Delaware. He also received postdoctoral training in neuropharmacology at the University of Illinois.

Paul Lombino is a freelance writer based in Somerville, Massachusetts.

Sandra L. Lowery is president and owner of Case Management Intervention, providing consultative services in medical case management. She received an AA in nursing from Saddleback College and a BS in nursing from the State University of New York at Albany. She is certified as an oncology nurse, a rehabilitative nurse and as a case manager. She has been published in *The Case Manager* and *The Journal of Health Care Benefits*. She is affiliated with many organizations and a frequent speaker at conferences.

Carol Malone is the manager of Health Decision Resource Group of Coopers & Lybrand in Washington, DC.

Patrick May is the director of communications for the National Leadership Coalition on AIDS, a non-profit organization of businesses and labor unions working together to stop the spread of HIV through effective workplace AIDS policies, practices and education programs on HIV/AIDS and U.S. business.

Rebecca Morrow is the benefits editor for the Institute of Management & Administration (IOMA), located in New York City.

Joyce M. Munsell, RN, MPA, is manager of health care resources for Parker Hannifin Corporation in Irvine, California.

Margeret E. O'Kane is the president of the National Committee for Quality Assurance and a prominent advocate of enhanced health care quality. Previously, she served as the director of Quality Improvement Management for the Group Health Association, a staff-model HMO in the Washington, DC area, and as a senior executive with the Group Health Association of America, a national trade association that represents the interests of health plans in Washington.

Monica E. Oss has extensive experience in the behavioral health and marketing fields. She is president of the managed behavioral health care industry research and consulting firm OPEN MINDS, based in Gettysburg, Pennsylvania. Her company's newsletter, also called OPEN MINDS, has more than 2,500 sub-scribers, including most of the nation's largest managed health care programs, and hundreds of employee benefit consultants, behavioral health providers, and corporate employee benefit managers. Its reputation for tracking and predicting financing, marketing and legal issues in the mental health and chemical depend-ency field is extensive and outstanding. Ms. Oss is also executive editor of AAHP News, the Behavioral Health Track chair of the National Managed Health Care Congress, a member of the Dialogue Advisory Board of the Institute of Be-havioral Healthcare, editorial director for a number of independent managed care publications, featured speaker at more than two dozen annual conferences and seminars, a lecturer at several institutions of higher learning, and a member of the Board of Directors of Adams County Head Start. Formerly marketing director for one of the nation's largest behavioral health care companies, she has written numerous books and magazine articles on marketing, behavioral health care management and provision, and health care policy.

Michelle Porter was formerly research director at InterStudy, and is now with Velocity Health Care Information, in Eden Prarie, MN.

Patricia Posey has been a registered professional nurse for more than thirty years and has been a rehabilitation counselor for workers' compensation claimants for more than fifteen years. She is a graduate of the Medical College of the Virginia School of Nursing, Virginia Commonwealth University. Ms. Posey has promoted an early intervention with injured workers and believes workers who fit a certain disability dependent profile need "day one" intervention. She completed a demonstration project for very early intervention in 1986 in which the disability dependent was found to be related to psychosocial factors inherent in the injured worker rather than the actual injury itself. Ms. Posey suggests that intervention should be directed to such factors as locus of control, job satisfaction, and the worker's ability to communicate needs. Ms. Posey is founder of West Virginia's first private rehabilitation firm. She serves on the Health Care Advisory Panel to the state workers' compensation division and is board secretary to the W.V. Board of Examiners in Counseling.

Richard D. Quinn, III, is director of corporate benefit planning and services for the Public Service Electric and Gas Company. Mr. Quinn has been involved in employee benefits since 1961, beginning his career as a health insurance claim processor and later as a benefits administrator. Since 1975, he has held several management positions in which he was responsible for corporate strategic benefits planning, cost containment strategies, communications, compliance, and legislative analysis. He has designed, implemented, and administered virtually every type of qualified plan and welfare benefit plan for both represented and salaried employee groups. He has extensive experience in labor negotiations and is actively involved in lobbying efforts with federal legislators. Mr. Quinn has written over 100 articles which have appeared in various national publications. He is currently contributing editor for the *Employers Health Benefits Bulletin.* Mr. Quinn co-edited *Employers' Handbook—Mandated Health Benefits* and *The COBRA Guide*, and was contributing editor for a *Practical Guide for Section 89 Compliance and Laws and Issues Affecting Personnel Management.* Mr. Quinn is an active member on several advisory groups at state level and for such organizations as the Conference Board.

Thomas S. Roos, BA, is corporate director of employee benefits at Parker Hannifin Corporation in Cleveland, Ohio.

Steve Schoen, FSA, CEBS, is assistant vice president at Excess Risk Products and Group Product Actuary, for the U.S. operations of Sun Life Assurance Company of Canada. A graduate of Worcester Polytechnic Institute, Schoen earned his Fellow in the Society of Actuaries designation in 1980 and his Certified Employee Benefits Specialist designation in 1984. He is also a member of the Academy of Actuaries.

Matthew Schuller, RRA, currently serves as the quality improvement manager for Community Care Network, Inc., a healthcare managed care organization that developed and operates the EPIqual Healthcare Program, a PPO Network. Previously, Mr. Schuller was a Quality Improvement and Health Information Management consultant for a quality improvement and resource management software corporation. In addition, he has also managed quality improvement activities for a 450 bed hospital in the greater Chicago area. Mr. Schuller has a BS in health information management and is an active member of the American Health Information Management Association's Quality Assurance Section.

Donna Sheerin is an assistant benefit consultant in the Group Consulting Services Department of Buck's New Jersey office. Ms. Sheerin joined Buck in 1988 after working as a benefit analyst for Noble Lowndes where she worked primarily on designing, marketing and implementing benefit plans for a number of small and large employers. Ms. Sheerin assists in traditional and flexible benefit plan design and pricing, and has been involved in the development and implementation of flexible benefit programs for a number of major employers such as Cushman & Wakefield, Avon Products, Inc., *The Washington Post,* Consolidated Edison, Dole Food, and Union Pacific. She is also responsible for statistical analysis of issues relating to the group benefits area. Ms. Sheerin is a frequent speaker on these topics and, in addition, has published articles on flexible benefit plan design and work and family issues in *Pension World* and *Compensation & Benefits Management.* Her most recent article deals with administrative issues pertaining to flex plans is published in *Journal of Compensation & Benefits.* Ms. Sheerin graduated from Lafayette College with a BS degree in mathematics. She is currently pursuing a certificate in the certified employee benefits program.

Scott P. Smith, MD, MPH, FACP, is board certified in internal medicine, preventive medicine, and medical management. He is currently vice president of Clinical Management Services and the national medical director for HealthCare COMPARE Corp. in Downers Grove, Illinois. He previously served as Great Lakes Regional medical director for Lincoln National, director of medical affairs at the Michael Reese Health Plan in Chicago, medical director for HealthAmerica of Georgia in Atlanta, and medical director for the county health department in Phoenix, Arizona. He trained at the University of California, the University of Colorado, and the University of Arizona. He practices as a volunteer internist with the Chicago City Health Department, and serves as a lecturer at the University of Illinois School of Public Health. Dr. Smith is a Fellow of the American College of Physicians and a member of the American Colleges of Physician Executives and Preventive Medicine. He served as a surveyor for the Ambulatory Care Accreditation Program with the Joint Commission from 1987 through 1992 and has been an NCQA reviewer since early 1991.

Martin Z. Sipkoff is a writer with extensive newspaper and magazine experience. He has written for several health care publications about behavioral health marketing, employee assistance programs, workers' compensation, legal issues in managed care, and health care financing. Prior to his work as a professional journalist, he spent a decade on the staff of a social service agency. Mr. Sipkoff is currently working on a book about continuous quality improvement in the behavioral health field.

Jonathan Stevens, director of analytical consulting, joined HealthCare COMPARE in 1992. He heads the Analytic Consulting department, which works with HealthCare COMPARE Corp. clients to identify and resolve health cost management issues through the use of data analysis. He received a BA in anthropology from Yale University, and received a masters in public health from the University of North Carolina. In 1992, Mr. Stevens earned his Certified Employee Benefit Specialist (CEBS) designation. Mr. Stevens came to COMPARE from Towers Perrin/Chicago where he was a benefits consultant with a specialization in managed care. Prior to that, he served as Director for PPO Development for John Hancock Mutual Life and established their PPO in the Chicago market. He also held the position of Executive Director for the Vermont State Data Center, which tracked hospital discharge information for the state. Mr. Stevens has 20 years experience in the health and benefit fields. Mr. Stevens serves as a board member and treasurer of Alivio Medical Center, a neighborhood health center serving Hispanic populations on Chicago's Southwest side. He is also president of the Yale Club of Chicago.

Lance D. Tane is a partner in Kwasha Lipton, Fort Lee, New Jersey, and head of the firm's flexible benefits operations.

Terry R. Tone is a clinic administrator at Owatonna Clinic in Owatonna, Minnesota. He is also an adjunct professor of finance at the University of St. Thomas, in St. Paul, Minnesota. Mr. Tone received a BS and MBA from Mankato State University, in Mankato, Minnesota and a BA from Luther College in Decorah, Iowa.

Susan Murray Young is an associate at Washington Business Group on Health, where she works on projects related to mental health, health promotion, and other worksite health issues. Ms. Young has authored and co-authored several WBGH publications, including *Access to Preventative Services: The Role of Employers* and *The Worksite Health Promotion Update*, a corporate newsletter published by Rodale Press. She received a BA from Wittenberg University in Springfield, Ohio, and an MS in wellness Management from Ball State University, Muncie, Indiana.

Carla R. Walworth, a partner in the employment law and employee benefits group of the law firm of Day, Berry & Howard, in Stamford, Connecticut, specializes in employment litigation in federal and state courts.

Carole F. Wilder, is an associate who practices in the area of employment litigation at Day, Berry & Howard in Stamford.

Brent A. Winans, CPCU, CIC, ARM, is presently employed as the vice president of risk management for Concord Services, Inc., a group of diversified international companies headquartered in Denver, Colorado. He began his insurance and risk management career twenty years ago as the youngest State Farm agent in Indiana. He since has worked as an independent broker, risk management consultant, and risk manager. Mr. Winans served as the president of the Colorado Self Insurers Association and has been an instructor for the Associate in Risk Management program. He received a BA from Lincoln Christian College. Mr. Winans speaks and writes frequently on risk management subjects.

Leonard E. Wood is president and CEO of Gallagher Bassett Benefit Administrators, a division of Arthur J. Gallagher & Co.

Contents

Part 1

REFORM

Part 1

REFORM

1. Coping with National Health Care Reform
Donald R. Levy

The Clinton Health Security Act was one of a number of proposals finally pulled together in 1993. Clinton's proposal was, of course, the most publicized. It was the cornerstone of a new President's domestic program and the part of that program on which he most heavily relied in his campaign for election the year before. Some form of it may be re-proposed in 1995. This article and appendixes offers an overview of the types of issues that, undoubtedly, will be discussed in the future.

Early in his presidency Mr. Clinton created a special study group or committee to examine the health care issues and develop a proposed plan. The President selected Hillary Rodham Clinton to chair the project.

The Clinton proposal called for a new approach to be implemented as early as 1995 but no later than 1998. This timetable assumed that Congress and the President would enact a bill in 1994 and that, thereafter, the plan would be implemented in stages. The broad purposes of the Clinton Health Security Act, which has now been killed in Congress, were:

- Universal coverage (for active employees, retire employees, and all others)
- Comprehensive benefits, and
- Cost control.

The Clinton Plan included approaches to minimum coverage, purchasing alliances, employee choice, maximum employer costs, state's choice for implementation, and benefit changes among other issues.

Reprinted from *Company Policy Manual: Special Report*, Donald R. Levy, 1994 No. 1. A Panel Publication, Aspen Publishers, Inc.

Minimum Coverage

Full-Time Employees

Employers are required to cover their full-time employees for no less than the comprehensive benefit package specified by law. This package approximates the current upper range of large employer benefit packages and will provide a better level of benefits than is now provided by Medicare.

Part-Time Employees and Dependents

Employer and employee contributions for some part-time employees are to be required, on a scaled back basis.

Where dependents of an employee are also employed, and by a second employer, they need not be covered as dependents through the first employer. But whichever plan covers them—whether one of the first employer's plans or one of the second employer's plans—the cost of coverage will be shared by the two employers. This will reduce the burden currently imposed on employers who provide dependent coverage that is better than the coverage offered by a dependent's own employer.

Retirees

Those retiring before age 65, when Medicare coverage begins, will have their benefits provided. There will be no cost to the employer unless the employer was previously contributing to the retirees coverage, in which case the employer may pay only 20 percent. The other 80 percent will be absorbed by the health care system. Employers that have been contributing will be subject to a tax during the first three years of the plan which will, at the minimum, assess the full amount by which retiree health costs have been reduced by health security for those three years.

Self-Employed Individuals

They would be required to provide medical coverage for themselves and covered family members. The dependent cost would then be shared under the usual approach with any other employer of a dependent. But the entire cost would be 100 percent tax-deductible rather than the present 25 percent.

Purchasing Alliances

The primary method chosen to achieve cost control is for the states to create purchasing alliances for each geographical segment of the country. Sometimes an alliance's territory will be a single state. The alliance will buy health care coverage for all employers with less than 5,000 employees. Employees with more than 5,000 employees (or such lower limit as may be agreed to) may remain independent, but if they do not join the alliance, they may be subjected to a new federal tax. If the states do not act in a timely manner, the federal government becomes involved in the process.

Premiums will be those negotiated by the regional alliance with plans available in the marketplace. Plans that bid may be excluded when cost is more than 20 percent higher than the alliance average. Under the alliance approach it would seem that self-insurance for small employers would be completely eliminated.

Employee Choice

Employees will choose a plan from among the plans offered through, and accepted by, the purchasing alliance. Therefore, an employer will no longer be able to limit the employee's choice. Choice of a doctor is limited under some plans, but an individual may be allowed to make a selection of a non-plan doctor, and there may then be a significant deductible and a higher than normal co-payment.

Minimum Employer Share of Cost

The employer will pay at least 80 percent of the average cost resulting from the individually made plan selections of its employees. The remaining cost will be the responsibility of the employee. Therefore, where the employer contributes 80 percent of the average cost, employees choosing a more expensive alternative will pay more than 20 percent, while those selecting a plan of less than average cost will be rewarded with a less than 20-percent contribution charge.

Benefits provided in excess of those prescribed will not be taxed at the outset. But, starting at a later date, employees would be taxed on employer-provided benefits that exceed the statutory minimums. The employer contributions would remain deductible.

Cost Controls

The Clinton Plan's cost control target for employer cost of the total package is a maximum 7.9 percent of payroll in the initial year of the new law. Small employers may receive a subsidy to meet the cost of the package. The subsidy would be on a sliding scale, for employers of less than 75 employees, and would reduce cost down to as little as 3.5 percent of payroll.

State Management

States will have latitude in how to implement health security but subject to the federal guidelines.

The single payer approach used in Canada would involve use of a single alliance rather than competing alliances. The Clinton Bill would allow any state that wishes to do so to adopt such a system, but the Canadian model would not become universal unless every state adopts it. This is not at all likely in the present political climate since the single payer system would seem to involve too much government control. However, it is quite possible that one or more states will adopt this approach.

Other Benefit Changes

Dental benefits will not be included in the mandatory benefit package except for preventive dental care for those under 21 years old. Dental benefits will be expanded and more fully phased in by the year 2001. In addition, COBRA will be superseded by the new law and flexible spending accounts will be phased out. Medicare benefits will be expanded to include coverage for prescription drugs.

Some Other Details

There will be a single claim form used by all carriers. Everyone will have the same coverage card which will be authorized by the federal government.

The program is to be financed by a tobacco tax as well as special taxes on large employers electing not to join an alliance. It is also anticipated that, as a result of the expected reduction in the previous rate of inflation for health care, costs for Medicare and Medicaid will be less than would otherwise have resulted. Some integration of Medicare, Medicaid, and workers' compensation medical benefits may also contribute to reduce costs or lessen cost increases.

Special affidavits will be required to institute malpractice suits and alternative dispute resolution efforts also will be required before an action can be brought. Attorneys' contingency fees cannot exceed 33.3 percent of any malpractice settlement. There would be practice protocols to guide doctors and prevent litigation.

Practicing physicians and medical students will be encouraged to become general practitioners rather than specialists. The effort will involve influencing medical school curricula. The objective is twofold: (1) to reduce the number of times specialists need to be utilized and (2) to improve the quality of care, particularly in areas where general practitioners as well as specialists are in short supply.

Insurance carriers will be prohibited from making unfavorable changes during the transition period, before health security goes into effect.

Since congressional and national interest has clearly been aroused, the health care issue is likely to remain near the top of the national agenda for a long time to come.

ALTERNATIVE PROPOSALS

A variety of alternative proposals were introduced. It is important for small employers to analyze these developments as a basis for decisions they will make and actions they will take concerning their own businesses. Appendix A details five of the alternative bills that were introduced. Others may yet be added. Some will be combined, and negotiations to that end will continue.

Three threads run through these alternatives. At the extremes are the single-payer approach and the no-basic-change approach. In between is a reform package—illustrated by the Chafee bill—that was more conservative than that proposed by the President.

The Single-Payer System

The federally mandated single-payer system is the health coverage plan most Americans would prefer according to some polls, although it is not clear how popular the necessary taxes and controls would be.

This alternative is illustrated by H.R. 1200, which was introduced by Congressman McDermott (see Appendix A). Under this approach, much of the Canadian pattern would be adopted. Although known as a State Health Security Program run by each state for its own citizens, each state would be required to comply with federal rules and regulations.

Senator Chafee's Approach

The proposal of Senator John Chafee generally followed the Clinton objectives of universal coverage, comprehensive benefits, and cost control. However, it would implement those objectives differently, by:

1. Making individuals responsible to cover themselves;
2. Leaving it to free market forces to fix rates;
3. Allowing more flexibility about how purchasing alliances would be established;
4. Relieving small and large businesses alike of Clinton-proposed employer mandates; and
5. Reducing mandatory benefits to a level the sponsors feel the nation can now afford, and then increasing benefits only as costs permit.

Individual Responsibility

The analogy here is to the requirement that individuals buy automobile insurance. Those failing to buy insurance would be subjected to penalties, which might even be collected by the IRS. Alternatively, for example, an uninsured individual arriving at a hospital would be treated but would be required to enroll and pay premiums due.

Free Market

Unlike the Clinton proposal which called for further action to be taken whenever costs rise above the cost cap (initially set at 7.9 percent of payroll for most employers), the approach here would be to shun any price caps, or price control guidelines, however worded and however indirect.

Purchasing Alliances

These are recognized as one of the methods that could be used but there will continue to be a free market.

Relief for Small Businesses

Since no employer would be required to insure its employees, small employers who wish to do so can have no medical plan for their employees. In this way they could avoid the cost of the standard plan which it has been argued could cause layoffs and business failures.

Comprehensive Benefits

The package of benefits is more limited than that proposed by the Clinton Administration. Employers going above the more modest package might lose the tax shelter on the excess piece as might their employees.

No-Basic-Change Approach

Insurance would remain optional. However, steps would be taken to encourage improved cost-control mechanisms, administrative simplicity, and to limit malpractice liability.

Most extensive malpractice reform would be emphasized. It is a common belief that one of the causes of high health care inflation is the feeling among doctors, hospitals, and other providers that all conceivable tests must be performed to assure that the provider will not be found liable for negligence. When juries look back to consider what might have been done they have the benefit of hindsight wisdom. Providers may be "overmedicating" to anticipate the hindsight that may later be applied. Limited malpractice liability could reduce cost by reducing provider overtesting.

The optional coverage approach would encourage managed care but with no federal mandate and little interference from government. There would be no employer mandates and no managed competition. Subsidies would be offered on a small scale.

Apart from administrative streamlining and malpractice reform, there is another element given great emphasis by the optional coverage approach: the introduction of medical savings accounts, like individual retirement accounts (IRAs), available for those who wish to trade lower benefits for a contribution (by employer and/or employee), to a tax-free accumulation fund to build up reserves that can be used later for health care during retirement.

Although the timing and details of the ultimate legislation cannot be predicted, the various alternatives (with the possible exception of a single payer) may be meshed with some of Clinton's ideas into a suitable compromise. Such a compromise may be necessary to enact any bill.

Under a compromise plan, the right to choose a doctor might be more protected than under Clinton's approach, malpractice reform might be more dramatic, and universal coverage might be accomplished without sweeping employer mandates. Another compromise might do more to encourage states that wish to do so to adopt a single payer approach.

APPENDIX A

Comparison of Health Reform Proposals

Martha Priddy Patterson

Appendix A compares President Clinton's health reform proposal with other proposals sponsored by Members of the 103rd Congress. The Comparison was prepared by KPMG Peat Marwick.

Martha Priddy Patterson, Esq. is Director of Employee Benefit Analysis, KPMG Peat Marwick, Washington, DC.

KPMG PEAT MARWICK COMPARISON OF HEALTH REFORM PROPOSALS
103rd Congress

	President Clinton H.R. 3600/S.1757	H.R. 1200 Cong. McDermott	H.R. 3222 Bipartisan Group on Health Reform (Cong. Cooper)	S. 1770 Senate Republican Task Force (Sen. Chafee)	H.R. 3080 House Republican Proposal (Cong. Michel)	Sen. Gramm
COVERAGE APPROACH	Universal coverage through health alliances with employers mandated to pay for 80% of average costs; regional alliances must negotiate with any willing state-certified plan, including fee-for-service plans.	Universal coverage through single-payer system, the State Health Security Program, run by each state; individual providers paid on a fee-for-service basis, hospitals and other institutions paid on an annually negotiated basis; care delivered by private providers reimbursed by states.	Universal coverage encouraged, but not required; all care delivered through pre-paid Accountable Health Plans (AHPs).	Universal coverage required through a mandate requiring individuals to purchase coverage.	Expansion of existing coverage encouraged by requiring all employers to offer at least one health plan and through guaranteed renewability of health insurance.	Expansion of existing coverage encouraged through guaranteed renewability of health insurance, deductibility for self-employeds and individuals, and credits for low income individuals.
EMPLOYER ROLE	Mandated payment for up to 80% of average premium; caps on percentage of payroll paid by employers with 75 or fewer employees.	None, other than paying a 7.9% payroll tax.	Employers of fewer than 100 employees would join health plan purchasing co-ops; employers not required to pay for benefits.	Employers must offer the standard benefits package, but not required to pay for benefits.	Employers required to offer health plan, but not required to pay for health benefits.	Current voluntary role.

Reprinted with permission of KPMG Peat Marwick.

KPMG PEAT MARWICK COMPARISON OF HEALTH REFORM PROPOSALS
103rd Congress

	President Clinton H.R. 3600/S.1757	H.R. 1200 Cong. McDermott	H.R. 3222 Bipartisan Group on Health Reform (Cong. Cooper)	S. 1770 Senate Republican Task Force (Sen. Chafee)	H.R. 3080 House Republican Proposal (Cong. Michel)	Sen. Gramm
BENEFITS	Benefits spelled out in the law; including hospitalization, emergency, physicians, preventive care, mental health and substance abuse, family planning, pregnancy-related services, hospice care, home health care, extended care, ambulance, labs, prescription drugs, medical equipment, vision and hearing care, children's preventive dental, and health education.	Benefits spelled out in the law; including coverage for all inpatient and outpatient services without limits on duration or intensity except as dictated by outcomes research and practice guidelines. Coverage for some dental services and long-term care. No coverage for cosmetic procedures. Employers or individuals may buy additional benefits.	Federal Health Care Standards Commission to establish standard benefit package which must include preventive and diagnostic benefits; package approved by Congress in an up or down vote.	Standard benefit package includes medical and surgical services, prescription drugs, rehab and home health care for acute care episodes, limited mental health services, substance abuse services, preventive care. A new Benefits Commission will "clarify" the standard benefit plan each year. An alternative "catastrophic benefit plan" integrated with a Medical Saving Account with high cost sharing can be purchased.	"MedAccess" Standard Benefit package to be determined by the National Association of Insurance Commissioners; an alternative "Catastrophic Plan" and a "MediSave" package consisting of a Medical Saving Account integrated with a catastrophic benefit plan with high cost sharing is also to be available.	Continues COBRA coverage; to maintain tax-exempt status of benefits to employees, employers must offer three options, (1) current health plan, (2) managed care plan and (3) a catastrophic plan coupled with a "Medical Savings Account" to which employers and employees could contribute pretax dollars.
PAYMENTS FOR COVERAGE	Employers pay 80% of average premium, individuals pay the remainder. Cost cap of 7.9% of payroll for most employers.	Federal government pays 85%, state government pays 15%.	Individual responsible for paying; individuals with incomes below 200% of poverty line receive federal subsidies; individuals at poverty level will pay no premiums and only a modest copayment.	Individual responsible for paying; federally paid coverage for low income will be phased in only as savings from the program are realized. Phase in would begin in 1995 for those with incomes of 90% of poverty level and below.	Individual responsibility. States could use Medicaid funds to subsidize those with incomes up to 200% of poverty; states could establish plans for low income.	Individual responsible; government would offer premium subsidy for those with preexisting conditions, if insurance costs more than 7.5% of income.

KPMG PEAT MARWICK COMPARISON OF HEALTH REFORM PROPOSALS
103rd Congress

	President Clinton H.R. 3600/S.1757	H.R. 1200 Cong. McDermott	H.R. 3222 Bipartisan Group on Health Reform (Cong. Cooper)	S. 1770 Senate Republican Task Force (Sen. Chafee)	H.R. 3080 House Republican Proposal (Cong. Michel)	Sen. Gramm
NEW TAXES, OTHER FINANCING	$89 billion in new revenues from increases in tobacco tax and payroll tax on employers who establish corporate alliance health plans; increase Medicare Part B premiums for high income participants; Medicaid and Medicare savings of $189 billion; increased revenues $71 billion.	7.5% surtax on taxable income; 7.9% payroll tax; other revenues increases.	$16 billion from capping employer deductibility; $6.5 billion reducing increases in provider fees under Medicare; $1.5 billion phasing out the Medicare Part B subsidy for upper-income recipients; $1 billion pre-funding federal retiree medical benefits.	Reducing the growth of Medicare from 12% annually to 7% annually over six years, in part by increasing Medicare Part B premiums and means testing Part B premiums.	Not specified in detail; some savings from increasing Medicare Part B premiums for high income individuals.	None. New tax credits paid for by savings from Medicaid and Medicare and reductions in use of medical deduction.
TAX STATUS OF BENEFITS	Benefits in excess of "standard package" taxable to employee after 2003; premiums for standard package fully deductible for self-employed individuals. Payments fully deductible to employers.	Not specified.	Employers may deduct amounts paid for employees up to 100% of the lowest price AHP; self-employeds and those who pay part or all of their premiums may fully deduct their AHP premiums; coverage from a nonqualified AHP is not deductible; no limit on tax-exempt status of employer provided health benefits.	Benefits in excess of the tax cap are taxable to the employee and nondeductible to the employer. Individuals and self-employeds can deduct the cost of premiums up to the tax cap. Tax cap is defined as average cost of the lowest 1/3 of plans in the area. Medical Savings Accounts for those with only catastrophic health plans can be funded on a tax free basis up to the tax cap.	Self-employeds and other individuals purchasing health insurance would be able to deduct full value of standard plans; contributions to Medical Savings Accounts would be tax exempt for contributions of $2,500 for individual or $5,000 for family. Provide the same tax treatment for long-term care insurance as for other health insurance.	Employer provided benefits tax exempt to employee only if employer offers three choices (see above); individuals and self-employeds deduct same amount of premium costs as national average employer contribution for premiums; low income individuals receive a credit for catastrophic coverage.

KPMG PEAT MARWICK COMPARISON OF HEALTH REFORM PROPOSALS
103rd Congress

	President Clinton H.R. 3600/S.1757	H.R. 1200 Cong. McDermott	H.R. 3222 Bipartisan Group on Health Reform (Cong. Cooper)	S. 1770 Senate Republican Task Force (Sen. Chafee)	H.R. 3080 House Republican Proposal (Cong. Michel)	Sen. Gramm
HEALTH CARE PURCHASING GROUPS AND HEALTH PLANS	Employers or collective bargained plans with 5000 or more may have Corporate Alliances; all others receive coverage through Regional Alliances; only one Regional Alliance per area; Regional Alliances are run by appointed boards of directors. Health plans deliver care.	Comprehensive health service organizations may furnish a full range of services on a pre-paid, capitated basis. Private providers may also deliver care.	Health Plan Purchasing Cooperatives will be state chartered organizations with only one HPPC per area; individuals and all businesses with fewer than 100 employees will purchase health care through the HPPC from various AHPs; all health care will be on a pre-paid basis through an AHP.	States would establish one or more "purchasing cooperatives" per area for individuals and employers with 100 or fewer employees. Participation in these co-ops is voluntary, but the co-ops must accept all applicants. The co-ops are governed by members. Co-ops collect premiums and pass them on to health care plans.	Would eliminate IRS rules preventing employer groups from offering tax exempt health insurance; provide incentives for multiple employer health plans.	Removes legal restrictions on pooling health care purchases for businesses and other organizations.

KPMG PEAT MARWICK COMPARISON OF HEALTH REFORM PROPOSALS
103rd Congress

	President Clinton H.R. 3600/S.1757	H.R. 1200 Cong. McDermott	H.R. 3222 Bipartisan Group on Health Reform (Cong. Cooper)	S. 1770 Senate Republican Task Force (Sen. Chafee)	H.R. 3080 House Republican Proposal (Cong. Michel)	Sen. Gramm
COST CONTAINMENT	Nationally targeted spending caps; streamline administrative processes; standardized forms; antitrust barriers to networks eliminated; malpractice reforms reduce costs of defensive medicine. Spending caps do not apply to individually purchased coverage in excess of standard benefits.	Global budgeting set by financing authority and limits on amount of money that can be spent on health care.	Cost savings will come from competition among AHPs, malpractice reforms, and administrative simplification.	Cost savings to come from tort reform, antitrust law changes, administrative simplification, and better information about the effectiveness of medical treatments.	Cost containment from merging Medicare Parts A and B; malpractice reform; administrative reform; antitrust reforms; antifraud provisions; and Medicaid flexibility.	Reforms in Medicaid (see below) and Medicare. Retirees may opt out of Medicare coverage and if new coverage cost less than Medicare, recipient keeps one half the difference in savings. Enhance efficiency through paperwork reduction; private carriers reimbursed only if use federal standardized forms. Antitrust reforms.
NATIONAL HEALTH BOARD	Interprets basic benefit package and recommends revisions; sets and enforces national budget for health care; oversees certain state actions; runs national quality management system and breakthrough drug committee.	American Health Security Board will approve state programs, establish policies and procedures for enrollment, quality, provider participation, data gathering, etc. Will be advised by an Advisory Council of providers and consumers and a Quality Council of providers.	A federal Health Care Standards Commission will establish a standard benefits plan, establish standards for reporting prices, outcomes and consumer satisfaction for AHPs, develop risk adjustment factors for AHPs; certify AHPs; provide administrative simplification.	A new Federal Administrative Standards Panel will be created to establish uniform data gathering and forms. A Benefits Commission will establish a standard benefit plan for recommendation to Congress.	None.	None.

KPMG PEAT MARWICK COMPARISON OF HEALTH REFORM PROPOSALS
103rd Congress

	President Clinton H.R. 3600/S.1757	H.R. 1200 Cong. McDermott	H.R. 3222 Bipartisan Group on Health Reform (Cong. Cooper)	S. 1770 Senate Republican Task Force (Sen. Chafee)	H.R. 3080 House Republican Proposal (Cong. Michel)	Sen. Gramm
ROLE OF STATES	States establish regional alliances; establish funding requirements and guaranty fund for AHPs; certify health plans; monitor quality of and access of care.	States design and administer the plan; states establish quality assurance programs and uniform data bases. States negotiate prices with health care providers.	Charter HPPCs; no role in Medicaid; retain responsibility for long-term care. State mandated benefits and restrictive laws on managed care are preempted.	Establish purchasing co-ops, continue to run Medicaid. States may establish alternative health delivery systems upon approval by HHS.	Gives states greater flexibility in Medicaid; allows states to establish group insurance for low income workers and early retirees. State mandated benefit laws are preempted and anti-managed care laws limited.	States given more flexibility to design Medicaid programs.
MEDICAID	Folded into regional alliances; former Medicaid eligibles subsidized.	Medicaid is superseded.	Medicaid is repealed; low income participants receive federal subsidies.	Continues as an existing program.	All Medicaid recipients could be placed in managed care plans without federal waiver process; certain Medicaid funds could be used to provide benefits to those with incomes of up to 200% of poverty level.	Medicaid payments to state on a per capita basis; states given flexibility to design own programs.
ERISA PREEMPTION	Would apply only to Corporate Alliances; states could apply nondiscriminatory taxes and cover such employers in single-payer plans.	Not addressed, but becomes largely irrelevant for health plans because employers are no longer providing health benefits.	No provision.	ERISA application to health plans limited; employers who simply provide plans to satisfy this Act will not be treated as covered by ERISA.	Department of Labor could exempt "multiple employer welfare plans" (MEWAs) from state insurance laws, upon application by MEWA.	No provision.

KPMG PEAT MARWICK COMPARISON OF HEALTH REFORM PROPOSALS
103rd Congress

	President Clinton H.R. 3600/S.1757	H.R. 1200 Cong. McDermott	H.R. 3222 Bipartisan Group on Health Reform (Cong. Cooper)	S. 1770 Senate Republican Task Force (Sen. Chafee)	H.R. 3080 House Republican Proposal (Cong. Michel)	Sen. Gramm
HEALTH INSURANCE REFORMS	No preexisting condition exclusions; community rating; plans must accept all applicants.	Not applicable.	No preexisting condition exclusions; community rating required; guaranteed renewability in most cases.	Guarantee availability and renewability to all applicants, no discrimination on basis of health status, require community rating, but phased in for groups of 100 or fewer.	All insurers must offer the Standard Plan, Catastrophic Plan and Medisave Plan to companies employing 2 to 50 employees; rate variations and increases to these groups would be limited. Risk pools would be established. MEWAS, multiemployer plans and insurance companies must provide guaranteed renewability; preexisting condition exclusions are limited.	Guaranteed renewability; premium increases based on illnesses not permitted; cancellation not permitted except for nonpayment or ceasing business in the state.
EARLY RETIREES	Retired individuals from age 55 to 64 would have premium subsidized by federal government; if former employer previously covered the individual, the employer must pay a portion of the liability to the government.	No provision, but all individuals would be covered regardless of employee status.	No provision.	No provision.	Early retirees could go into a state Medicaid plan.	No provision.

KPMG PEAT MARWICK COMPARISON OF HEALTH REFORM PROPOSALS
103rd Congress

	President Clinton H.R. 3600/S.1757	H.R. 1200 Cong. McDermott	H.R. 3222 Bipartisan Group on Health Reform (Cong. Cooper)	S. 1770 Senate Republican Task Force (Sen. Chafee)	H.R. 3080 House Republican Proposal (Cong. Michel)	Sen. Gramm
TORT REFORM/ MAL-PRACTICE REFORM	Mandatory Alternative Dispute Resolution (ADR) as a first step; attorneys fees limited to 1/3 recovery; outcomes research; practice protocols which if followed would insulate physician from malpractice suits; expert medical affidavit required to file suit.	No provision.	Preempts state laws, except where such laws are more stringent than federal law. Mandatory use of ADR as first step. Non-economic damages are limited to $250,000; attorneys fees are limited; statute of limitations is two years.	Mandatory ADR as first step, after ADR if litigated losing party pays all fees; non-economic damages limited to $250,000; damages reduced by payments from other sources; 50% of punitive damages paid to the state; two-year statute of limitations. Following practice guidelines creates a rebuttable presumption of appropriate care.	Mandatory ADR as first step, after ADR losing party pays all fees, except court costs; non-economic damages limited to $250,000; seven-year absolute statute of limitations; no punitive damages permitted against manufacturers of medical devices; other punitive damages awarded to the state. Contingency fees limited.	Losing plaintiff pays health care provider costs, including losses from being away from practice. Non-economic damages limited to $250,000; contingency fees limited to 25%; awards reduced by any other payments plaintiff receives; two-year statute of limitation from discovery, but in no event more than four years from discovery. No punitive damages if drug or device approved by FDA.
COST TO FEDERAL BUDGET	Estimated savings of $58 billion over first five years	Estimated savings of $14.2 billion per year, assuming using adjusted Medicare rates for comparison.	Approximately $25 billion per year paid for by financing mechanisms outlined above.	Not specified. Presumably no net cost as subsidies are delayed if savings do not occur.	Not specified.	Estimated $45.5 billion in deficit reduction over five years.

KPMG PEAT MARWICK COMPARISON OF HEALTH REFORM PROPOSALS
103rd Congress

	President Clinton H.R. 3600/S.1757	H.R. 1200 Cong. McDermott	H.R. 3222 Bipartisan Group on Health Reform (Cong. Cooper)	S. 1770 Senate Republican Task Force (Sen. Chafee)	H.R. 3080 House Republican Proposal (Cong. Michel)	Sen. Gramm
EXAMPLES OF NOTABLE SUPPORTERS	Chairs of jurisdictional committees will co-sponsor; Republican Senator Jeffords; American College of Physicians, Former Surgeon General Koop.	89 members of the House; Americans for Democratic Action; 913 grassroots organizations. Sen. Wellstone has companion bill in the Senate.	49 members of the House from both parties; Jackson Hole Group; Conservative Democratic Forum; Democratic Leadership Council. Sen. Breaux has a companion bill in the Senate.	Members of the Senate Republican Task Force on Health.	106 Republican members of the House.	10 Republican Senators, including Hutchison and Helms.

APPENDIX B

Comparison of the Clinton Plan Standardized Benefit Package and Health Benefits of Small, Midsize, and Large Firms, 1993

In the Spring of 1993, collaborating with researchers from Wayne State University, KPMG Peat Marwick conducted the telephone interviews with a sample of the nation's employers. The sample included small, medium, and large employers, and was drawn from a listing of the nation's employers compiled by Dun & Bradstreet. The interviews were with human resource managers.

The table displays essential features of health benefits offered in 1993 by small, medium, and large employers and compares them with the standardized benefit package required under the Clinton Plan. The table also compares the annual cost of premiums between today's plans and the Clinton Plan. One may reach one of two conclusions after analyzing the survey results shown in the table. The first is that the Clinton Plan offers rich benefits at a lower premium cost, particularly for small employers. The opposing conclusion is that the Clinton Administration has underestimated the cost of coverage, which will require the Administration to alter its plan for financing the uninsured.

Benefit	White House Health Care Reform Blueprint	Firms with 1 to 49 Employees
Premiums	Employer pays: 80% of average plan. the remainder (20%) is employee paid. Firms have option of paying a larger percentage of the premium.	Employer pays: FFS 61% individual, 54% family HMO 65% individual, 52% family PPO 67% individual, 48% family
Deductibles	$200 single, $400 family	FFS $330 individual, $717 family PPO In-plan $264 Out-Plan $1,139
Coinsurance	20% employee paid, or 80-20	35% of PPO plans pay 80-20 when in-plan provider used (36% < 80-20). 45% of PPO plans pay 80-20 when out-plan provider used (5% < 80-20)**
HMO Visit Fee	$10	25% have $10 fee; 53% have lower or no fee
Preventative Care	Well-baby care required Well-child care required	Currently provided in: FFS 57% HMO 97% (no data for PPO plans on preventive benefits)
Physical Exams	Adult physicals every two to five years	Currently provided in: FFS 49% HMO 94%
Out-of-Pocket Limits	$1,500 for individuals	FFS $1,000 or less 25% $1,001–$2,000 26% More than $2,000 24% PPO $1,000 or less 24% $1,001–$2,000 33% More than $2,000 17%
Lifetime Maximum Benefits	None	16% of FFS plans have no lifetime maximum benefit. 11% of PPO plans have no lifetime maximum benefit.
Pre-existing Condition Limitations	Prohibited	59% of FFS, 19% of HMO, and 65% of PPO plans have pre-existing condition limitation clauses.
Percent of plans with limits		
Cost		
Conventional (FFS)	Estimated average annual cost for all plan types is $1,800 single, $4,200 family	$2,235 single $5,141 family
HMO	Estimated average annual cost for all plan types is $1,800 single, $4,200 family	$1,866 single $4,652 family
PPO	Est. average annual cost for all plan types is $1,800 single, $4,200 family	$2,024 single $4,620 family

Excerpts from Employee Benefits Survey (1993) contained in the "American Health Security Act Summary and Analysis" by KPMG Peat Marwick. Reprinted with permission.

* KPMG Peat Marwick/Wayne State University Survey of 750 firms, Spring 1993

** FFS data not available

Firms with 50 to 199 Employees*	Firms with 200+ Employees*
Employer pays: FFS 77% individual, 63% family HMO 68& individual, 54% family PPO 73% individual, 55% family	% of Premium employer pays:* FFS** 86% Single, 76% Family HMO 81% Single, 71% Family PPO 81% Single, 72% Family
FFS $263 individual, $580 family PPO In-plan $242 Out-plan $362	FFS $224 Single, $545 Family PPO In-plan $145 Out-plan $242
29% of PPO plans pay 80-20 when in-plan provider used (44% < 80-20). 28% of PPO plans pay 80-20 when out-plan provider used (0% < 80-20)**	Employee pays 20% in 77% of plans; another 12% have lower coinsurance
44% have $10 fee; 32% have lower or no fee	28% of HMO plans charge $10; 62% have lower or no fee
Currently provided in: FFS 67% HOM 99% (no data for PPO plans on preventive benefits)	Percent of plans covering: FFS 55% PPO 72% HMO 97% percent of plans covering: FFS 42% PPO 55% HMO 95%
Currently provided in: FFS 63% HMO 99% (no data for PPO plans on preventive benefits)	Percent of plans covering: FFS 37% PPO 50% HMO 97%

FFS $1,000 or less   33%
          $1,001–$2,000   30%
          More than $2,000   13%
PPO $1,000 or less   39%
          $1,001–$2,000   37%
          More than $2,000   12%
	FFS $1,000 or less 35%
	          $1,001–$2,000 34%
	          $2,000 or more 17%
	PPO $1,000 or less 39%
	          $1,001–$1,999 22%
	          $2,000 or more 22%

Have no lifetime maximum benefit 18% of FFS plans; 19% of PPO plans	Have no lifetime maximum benefit 15% of FFS plans; 19% of PPO plans
59% of FFS, 3% of HMO, and 82% of PPO plans have pre-existing condition limitation clauses.	Prohibited FFS 64% PPO 71%
$2,205 single $5,258 family	$2,050 Single $5,292 Family
$1,718 single $4,638 family	$1,896 Single $5,064 Family
$1,870 single $4,564 family	$2,172 Single $5,448 Family

* KPMG Peat Marwick Survey of 200 Firms, Spring 1993

** FFS data not available

*Based on KPMG Peat Marwick Survey
of 1.003 firms, Spring, 1993*

* Note: definitional difference
  —"Family" as defined in the KPMG Peat Marwick Survey
    means 4 people
  —"Family" as defined in the Clinton Plan refers to either
    a couple, a single parent with dependents, or a married
    couple with children.

** FFS = fee-for-service conventional plan

2. State Health Reform Activity in 1994: Less Comprehensive, More Incremental

Carol Malone

Although most states have put their health reform measures on the back burner while they wait for the federal government to act, a number of states are going ahead with their own versions of health care reform. Because of the political climate and a number of other factors, most of these state reform measures are incremental rather than comprehensive. Nevertheless, the types of programs and financing mechanisms some states are acting on today—and more importantly, the voters' reactions to them—are probably indicative of the future of health care in America.

The pace of health care reform at the state level slowed considerably during the first six months of 1994. Rather than enacting comprehensive reform legislation as they did in 1992 and 1993, states, for the most part, have opted to restructure their health care delivery and financing systems in incremental stages. Many states are doing this through reform of the health insurance industry—in particular, the small group market—as well as through the introduction of purchasing cooperatives. A number of states have actually scaled back or delayed their earlier, more comprehensive initiatives, and even those that did pass moderate reform measures during 1994 left the tough financing decisions for future sessions.

Several factors may account for this slowdown: Many state governments have turned their attention to other, more immediate issues, such as violent crime, the economy, welfare reform, and education. Also, shortened legislative sessions during this election year have kept many state health reform initiatives bogged down in partisan politics.

The possibility of federal health care reform has also put the brakes on reform at the state level, with several states debating whether to wait until Congress acts or to move ahead with their own plans. If reform occurs at the federal level, what would happen to their plans? Should they be ready to implement their own plans if Congress is unable to pass a national health care reform bill?

ERISA: STILL A MAJOR IMPEDIMENT

Even states that have enacted—or have proposed—legislation that would provide universal coverage to state residents have a major hurdle to overcome before their laws are effective. The Employee Retirement Income Security Act of 1974 (ERISA) makes it difficult for states to implement comprehensive health reform legislation within their borders. Specifically, ERISA prohibits states from establishing or imposing approaches such as single- or all-payer rate-setting systems, employer mandates, premium taxes on self-insured plans, provider taxes earmarked for health programs for uninsured or low-income individuals, minimum guaranteed benefits packages for all employees, and standard data collection systems and uniform administrative processes. While Oregon, Massachusetts, Minnesota, Vermont, and Washington, for example, have enacted universal health care legislation, they are prohibited from actually implementing it. In fact, Congressional representatives from Oregon and Washington submitted proposals in 1993 requesting waivers from ERISA, but little action has been taken on these measures. Hawaii is the only state with a limited ERISA waiver because its universal coverage program was established before ERISA's enactment.

While states may chafe under ERISA preemption, large self-insured employers view it favorably. ERISA does permit states to regulate insured plans through state insurance laws, but preempts regulation of self-insured health plans. As a result, self-insured plans are not subject to state mandated benefits, taxes on premiums, and participation in state risk pools or uncompensated care plans, as are insured plans. Because of this, self-insured employers with operations in multiple states are able to offer a standard health benefits package to employees in all states in which they do business, rather than different plans that conform to the health care delivery and financing requirements of each state. Employers contend that without ERISA preemption, the costs of administering health plans would skyrocket because businesses would have to comply with differing laws in each state.

NATIONAL POLITICS AFFECT STATES, AND VICE VERSA

Meanwhile, lawmakers in Washington are paying close attention to progress and setbacks in health care reform in several states. According to some health policy experts, the substance of reform at the state level is a good barometer of public sentiment about some of reform's more controversial aspects. In the opinion of experts, the roadblocks that states face may reflect those that Congress will grapple with as it moves forward with the debates about reform at the national level. For example, several states have defeated employer mandates and mandatory purchasing alliances, sending a clear message to Washington about the role of mandates in providing universal coverage. In California, residents will vote in November on a statewide initiative calling for a single-payer system to provide universal coverage for state residents.

Congress is also keeping tabs on the partisan politics being played out in state legislatures around the country this election year. In Florida, for example, a special health care reform session ended prematurely when legislation that initially enjoyed broad bipartisan support was blocked strictly along party lines. Eventually, the legislation died in committee. Following its demise, Democratic Governor Lawton Chiles, who is up for reelection this fall, and other Florida Democrats claimed that Republicans in Washington leaned heavily on their party's state legislators to block the proposed health reform bill. In Chiles' view, a vote for his plan was a vote for the Clinton plan.

A similar fate befell the health reform proposal of Vermont Governor Howard Dean, a Democrat. Dean's bill would have achieved universal coverage, financed through a combination of individual and employer mandates. Under his proposal, all residents would have been required to purchase health insurance, and employers would have to pay 50 percent of the insurance costs for employees. A subsidy program for the uninsured would have been financed through a 5 percent tax on insurance premiums.

According to many analysts, heavy lobbying by small businesses and other special interest groups—and exhaustive local media coverage—doomed Vermont's proposal. The more the public understood about the bill's provisions and its cost, the more nervous they became. Governor Dean, also up for reelection this year, has long been a proponent of states adopting their own solutions to local health delivery problems. However, his recent defeat has altered his perspective, and today, Dean supports the need for a federal framework.

STATES ENACT, IMPLEMENT, AND PROPOSE

Despite the slowdown, some states have enacted significant legislation in 1994, while others have started to implement laws passed in 1992 and 1993. A handful of states have proposed health care reform legislation to be voted on in the fall.

Reforms Enacted   *15-3, 170*

Kentucky, Minnesota, Connecticut, and Colorado enacted significant legislation in the first six months of 1994.

Kentucky. So far, Kentucky has set the benchmark in 1994 for health care reform initiatives at the state level. After several years of pushing a comprehensive health reform agenda, Governor Brereton Jones, a Democrat, in April signed into law an incremental reform proposal. The legislation falls far short of meeting two of the governor's original goals: universal coverage and provider rate setting.

Kentucky's law establishes a hybrid voluntary-mandatory statewide health purchasing alliance, effective in 1995. The alliance is open to individuals and to employers with 100 or fewer workers. State employees and Medicaid recipients will be required to join by 1995. And public health, state, higher education, local government, and judiciary employees must join by 1996. Until the alliance is operational, the law calls for the creation of a state employee insurance buy-in program to allow eligible state residents to purchase insurance. Also, as part of the plan, all health care providers will now be required to post their maximum charges for certain procedures, services, and products.

Minnesota. In May, Republican Governor Arne Carlson signed into law a weakened health reform bill that would provide universal coverage for state residents. The law also calls for minor health insurance reform, with an extended phase-in for portability and guaranteed issuance. In addition, the bill delays to 1997 the reform provisions enacted in 1992 and 1993 under the MinnesotaCare law.

The law's universal coverage provision would become effective July 1, 1997, through an individual mandate requiring individuals to buy coverage. However, Minnesota's new law has no financing mechanism. Over the next several months, studies will be conducted to analyze alternative ways to pay for universal coverage. If cost analyses indicate too high a price tag, Carlson may halt further progress of the universal coverage concept. Otherwise, in 1995 Minnesota's lawmakers are required to determine ways to pay for universal coverage.

The new law also moves the state closer to implementing two systems of health care: Integrated Service Networks (ISN), or managed medical networks, and Regulated All-Payer Option (RAPO). Both would help control costs in accordance with previously established targets. The majority of Minnesotans are expected to obtain their care through ISNs, while those who seek fee-for-service care would pay regulated fees. The state postponed for three years, until July 1997, the date for licensing ISNs and full implementation of the program. This summer, Minnesota will begin licensing smaller networks, called community ISNs (CISNs), which have 50,000 members or fewer.

The Minnesota legislature also worked out a compromise over the hotly debated "any willing provider" provision, which gives consumers expanded access to about 20 types of allied health providers. The compromise allows all providers to join managed care plans as long as they comply with plan rules and prices. However, it also allows managed care plans to sell these products separately and at actuarially justified higher prices. Exempt from this rule are staff model HMOs and the new CISNs.

Connecticut. Early this year, Connecticut enacted legislation that deregulates hospital pricing and creates a new method for calculating reimbursements to hospitals for the cost of uncompensated care. The new law repeals Connecticut's uncompensated care surcharge and pool, eliminates the state's regulation of hospital charges, and allows all payers and hospitals to negotiate the price and delivery of care. Uncompensated care is now reimbursed through a tax imposed on hospital services and revenue.

The law was the outcome of a recent federal court decision that ruled that the state's practice of assessing the hospital bills of individuals who have health coverage to pay for uncompensated hospital care violated ERISA. The suit was brought by a union health plan, which argued that ERISA prohibits states from creating any mechanism that makes health coverage more costly to self-insured employers and their workers.

Colorado. In June, Colorado Governor Roy Romer, a Democrat, signed a health insurance reform bill that requires carriers for small employers (those with two to 50 employees) to offer at least two uniform benefit packages. The new law also limits preexisting condition waiting periods and requires that premiums be based only on age, family size, and location. Romer also signed a bill that allows the creation of private, voluntary purchasing alliances and provider networks.

Reforms Implemented

Some states—including Florida, New York, Tennessee, Texas, and Oregon—have been implementing legislation passed between 1989 and 1993.

Florida. In May, Florida began moving ahead with implementing 11 new Community Health Purchasing Alliances (CHPAs) by enrolling a limited number of small employers. Established under the 1993 health reform law, CHPAs are non-profit corporations that pool, on a voluntary basis, the purchasing power of self-employed individuals and businesses with 50 or fewer employees. In addition, CHPAs offer small employers a choice of health benefit plans and provide detailed information about prices, utilization rates, and outcomes of plan providers. Small businesses are expected to save an average of $100 to $300 a month in total health insurance costs by purchasing through a CHPA plan.

New York. New York State Insurance Department figures released in May showed that the number of individuals with health insurance coverage actually decreased by approximately 26,000 after the state's community rating laws for individuals and small businesses went into effect. The costs of covering high-risk individuals have reportedly increased the costs of policies for younger, healthier individuals, many of whom dropped coverage.

Also, insurance companies in New York have sued the insurance commissioner in federal court to overturn the pooling mechanism established under the state's community rating law. Under the regulations imposed by a 1992 health reform law, insurers and HMOs with healthier, lower risk subscribers are required to contribute to two pools, which are then used to pay insurers that have sicker, higher risk subscribers. The lawsuit alleges that ERISA preempts the state from establishing community rating pools and enforcing regulations because they directly impact employee benefit plans.

Tennessee. TennCare, Tennessee's ambitious managed care program designed to replace Medicaid, went into effect on January 1. Individuals who qualify for Medicaid and Tennessee residents who were uninsured as of March 31, 1993, may apply for TennCare. Any Tennessean with an income below 100 percent of the federal poverty level may join TennCare and pay no premium charges, deductibles, or copayments. Individuals with incomes between 100 and 200 percent of the poverty level qualify for TennCare on a sliding scale, and their premiums, deductibles, and copayments rise in proportion with their higher incomes. Residents with incomes above 200 percent of the poverty level are required to pay the full premium, deductible, and copayments.

The program has been popular: By the end of the first quarter 1994, TennCare received 250,000 applications, eight times the number predicted. So far, Tennessee's physicians have been less than enthusiastic about the program, citing a so-called "cram down" policy imposed by Blue Cross and Blue Shield (BCBS) in Chattanooga and sanctioned by the state. The policy requires physicians who want to participate in the state employee BCBS Tennessee Provider Network (a PPO) to accept TennCare patients also.

Texas. The Texas Insurance Purchasing Alliance, created by legislation signed in 1993, began in May to sell policies to small businesses—those with three to 50 employees—in the Gulf Coast region. Alliance policies are expected to be available throughout Texas by the fall of 1994. The voluntary purchasing alliance pools thousands of small employers, enabling them to negotiate lower cost premiums, and offers a choice of six standard benefit levels. Employers are required to contribute at least 75 percent of the lowest cost option available, and employees are required to pay the remaining 25 percent.

Oregon. Phase one of Oregon's universal coverage plan went into effect on February 1. The plan expands Medicaid eligibility to a greater number of poor residents—an estimated 120,000 people under the poverty level—places them in managed care plans, and covers a limited list of priority services.

So far, enrollment in the plan has exceeded original estimates. As of June 1, more than 65,400 poor and uninsured residents have signed up—14,000 more people than originally projected. State officials also report that the majority who have signed up are in traditional families, rather than the single, the unemployed, and childless couples that the state had expected.

To help pay the costs of extending free health services to a greater number of poor Oregonians, the plan will cover only 565 of the 696 medical conditions normally covered by Medicaid. In 1994, the reduced list of services covered applies to Medicaid-eligible pregnant women, mothers, and their children. Medicaid-eligible blind, elderly, disabled, and children in foster care will be part of the plan in 1995.

Reforms Proposed

Despite the current debate in Washington over federal health care reform, some states are asking voters to voice their preferences in elections this fall. Three of the more significant proposals have been drafted by California, Massachusetts, and Pennsylvania.

California. A single-payer plan modeled on Canada's system has qualified for the ballot in California this November. More than one million signatures gathered by voter registrars have been audited and validated. The plan would cover all inpatient and outpatient care, full mental health benefits, long-term care, prescription drugs, and some dental care for all legal California residents. As drafted, the plan would require no copayments or other out-of-pocket costs. California would finance its single-payer plan by increasing taxes on individuals, cigarettes, and company payrolls.

Massachusetts. Governor William Weld, a Republican, and Democratic legislative leaders introduced competing bills that would expand health care coverage and provide subsidies to 600,000 uninsured low-income state residents. Both proposals would reform the insurance industry for small groups. Weld defines small groups as those with 50 or fewer participants, while the Democrats defines them as 100 or fewer.

Weld's proposal would repeal the employer mandate set to kick in by January 1995 under the pay-or-play plan passed in 1988 under the Dukakis administration. The Democratic version would maintain the mandate. Under the 1988 law, employers would have been required to provide health coverage to their employees or pay up to $1,680 per worker into a state insurance pool. The plan was to have begun in 1992 but has been delayed for political reasons.

Pennsylvania. A compromise health reform bill that includes elements of both a single-payer plan and Democratic Governor Robert Casey's managed competition proposal is expected to be ready for a vote when the state House returns in the fall. The single-payer plan addresses the needs of residents in Pennsylvania's rural areas. To obtain passage, the governor and his supporters reportedly need to win some Republican votes and solidify a splintered Democratic caucus in the House.

1994: ALIGNING EXPECTATIONS AND RESOURCES

With few exceptions, state health care reform activity will be on the back burner for the rest of 1994. Analysts read many messages in this slowdown in state health reform activities. The shift away from comprehensive measures to more incremental reforms suggests that states may be approaching health care reform more pragmatically. Working with limited resources and in a climate not conducive to further tax increases, state legislatures have had to rethink their priorities and reapportion state funds and legislative resources among the numerous problems pressing in on them. Even states with ambitious programs promising universal coverage must wait for Congress to decide on whether to grant ERISA exemptions. States seem to have decided to proceed with incremental reform rather than spend valuable resources working out comprehensive legislation that cannot be implemented as long as the ERISA preemption takes precedence over state law.

By enacting less comprehensive, more incremental legislation, perhaps states can be viewed as sending loud messages to Congress about what they expect from federal reform: The American public may be reluctant to vote for sweeping change without first testing the impact of smaller reforms. Voters may also be telling their legislators in Washington to align expectations with available resources. The American public's advice to Congress seems to be: Go slowly.

3. Backdrop of Reform: The Evolving Health Care Delivery System

William S. Custer

The evolution of the health care delivery system in this country in recent years has been nothing short of dramatic. The very changes to the system that are the central tenets of many politicians' health care reform plans—increasing managed care, reorganizing the structures and administration of medical organizations, changing the sites of medical services, and others—are already taking place, due largely to natural market forces like inflation. Understanding the evolution of the health care delivery system so far is the best way to understand the way health care reform will change it in the future.

The debate about health care reform has taken place against the backdrop of a rapidly evolving health care delivery system. Increasing health care costs have led both private and public purchasers of health care services to change their relationships with the health care services market. This in turn has affected the practice of medicine. Care has moved out of the hospital to a variety of sites, referral patterns of physicians have been affected, the relationship between hospitals and their medical staffs has been altered, and the way providers market themselves has changed due to changes in the way payers purchase health care services. A cost management industry has arisen composed of utilization review firms, provider networks, data analysis firms, and other vendors whose services track medical decision making and assess the quality of care.

Rising health care costs have resulted in an increasingly segmented health insurance market, leading fewer employers, especially small employers, to offer health insurance as an employee benefit, and resulting in an increase in the number of Americans without health insurance coverage. Changes in health care financing have limited providers' ability to provide uncompensated care, limiting the access to care of uninsured people.

The number of Americans without health insurance increased slowly through the 1980s, reaching 38.5 million individuals in 1992. The shift in the number of nonelderly individuals with *employment-based* health insurance has been more dramatic in recent years. Partly as a result of the recession beginning in 1990, 2 million fewer Americans had employment-based health insurance in 1990 than 1989. That event coincided with the rise in health care reform as an important political issue. While a number of proposals for reforming the health care delivery system had been advanced before the 1992 election campaign, none of them garnered enough support to suggest that they might be implemented. Since the election, the Clinton administration and congressional groups of both parties have advanced health care reform proposals that incorporate elements of managed competition models.

Managed competition is a model of health care reform that reorganizes the market for health care services. As a general concept, managed competition is appealing to a wide variety of groups because managed competition models can have varying levels of government regulation built in. Thus, those who believe that the market for health care services can never work efficiently can design a model with a high degree of regulation, while other models can be designed with much less government regulation.

While health care reform will have important effects on the future evolution of the health care delivery system, the promise (or threat) of health care reform has already had an impact on the health care delivery system. Health care cost inflation has set in motion forces that are moving the health care delivery system toward a more concentrated, more vertically integrated, system. The increasing likelihood that some type of health care reform proposal will be enacted has accelerated the evolution of the health care delivery system. It is widely believed that vertically integrated coordinated systems of care will be in the best position to compete in a managed competition system. Although it is unclear whether a health care reform proposal will be enacted, there has been an increase in the number of mergers and cooperative agreements among health care providers and health services organizations.

This paper examines the changes the health care delivery system has undergone in the past decade and discusses the elements of health care reform and their implications for the evolution of the health care delivery system.

REASONS FOR HEALTH CARE COST INFLATION

The present system of financing health care services began with the spread of health insurance after World War II. Unlike other types of insurance, health insurance benefits are based on expenditures for health care services rather than on the actual loss due to a particular ailment. As a result, health insurance lowers the relative price of medical services to insured individuals, increasing patient demand for health care services. This change in consumer behavior due to the presence of insurance is a form of "moral hazard." The increased demand for health care services due to moral hazard is one source of health care cost inflation.

The characteristics of provider reimbursement policies of private and public insurers have had important implications for the health care delivery system. Hospitals have been regarded as quasi-public institutions and as such were traditionally reimbursed on a cost-plus basis to ensure that they were able to maintain high quality services. However, reimbursement under fee-for-service for physicians or cost-plus systems for hospitals gives providers little incentive for limiting the potential range of diagnostic and therapeutic services available to a patient, or to limit the quantity of services they provide. Increased health insurance coverage has raised the demand for medical services. All of these features of the health care delivery system have been cited as contributing to increasing costs.

The increasing demand for health care services has led to a corollary increase in the demand for new medical technology. Medical researchers, with financial assistance from the government and other sources, have responded impressively. The number of diagnostic tools a physician can employ on a given set of symptoms and the number of potential therapeutic procedures for a given diagnosis have increased dramatically in the last 25 years.

New technology lengthens the list of procedures a physician can perform for a given condition and increases the number of conditions a physician can treat, increasing the number of services purchased. Concurrently, as the supply of physicians increases, they tend to specialize, performing fewer types of procedures.[1]

The sensitivity of the demand for health care services to changes in price is lessened by the spread of health insurance, which lowers the effective price of health care services to patients. Physicians have long considered price competition unethical. Providers have competed in quality or, more accurately, in quality signals. Lacking the information necessary to evaluate the technical quality of care, patients look for signals they hope relate to technical quality, such as location, office attributes, and the physician's hospital affiliation. Hospitals compete with each other for physicians and patients by offering the ability to perform more procedures and to deliver more amenities.[2] The cost of the more expensive new technology required to perform new procedures is often spread across all other procedures.[3]

The result is that new technology is introduced with little or no evaluation of its benefits relative to costs. Providers adopt practices based on personal preferences, resulting in the well-documented variation in practice patterns among physicians practicing in the same geographic area. Patients and payers lack the information necessary to evaluate the quality of care they received before, during, or after an episode of illness. Medical researchers have had little or no incentive to assess the relative benefits of the procedures they developed; to be adopted, new procedures did not have to be more effective or less expensive than existing procedures.

Medical research has produced a rapid expansion in treatment options without concurrent research on the relative efficacy of each option. This has prevented the formation of a medical consensus on the proper treatment of a given set of symptoms. Large variation in practice patterns has been documented among physicians practicing in the same geographic area.[4] Many physicians see too few patients with any specific condition to evaluate the relative efficacy of competing treatments. The paucity of research on medical outcomes results in the practice of medicine as an art rather than a science and limits the ability of purchasers of health care services to differentiate among providers on the basis of quality.

COST MANAGEMENT STRATEGIES

The preceding discussion provides some of the reasons health care costs have risen so rapidly over the last 20 years. Private health plans and public programs have been evolving rapidly in the last decade in response to health care cost inflation. The reaction of employers to increases in health care costs has varied depending on the labor market they face, the amount of competition in their product market, and their level of power in their specific health care services markets. In general, employers have adopted four types of cost management strategies:

1. Cost sharing,
2. Utilization review (UR),
3. Provider services packaging, and
4. Selective contracting with providers.

These strategies have been combined in the various managed care plans employed by many employers.

Cost sharing is effective in reducing health care expenditures by reducing the utilization of health care services. For example, the Rand Health Insurance experiment found that individuals in plans with a 25 percent coinsurance rate had 15 percent lower per capita costs than individuals in plans with a zero coinsurance rate.[5] Cost sharing is most effective in reducing the use of outpatient care. However, some of the care forgone may include preventive care, the lack of which may result in larger inpatient costs. The Rand study found that low-income individuals with lower coinsurance rates experienced specific health gains for three prevalent chronic problems—high blood pressure, myopia, and dental care—that are relatively inexpensive to diagnose and treat.

UR includes a number of strategies for intervening in the decision to purchase health care. These may include pre-admission certification, in which care is reviewed before it is given to determine its appropriateness; concurrent review, or case management, in which care is monitored as it is provided; and retrospective review, a system of reviewing care after it is given. In all cases, care is reviewed against criteria to determine if it is necessary and appropriate. These criteria are either developed by UR firms internally or are licensed from outside sources and modified by the firms.

Another strategy for managing health care costs attempts to steer patients to cost-effective providers. Under this approach, plans reward patients for choosing cost-effective sites of care; examples of this approach include ambulatory surgery provisions and use of preferred provider organizations (PPOs). Although the actual structure of PPOs differs greatly, in theory PPOs combine three broad cost management strategies: a limited panel of providers, negotiated fee schedules, and UR.

Finally, many employers offer employees a choice of an indemnity plan and a health maintenance organization (HMO). Depending upon the HMO, total costs for enrollees have been found to vary between 1.4 percent and 31.8 percent lower than more traditional health insurance programs (see Table 1).[6] These costs differences result from lower rates of service, especially lower hospital admission rates.

There are a number of HMO models, but they generally fall into two categories: group (or staff) models and independent practice arrangements (IPAs)

Table 1. 1992 Indemnity Plan Costs vs. Managed Care Plan Costs (Selected U.S. Cities)

City	Indemnity plan	Average cost per employee	HMO cost vs. indemnity cost	Average cost per employee	PPO cost vs. indemnity cost
Atlanta	$3,729	$3,311	−11.2%	$3,363	−9.8%
Chicago	4,245	3,088	−27.3	3,684	−13.2
Cleveland	4,027	3,727	−7.4	3,459	−14.1
Dallas/Fort Worth	3,917	3,330	−15.0	3,837	−2.0
Houston	3,627	3,575	−1.4	4,091	+12.8
Los Angeles	4,350	3,189	−26.7	4,457	+2.5
Minneapolis/ St. Paul	3,347	2,969	−11.3	3,121	−6.8
New York Metro	4,852	3,448	−28.9	3,871	−20.2
Orange County	4,276	3,124	−26.9	4,315	+0.9
Philadelphia	4,696	3,319	−29.3	3,708	−21.0
Richmond	3,578	3,074	−14.1	3,183	−11.0
San Francisco	4,531	3,092	−31.8	4,459	−1.6
Seattle	3,554	3,092	−13.0	3,114	−12.4

Source: A. Foster Higgins & Co., Inc., *Health Care Benefits Survey, 1992* (Princeton, NJ: A. Foster Higgins & Co., Inc. 1993).

or network models. In group models, the physician is either an employee of, or receives a majority of his/her patients from, the HMO. In an IPA model, the HMO contracts with physicians or physician groups who also maintain a fee-for-service practice. Physicians in IPAs are typically reimbursed on a blended fee-for-service/capitation basis.

Although IPAs have been the fastest growing HMO model, the research literature has generally focused on the older, more established HMOs, which are more likely to be group or staff models. The few studies of IPAs that have been done suggest that these HMOs have more admissions per thousand members and thus are less effective than group or staff models in constraining costs.

Some employers offering an HMO option in addition to an indemnity plan have claimed that employees who represent lower risk opt for the HMO, while higher-cost patients remain in the comprehensive plan, resulting in higher overall health care costs. Buchanan and Cretin found that families selecting HMOs were younger, had lower income, and had lower claimed health care expenses before enrollment than families selecting a fee-for-service plan.[7] Studying the impact of various benefit options on premiums, Jensen and Morrisey found that a group health plan offering an HMO option had significantly higher premiums for its fee-for-service plan.[8]

Finally, two widely cited studies using data from the late 1970s or early 1980s have found that the rate of cost inflation is the same for HMOs as it is for more traditional insurance plans. The authors of one of these studies argue that this result indicates that HMOs must adopt new technology at the same rate as the fee-for-service plans. One possible explanation of this result may be that the information necessary to evaluate the cost effectiveness of a new procedure is simply not available, even to providers with a clear financial incentive to adopt cost reducing techniques. Another possibility is that maintaining the HMOs' market share in competition with fee-for-service care requires the adoption of the same types of practices. Conversely, recent surveys of employers found that HMO premium increases have been about 5 percentage points lower than indemnity plan premium increases (see Table 2).

The enrollment in HMOs of all types has increased from 9.1 million Americans in 1980 to 37.2 in 1992. This increase in market penetration by HMOs has not been evenly distributed. HMOs have not been established in rural areas, in large part because these areas lack the population size necessary to maintain an independent health plan. The market penetration of HMOs also differs considerably by region. Almost 30 percent of Californians were enrolled in an HMO in 1989, and just under 24 percent of the residents of Massachusetts, but only 10.6 percent of Floridians and 7 percent of Texans. In less populous states the percentage of residents enrolled in HMOs was even smaller, with less than 1 percent of the citizens of Alaska, Montana, and Wyoming.

The need to evaluate providers for selective contracting and to evaluate care as it is being provided has led to the development of a health information industry.

Table 2. Health Maintenance Organization (HMO) Enrollment by State. Combined Pure and Open-Ended Enrollment in HMOs,a by State, July 1991 and July 1992.

State[b]	July 1991 Total Enrollment	July 1991 Percentage of State Population in HMOs[c]	July 1992 Total Enrollment	July 1992 Percentage of State Population In HMOs[D]
Total United States	36,482,090	14.7	38,841,693	15.2%
Alabama	240,361	5.9	217,314	5.3
Alaska	0	0	0	0
Arkansas	63,073	2.76	5,574	2.7
California	9,394,346	31.6	9,769,031	31.6
Colorado	698,634	21.2	740,994	21.4
Connecticut	658,703	20.0	652,270	19.9
Delaware	122,440	18.4	115,476	16.8
District of Columbia	477,539	e	488,594	e
Florida	1,562,398	12.1	1,819,577	13.5
Georgia	383,543	5.9	378,685	5.6
Guam	39,789	e	74,137	e
Hawaii	253,072	22.8	259,671	22.4
Idaho	20,351	2.0	20,351 1.9	
Illinois	1,486,422	13.0	1,716,593	14.8
Indiana	339,735	6.1	359,313	6.3
Iowa	282,937	10.2	107,178	3.8
Kansas	182,734	7.4	165,444	6.6
Kentucky	300,952	8.2	248,955	6.6
Louisiana	264,757	6.3	258,510	6.0
Maine	24,325	2.0	48,663	3.9
Maryland	975,829	20.4	1,154,725	23.5
Massachusetts	1,829,956	30.4	2,024,758	33.8
Michigan	1,474,528	15.9	1,578,218	16.7
Minnesota	1,265,346	28.9	1,200,817	26.8
Mississippi	0	0	0	0
Missouri	565,785	11.1	615,386	11.9
Montana	8,166	1.0	10,731	1.3
Nebraska	97,601	6.2	110,432	6.9
Nevada	115,877	9.6	143,075	10.8
New Hampshire	110,292	9.9	126,058	11.3
New Jersey	921,564	11.9	921,438	11.8
New Mexico	212,279	14.0	239,959	15.2
New York	2,897,200	16.1	3,200,733	17.7
North Carolina	330,625	5.0	379,572	5.5
North Dakota	6,839	1.1	6,072	1.0
Ohio	1,427,251	13.2	1,519,249	13.8
Oklahoma	208,186	6.6	221,990	6.9
Oregon	739,987	26.0	777,812	26.1
Pennsylvania	1,485,489	12.5	1,705,179	14.2
Rhode Island	151,183	15.1	154,669	15.4
South Carolina	83,974	2.4	96,433	2.7
South Dakota	21,653	3.1	20,510	2.9
Tennessee	211,090	4.3	215,756	4.3
Texas	1,466,453	8.6	1,458,854	8.3
Utah	266,194	15.5	329,169	18.2
Vermont	46,344	8.2	53,966	9.5
Virginia	355,395	5.7	408,223	6.4
Washington	656,971	13.5	809,811	15.8

State[b]	*July 1991*		*July 1992*	
	Total Enrollment	Percentage of State Population in HMOs[c]	Total Enrollment	Percentage of State Population In HMOs[D]
West Virginia	74,077	4.1	72,805	4.0
Wisconsin	1,057,991	21.6	1,064,161	1.3
Wyoming	0	0	0	0

Source: Interstudy, *The Interstudy Competitive Edge,* Vol. 1 No. 2, 1992 and *The Interstudy Competitive Edge Databook*, Vol. 2 No. 2, 1993 (Excelsior, MN: InterStudy, 1992 and 1993).

a. Pure HMO members include all categories of prepaid membership (employer groups; individual, direct-pay, members; Medicare; Medicaid; and Federal Employee Health Benefits Program (FEHBP). Pure enrollment figures reflect the number of "covered lives"; covered dependents are included in these data. Self-insured enrollees are not included in these data. Open-ended members meet all of the requirements of pure members, but enrollees have the option of self-referring to providers outside of the HMO network at any time (at point of service).

b. The District of Columbia has been excluded from the state ranking due to the cross-state nature of its enrollment. Guam has also been excluded. However, enrollment for both D.C. and Guam remain in the U.S. total enrollment figure.

c. April 1, 1990 population figures provided by the U.S. Department of Commerce, Bureau of the Census. HMO enrollment represents July 1, 1991 data.

d. July 1, 1992 population figure provided by the U.S. Department of Commerce, Bureau of the Census. HMO enrollment represents July 1, 1992 data.

e. Data not available.

This industry supplies providers, insurers, employers, and consumers with information on the quality, appropriateness, and cost effectiveness of the care they are producing or consuming.

New health care plans have been developed that combine attributes of PPOs and HMOs with UR and objective performance criteria for selecting providers. One of the most important features of the selectively contracted networks is the criteria used to identify providers for inclusion in the network. Most networks require that providers agree to accept UR procedures, refer patients only to other providers in the network, and accept the network's reimbursement procedures. The networks also have quality standards, such as board certification, that the provider needs to meet in order to be considered for participation. Finally, providers' practice patterns may be monitored while they are in the network to identify and remove providers with unjustifiably high costs.

Objective information on the quality of care is being used by some employer plans to identify providers for selective contracting. Employers are contracting with specific hospitals for high cost procedures such as open heart surgeries and transplants and are using a number of criteria, including mortality and morbidity rates, to select hospitals. In selectively contracting on the basis of these criteria, employers are explicitly using outcome measures for determining reimbursement.

Managed care networks typically employ medical directors who develop or implement treatment protocols. These protocols determine the practice patterns of physicians employed or under contract with the network. Many of these new networks and network models of HMOs also employ primary care physicians to act as gatekeepers to manage health care costs. These gatekeeper physicians provide primary care for insured patients and control their access to specialists and sometimes to hospital care. A number of different financial arrangements have been developed between networks and gatekeeper physicians. Under some of these arrangements, the gatekeeper bears some of the risks. For example, the gatekeeper might be reimbursed on a capitated basis. As a result, the gatekeeper physician has a financial incentive to manage the patients' care as cost effectively as possible. Gatekeepers thus have an incentive to limit patients' access to specialists and other expensive health care services.

CHANGES IN THE MEDICARE PROGRAM

The federal government's efforts at controlling costs in the Medicare program has differed greatly from efforts by private payers. The Medicare program instituted the prospective payment system (PPS) for reimbursing hospitals in 1983 and began reimbursing physicians using a relative value fee schedule in 1992. Prior to the 1983 Social Security Amendments, Medicare paid hospitals retrospectively on a cost basis. That is, a hospital's reimbursement rate was determined by its historic costs. PPS represented a fundamentally different method for reimbursing hospitals than was commonly used by either public or private payers. The PPS hospitals moved from being reimbursed per day based on the hospital's historic costs to being reimbursed per admission at a prospectively determined rate. Thus, the incentives that Medicare's reimbursement methodology presented to hospitals changed in two distinct dimensions.

The change from a reimbursement rate based on the individual hospitals' historic costs meant that hospitals could no longer influence future reimbursement rates by incurring higher costs in the present. PPS thus removed one disincentive for hospitals to restrain their costs of provided health care services.

The second dimension along which PPS changed hospital incentives was the bundling of the services provided a patient during a single admission. Historically, cost-based, per diem reimbursement provided hospitals with a financial incentive both to lengthen the hospital stay of Medicare patients and to provide more services per stay. Conversely, under PPS, hospitals have an incentive to reduce the length of stay and provide the minimum services necessary to care for the patient.

In fact, a number of studies have found that PPS reduced both the average length of stay per admission and the number of admissions. Findings of a recent study by Schwartz and Mendelson, for example, indicate that the PPS may be responsible for a reduction in the average number of inpatient hospital days between 1981 and 1988. The cumulative reduction was 28.1 percent. The study also found that PPS is responsible for reducing the number of inpatient admissions. Between 1981 and 1988, the cumulative percentage decrease was 23.6 percent. Other studies indicate that there has not been a concurrent reduction in the quality of care provided to Medicare patients. While PPS reduced the rate of increase in Medicare Part A costs, it may have increased the rate of growth in Part B costs.

Growing concern about increases in physician service expenditures, exacerbated by the shift from outpatient care to inpatient care due to the advent of PPS in Medicare Part A, resulted in legislation in the Omnibus Budget Reconciliation Act of 1989 (OBRA '89) to change Medicare's methodology for reimbursing physicians. In 1992, Medicare began reimbursing physicians using a resource-based relative value scale (RBRVS), which is an index of the resources necessary to provide a given medical service. The relative value scale used in determining reimbursement is based on research performed at Harvard Medical School. Like the PPS for hospitals, RBRVS makes physician reimbursement prospectively determined. It removes incentives for physicians to charge higher fees this year in hopes of achieving higher reimbursement levels next year. Unlike PPS, the new physician reimbursement methodology does not bundle services. Physicians are still reimbursed on a fee-for-service basis. The financial incentive to provide as many possible services within each episode of care remains.

THE MARKET FOR HEALTH CARE SERVICES

The efforts of private and public payers to manage their health care costs has affected the insurance markets, the market for hospital services, physician practice arrangements, and treatment patterns. The growth of enrollment in staff and group model HMOs in the early 1980s and the development of UR techniques set the stage for the evolution of managed care plans that combined some of the reimbursement features of HMOs with selective contracting, gatekeepers, and treatment protocols. These developments have resulted in changes in the marketing strategies of hospitals, consolidation of hospitals and sharing of equipment, changes in hospital/medical staff relationships, rise of physician groups with a corresponding decrease in the number of solo practitioners, and changes in the career paths of young physicians.

Hospital care accounted for 38.4 percent of the nation's health expenditures in 1991. That is a decrease from the almost 41 percent of national health expenditures devoted to hospital care in 1980. Hospitals have generally competed with one another for physicians (and the patients they admit) on the basis of quality signals. These quality signals included the range of services or technologies available at the hospital. Hospitals thus have an incentive to invest in new technologies as they are introduced, to create excess capacity, to provide instant access to care, and to create amenities that are attractive to patients and physicians. As a result, 36 percent of hospitals with more than 200 beds have magnetic resonance imaging equipment and 86 percent have CT scanners—expensive technologies that in many cases are underutilized.

Changes in the reimbursement methodologies used by public and private payers have altered the incentives for hospitals to invest in new technologies, reduced their ability to subsidize uncompensated care, and changed the relationship between hospitals and physicians. Changes in reimbursement have lowered hospital operating margins and reduced their ability to finance the purchase of new technologies. Concurrently, many hospitals faced with prospective payment from public payers and selective contracting by private payers are attempting to restrict access to their services by the uninsured and are placing limits on their medical staffs' treatment patterns. Physicians, partly in response, are giving more care on an outpatient basis and are treating patients they have admitted to the hospital more intensively.

The number of hospitals decreased by 8 percent between 1981 and 1991, while the number of admissions fell by 14.7 percent and the number of inpatient days fell by 20 percent in the same period. During that same time period, the number of outpatient visits to hospitals increased by 58 percent. This increase does not include utilization in physician offices, independent surgery centers, and other facilities, which also experienced an increase in utilization during this period.

Hospitals have been confronted by: employers and insurers seeking to selectively contract, competition from managed care plans, changes in public plan reimbursement methodologies, and changes in technology that permit care to be moved to outpatient settings. As a result, they have had to change the way they market their services.

Hospitals rely on their medical staffs to provide patients and determine the volume of hospital services they will purchase. Both hospitals and physicians supply inputs to the production of hospital services. Yet the relationship between hospitals and their medical staffs is complex and not usually determined by an explicit market relationship. As the health care delivery system has evolved, the relationship between hospitals and their medical staffs has changed as well.

Changes in the health care delivery system have also changed physicians' practice arrangements. The percentage of physicians in groups increased from 26 percent of physicians in 1980 to 32.6 percent in 1991. The size of the groups also increased, from an average of 8.2 full-time equivalent physicians per group in 1980 to 11.5 in 1991. The number of employed physicians increased from 426,000 to 575,000 during this period.

Pharmaceutical and medical technology companies have begun to change both the content of their marketing materials and their targets. Historically, they have marketed their prescription products to physicians on the basis of efficacy. Increasingly, their marketing efforts are based on the cost effectiveness of treatment, and these efforts are often targeted toward medical directors of managed care networks.

The evolution of the health care delivery system led to the creation of relatively concentrated organizations. The threat/promise of health care reform has accelerated the trend toward vertical integration in the health care delivery system. Recent mergers in the pharmaceutical industry and the hospital industry demonstrate the desire of many stakeholders in the health care market to position themselves for health care reform.

HEALTH CARE COST INFLATION

All of these changes are having profound effects on the health care delivery system. It is not clear however, if those effects include a slowing of health care cost inflation. Health costs have moderated in the last two years, with employer health costs rising only 8 percent between 1992 and 1993.[9] This rate is still more than twice the annual rate of general price inflation, however. There are good reasons to be cautious about declaring victory over health care cost inflation.

The market for health care services appears to be evolving toward a more efficient, competitive market, but it still contains many of the characteristics that fuel health care cost inflation. Many managed care plans that hold the potential for constraining costs adopt less effective cost management strategies—at least initially—in order to establish themselves in local health care markets. The information systems needed to identify cost-effective new technologies to both producers and consumers of health care services are not yet in place. Purchasers of health care services do not yet have the tools to reward cost effective providers with increased business and to punish those less cost effective providers with decreased business.

It is, in fact, unreasonable to expect the market to have evolved to a point where health care costs inflation can be controlled. The changes in the health care delivery system that have occurred over the last five years are profound, but are only the beginning of a long road. Changing the way 14 percent of the economy operates is a difficult and ultimately lengthy process. The future of the health care delivery system and the speed with which it evolves will depend in large part on the shape of health care reform.

HEALTH CARE REFORM

The Clinton administration developed a health care reform model loosely based on managed competition. The basic element of managed competition is the creation of sponsors who act as collective purchasing agents for large groups of individuals. These sponsors negotiate with insurers or health plans and then offer their subscribers a menu of choices among different insurance plans, with information on each plan's quality of care and price. Managed competition is intended to shift the market for health insurance from competition based on risk to price competition. As a result, competition in the health care services markets will also theoretically move toward price competition.

By the time this article is published Congress will have either acted on one of the proposals presently before it, or postponed health reform for another year. Whatever the political process has produced this year, it seems likely some type of health reform will be enacted before the next presidential election. Following is a discussion of the various elements of health care reform and some of their effects on the health care delivery system.

Insurance Reform

Small groups often face higher costs per participant because of their higher per capita administrative cost and insurance companies' limited ability to pool risks. By removing barriers that prevent insurers from pooling small groups, employment-based coverage may expand to include many of the uninsured who are employed in small firms as well as the dependents of these employees (who constitute 39 percent of the nonelderly uninsured).

Although there are significant differences among small group reform proposals, there is agreement on some basic principles, including the following:

- Small groups should be guaranteed access to insurance
- Restrictions on preexisting conditions should be limited
- New restrictions should not be imposed when individuals change jobs or when groups change insurers
- Coverage should not be canceled because of high utilization of services
- Insurers should be required to offer coverage to all small groups (if they offer insurance to any)
- Premium rates should be stabilized
- Policies should be renewable (except for reasonable cause such as nonpayment of premiums)

Most proposals include some means for guaranteeing that all small groups have access to insurance and are not denied coverage based on individual characteristics. However, proponents of insurance market reform recognize that guaranteed availability alone accomplishes little unless premium rates for small groups are stabilized. Without some limits, insurers could use rating practices to raise the cost of coverage for riskier groups until the price becomes so high that these groups choose not to purchase insurance. Some proponents suggest moving toward community rating so that insurance would be offered to all small groups at fixed rates. Others would allow insurers to adjust community rates for factors such as age, sex, geographic location, and industry type (class rating). Generally, proposals would limit medical underwriting and restrictions on preexisting conditions.

Implications

It is generally accepted that moving to a community-rated insurance market will reduce the number of insurers in the market because of the need to create larger risk pools. In order to remain viable in a community-rated market, an insurer must have a sufficient market share to ensure that enough good risks are in the pool to make the costs of the coverage affordable. The result is likely to be fewer insurers in any given market, with each remaining insurer commanding a significant market share. Fewer insurers in more concentrated markets may increase the speed with which managed care networks are introduced and increase leverage of the payer over provider behavior.

Managed Competition

Under managed competition, the health insurance market would be altered by the substitution of the sponsor as a knowledgeable negotiator, with health insurance plans in the place of individual consumers or employee benefit managers. The sponsor would represent a group of consumers, whether they be the employees or dependents of employees of large employers or all individuals in a geographic area. Insurers would be required to accept any individuals who purchase health coverage through the sponsor. In theory, the health insurance market would be fundamentally changed under managed competition in that insurers could no longer attempt to avoid poorer risks and would need to find ways to control the costs of providing care.

Individuals under managed competition would be offered a menu of choices of health plans and given price and quality of care information for each plan. Theoretically, they could then choose the plan whose price and quality combination most suited their preferences. Such a choice requires that insurance policies be standardized to facilitate consumer choice, consumers be given a financial stake in their choice, and quality measures be developed that consumers can use to make choices.

Implications

The creation of a health alliance or sponsor changes the way health insurance plans are marketed. The alliance presents consumers with prices of standardized health plans and measures of quality of care and patient satisfaction. Insurance plans will thus compete on the basis of costs and those quality measures. The insurers' increased market power in the health care services market will force providers to alter treatment patterns to conform to the insurers' desire to attract patients on both the cost and quality dimensions. It seems likely that one result of these pressures will be lower real physician incomes, at least for some specialties.

The net effect on the health care delivery system will depend on the measures of quality used to evaluate plans and on relative values consumers place on these measures. If consumers value unlimited choice of providers, the ability of insurers to affect the health care services market may be constrained. While this may be an important factor in some markets, the growth of HMOs and managed care networks implies that consumers are willing to make some tradeoff between costs and choice. The need to assess the quality of care may hasten the development of quality assessment tools, and the use of these quality assessment tools may standardize the practice of medicine, resulting in higher quality, lower cost care.

The regulation of quality assessment techniques may also limit the ways that the quality of care is evaluated. Once put in place, these measures may be difficult to amend or replace. The measures of quality actually employed in the health care system will determine in large part the incentives faced by insurers, providers, and consumers. Once a definition of quality is developed, health plans will be required to provide the alliance with specific information that will be used to ascertain the quality of care, and the plans will then compete along the dimensions of quality defined by the system. To the degree that they are inaccurate or inadequate, lower quality care may be mandated into the system.

Universal Coverage

The Clinton plan mandates that all employers contribute to their employees' health insurance coverage, and that all individuals purchase coverage. It requires that all Americans not covered by Medicare purchase coverage through either one of the regional health alliances or an employer health alliance (which the employer can form only if it employs more than 5,000 individuals).

Implications

This requirement clearly redistributes income in the financing of health care services in two ways. First, employers who do not now offer health insurance coverage and individuals who do not now purchase health insurance would be required to contribute. Second, the move to community rating and inclusion in the insurance risk pools of individuals now excluded from the insurance market due to poor health or low income means that the cost of insurance would change for most Americans.

Universal coverage would also redistribute income on the provider side. The currently uninsured, those covered by the Medicaid program, and those with employment-based health insurance coverage would all present similar financial incentives for treatment to providers. Providers would no longer have an incentive, or the ability, to price discriminate across different payer groups.

Universal access would obviously increase the demand for health care services, although the degree to which that would occur is unclear. Currently, the studies have found that the uninsured use on average between 63 percent to 73 percent of physician services and 31 percent to 81 percent of the inpatient hospital resources used by privately insured individuals. A number of studies have estimated that providing universal coverage would increase the amount of money in the health care delivery system by between $40 billion and $60 billion annually.

Budget Caps

The Clinton health plan caps the amount of money going into the health care delivery system in two ways. First, there is a limit on the amount that individuals and employers would pay for health insurance. This limit is set at 7.9 percent of payroll for employers. Employed individuals and families would pay 20 percent of the premium, while nonworkers and self-employed individuals would pay the full premium. The cap on employer contributions would significantly decrease the amount of money going into the system. Currently, employers' contributions average over 10 percent of payroll.

Second, the proposal would cap insurance premium growth over the base projected premium to the growth in consumer prices. It seems unlikely that health care costs would not grow faster than consumer prices in the near term for several reasons, and if the base premium is estimated without taking into account the new populations being insured and the new community rating system, insurance premium growth may exceed the cap in the first or second year of implementation. Once the premium cap is exceeded, insurance premiums would be rolled back to the level of the cap.

Implications

The intent of the budget cap is to force insurers to manage health care costs. Given that price would no longer be a factor for competition, health plans would need to find a way to lower costs without reducing the quality of care in such a way as to reduce the number of individuals desiring to enroll in the plan. Alain Enthoven has suggested that global budgets would rob managed competition of its major cost management feature: price competition. Since the intention of managed competition was to develop a mechanism that would allow the market for health care services to operate efficiently, imposing price controls on that market means that the market would not determine the allocation of health care resources.

The reduction of resources flowing into the health care system would inevitably reduce the amount of capacity in the system. In the short run, the excess capacity of the U.S. health care system would probably mitigate some of the adverse affects on the quality of care that many analysts have suggested would be the result of binding budget caps. Budget caps would also slow the introduction of new technology. Again, there may be benefits to society if the new technology that is not introduced is of small marginal benefit.

It seems likely that budget caps of this type would lower the incomes of workers in the health services industry. One of the results of the wage and price controls imposed by the Nixon administration was a decrease in the real wages paid to hospital workers. It seems likely again that physicians and other professionals would also see their incomes decrease.

The net effect of a budget cap on the quality of care would depend critically on the measures of quality used by the alliances to assess care within the plans. If these measures do not adequately capture some dimensions of quality, then restricting the amount of resources that flow into the health care delivery system is likely to reduce quality of care along those dimensions. If the measures capture all relevant dimensions of quality competition among health plans for enrollees, they may prevent a reduction in the quality of care. However, many areas of the country would not have an adequate population to support competition among health plans. In those areas, regulatory oversight would be necessary to assure that quality does not erode as a result of budget caps.

CONCLUSION

The health care delivery system is evolving rapidly. There have been changes in the way health care is financed, the types of treatments available, the sites of care, and the physician-patient relationship. These changes have resulted primarily from reactions to health care cost inflation.

Health care reform is likely to accelerate some of these changes. The threat/promise of health care reform has already accelerated the consolidation of the health care services market. Health care reform is likely to reduce the number of insurers, increase the number of Americans in managed health care plans, increase the number of physicians in group practice, change provider income, and in general make the health care delivery system more concentrated and vertically integrated.

1. See JR Baumgardner, "Physicians' Services and the Division of Labor across Local Markets," *J of Political Economy* (Oct 1988): 948-982.

2. WS Custer, "Hospital Attributes and Physician Prices," *Southern Economic J 52* (Apr 1986): 1010-1027.

3. DR Cohodes and BM Kinkead, *Hospital Capital Formation in the 1980s* (Baltimore, MD: The Johns Hopkins University Press, 1984).

4. For a review of the evidence, see J Wennberg and A Gittelson, "Variations in Medical Care Among Small Areas," *Scientific American,* 246 (1982): 120-135.

5. WG Manning, et al., "Health Insurance and the Demand for Medical Care," *Amer Economic Rev* (June 1987): 251-276.

6. A. Foster Higgins & Company, Inc., *Health Care Benefits Survey, 1992* (Princeton, NJ: A. Foster Higgins & Company, Inc., 1993).

7. JL Buchanan and S Cretin, "Risk Selection of Families Electing HMO Membership," *Medical Care* (Jan 1986): 39-52.

8. GA Jensen and MA Morrisey, "The Premium Consequences of Group Health Insurance Provisions," *Rev of Economics and Statistics* (Feb 1990).

9. A. Foster Higgins & Company, Inc., *National Survey of Employer-Sponsored Health Plans/1993* (Princeton, NJ: A. Foster Higgins & Company, Inc., 1993).

Part 2

MANAGED CARE

---

4.   Trends in HMO Development

Richard Hamer   Michelle Porter

Health maintenance organizations are a widespread alterative to traditional health services. The authors examine the various types of HMOs, trace patterns and causes of enrollment growth, analyze current trends, and forecast future developments in the delivery of managed health care.

Pre-Paid Health Maintenance organizations (HMOs) represent one alternative, developed over the past 20 years, to traditional fee-for-service medicine—the other most familiar alternative being preferred provider organizations (PPOs). These organizations are described as providing "managed care" because they establish structures that seek to control and manage the delivery and financing of medical services. It is said that the greatest control over the medical care process is achieved by prepaid plans because these plans place the provider at financial risk for over-treatment of patients or over-utilization of medical services. In this article we present an analytical perspective on the health care system and on the growth of the HMO industry, based on data reported by InterStudy as of July 1, 1992.

HMOS AND THE HEALTH CARE MARKET

While the prepaid financing of HMOs is considered a radical departure from tradition, the HMO cannot be understood without considering the overall system and the forces within it that are driving up costs.

Reprinted from *Compensation & Benefits Management*, Vol 9, No. 3, Autumn 1993. A Panel Publication, Aspen Publishers, Inc.

Prepayment for medical services reverses the traditional fee-for-service financing of medical care by making the healthy patient an asset to the physician or medical group. Because healthy patients do not consume as many medical services, their enrollment in the HMO improves the earnings of the prepaid provider. As a result, the provider has a financial incentive to keep people well, to encourage early detection and treatment of disease, and to provide the most cost-effective care.

The growth of alternative health care plans in the mid-1970s created competition in the health care market. In order to compete on premium price, health plans, HMOs, and other systems sought to identify individuals most likely to use few medical resources. Reasoning that individuals who did not expect to require much medical care would not want to pay a great deal for insurance, health plans identified low-risk individuals by letting them self-select a low-cost, no-deductible package of basic services. Conversely, the reasoning went, those who expected to require much medical care should choose a more expensive, more extensive policy, even at the risk of incurring high out-of-pocket expenses.

This competitive strategy caused the market to become segmented into individuals and groups identified as higher or lower risks to health plans. When premiums were calculated with a community rating, market segmentation allowed some plans to do very well financially; they were "favorably selected." Others faced "adverse selection" and did poorly.

By the late 1970s it was clear that risk was not being spread evenly over the population and the market was not reaching price equilibrium. To this day, premium charges continue to cycle upward, in part because adversely selected plans raise premiums to cover their losses. This allows other health plans to "shadow price" the highest priced plans and, ultimately, high prices cause some high-risk individuals to switch insurance. These individuals move into plans that once were favorably selected, consequently upsetting the finances of these plans. As costs are driven upward, both low-risk and high-risk individuals tend to demand more benefits.[1]

Other equally important factors also contribute to the upward spiral of health care costs. Some of these can be controlled, and some cannot. First, as medical technology has expanded, most health problems now have several diagnoses and treatment options. For example, gallstones can be treated with drugs, ultrasound, and different kinds of surgery. However, it is generally not known or agreed upon which treatment will be the most effective and at what point the health benefit received is no longer worth the expense. With the current system, medical care is an open-ended proposition—there is no set end-point to treatment. Unfortunately, high technology medicine, expensive as it is, is favored in our culture and is in high demand by insured patients.

Second, consumers are mostly indifferent to price, so additional treatments are not an economic concern to them. Even if there was widespread interest in pursuing higher quality or greater value for the dollar, there is very little information that would distinguish the performance of one health plan from another.

Third, the population is aging. Even if the cost per unit of service is controlled, the average patient needs more services; therefore the average cost per patient increases.

Fourth, the full range of options available for treating patients is not properly used. The evolution of the health care system started in an age when acute illness was the primary concern. Prior to the development and widespread use of vaccines, antibiotics, and public health measures, the work of the physician was to intervene in the progress of serious maladies, such as tuberculosis and other infectious diseases. With these diseases, the onset was sudden and the resolution was definite—either patients were cured or they died. As a result, acute problems were the focal point in the development of health care facilities.

In the present day, infectious disease has all but been conquered, and the burden of care has shifted to chronic diseases—such as hypertension, heart disease, and diabetes—that are not easily resolved. Because treatment of ongoing health problems is often not efficient in the acute care, high-tech hospital setting, the challenge of the next decade is to develop managed care systems that allocate treatments to more resource-efficient settings. The setting represents care at various levels of intensity, including ambulatory treatment, home care, nursing homes, and hospice.

HOW HMOs CONTROL THE DELIVERY OF CARE

InterStudy data collected in 1992 show that 90 percent of HMOs use all of the following to control costs and manage medical services: inpatient utilization review, outpatient utilization review, hospital preadmission certification, concurrent review of hospital stays, referral authorization for nonplan providers, catastrophic case management, hospital discharge planning and cost\utilization feedback to physicians. These techniques represent the managed care equivalent to the control function of any business: information about the production process is collected, assessed, and fed back to producers and managers in order to guide the organization toward the desired quality and efficiency.

Inpatient and outpatient utilization review, preadmission certification, and concurrent review of hospital stays are the most venerable of cost-control efforts. A key success factor in their implementation is the degree to which the health plan and provider group can agree on the financial goals of the organization and the means by which these goals can be obtained. Without this agreement, these review procedures serve only as portholes through which reimbursement for medical services is obtained or denied. If the relationship between health plan and providers has withered to the point where "yes" and "no" are the only functions of utilization review, the system opens up to manipulation.

Cost-saving initiatives have focused on reducing the length of hospital stays. This has happened for two reasons: accumulated evidence indicates that additional days in hospital do not improve patients' health status; and overall hospital costs have increased to the point where they represent more than half of the medical expenses of most health plans; therefore hospitalization is the most fruitful area for cost-controlling attention.

According to Arnold Milstein, M.D. and his associates at National Medical Audit Services, the provider and payor relationship contains implicit standards for annual hospital days per 1,000 patients. The following standards are based on National Medical Audit Services' experience with utilization reviews for many organizations over several years:

1. Under a fee-for-service system, where physicians are not penalized for high utilization, populations are fully insured, and elective surgeries are routinely accepted, one can expect over 700 annual hospital days per 1,000 covered lives.
2. Under a managed fee-for-service system, where utilization is reviewed against a standard of average or prevailing practices, on e can expect 450 to 550 annual hospital days per 1,000.
3. Under a system associated with the most successful prepaid group practice HMOs, one can expect 200 to 350 annual days per 1,000.[2]

One way of controlling hospital use is to limit both the number of providers that serve the health plan's enrollees and the availability of hospital beds. According to a report by the U.S. Department of Health and Human Services,[3] staff and group model HMOs were staffing with a ratio of 1 physician per 1,000 enrollees. This contrasts to the United States generally, where the ratio is 1 physician to 410 people (based on U.S. Census Bureau population estimates and American Medical Association estimates for the number of physicians). The difference in resource allocation also holds for hospital beds: approximately 5.8 hospital beds per 1,000 people are allocated nationally, but, according to Robert Shouldice, HMOs planning for hospital services use a ratio of 1.5 to 2 beds per 1,000 enrollees.[4]

These figures have generated debate among pragmatists, who argue that HMOs are better able to plan and therefore need fewer beds, and materialists, who argue that the existence and availability of more hospital beds leads to more use by fee-for-service physicians. One would expect that if HMOs plan for the care of their enrollees, they would substitute ambulatory care for hospitalizations, and there would be more physician encounters by HMO enrollees. However, InterStudy data on HMOs published in 1989, report an estimated average of 5.1 ambulatory encounters per enrollee per year, whereas the average for the general population in the same period was 4.7 encounters per person.[5] The small difference would tend to support the materialists' argument that the material structure of the system determines, in part, the behavior of physicians. To the extent that restricting access to resources allows the HMO to define the structure of its health care microsystem, costs are controlled.

Operating as a smaller part of the overall system, HMO initiatives have produced both successes and failures. For example, efforts throughout the 1980s to reduce costs by limiting length of hospital stay, and using diagnostic-related groups, have resulted in provider incentives to unbundle clinical procedure and treatment codes in order to maximize reimbursement. Likewise, the attack on costs in specific areas of care has led to cost-shifting, or "gaming" the system, which creates an environment of mistrust and manipulation between providers and health plans. HMOs have succeeded most notably in controlling the cost per unit of many medical treatments. They have not succeeded in curbing the exponential rise in overall health care costs, nor the instability of health care premiums. Yet prepaid managed care has become the dominant strategy for redeeming the private system without the introduction of massive government regulatory and financing programs.

TRENDS IN HMO DEVELOPMENT

1992 Highlights of Enrollment Growth

Total HMO enrollment—including all pure open-ended, supplemental Medicare and other enrollment—was reported to be 39,175,665 as of July 1, 1992. This figure is usually divided into two key parts for the purposes of tracking develop-ment. The first part, "pure HMO enrollment," is defined as the traditional form of HMO business whereby the health plan offers comprehensive services, by a specific set of providers, to a defined population of enrollees. Unless specifically stated in the contract, pure enrollees are not covered for nonemergency care received a nonpanel provider. The second part, "open-ended HMO enrollment," is defined as a product that offers the patient an option to see a nonpanel provider or be referred to a nonpanel provider.

Between July 1991 and July 1992, pure HMO enrollment grew at its fastest annual rate since 1988—6.1 percent. During this period, HMOs gained 2,147,495 new pure enrollees, bringing the national total pure enrollment to 37,199,140. The rate of increase slowed somewhat in the first half of 1992, with HMOs reporting 2.9 percent semiannual growth compared to 3.1 percent growth for the previous six months. This is the first time since January 1991 that the semiannual growth rate has not increased. While the rate of enrollment growth continues to increase in the Northeast and the South, HMOs in the Midwest and West reported lackluster semiannual growth rates of 1.5 percent and 1.4 percent, respectively. Overall our survey showed that 60 percent of all HMOs gained pure enrollees at an annual rate greater than 0.5 percent increase; 42 percent reported annual growth rates greater than 10 percent.

The annual rate of enrollment growth for open-ended HMO products has dropped from its peak of nearly 40 percent in 1990 to 14.8 percent growth from July 1991 to July 1992. During this period 212,108 new enrollees were added to open-ended plans, bringing the national total to 1,642,533. For the past five years the strongest growth in this product has been in the South, where 102,200 enrollees, or 48 percent of all new members, were added during this period. If the present trend continues, the South will surpass the Midwest in 1993 as the region with the most open-ended HMO enrollees. Thirty HMOs introduced new open-ended products in the first half of 1992.

Our survey also showed that 9 out of 10 enrollees are in HMOs that are six years old or older. In 1991 older HMOs represented 75 percent of open-ended enrollment, and in 1990, 72 percent. Over this same period, the net change in the total number of HMOs was less one. The growing concentration of enrollees in older, and presumably more established, plans plus the lack of new entries into the market is an indication of a mature industry in a phase of flat growth. Mature industries often require a paradigm shifting innovation or some other external stimulus to cause their growth curves to steepen (see Table 1).

The History of Model Type

One of the key characteristics that defines the relationship between the health plan and its providers is the model type. Four models have been identified that generally outline the basis of the relationship:

1. *Staff model.* An HMO delivers health services through a group of physicians who it employs.
2. *Group model.* An HMO contracts with one independent group practice to provide health services.
3. *Network model.* An HMO contracts with two or more independent group practices, possibly including staff physicians, to provide health services.
4. *IPA model.* In independent practice associations, an HMO contracts directly with physicians in independent practices; and/or one or more associations of physicians in independent practice; and/or one or more multispeciality group practices.

Philosophically and historically, the group-based models—staff, group, and network—most closely reflect the original principles on which the first HMOs were founded: to use the group practice approach as a means to ensure the highest quality of care, to practice preventative medicine, to use prepaid financing, and to foster consumer participation in the form of board membership and advocacy processes. The first HMOs and their prototypes were group and staff models. These plans still exist as dominant forces in the areas where they began. They include Group Health Cooperative of Puget Sound and Health Insurance Plan of Greater New York (both staff model HMOs), and Group Health Association and

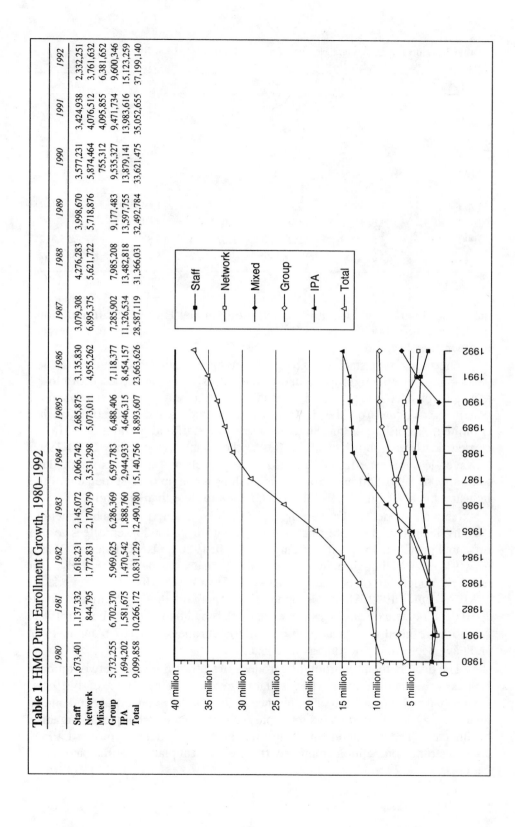

Table 1. HMO Pure Enrollment Growth, 1980–1992

	1980	1981	1982	1983	1984	1895	1986	1987	1988	1989	1990	1991	1992
Staff	1,673,401	1,137,332	1,618,231	2,145,072	2,066,742	2,685,875	3,135,830	3,079,308	4,276,283	3,998,670	3,577,231	3,424,938	2,332,251
Network		844,795	1,772,831	2,170,579	3,531,298	5,073,011	4,955,262	6,895,375	5,621,722	5,718,876	5,874,464	4,076,512	3,761,632
Mixed											755,312	4,095,855	6,381,652
Group	5,732,255	6,702,370	5,969,625	6,286,369	6,597,783	6,488,406	7,118,377	7,285,902	7,985,208	9,177,483	9,535,327	9,471,734	9,600,346
IPA	1,694,202	1,581,675	1,470,542	1,888,760	2,944,933	4,646,315	8,454,157	11,326,534	13,482,818	13,597,755	13,879,141	13,983,616	15,123,259
Total	9,099,858	10,266,172	10,831,229	12,490,780	15,140,756	18,893,607	23,663,626	28,587,119	31,366,031	32,492,784	33,621,475	35,052,655	37,199,140

Table 2. Number of HMOs and Members Enrolled 1980, 1985, 1990, 1992

	Staff	Group	Network	IPA	Mixed
Plans					
1980	63	76	—	97	—
1985	55	71	86	181	—
1990	50	62	82	350	12
1992	41	54	61	339	61
Membership					
1980	1,673,401	5,732,255	—	1,694,202	—
1985	2,685,875	6,488,406	5,073,011	4,646,315	—
1990	3,577,231	9,535,327	5,874,464	13,879,141	755,312
1992	2,332,251	9,600,346	3,761,632	15,123,259	6,381,652

the Kaiser Foundation Health Plans (all group model HMOs). Staff and group models are more likely to be nonprofit, 56 percent are, compared to 29 percent of other model types.

The number of staff and group models has decreased over the past ten years—generally thought to be due to public resistance to the used of closed panels of physician providers. Under this structure, enrollees must receive all nonemergency care from the HMO's panel of providers; the choice of physician is limited. According to InterStudy data, in 1980 staff and group model HMOs carried nearly two-thirds of all HMOs in the country (see Table 2). In 1992, however, less than one-fifth of the HMOs were exclusive staff or group models. Similarly, in 1980 staff and group memberships made up over 80 percent of the industry, but as of July 1, 1992, they accounted for less than one-third.

Network model HMOs were able to partially solve this problem by widening the physician base to more than one group and by allowing enrollees to use off-panel providers in specific circumstances. In 1980 no HMO listed itself as a network model (though a number of HMOs that now define themselves as network models are older than 12 years); 21 HMOs were listed as networks in 1981. As of July 1992, 61 HMOs reported being network models. Similarly, while 1980 data indicate no enrollees, network models had 844,000 enrollees in 1981. Networks reached their peak with 6.9 million enrollees and 107 plans in 1987 and have been slowly declining since that time.

The drop in the proportion of enrollees in staff, group, and network model HMOs corresponds to market forces that favored IPA plans. By the early 1980s, HMOs had become enough of a presence in the market to encourage indemnity insurers, physicians, and others to employ managed care techniques to organize health care. The development of insurance- and physician-sponsored PPOs created strong competition among alternative medical plans to attract and retain patients.

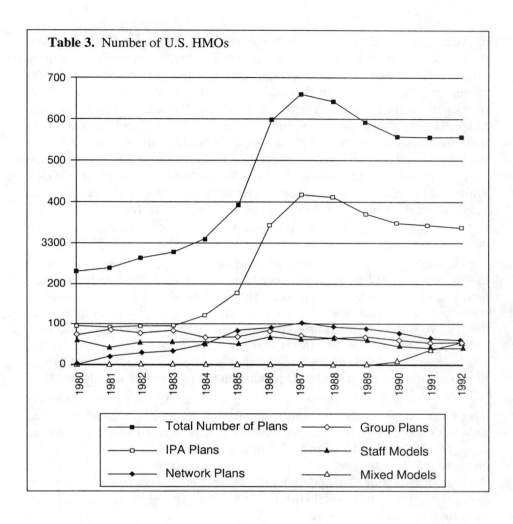

Table 3. Number of U.S. HMOs

While IPAs have been in existence for many years, it was not until the mid-1980s that their dominance in the industry became clearly evident (see Table 3). In 1980 IPA model HMOs accounted for 40 percent of the operational plans; in 1992 data indicate that over 60 percent of all HMOs are IPA models. Similarly, less than 20 percent of all enrollees were members of an IPA in 1980; however, by 1992 IPA market share had doubled to more than 40 percent of the membership. Since 1983 the IPA model has been the most common new entrant into the industry. In the most recent period, of 151 HMOs that are less than six years old, 82 percent are IPAs. In the same six-year period, only one staff model and seven group model plans were started.

Several factors contribute to the growth of the IPA model HMO. First, the IPA allows physicians to continue their practices in their own settings, thereby facilitating physician and patient recruitment. According to July 1, 1992, data from InterStudy, IPAs held an estimated 117,000 contracts with primary care physicians and 420,500 contracts with specialty care physicians. By comparison, the HMO industry as a whole held an estimated 257,000 contracts with primary care physicians and 660,700 contracts with specialists. (According to recent survey results published in *Medical Economics*, nearly 40 percent of all physicians contract with two HMOs.) Second, the IPA does not require as large a capital outlay as that required to start a group-based plan. Third, IPAs are more organizationally compatible with the existing health care system, including traditional insurance companies. Several of the largest national managed care firms are established health insurers. They include Aetna Health Plans; CIGNA Employee Benefits Companies; MetLife Health Care Management Corporation; Principal Health Care, Inc.; Prudential Health Care Plans, Inc.,; and Travelers Health Network, Inc. All use the IPA model, exclusively or in conjunction with other models.

In more recent years the complexity of delivering health care and the need to organize a broad base of providers has made it more difficult to limit model definitions to one type. For this reason a fifth model was added to the typology—the mixed model. This type of HMO is actually a hybrid of the other models. In the past two year, since it was first reported in *Managed Care: A Decade in Review 1980-1990*[6], the number of HMOs that list themselves as mixed models has grown from 12 to 61. Similarly, membership in mixed-model HMOs has grown from a mere 2 percent of the HMO population to 11 percent as of July 1992.

While six new HMOs have organized as mixed models since 1990, 55 others have changed their standing from a singular model type to a combination of several. Of those switching to mixed models, 21 were formerly networks, 16 were IPAs, 15 were staff and 3 were group models. Of those models that were added on to the existing structure, IPA was clearly the most attractive; 28 plans added this provider structure to their definition. The other three model types were added in equal numbers: staff model HMOs to 12 plans, network models to 11 plans, and group models to ten plans.

Two combinations captured over half of the mixed plans—the network/IPA combination—and the staff/IPA combination—with 19 and 18 plans, respectively. Similarly, these two combinations also enroll nearly one-third of the mixed-model HMO membership between them. The third most common combination, which is used by only one HMO, ranks fourth in mixed-model membership, with slightly under 10 percent of enrollment. Network/staff HMOs rank fourth in number of plans (8 out of 61 HMOs), but they account for only 7 percent of the membership. There is one network/IPA and two network/group mixes; combined they account for less than 5 percent of the mixed-model enrollment.

While it is apparent that the IPA model is the organization of choice for the most HMOs, particularly those just starting up, the trend seems to be away from the exclusive use of one model type. Instead, the steady growth of interest in combined model types seems to confirm that the increased complexity of health care organization cannot be served by any single model type.

Table 4. HMOs and Pure Enrollment by Affiliation/Sponsorship, July 1, 1992

Affiliation	Number of Plans	% of All Group	Enrollment	% of Total Enrollment
National Managed Care Firm	280	50.1%	21,603,067	58.1%
Blue Cross/Blue Shield	82	14.7	5,579,877	15.0
Independent HMO Ownership/sponsorship:				
Business/corporation	52	9.3	3,741,017	10.0
Hospital(s)	39	7.0	1,463,180	3.9
Community/cooperative	19	3.4	1,266,970	3.4
Joint hospital and physician(s)	17	3.0	853,142	2.3
Medical society, IPA, or foundation	15	2.7	1,598,147	4.2
Commercial insurer	13	2.3	149,278	0.4
County Government	4	0.7	63,705	0.2
Union	2	0.3	41,406	0.1
Physician group (not IPA)	1	0.1	23,316	0.1
Other Combinations of the above	35	6.2	816,035	2.2
TOTAL	559	100.0%	37,199,140	100.0%

Affiliation/Sponsorship

HMOs are also characterized by their affiliation/sponsor relationship. Generally, there are three categories: national managed care firms (NMCFs), Blue-Cross/Blue Shield, and nonaffiliated or independently owned. InterStudy defines a NMCF as a company that operates HMOs in two or more states.

In 1980 NMCFs sponsored 26 of the 236 operating HMOs—11 percent of the industry. The total number of national firms operating at that time was seven. Surprisingly, even at that time, the proportion of HMO members enrolled in a national firm was over 50 percent. By 1985 the number of affiliated plans had reached nearly 40 percent (153 of 393 HMOs), and the actual number of firms operating had more than tripled. Though NMCFs have dominated the industry, during the mid-1980s, when industry growth was at its peak, the actual percentage of membership that was under the umbrella of NMCFs dropped from that of 1980 because new plans were being added so quickly. As of July 1, 1992, NMCFs and Blue Cross/Blue Shield accounted for 65 percent of HMOs and 73 percent of the membership (see Table 4).

National managed care affiliates comprise the majority of plans offering open-ended HMOs and other managed care products. They account for:

- 67 percent of the HMOs offering open-ended products;
- 74 percent offering point-of-service;
- 68 percent offering PPOs;
- 73 percent offering managed fee-for-service;
- 67 percent offering self-insured.

NMCFs account for the majority of IPA, group, and mixed-model HMOs. In contrast, only 17 percent of staff models and only 29 percent of network models are affiliated with a NMCF. Slightly more than one-third of all NMCF-affiliated HMOs are in the South. Of the largest firms, CIGNA, Prudential, Travelers, Humana, and Principal have 40 percent or more of their HMOs in this region. Although NMCFs seem to favor IPA and mixed-model organization, there is no evidence that they are fueling growth in the number of HMOs. NMCFs are only slightly more likely to operate HMOs younger than six years. Thirty percent of NMCF-affiliated HMOs, other than Blue Cross/Blue Shield, are less than six years old, compared to 25 percent of independents and 22 percent of Blue Cross/Blue Shield plans. NMCFs are also no more likely to sponsor smaller plans.

Blue Cross/Blue Shield, while considered to be an NMCF, is not wholly comparable to the other national firms in organizational structure, because it is an *association* of HMOs rather than a company. Therefore, for most administrative and managerial duties, each HMO acts as an independent entity. The Blue Cross/Blue Shield Association offers technical assistance, marketing, administrative and, occasionally, financial support.

PATTERNS OF PURE ENROLLMENT GROWTH

Differences by Region

As reported in *The InterStudy Competitive Edge,*[7] there appears to be a correlation between geographical region and the model type of the HMO in terms of enrollment growth. In the Northeast, declines in enrollment were reported most often by staff models—three of the eight staff models reported declines of more than 0.5 percent. Plans in the Northeast were more likely to cite decreasing enrollment in existing groups as a reason for enrollment decline; this reason was offered by 71 percent of the plans in the Northeast, by 57 percent in the West, 43 percent in the Midwest, and 38 percent in the South. Other model types seemed to fare better. Sixty percent (40 HMOs) of the IPAs reported increases of over 10 percent. Of network models, group models, and mixed models, the majority (15 HMOs) reported enrollment increases of 10 percent or more.

In the South, group models seemed to fare less well; 39 percent (9 HMOs) reported declining enrollment. Southern plans were less likely than northeastern or western plans to report enrollment increases of over 10 percent; 42 percent did, as compared to 57 percent of northeastern and 47 percent of western plans.

HMOs in the West, were least likely to report pure enrollment loss; 24 percent reported declines of more than 0.5 percent. In contrast, 47 percent of all HMOs reported increases of more than 10 percent—including 50 percent of the IPAs. What distinguished the West from the Northeast and the South is that group-based models did very well: all of the western staff models reported enrollment increases of more than 4 percent. Similarly, 88 percent of the group reported increases of more than 0.5 percent.

In the Midwest, 54 percent of the group models, 39 percent of the mixed models, and 30 percent of the network models reported declines of more than 0.5 percent. Pure enrollment gains were more commonly in the 0.5–10 percent range in the Midwest than in any other region. Twenty-nine percent of the midwestern plans reported pure enrollment increases of more than 10 percent.

Differences by HMO Size

The pattern of enrollment increase also showed significant differences according to the size of the HMO's pure enrollment, as shown in Table 5.

HMO Size	Mean Rate
Less than 5,000	21.2%
5,000 to 14,999	10.8%
15,000 to 24,999	10.8%
25,000 to 49,999	18.8%
50,000 to 99,999	15.2%
More than 100,000	9.7%

It was also observed that medium-sized HMOs, those with between 5,000 and 50,000 members, lost nearly 120,000 enrollees during the year July 1991 to July 1992. In citing reasons for enrollment changes, medium-sized HMOs were less likely than others to report new contracts with groups previously covered by other local HMOs, PPOs, indemnity insurers, or self-insured arrangements. Larger sized HMOs were more likely to report new groups from self-insured arrangements (over 45 percent of plans with 50,000 members or more responded that this was one of their reasons) than were HMOs with less than 15,000 members (less than 10 percent indicated this source).

REASONS FOR PURE ENROLLMENT CHANGES

Survey respondents were asked to cite reasons for the increases in their pure enrollment. Two-hundred eighty-two, or 88 percent, of all HMOs whose pure enrollment did increase responded to these questions.

Table 5.

	Percent of Plans	Number of Plans
>10% Decline	20%	107
4% to 10% Decline	9%	47
0.5% to 4% Decline	9%	47
0.5% Decline to 0.5% Growth	4%	21
0.5% to 4% Growth	9%	48
4% to 10% Growth	10%	56
>10% Growth	42%	232

Percent of HMOs by Rate of Decline or Growth
in Pure Enrollment - July 1, 1991 to July 1, 1992

In general the results showed that HMOs have relied on increases in the number of group contracts they carry, and increases in the number of enrollees in existing groups, to fuel growth. These two reasons were cited far more often than increasing Medicare or Medicaid enrollment or any other reason.

In looking at the sources of new groups, other local HMOs were mentioned most often as the source of new groups (see Table 6). This indicates that HMOs are frequently in competition with each other, rather than other alternatives, for group business. The regional nature of the medical care market often makes it difficult for plans to escape the bounds of their networks of providers and expand to new geographic markets. The environment that makes an area attractive for one HMO makes it attractive for many HMOs; therefore competition is within, rather than between, alternative groups of health care plans.

Differences by Model Type

It appears that mixed, network, and IPA models had experiences that were more similar to each other than to group or staff models. For example 69 percent of mixed,

Table 6.

	Percent of Plans	Number of Plans
Other managed care product	31%	75
Formerly Self-Insured	35%	85
A local PPO	42%	102
Indemnity Insurer	65%	159
Another local HMO	68%	165

Percent of HMOs Citing Sources of New Groups

network, and IPA models reported gaining new groups previously covered by indemnity insurers, compared to 52 percent of staff and group models who reported similar gains. Mixed, network, and IPA models were also more likely to indicate that new groups were previously enrolled with another local HMO. Mixed, network, and IPA models were most likely to cite PPOs, as a source of new contracts; 45 percent reported such gains. Staff and group models were most likely to report increasing Medicare/Medicaid enrollment as a reason for enrollment growth.

Differences by Size of HMO

Moderately sized HMOs, those with between 5,000 and 50,000 members, had a more difficult time maintaining their levels of enrollment. Plans of this size lost nearly 120,000 enrollees during the year July 1991 to July 1992. These plans also reported lower average rates of enrollment change.

In citing reasons for enrollment changes, medium-sized HMOs were less likely than others to report new contracts with groups previously covered by other local HMOs, PPOs, indemnity insurers, or self-insured arrangements.

LOOKING AHEAD

Health care organizations are evolving from a management model based on utilization review to one based on quality management designed to serve the demand for accountability and evaluation. New management information systems will analyze how appropriately the health plan is utilizing resources from multiple levels of analysis—the setting, the process of care, and the outcome.

The setting in which medical care takes place is also representative of the level of intensity, in terms of the technology available and the personnel required. Assessment of the appropriateness of setting will be a key feature of quality management systems. These settings will include hospitalization, outpatient treatment, home care, hospice, and nursing home.

To achieve quality control of the process of care, the use of hospital days per 1,000 patients as an indicator of efficiency will be replaced by measures of services such as physician services, allied health services, or chiropractic services. Measures of the outcomes of care will serve as the common denominator, providing indications of whether or not patients' health improved and what aspects of setting and process contribute most to health improvement.

In conflict with the trend to sharpen management control functions is the public's continued demand for wide provider choice, coupled with distrust of proposals that would limit benefits or health plans. The optimal use of resources will require hospitals, groups practices, and health plans to more fully integrate their operations within organizations that can provide the variety of care at these many levels. We have seen this happen over the past ten years as HMOs have shifted from group-based models to models that allow a wider network of providers. We are also seeing this trend plan itself out in many cities, where health plans are expanding to include dental care and chiropractic services, and are consolidating or entering into joint ventures. Hospitals, too, are purchasing group practices and home care agencies as they strive to become total centers of care. In order to be totally accountable, a health plan must have the ability to deliver care at all of the various levels listed above.

Presently HMOs are at a critical juncture. They commonly compete against one another, indicating that they may be marketing to the same, rather than new, populations. Since 1988 HMO enrollment growth has been modest, although the rate of growth appears to be increasing. To some, the rate of growth and the ability to penetrate markets are disappointing. Yet HMOs have a significant role as the most highly developed organizational alternative in our health care system. The HMO provides more than a financial scheme and a management control mechanism for delivery of care; it is a framework in which to plan different combinations of services.

---

1.   For an excellent discussion of the political economy of health care competition, we recommend Mark V. Pauly, "A Primer on Competition in Medical Markets," in H.E. Frech, ed., *Health Care in America*, San Francisco: Pacific Research Institute for Public Policy, 1988.

2. Arnold Milstein, Linda Bergthold, and Leslie Selbovitz, "Utilization Review Techniques," in Peter Boland, ed., *Making Managed Healthcare Work* (Gaithersburg, MD: Aspen Publishers 1991) 377.

3. Office of Health Maintenance Organizations, "Medical Care Data from HMOs, *National Trend Data Issuance 2* ((Rockville, MD: U.S. Department of Health and Human Services 1980).

4. Robert G. Shouldice, *Introduction to Managed Care* (Arlington, VA: Information Resources Press 1991) 295.

5. National Center for Health Statistics, *Health in the United States, 1988* (Hyattsville, MD: U.S. Department of Health and Human Services 1988).

6. InterStudy, 1990.

7. Vol. 2(2) 1993.

5.   An Approach to Managing
Health Maintenance Organizations
Kathleen Angel

Due to rising costs and pending legislative reform, national health care promises to be one of corporate America's most topical issues of the 1990s. While large, global employers—like Digital Equipment Corporation—may have different concerns and approaches from many companies, all employers have come to accept health care as a long-term, critical item on today's ever-shifting business agenda.

The health care issues facing corporate America are numerous:

- Medical costs are escalating for all services.
- Cost of medical care threatens to become an issue of affordability for employees and for the company.
- The health care industry has not been held accountable for the delivery and financing of care.
- Data standards necessary to capture health care information and outcomes have been non-existent.
- Much of the medical care that employees receive may be inappropriate, or may be delivered at an inappropriate level within the health care delivery system.

In addition, other issues affecting corporate costs are virtually impossible to measure or control, such as the shifting of government cost to the private sector, or coverage for the uninsured.

BACKGROUND

In response to skyrocketing health care costs, Digital determined in 1990 that, to meet the diverse needs of its U.S. employee population, offering a choice of health plans was a requirement. The following year, Digital offered a new series of point-of-service, managed care health plans to its U.S. employees. The plans included options for traditional indemnity plans and health maintenance organizations (HMOs).

When Digital began considering implementing a point-of-service plan, there was no off-the-shelf program that could fulfill the requirements of the company and its U.S. employees: a program that met our objectives of optimizing the balance between quality and cost, while providing employee choice. Consistency across the company—in plan designs, customer service, and administration of Digital's out-of-network claims processing—was also an important factor. As a result, Digital decided to design its own managed care structure.

As the company began its work in providing managed health care for employees, we chose to focus on a number of issues: we set out to design a program that delivers value to our employees and to the company. At the same time, we felt it was important to offer employees a choice of care providers and health care programs to meet their different needs, while providing a structure for accountability in the delivery of health care.

In designing our strategy for managed care, we kept a number of objectives in mind—from a quality of care and employee relations perspective, as well as from the perspective of corporate fiscal responsibility:

- Since Digital will assume greater responsibility for the delivery of health care services, HMO performance standards were developed for selecting providers and delivering health care services.
- Quality health care will be delivered in an integrated system that uses the primary care physician as the coordinator of care.
- Quality will be measured through a formal quality improvement program to ensure ongoing delivery of quality health care.
- Satisfaction will be measured through periodic assessments.
- Since well-organized, technologically advanced managed care plans should be able to deliver health care efficiently, they should be held accountable for the quality and cost-effectiveness of care.
- A managed care program should continue to offer employees meaningful choice in quality providers of health care and at competitive levels that are affordable.
- Employees will be encouraged to access the managed care delivery system through quality aspects of the program, such as administrative ease and coordination of care.

- Digital will communicate managed care objectives and continue to educate employees on health care issues, so that they can make decisions appropriate for them.

DIGITAL'S SOLUTION

Digital's responded to escalating U.S. health care costs and concerns by becoming an active and creative purchaser of health care services. Based on our experiences, we believe that a managed care system—a network of health care professionals providing necessary and appropriate care, under active management for quality, access, and price—offers the greatest potential to control costs, while maintaining and improving the quality of health care.

With this approach, our first step was to define "managed care." For Digital, managed health care grew to mean:

- Coordinating the approach to the design, financing, and delivery of health care; and
- Balancing price and utilization controls with access to high quality care.

Using John Hancock Mutual Life Insurance Company as its network manager, Digital has designed its current managed care structure around a model that enables partnerships with well-organized, well-managed, and efficient HMOs as the key delivery channel.

As a result, Digital's managed care strategy has been responsible for providing flexible, high-quality health care to a diverse U.S. employee population of 43,000 individuals, while controlling health care costs and saving Digital additional costs of $35 million between 1991 and 1993.

FLEXIBILITY AND CHOICE

Through the Digital point-of-service program, employees retain the flexibility to choose any doctor, hospital or eligible health care provider. Digital has not eliminated any medical plan choices. However, benefits and levels of coverage depend on how members choose to receive their medical care—either at a program HMO or outside the HMO.

If employees choose a provider outside the HMO, they are responsible for paying a larger portion of their medical expenses through deductibles and co-payments, similar to an indemnity plan. This means that employees who receive their services at the program HMO can receive significant savings on medical expenses.

Implementing the point-of-service program involved extensive negotiating arrangements with HMOs that were capable of meeting specific performance criteria developed by Digital. Digital has found that its managed care delivery system has already contributed significantly to controlling health care costs, while maintaining and improving the quality of care provided to employees and their families.

From a cost-sharing perspective, Digital's share of medical costs is based on the lowest-cost HMO in each geographic area that meets Digital's HMO standards of care. Employees who choose less efficient, more costly plans must pay the incremental costs of these programs. As a result, Digital's cost is the same regardless of the plan the employee chooses.

DIGITAL'S HMO STANDARD OF CARE

Digital's HMO performance standards are today the hallmark of the company's quality approach to managed care. The standards of care, which can be described as "purchasing specifications" for health care services, have been developed by Digital for the management of the participating HMOs.

Adherence to Digital's HMO standards is the key to the HMO management program. The standards provide the framework for developing relationships with new HMO partners and for influencing the ongoing management of the HMOs.

The standards of care are based on the principles of total quality management (TQM), focusing on major areas of specific concern to Digital:

- Access to Care Standards—Choice of primary care physician in defined geographic areas; established ratios of providers to patients; availability of urgent care and telephone response time.
- Quality of Care Standards—Maintenance of a provider selection and credentialing process; adhering to board certification and accrediting standards; monitoring and evaluating provider practices and treatment protocols, such as outcomes management and automated medical records; commitment to the process of total quality improvement.
- Data Collection and Analysis Standards—Prescribed formats on a timely basis of reports on patient satisfaction surveys; patient utilization; and audited financial statements. Digital was an original participant in the development of the National Committee for Quality Assurance's Health Plan Employer Data and Information Set (HEDIS), a core set of performance measures developed to systemize and evaluate health care standards.
- Financial Controls and Stability Standards—Detailed financial reporting, measures, and a statement of liability protection.
- Mental Health and Substance Abuse Standards—Ability to offer a continuum of care; willingness to change the limits of coverage for inpatient and ambulatory visits; availability of alternative treatments settings; presence of an active triaging and case management program; ability to track outcomes.

As of October 1993, HIV/AIDS care standards are now included in Digital's HMO standards of care. These standards were developed by Digital, John

Hancock, and Digital's HMO partners to help assure consistency of care for Digital employees and families who are living with, or are affected by, the HIV disease. This leading initiative in HIV/AIDS care attests to Digital's commitment to provide effective and appropriate health care to all of its employees and members.

MEASURABLE RESULTS

By 1993, 70 percent of Digital's U.S. employees were enrolled in HMOs, up from 28 percent in 1990. Currently there are 26 participating point-of-service HMOs across the country, compared with just four HMOs offering plans to Digital in 1991. A 1991 national survey of Digital employees indicated continuing satisfaction with HMOs, with satisfaction levels measurably greater than those for the fee-for-service system.

After implementing this new health care strategy focused on HMOs in 1991, the company has seen U.S. annual health care cost increases fall from 16 percent in 1990, to 9.5 percent in 1993, and down to approximately 4 percent in 1994.

The company estimates U.S. cost savings in the first year of implementation (1991) to have been about $4 million, growing to as much as $28 million for 1994, and totaling approximately $62 million.

PARTNERING FOR QUALITY HEALTH CARE

In an effort to encourage continuous quality improvement in the delivery of health care to its employees, Digital is partnering with several of its HMOs, and in some cases, other employers, in several leadership efforts:

- As a precursor to HEDIS, Digital has initiated HMO partnering activities with several of its larger HMOs. Called the Clinical Indicators Project, its goal is to establish benchmarks for cross-plan comparisons of Caesarean section, prenatal, asthma admission, hypertension screening, mammography, and mental health readmission rates.
- Through HEDIS, Digital and other participants have begun to compare HMOs' performance in 60 key categories. The goal through this scorecard procedure is to capture comparable data on each HMO on utilization, quality measures, and financial reporting.
- Digital has facilitated the collaboration among three major competing HMOs in the design and implementation of the New England Psychiatric Outcomes Project. The study has been designed to include all inpatient mental health admissions at several local facilities. This is a significant project in that it addresses the need for consistent treatment approaches and outcomes

measures in order to allow for the return of productive employees to the workplace.

- In partnering with other Fortune 500 companies and the nation's leading health plans, Digital is participating in a landmark study, the Managed Health Care Association (MHCA) Outcomes Management Study, for the treatment for angina and asthma. The conclusions thus far are that: outcomes measures can be collected and information pooled; competing companies can cooperate for a common goal; instruments are reliable and valid; and standardization of data collection processes across organizations is needed.
- Digital has a representative on the Board of Directors of the Washington Business Group on Health (WBGH), and chairs its Organized Systems of Care Committee. Digital also holds a seat on the Advisory Board for the Institute for Behavioral Health.
- Digital has joined forces with a consortium of large national employers to implement a member satisfaction and health risk assessment survey of employees across a broad spectrum of health plans. The goal is to compare satisfaction levels across health plans and model types, as well as to: identify areas of improvement through performance monitoring, assess the health risk of employees across these plans, and coordinate this work under the HEDIS umbrella.

In June of 1993, a "Special Presidential Commendation" was awarded to Digital by the American Psychiatric Association (APA) in recognition of outstanding leadership in providing high-quality mental health services for its employees and their spouses, both at the work site and through organized systems of care.

LOOKING AHEAD

Digital is implementing its strategy to provide a more viable, long-term solution to the health care cost issues that continue to face the company and its employees by:

- Developing long-term partnerships with HMOs;
- Establishing a proactive management process that clearly articulates performance standards and balances quality and cost; and
- Offering expanded medical plan choices to employees.

Digital also believes that its experience will serve as a working model for other health care system planners.

Having built this successful track record in managed care, Digital believes that it is essential that any national health care reform legislation—in addition to working toward providing access to affordable, necessary, and appropriate health care for all—should embody the following principals:

- The role of large employers as active purchasers of health care must be maintained to ensure competition and innovation in the marketplace.
- All employers must offer coverage to their employees, funded through a combination of employer and employee contributions.
- Since large employers such as Digital have demonstrated the ability to encourage innovation in the health care delivery system by motivating plans to compete for membership on the basis of quality and cost, any health care reform proposal should provide the flexibility to employers to act as their own health alliances. In addition, employers should be permitted to select and mange those accountable health partnerships that offer appropriate benefits and services for their employees.
- Employers that act as their own Health Alliance should be able to negotiate premiums with accountable health plans that reflect the health status of their employee populations.
- Any health care reform proposal should encourage employee education on disease prevention, health promotion and wellness by providers, employers, and health alliances.
- Employers should be able to base their share of the premium costs on the most efficient accountable health plan in a region, to encourage competition among plans and the use of efficient delivery systems. Informed consumers should have a reasonable choice of accountable health plans but bear the cost of that choice if they join inefficient plans.
- The cost of extending coverage to all should be fairly and equitable distributed across all parties, including employers, employees, government, and providers.
- Any health care reform proposal should recognize the inefficiencies of high-cost delivery systems and support the utilization of high quality, cost-efficient delivery systems.
- Quality and cost efficiency in health care can best be achieved through organized, technologically advanced accountable health plans that integrate the financing and delivery of comprehensive, appropriate, and necessary care to their members and compete for membership based on comparable performance measures.
- National standards for accountable health plans should be rigorous, encourage continuous improvement, and produce comparable measures that enable purchasers and consumers to make informed decisions about the value of a plan.
- The health care system should promote the development and use of information technology to enhance the quality of care and efficient administration of health services, resulting in cost-effective health care delivery. Information technology can be used to generate comparable data across plans, so that employers and employees can purchase health care on the basis of quality and cost.

- National employers must have the ability to operate in a consistent manner throughout the United States to ensure employee mobility and maintain their global competiveness.

CONCLUSION

Digital's goal is to ensure that its health care programs meet the diverse needs of its employees and their families—while being cost-effective for the employees and for Digital.

In developing and implementing health care strategies, each company has to look at the needs of their employees, and their own philosophical beliefs in the delivery of care. We believe that our HMO partners appreciate our approach and share our concerns and our ideas. We work toward translating this back to employees through high-quality health care—resulting in satisfied health care customers.

6.   USAir's Experience in Moving Toward Managed Care
Virginia M. Gibson

No one expected a "problem-free" transition to managed care, but USAir underestimated the extent of the potential conflict between the various affected parties—USAir health benefits department, and The Travelers.

Unlike most employers, USAir had escaped the negative impact that rising healthcare costs had on many businesses during the 1980s. An extremely profitable company, USAir shared the prosperity with its employees. Benefits—particularly healthcare benefits—remained "top shelf" as the 1990s began. They were fully paid by the company, including 100 percent coverage for many services and low deductibles. Healthcare costs were just not an issue at that time.

Then came 1991. Severe economic conditions and record losses forced a drastic change in how the company was managed. Healthcare was identified as one of the most significant expenditures the company could better control. Like many employers across the nation, USAir decided to introduce managed care to its employees. Here's what happened and what management learned from the experience.

BACKGROUND

Faced with record losses of almost $850 million during 1990 and 1991, managed care was introduced as part of a broad-based series of initiatives designed to trim costs. Merit raises were suspended; the defined benefit plan had been frozen and

Reprinted, by permission of publisher, from *HR Focus,* November 1993 © 1993.

replaced with a defined contribution plan. Base salaries were reduced with higher wage earners taking the largest reductions, and 9,000 employees were laid off. In a drastic attempt to get costs immediately under control and to have the ability to more effectively predict and manage future expenses, the decision to introduce managed care was made in early 1991. The new program would be introduced to 24,000 non-contract employees effective January 1, 1992. Mechanics and pilots would be introduced to changes the following January, followed by flight attendants and baggage handlers in June of 1993. As expected, employee concerns were great. What management underestimated, however, was the magnitude and volume of these concerns and their direct impact on employee morale and productivity.

IMPLEMENTATION

Once the decision to act was made, USAir, with assistance from the management consulting firm Alexander & Alexander, set out to design a program that would meet the needs of a diverse workforce, manage costs and maintain quality. After intense analysis, a decision was made to introduce a point-of-service (POS) option to the program, which already included health maintenance organizations (HMOs) and an indemnity plan.

"We went from a base plus major medical plan with a $100 deductible and 80 percent co-payment to a point-of-service plan that paid 90 percent in network and 70 percent out of network for most services," said James C. Davis, senior director, employee benefits at USAir. "If an employee chooses in-network services, there are no deductibles and a $700 out-of-pocket maximum. Preventive care—such as physical and well-women exams and well-child care—are covered after a small co-payment. If an employee chooses to go out of the network, the costs are significantly higher," Davis emphasized.

In addition to the plan change, The Travelers assumed the role of third-party administrator after a thorough assessment identified the insurance carrier as the strongest candidate to administer this managed care program.

Shortly after the program's introduction, USAir management at all levels began to receive an unacceptable volume of telephone calls, letters and verbal complaints. "The implementation was fraught with problems that were unanticipated," Davis recalled. "The largest single setback was that our previous carrier was extremely uncooperative in providing past and current claims data to The Travelers. This was just something that we hadn't planned for, and it caused a ripple effect throughout the rest of the implementation process." To quell the discontent, USAir management enlisted the services of Chesapeake Consulting Group/Macro International (CCG/Macro) in October of 1992. A task force was commissioned, which included representatives of USAir, The Travelers and CCG/Macro, with a mission to identify the root causes of the employee complaints and to address each issue through short-, medium-, and long-term quality improvement actions.

"Implementing managed care is an extremely complex process," observed Simon H.B. Hewat, president of Chesapeake Consulting Group. "There are very definite issues that must be addressed in the planning, introduction and on-going phases. Failure to embrace these concerns globally can result in disaster."

"The USAir program is the most ambitious initiative to date within the industry to contain the rapidly increasing financial burden of employee medical costs," added Albert D. Alexander, vice president at The Travelers. "Managed care requires more intensive interventions on the part of the carrier before paying a claim. We were challenged to design a program and an administrative system that cut out extraneous costs while at the same time allowed claims to be paid quickly and accurately."

Using total quality management tools for process improvement, the task force began to assess the issues. Thirty-three problem areas were identified, which included claims, eligibility, customer service, communications and provider relations. "CCG/Macro was extremely valuable to the overall process," Davis said. "Because of their non-biased position, Simon Hewat and the CCG/Macro team were able to provide agendas and reach solutions that worked.

"Not only did they provide consulting advice, they were hands-on participants in the process, picking up the slack where needed and making things happen," Davis added.

Eligibility information was one of the processes which actually contributed to the problems. Originally, USAir would prepare the eligibility tape and forward to The Travelers, which then would run a series of edits and forward any questions back to USAir for review and "cleaning up." Once corrected, the information could be sent back to Travelers. The cycle times independently did not seem too long, but when the process was looked at in its entirety, it actually took over one month for eligibility changes to be accurately reflected in The Travelers file. In the meantime, the employee who was trying to access the system was denied care, adding to his or her frustration.

"We were able to look at the process in aggregate and streamline procedures," Simon noted. "For example, Travelers worked with USAir programmers to establish an edit process on their end. Now when Travelers gets an eligibility tape from USAir, it has been processed through the edit phase and is error-free. The information is ready to be inputted directly into The Travelers eligibility system. This step cut the update time in half."

"We learned some very valuable lessons with USAir," Alexander noted. "So often the focus is on plan design, when in reality the emphasis must be on how the program works and to ensure that there are systems in place to support these increased demands. As a result of our experience, all of our clients will benefit. We've incorporated what we've learned with USAir into our everyday business operations."

MANAGED CARE: THINK BEFORE YOU LEAP

James C. Davis, senior director for employee benefits at USAir, offered the following advice to employers that are considering managed care:

1. Talk to other employers that have implemented managed care. Ask tough questions about the process.
2. Asked detailed questions about what can and did go wrong.
3. Don't overlook the systems interface and the integration needed between the carrier and the employer. This is critical to the success of the program.
4. Assess the relationship between the carrier and the providers. Review any provider satisfaction surveys and ask questions about the carrier's provider relations efforts.
5. Communicate, communicate, communicate. Prepare employees for what is going to happen. Be sure employees understand how the changes will impact their access to medical care. When you think you have communicated enough, communicate some more!
6. Be prepared for increased employee interest. As their levels of accountability and financial contribution increase, so will their need for information.
7. A third-part consultant, if needed, should be selected by both the employer and the vendor, and the fees should be shared. This encourages open lines of communication and focuses the attention of the consultant on the big picture, not just on the needs of the party that pays the fees.

WORKING RELATIONSHIPS

One area often overlooked by employers is the relationship between the insurance company and the providers. "The doctors play such a critical role in the success of managed care," Davis said. "Yet what we found was an extremely adversarial relationship between the provider and The Travelers. This attitude can't help but be conveyed to the patients—our employees—when they are receiving healthcare. We found that a negative attitude on the part of the provider contributed significantly to employee dissatisfaction with the plan." The Travelers, once it was made aware of the problem, took definitive action. It formed targeted focus groups and generated feedback through provider satisfaction surveys.

Despite the growing pains. USAir believes the initial transition has been successful. Preliminary cost savings for 1992 are estimated at $37 million in actual medical care and another $5 million for psychiatric and substance abuse costs. Employee contributions accounted for an additional $16 million in savings. An interesting observation: Although consultants and employers have recommended introducing changes in plan design and contributions over a period of several years to give employees time to become familiar with the new requirements and to gradually shift to managed care options, the USAir experience has been just the opposite. "Our employees almost never choose the out-of-network option," Davis said. "The feedback we're getting suggests that within our culture, where employees are used to high-option coverage with little or no out-of-pocket costs, they are very prudent purchasers when it comes to getting the best value for their money. Simply put, they just won't spend more for out-of-network services when they can get the same benefits in the network at little or not cost," Davis added.

With the cooperation from all involved parties, tangible and meaningful progress was made almost immediately. Claims processing was faster and more accurate. Employee eligibility updates were processed in less than half the original time, and employee complaints were almost non-existent by the first quarter of 1993. "Based on our initial experiences, we were able to put the necessary procedures and communication efforts in place for the conversions in January and June of this year," Davis noted. "As a result, these implementations were virtually problem-free."

Many employers make the mistake of assuming that once managed care is implemented, the worst is over. "We realized this is a continuous process, and we are looking for ongoing improvement and ways to enhance the product and services delivered to our employees," Davis said. "The ongoing team involves USAir, The Travelers, employees and providers. With this cooperative partnership, we believe we can make managed care work for everyone involved."

WHAT'S NEXT?

USAir plans to continue to improve employee communications efforts and it looking into the advantages of using high-tech options, such as teleconferencing and touch-screen technology. Customer service remains paramount. Even the HR staff is being educated in state-of-the-art customer service techniques and the importance of their role in making managed care a success. Of equal importance is establishing a nurturing and open dialogue with providers, and encouraging improved relationships with The Travelers and USAir.

7. Employer Liability in the Managed Care Setting

David M. Ermer

Managed care may present legal risks for employers. To avoid potential liability, employers should engage in due diligence and carefully draft plan documents, vendor contracts and employee communications.

THE TRANSITION FROM TRADITIONAL INDEMNITY COVERAGE TO MANAGED CARE

Since the 1930s, employers have sponsored fee-for-service (FFS) health benefit plans that serve as a health care financing system for their employees. Under an FFS plan arrangement, employees are free to choose their own providers of care. FFS plans simply reimburse those employees for all or a percentage of the provider's covered charges. Consequently, FFS plan costs usually increase in lock step with health care charges in the community.

Beginning in the 1970s, health care costs for employers began to skyrocket due to constant medical cost inflation and increased utilization. Health care prices have grown at almost twice the overall inflation rate since 1980.[1] The provision of health care services dramatically increased due to technological advances, inefficiencies associated with the widespread availability of health insurance, the rise of epidemic diseases such as AIDS, an aging population and the practice of "preventive medicine" to avoid malpractice suits.[2] Finally, the federal govern-

"Employer Liability in the Managed Care Setting," by David Ermer, which appeared in the June 1993 issue, was reprinted with permission from the *Employee Benefits Journal*, published by the International Foundation of Employee Benefit Plans, Brookfield, WI. Statements or opinions expressed in this article are those of the author and do not necessarily represent the views or positions of the International Foundation, its officers, directors, or staff.

ment began in 1982 to shift Medicare costs to the private sector by placing significant limits on Medicare reimbursement to hospitals and other covered providers. In fact, a recent study indicated that hospitals now lose twice as much money on their Medicare business as they do on charity care.[3] Hospitals routinely recoup these losses by increasing charges to patients with private sector coverage. As a result, from 1984 to 1992, total per employee health plan costs increased from $1,645 to $3,968 per employee.[4]

In response, employers sought to manage health care costs through an alphabet soup of devices: UR-utilization review, PPO-preferred provider organization, HMO-health maintenance organization, POS-point of service and EPO-exclusive provider organization. By 1992, a majority of employees (55 percent) were enrolled in HMO, PPO, POS and EPO plans.[5]

MANAGED CARE SETTINGS

Health Maintenance Organizations

HMOs, the first form of managed care, offer comprehensive health care services to persons living in a specific geographic area. Services are rendered through a panel of health care providers who are compensated at a capitated or other "at risk" rate. (A *capitated rate* involves the payment of a lump sum per member, per month, regardless of the actual number of services rendered to each member.)

Four types of HMOs are recognized: (1) the staff model, in which the HMO hires a staff of physicians and other allied health care professionals; (2) the group model, in which the HMO contracts with an independent group medical practice; (3) the individual practice association (IPA) model, in which the HMO contracts with an IPA, which in turn contracts with independent contractor physicians who provide care both to HMO members and other patients; and (4) the network model, which is a combination of two or more of these other approaches. The majority of the 552 HMOs in the United States are IPA model.[6]

HMO subscribers are required to utilize HMO physicians who often are subject to strict utilization controls. Of course, HMOs vary in the degree to which they restrict a patient's choice of physician. In an HMO setting, patients generally do not have free access to specialists. The patient's primary care physician must refer the patient to a specialist. This is known as a *gatekeeper* function. Most HMOs permit members to choose their primary care physician from a list. Certain HMOs, however, designate the gatekeeper or primary care physician for the patient.

PPO, POS and EPO Plans

PPOs are an HMO/FFS plan hybrid. A PPO is a network of providers who are willing to accept participating FFS plan members as patients at a negotiated rate.

In return, the participating FFS plan offers its members a financial incentive, i.e., a reduced or waived deductible or more generous copayments, to utilize the preferred providers. PPO networks may be established by an insurer or other sponsoring organization, or through direct contracts between the provider and the employer, or through contracts between coalition(s) of employers and providers. There are approximately 800 operational PPOs in the United States.[7]

POS plans are an HMO/PPO hybrid. These plans permit their members to receive care outside of the plan's provider network at a significantly lower reimbursement level than for in-network providers. The distinction between POS plans and PPOs is a fine one. Most POS plans evolve out of HMOs, which traditionally limit access to nonnetwork providers. PPOs are an outgrowth of FFS plans, which generally emphasize freedom of provider choice. Thus, POS plans tend to use the "stick" instead of the "carrot" when encouraging their members to use network providers.

EPOs essentially are HMO clones usually offered by insurers. Thus, EPOs require their members to utilize a panel of physicians and provide extremely limited out-of-network coverage.

UR—An Essential Managed Care Component

UR and other quality assurance tools are an integral component of any managed care system. UR assesses the medical necessity of inpatient hospitalizations and surgeries and reviews the lengths of stay of covered admissions. UR normally is coupled with catastrophic case management programs.

BASES FOR EMPLOYER EXPOSURE TO MANAGED CARE LIABILITY

The Effect of Limiting Freedom of Provider Choice

Managed care, as the name suggests, requires employers to become more involved with health care delivery to their employees. This fact potentially exposes employers to becoming swept up in the flood of medical malpractice litigation in the United States.[8]

When a person visits a lawyer to discuss bringing a medical malpractice lawsuit, the discussion eventually will turn to the process of identifying the potential defendants in addition to the treating physician, or otherwise stated, finding all of the available "deep pockets." The attorney will consider joining as defendants all those entities whom the law deems to share liability for the malpractice. Likely candidates, of course, are the hospital, clinic or HMO where the patient received the negligent treatment.

When the patient has traditional health insurance coverage, it is unlikely that the insurer or employer ever would become a topic of this conversation because the patient freely chose his or her own physician. (A patient's choice of a hospital, however, usually is linked to his or her physician's staff privileges—except at mental health and substance abuse facilities that accept self-referrals.)

In the managed care setting, however, freedom of physician choice is increasingly restricted over a continuum from PPOs, which are the least restrictive, to POS plans, and ultimately to HMOs and EPOs, which are the most restrictive. If, as a result of such restricted choice, a malpractice victim links his or her physician with a certain managed care organization or the employer, then the attorney likely will add those entities to the list of potential defendants. An attorney, however, usually will not actually name the managed care organization or employer as a defendant unless an arguable basis for liability exists.

We turn next to the theories of liability that generally are available under state law to an attorney in such circumstances, followed by a discussion of the available defenses—most importantly the ERISA preemption defense—and liability avoidance strategies.

Vicarious Liability Theories

Respondeat Superior/Actual Agency

A person or entity is liable vicariously for the negligent acts of its employee (or agent) committed within the scope of his or her employment. Thus, when a truck driver employed by a department store is responsible for an on-the-job collision, any person injured in that collision may recover from both the driver and the department store. This doctrine is known as *respondeat superior.*[9]

When assessing liability for negligent acts, the law draws a sharp distinction between employees (and agents), on the one hand, and independent contractors, on the other. It is axiomatic that a person who retains an independent contractor's services is not liable vicariously for the independent contractor's negligent conduct.[10]

The employee/independent contractor distinction turns on whether or not the alleged employer has retained control, or right of control, over the details of the work. Retaining control creates an employment relationship. When called upon to draw this distinction, courts will consider such factors as whether or not the person employed is engaged in a distinct business or occupation, the skill required in that occupation, whether the employer or the worker supplies the tools and place of work, the length of employment, the method of payment, i.e., by time or by the job, and the parties' intent. In sum, the question boils down to whether the employer has hired services or has purchased the product of those services. Purchasing the product of services reflects an independent contractor relationship.[11]

Until recently, courts have had little difficulty applying these rules in the health care setting. Physicians traditionally have worked in settings that are characteristic of an independent contractor relationship. They have owned their own facilities, received payment on a fee-for-service basis and, of course, exercised independent judgment based on many years of professional training and education.

Over the past 40 years, however, physicians increasingly have found themselves in a nontraditional employment relationship with hospitals, HMOs and other entities. Moreover, even those physicians who continue to maintain their own offices find themselves in contractual relationships such as IPAs that subject their performance to rigorous peer review.[12]

The courts have recognized this trend by holding hospitals and staff model HMOs liable under the *respondeat superior* doctrine for the malpractice of staff and resident physicians whom they employ.[13] In *Schleier v. Kaiser Foundation Health Plan,* 876 F.2d 174 (D.C. Cir. 1989), this *respondeat superior* doctrine was extended beyond the standard employment relationship to the conduct of an HMO's consulting specialist.

In that case, Kaiser, a group model HMO, had retained a cardiologist with a private practice to consult with one of its employee primary care physicians on a patient's condition. The cardiologist misdiagnosed the patient, who later died because he did not receive appropriate care. The appeals court affirmed the lower court's verdict that Kaiser was responsible for the consultant's malpractice principally because the consultant reported to a Kaiser physician and the consultant's work was part of Kaiser's regular business. The court stressed that the consultant "acted neither on his own initiative nor independently of the Kaiser physician. To the contrary, [he] only made recommendations to the Kaiser physician." 876 F.2d at 178.

The *Schleier* case currently represents the furthest extension of the *respondeat superior* doctrine in the managed care context. It no doubt raises concerns for nonstaff model HMOs and other managed care organizations that are engaged primarily in the health care delivery business. Those entities, however, can find solace in two more recent state court decisions, *Raglin v. HMO Illinois, Inc.,* 595 N.E.2d 153 (Ill.App. 1992), and *Chase v. Independent Practice Association, Inc.,* 583 N.E.2d 251 (Mass.App. 1991).

Both *Raglin* and *Chase* involved malpractice actions against IPA model HMO participating physicians. The plaintiffs also sought to hold the HMO and IPA liable based on the *respondeat superior* doctrine, but the courts ruled for the HMO and IPA. The Massachusetts court explained (583 N.E.2d at 254) that:

> While IPA did check the credentials of the [clinics] with whom it contracted, it did not have the right to hire and fire individual physicians, nor to set their salaries, work schedules, or terms of employment. More importantly, the IPA did not control the actual medical decisions made by [the contracting clinics and their physicians]. Although the agreement between IPA and the [clinic]

does provide for certain cost containment and utilization review measures, it makes clear that responsibility for the actual provision of medical treatment rests with [the clinic] and its employee-physicians.

Both opinions stress that utilization review and cost-containment measures that the IPA applied to its contracting physicians do not rise to the level of control necessary to create an employment or agency relationship. These cases are good news for the managed care organizations and employers because they suggest that the *Schleier* decision is not a judicial trendsetter.

Employers are more sheltered than managed care organizations from liability under the *respondeat superior* doctrine because they are not primarily in the health care delivery business. Unlike a hospital or an HMO, when an employer contracts with a provider of care directly or through a PPO sponsor, it essentially is purchasing a product with no intention of controlling the details of the work. Moreover, in a cafeteria or flexible benefits setting, it ultimately is the employee's choice to enroll in a particular HMO or other managed care option. This fact, particularly when it is made clear to employees in writing, should serve to sever any possible agency linkage between the employer and the HMO/managed care option. (The clearest example of such severance occurs when a federally qualified HMO mandates the employer to offer its coverage.) Thus, provided that an employer engages in prudent contracting practices (see below), an employer is unlikely to be held liable under the *respondeat superior* doctrine for the malpractice of a hospital or physician that its employees utilize in a managed care setting. However, that is not the end of potential vicarious liability exposure.

Ostensible Agency

Under the *ostensible agency* doctrine, a person may be held liable for the conduct of independent contractors whom the person hires and holds out as one of his or her employees. This doctrine was developed in the health care setting in cases in which hospitals were held liable for malpractice committed by emergency room doctors whom the hospital did not employ, and who technically were independent contractors. The *Restatement (Second) of Torts* § 429 describes the ostensible agency doctrine as follows:

> One who employs an independent contractor to perform services for another which are accepted in the reasonable belief that the services are being rendered by the employer or his servants, is subject to liability for physical harm caused by the negligence of the contractor in supplying such services, to the same extent as though the employer were supplying them himself or by his employees.

In the emergency room setting, this doctrine becomes applicable when the patient looks to the hospital—rather than the individual physician—as the caregiver, and the hospital holds out the physicians as employees by, for example, providing them with facilities.

Several federal district courts in Pennsylvania have extended the ostensible agency doctrine from the hospital to the HMO setting.[14] These courts have ruled that the HMO theoretically may be held liable for a panel member's malpractice where the patient proves that he or she looked to the HMO as an institutional caregiver and that HMO created the impression that the panel physicians were HMO employees. To our knowledge, however, no plaintiff actually has proved such a case against an HMO. Indeed, in the *Raglin* and *Chase* cases discussed above, the courts ruled on summary judgment that the IPA model HMOs were not liable on ostensible agency grounds because their subscriber literature quite explicitly stated that the participating physicians are independent contractors.

It certainly is well within the realm of possibility that courts may extend this doctrine beyond the hospital or HMO setting to PPOs or to employers, particularly when an employer engages in direct contracting with hospitals and physicians. The *Raglin* and *Chase* cases remind us of the essential point that the ostensible agency doctrine only becomes applicable when an entity fails to protect itself by affirmatively informing patients that an independent contractor relationship exists. As is discussed in more detail below, summary plan descriptions and other employee communications afford employers an excellent opportunity to communicate this fact to plan participants and nullify potential vicarious liability.

Direct Liability Theories Based on Contract Law

Employers sponsoring FFS plans with managed care components obviously are exposed to breach-of-contract liability based on a managed care organization's refusal to authorize payment of benefits. This problem arises most frequently in the context of UR denials of pre-authorizations for certain medically unnecessary procedures, such as hysterectomies, or experimental/investigational procedures, such as bone marrow transplant/high-dosage chemotherapy for solid tumors. Such actions will be governed by the Employee Retirement Income Security Act of 1974(ERISA), 29 U.S.C.§ 1001 et seq., which is discussed in more detail below.

Employees also may have enforceable rights as third party beneficiaries of the managed care contracts between employers and managed care organizations. For example, it is reported that in *Shelmach v. Physicians' Multispecialty Group,* an unreported decision from 1989 (No. 53,906), a Missouri state appellate court held an HMO liable, on this basis, to an enrollee who claimed that the HMO had promised in its contract to provide "good quality" care. Such undertakings, however, generally create liability solely for the managed care organization.

Direct Liability Theories Based on Tort Law

A tort claim alleges a violation of a duty that the law involuntarily imposes on a person. In contrast, a breach-of-contract claim concerns violation of a legal obligation voluntarily undertaken by a person. This article will focus on tort claim liability because of the substantially greater scope of available monetary relief. Contract damages generally are limited to compensation for economic injuries, i.e., unpaid benefits. Tort damages compensate plaintiffs for both economic and noneconomic injuries, such as pain and suffering and, in cases involving malice, include punitive damages. Consequently, tort claims present much greater potential liability exposure than do contract claims.

Corporate Negligence

Applying the *corporate negligence* doctrine, courts have held hospitals liable for the malpractice of an independent contractor physician with staff privileges on the theory that the hospital negligently extended such privileges to, or did not timely remove such privileges from, the physician. The policy rationale is that the hospital is better qualified than the patient to judge the physician's competence.[15]

In the leading case of *Harrell v. Total Health Care, Inc.* 781 S.W.2d 58 (Mo. 1989), the corporate negligence doctrine was extended to HMOs. The Missouri Supreme Court reasoned that by limiting its members' choices of available physicians, an HMO creates an unreasonable risk of hardship to its membership if the HMO selects physicians who are unqualified or incompetent. The court therefore decided that an HMO owes its members a duty to conduct a reasonable investigation of a participating physician's credentials and reputation. (The court, however, ultimately excused the HMO from liability based upon a state statutory immunity.)

More recently, a Pennsylvania state court reached the same result in a case involving an IPA model HMO.[16] The court held that the HMO had a nondelegable duty to "exercise reasonable care in selecting, retaining, and/or evaluating the plaintiff's primary care physician."

On the same basis, a malpractice victim could allege a corporate negligence claim against a PPO, EPO or an employer that engages in direct contracting on the theory that the organization or employer should not have included the negligent physician in, or should have removed him or her timely from, its provider network. A malpractice victim further could allege that an employer negligently selected a particular HMO or PPO for its employees.

To avoid corporate negligence liability, managed care organizations and employers that engage in direct contracting must implement a quality assurance program for their participating health care providers. Employers that contract with managed care organizations also should assure themselves that their contractors utilize sound quality assurance programs. The important components of such a program are discussed below.

Negligent Operation of a Managed Care Program

The California Court of Appeals in two decisions has recognized that managed care organizations and third party payers, under the appropriate circumstances, may be held liable for the consequences of a negligently designed or operated program. In *Wickline v. California,* 228 Cal. Rptr. 661, 670-71 (Cal.App.2d 1986), the court noted that a third party payer

> can be held legally accountable when medically inappropriate decisions result from defects in the design or implementation of cost containment mechanisms as, for example, when appeals are made on a patient's behalf for medical or hospital care are arbitrarily or unreasonably disregarded or overridden.

The court of appeals revisited this issue in *Wilson v. Blue Cross of Southern California,* 271 Cal. Rptr. 876 (Cal.App. 2d 1990).

In *Wilson,* a teenage boy covered under an Alabama Blue Cross policy was admitted into a psychiatric facility in California on March 11, 1983. Alabama Blue Cross contracted with Blue Cross of Southern California (BS/SC) to process its California claims. The psychiatric facility contacted BC/SC at the time of admission, and BC/SC imposed a concurrent utilization review requirement on the stay. The facility requested approval from BC/SC's UR vendor, Western Medical Review, for three to four weeks of care. Western authorized only ten days, and the boy was discharged on the tenth day. The boy committed suicide a week later, and the boy's parents then sued BC/SC, Western and Blue Cross of Alabama for wrongful death. The defendants' problem here was that the boy's Alabama Blue Cross policy did *not* require concurrent UR. The court held that under such circumstances a triable issue existed as to whether the improper utilization review action was a "substantial factor" in the boy's death.

On April 21, 1992, the *Wall Street Journal* (p. B5) reported that, following a trial in the *Wilson* case, a Los Angeles jury had ruled in the defendant Blue Cross plans' favor on the wrongful death claim. Evidently the jury refused to link the boy's death to the UR decision. (Western Medical Review had settled out of court before trial.) The jury found that BC/BS had breached its contract by unnecessarily requiring UR but that there had been no causal link between this breach and the boy's death. Accordingly, the jury awarded no damages.

A similar case went to trial last year in Greensboro, North Carolina, with a dramatically different result. In *Muse v. Charter Hospital,* No. 88-CV-7329 (N.C. Superior Ct.), the parents of a 16-year-old boy who had committed suicide after his release from a psychiatric hospital brought a wrongful death action against the hospital. The parents claimed that the hospital had released their son solely because his insurance coverage had run out. The hospital records showed that four days before the boy's release, he was having auditory hallucinations, had been diagnosed as psychotic and had been given antipsychotic drugs. At the time of discharge, the boy was talking about committing suicide. The jury found that the hospital did not advise the parents of their son's true condition and that the hospital's discharge policies interfered with the treating physician's medical judgment. The jury awarded the parents a judgment against the hospital for $1 million in compensatory damages and $6 million in punitive damages, the largest medical malpractice award in North Carolina history.[17] Even though a UR vendor's decision was not involved in this case, this result illustrates the potential risks of negligently operating a managed care program.

The *Wilson/Wickline* line of authority instructs employers to select well-qualified managed care organizations that emphasize quality assurance within their own operations, including an easily accessible physician-to-physician appeal process. However, neither *Wickline* nor *Wilson* involved employer-sponsored health plans, and thus the defendant managed care organization could not invoke the potent ERISA preemption defense available to employers that is discussed below.

Improper Design of a Managed Care Program

A handful of cases have raised state-law-based public policy objections to managed care programs. None of those cases, however, have resulted in a judgment against a managed care organization or an employer. For example, in *Bush v. Dake,* No. 86-25767 (Mich. Cir. Ct., Saginaw Cty., April 27, 1989), a Michigan state court denied an HMO's motion to dismiss the plaintiff's claim that the HMO's cost-containment system of financial incentives, risk sharing and utilization review violated state public policy and contributed to her medical malpractice damages. That case reportedly was later settled under a gag order.[18]

Other federal and state courts, however, have dismissed similar claims based on the fact that federal and state laws regulating HMOs encourage the development of such systems.[19] Similarly, as discussed later, courts interpreting the federal law governing employer-sponsored health plans, ERISA, have recognized that ERISA allows employers to incorporate managed care provisions in their health plans without restriction.

State legislatures have responded to the hue and cry about managed care interference with the physician-patient relationship. Several states have passed laws regulating UR and PPO activities.[20] Managed care organizations and employers are expected to challenge the more restrictive laws in court on ERISA preemption grounds.[21] It is to that subject—the ERISA defense—that we now turn.

LEGAL DEFENSES TO MANAGED CARE LIABILITY THEORIES

The ERISA Defense

Overview of ERISA

Private employer-sponsored health plans, with one principal exception, are governed by ERISA. Excepted from ERISA coverage are plans created solely to comply with state workers' compensation, unemployment insurance or disability insurance laws (29 U.S.C. § 1003).

"ERISA is a comprehensive statute designed to promote the interests of employees and their beneficiaries in employee benefit plans."[22] ERISA requires that health plans be reduced to writing and be communicated to plan participants in a written document known as a *summary plan description (SPD)*. The written plan document, at a minimum, must establish:

1. One or more named fiduciaries to operate and administer the plan;
2. Procedures for establishing and carrying out a funding policy, allocating fiduciary responsibilities, internally resolving disputed claims and amending the plan; and
3. The basis upon which payments are made to and from the plan.[23]

ERISA imposes few plan design requirements on health plans, other than compliance with COBRA continuation coverage requirements.[24] All courts that have considered the issue agree that employers are free to incorporate managed care provisions, including noncompliance penalties, in their ERISA-governed health plans.[25]

ERISA also includes a detailed civil enforcement scheme.[26] That scheme allows a plan participant to bring a civil lawsuit for the following purposes:

1. To recover benefits or enforce, or clarify, the participant's rights under the terms of the plan;
2. To obtain requested information from the plan and where deemed judicially appropriate receive a $100 a day penalty from the plan administrator over the period of delay;
3. To redress a breach of fiduciary duty; and
4. To enjoin any act or practice that violates ERISA or the terms of the plan and to obtain other appropriate equitable relief to redress such violation or to enforce ERISA or the terms of the plan.

The federal courts of appeals generally agree that monetary relief for any breach of ERISA fiduciary duty is payable only to the plan itself and that monetary relief to plan participants for any breach of the terms of the plan is limited to the benefits in dispute plus attorney fees.[27] Finally, as the Supreme Court emphasized in *Pilot Life Insurance Co. v. Dedeaux,* 481 U.S. 41, 54 (1987), ERISA's remedial scheme is exclusive:

> The [Congressional] policy choices reflected in the inclusion of certain remedies and the exclusion of others under the federal scheme would be undermined completely if ERISA-plan participants and beneficiaries were free to obtain remedies under state law that Congress rejected in ERISA.

This brings us to the topic of ERISA preemption of state law.

How ERISA Preemption Works

Congress enacted ERISA to encourage and preserve the financial stability of employee benefit plans and thereby ensure that those plans will fulfill their principal purpose of paying benefits to participants and beneficiaries. To this end, and its corollary objective of uniform plan administration, ERISA broadly preempts state laws, including statues, regulations and theories of liability that "relate to" employee benefit plans.[28]

ERISA saves, or exempts, state insurance laws from preemption.[29] For this reason, HMOs and often EPOs are subject to state insurance laws. However, the Supreme Court has interpreted this savings clause narrowly as applying only to laws that regulate risk sharing practices in the insurance industry.[30] This "savings" clause further is limited by ERISA's requirement that states not "deem" employee benefit plans to be insurance companies for purposes of coverage by their insurance laws.[31] Thus, the Supreme Court has recognized that the savings clause does not permit states to apply their insurance laws to self-insured ERISA plans.[32]

ERISA's preemption provision is "conspicuous for its breadth."[33] It reaches all state laws that have a "connection with or reference to" such plans.[34] Under this "broad common sense meaning," a state law may "relate to" a benefit plan, and thereby be preempted, even if the law is not designed specifically to affect such plans or the effect is only indirect. Moreover, the fact that the state law may be consistent with ERISA's substantive requirements simply is irrelevant to the preemption analysis.[35] Thus, the Supreme Court in the *Pilot Life, FMC Corp., Greater Washington Board of Trade* and *Ingersoll-Rand* cases has ruled that ERISA preempts state bad faith tort laws, antisubrogation laws, provisions of workers' compensation laws that refer to ERISA plans and wrongful discharge laws.[36] In sum, "Congress constructed ERISA so that the statute will preempt most state law claims."[37]

ERISA preemption, of course, ultimately has its limits. The Supreme Court has recognized that state laws that have a remote or tangential relationship to employee benefit plans are not preempted. For example, in *Mackey v. Lanier Collections Agency,* 486 U.S. 825 (1988), that Court ruled that ERISA does not bar a state law-based garnishment action against a vacation benefits fund. The Court reasoned (id. at 833) that:

> [L]awsuits against ERISA plans for run-of-the-mill state law claims such as unpaid rent, failure to pay creditors, or even torts committed by an ERISA plan are relatively common place. Petitioners and the United States (appearing here as *amicus curiae*) concede that these suits, although obviously affecting and involving ERISA plans and their trustees, are not preempted by ERISA.

The *Mackey* decision, in particular, causes us to differentiate for ERISA preemption purposes between the direct and vicarious liability theories discussed above.

ERISA Preemption Applies to the Direct Liability Theories

Breach-of-Contract Theories. Earlier we explained that managed care vendor decisions may result in breach-of-contract lawsuits against employers and/or their self-insured plans for unpaid benefits. ERISA clearly preempts state-law-based breach-of-contract claims. Instead, these cases will proceed under ERISA's civil enforcement scheme discussed above. Except in the Sixth Federal Appellate Circuit Court (which covers Michigan, Ohio, Kentucky and Tennessee), relief under ERISA currently is limited to the unpaid benefits plus attorney fees in the court's discretion.[38]

To reduce such litigation, employers should insist that managed care vendors adhere to a user-friendly and readily accessible physician-to-physician disputed claims procedure. Furthermore, in the written plan documents, employers should afford the plan administrator and all claims administrators, including, whenever appropriate, managed care vendors, discretionary authority to interpret the plan. This action entitles the benefit decision to limited judicial review under an "abuse of discretion standard."[39]

A recent decision from the U.S. Court of Appeals for the Fifth Circuit, *Salley v. E.I. DuPont de Nemours & Co.,* 966 F.2d 1022 (5th Cir. 1992), emphasizes the importance of integrating a plan's UR/managed care mechanisms with its claim decision making procedure. That case stemmed from the decision of du Pont's UR vendor rejecting the treating physician Dr. Blundell's proposed course of treatment and refusing to certify the continued psychiatric hospitalization of a teenage girl, Danielle Salley. Danielle remained hospitalized for three-plus months after the certification terminated. her father thereafter sued du Pont for benefits due on the hospital charges for the noncertified portion. The court subjected this claims decision to review under the abuse-of-discretion standard because du Pont had afforded itself the requisite discretionary authority in its plan document and "the contract between du Pont and [the UR vendor] explicitly states, 'du Pont reserves final authority to authorize or deny payment for services to beneficiaries of a plan'" (id. at 1014). The court added that "[a]s long as a company maintains the ultimate decision on denial of benefits, it can be beneficial for it to have experienced agents assist in the determination" (id.).

The court nonetheless concluded that the du Pont/UR vendor's claim decision had been an abuse of discretion. The court stated that "the plan administrator may rely on the treating physician's advise or it can independently investigate medical necessity" (id. at 1015). here, the plan administrator failed to conduct an independent investigation—either an independent medical evaluation or a review of the hospital records—and instead relied on a portion of the treating physician's advise to justify its decision. This approach, in the court's opinion, was an abuse of discretion. The court held as follows (id. at 1015–1016).

> [A]lthough DuPont followed the prescribed procedures, it abused its discretion in relying upon [the UR vendor's] recommendation to terminate Danielle's benefits. Because they chose to follow Dr. Blundell's diagnosis, [the UR vendors] were required, absent independent inquiry, to follow all his advice, not just part of it. If they decided to deviate from his diagnosis, they were required to investigate further the medical necessity of in-patient hospitalization. Whether this investigation included an examination of Danielle

or an analysis of hospital records depended on the particulars of each case. At the very least, however, administrators relying on hospital records obviously must review the most recent records. The [UR vendor] conceded at trial that they did not do so.

Salley thus calls attention to the importance of rationally based, thoroughly investigated and well-documented UR decision making.

Tort Theories. Above we described three state-law-based theories of direct tort liability applicable to managed care programs: (1) corporate negligence or the tort of negligent selection/retention of a managed care organization, (2) negligent operation of a managed care program and (3) improper design of a managed care program. In our opinion ERISA would preempt such claims because these causes of action relate to the essence of the health plan itself—furnishing health care coverage/services to participants and beneficiaries.

When an employer incorporates a managed care component into its plan and selects a particular managed care vendor, it is engaging in plan design and administration functions that, as discussed above, lie at the core of ERISA's substantive provisions. Moreover, as the Supreme Court ruled in *Pilot Life,* errors made in the administration of an ERISA-governed plan, which would include its managed care components, are not remediable under state law.

This conclusion is supported by a recent decision of major significance in the U.S. Court of Appeals for the Fifth Circuit. In a case captioned *Corcoran v. United Healthcare Corp.,* 965 F.2d 1321 (5th Cir. 1992), that court ruled that ERISA preempts a plan participant's medical malpractice action against an ERISA-governed plan's utilization review vendor, United Healthcare Corp. (United).

The *Corcoran* case arose from United's refusal to certify the medical necessity of an inpatient hospitalization for Peggy Corcoran, who was enduring an "at risk" pregnancy. Instead, the review organization authorized ten hours per day of private nursing care at Mrs. Corcoran's home. One day, while the nurse was not present, Mrs. Corcoran suffered a miscarriage in her home. The Corcorans contended that the review organization had given her erroneous medical advice and should be held liable for medical malpractice. In their view, their medical malpractice action was a run-of-the-mill tort action exempt from ERISA preemption under *Mackey.*

United argued that it had made a routine benefit decision, and that Mrs. Corcoran and her physician were responsible for choosing not to have her enter the hospital at her expense. The court did not entirely accept United's argument:

A prospective decision is different in impact on the beneficiary than a retrospective decision. . . . When United makes a decision pursuant to the QCP [the UR program], it is making a medical recommendation that—because of the financial ramifications—is more likely to be followed. 965 F.2d at 1331–1332.

Nevertheless, the court found a sufficient relationship between the malpractice action and plan administration to warrant ERISA preemption:

> Although we disagree with United's position that no part of its actions involves medical decisions, we cannot agree with the Corcorans that no part of United's actions involves benefit determinations. In our view, United makes medical decisions as part and parcel of its mandate to decide what benefits are available under the employee welfare benefit plan. When United's actions are viewed from this perspective, it becomes apparent that the Corcorans are attempting to recover for a tort allegedly occurring in the course of handling a benefit determination. . . . The principle of *Pilot Life* that ERISA preempts state law claims alleging improper handling of benefit claims is broad enough to cover the cause of action asserted here. Id. at 1332.

The court proceeded to rule that the Corcorans had no viable cause of action against United under ERISA itself. The court held that ERISA makes no provision for extra-contractual remedies—that is, any compensatory damages other than unpaid benefits or punitive damages—to be paid to plan participants in the event that a plan mishandles their claims. While expressing some concern that Congress may not have foreseen this result because ERISA was enacted before the advent of the managed care era, the court concluded that the Corcorans' lawsuit must be dismissed. The protection afforded UR vendors by the Corcoran holding necessarily extends to employers, given their seminal position in ERISA plan design and administration.[40]

The *Corcoran* holding, of course, equally is applicable to other, less dramatic situations in which a managed care vendor inconveniences a plan participant. For example, in *Disney v. Continental Assurance Co. et al.,* No. CIV-92-674-W, slip op. (W.D. Okla. July 1992), the plaintiff complained that she had lost wages and endured unnecessary pain and suffering because her hysterectomy had been postponed during a five-month long review by a federal employee plan's UR vendor. The court, invoking the preemption provision of the Federal Employees Health Benefits Act, 5 U.S.C. § 8902(m)(1), which is analogous to ERISA's, held that plaintiffs' state-law-based damages claims were preempted by federal law.

In sum, the *Corcoran* decision and several federal district court decisions reaching the same result confirm that an employer successfully may invoke the ERISA preemption defense in the event that it is joined as a defendant in a managed care liability/medical malpractice action on a direct liability theory.[41]

ERISA Preemption Does Not Apply to Vicarious Liability

In our view, the ERISA preemption defense will not find judicial support when a plaintiff proceeds with a managed care liability/medical malpractice claim based on a vicarious liability theory, either *respondeat superior* or ostensible agency. As the U.S. Court of Appeals for the Third Circuit has observed, medical malpractice actions are the type of run-of-the-mill litigation that ERISA generally does not preempt.

Several federal district courts and a state court have held that ERISA does not preempt medical malpractice claims against HMOs based on vicarious liability theories.[43] In those cases, the patient was covered under an employer-sponsored plan that provided HMO coverage. The patient allegedly received negligent care from an HMO physician. The courts held that the vicarious liability claim against the HMO was only tangentially related to the ERISA-governed plan and thus was not preempted.

In *Corcoran,* the Fifth Circuit distinguished these Pennsylvania cases as follows (965 F.2d at 1333, n. 16):

> [T]he medical decisions at issue [in the Pennsylvania cases] do not appear to
> have been made in connection with a cost containment feature of the plan or
> any other aspect of the plan which implicated the management of plan assets,
> but instead were made by a doctor in the course of treatment.

This reasoning suggest that, under appropriate circumstances, employers that contract directly for health care services or actually employ health care providers may be held liable based on vicarious liability theories.

As previously stated, employers that purchase managed care products, such as UR or PPOs, have minimal exposure to *respondeat superior* liability. However, such employers, if careless, may expose themselves to ostensible agency liability. Of course, no employer to date has been subjected to liability on any vicarious liability basis.

PRACTICAL DEFENSIVE STRATEGIES FOR EMPLOYERS

The Importance of Due Diligence

ERISA preemption is a valuable shield against managed care-based liability. To position themselves to assert an ERISA preemption defense in good faith, employers must ensure that their plans conform with ERISA's various requirements, i.e., that they have a plan document that conforms with ERISA's requirements, and that the plan administrator complies with ERISA's reporting and disclosure requirements. Advice on these specific ERISA compliance issues should be obtained from an attorney.

However, the scope of ERISA preemption is under attack in the courts and on Capitol Hill, and it may well be narrowed in the current Congress.[44] In any event, courts are likely to rule that ERISA preemption does not reach vicarious liability claims. Therefore, prudent employers should not rely exclusively on an ERISA preemption defense when gauging their managed care liability exposure. Furthermore, imprudent managed care administration may be found to constitute a breach of fiduciary responsibility under ERISA.

Persons who exercise discretion with respect to ERISA plan administration or asset management as plan fiduciaries are obligated to comply with ERISA's fiduciary responsibility provisions. ERISA essentially requires plan fiduciaries to act solely in the interest of the plan's participants, to expend plan assets only on benefit and reasonable administrative expenses, to perform their responsibilities prudently and to comply with the plan's governing documents.[45] Although plan design, i.e., the decision to incorporate a particular managed care feature in a plan, is a *settlor*—not a *fiduciary*—function, a court likely would deem the selection of a managed care vendor to be a fiduciary decision.[46] ERISA's fiduciary responsibility provisions require the decision maker to engage in due diligence when selecting a vendor and to monitor the vendor's actions.[47] In other words, ERISA obligations essentially overlap the responsibilities that the state law tort of corporate negligence imposes.

The Supreme Court has ruled that damages for breach of fiduciary responsibility are payable only to the plan.[48] If the plan is unfunded and has no assets, as is the case with many self-insured corporate health plans, there may be no financial injury to the plan arising from an imprudent selection of a managed care vendor. The loss instead would be to the company for spending money unwisely on the administrative fees of an ineffective managed care vendor.[49] Thus, every reason exists to engage in due diligence whether or not the threat of an ERISA breach of fiduciary duty action exists.

Quality Plus Savings Equals Value for Your Health Care Dollar

The initial emphasis in managed care was on cost reduction for its own sake. Corporate health care managers now understand that value for the company's health care dollar can only be achieved by linking cost reductions with quality health care vendors whom employees are likely to utilize. As we have seen, there is an inherent legal risk in contracting with managed care vendors that simply are "cheap." Due diligence, therefore, is achieved by analyzing the managed care vendor's cost savings achievements, its quality assurance program, its administrative capabilities and its financial stability.

Applicable federal and state law generally obligate hospitals, HMOs and EPOs to implement such programs. When considering whether to contract with a hospital, HMO, EPO or PPO, a company should investigate the vendor's quality assurance programs.[50]

Finally, over 300 HMOs participate int he federal Employees Health Benefits (FEHB) program that imposes the following quality assurance program requirement on participating HMOs:

(a) The [HMO] shall develop and apply a quality assurance program specifying procedures for assuring contract quality. At a minimum the program should include procedures to address:

   (1) Utilization of inpatient services, outpatient services and referral services which:

      (i)   verify the medical necessity of inpatient nonemergency treatment or surgery;

       (ii)   establish whether services must be performed in an inpatient setting or could be done on an outpatient basis; and

       (iii) determine the appropriate length of stay for inpatient services, which may involve concurrent and/or retrospective review.

  (2) Credentialing of providers.

  (3) Risk sharing with respect to primary care physicians, referral physicians, hospitals and/or ancillary providers.

  (4) Member satisfaction.

(b) The [HMO] shall make available to the [OPM] Contracting Officer upon request a current copy of the Member Handbook or other information used to instruct members and providers about the use of the Plan.

(c) The [HMO] shall make available to the [OPM] Contracting Officer upon request reports which demonstrate results of the Quality Assurance Program.

(d) The [OPM] Contracting Officer may order the correction of a deficiency in the [HMO]'s quality assurance program. The [HMO] shall take the necessary action promptly to implement the [OPM] Contracting Officer's order. (U.S. Office of Personnel Management (OPM) Standard HMO Contract for the FEHB Program, § 1.9).

This OPM contract provision describes the necessary components of a sound quality assurance program for most types of managed care vendors as well as employers that engage in direct contracting.[51]

A critical component of a valid quality assurance program is its provider credentialing process. Managed care vendors should ascertain at a minimum that participating hospitals are properly licensed and are certified by the Hospital Accreditation Program of the Joint Commission on Accreditation of Health Care Organizations. Managed care vendors also should make onsite assessments of the facilities.

Physician credentialing is a more time-consuming yet equally important process. The managed care vendor should verify the physician's licensure, staff privileges and board certification, investigate any licensing challenges or malpractice lawsuits against the physician and obtain evidence of adequate malpractice insurance. The process also may require the physician to furnish his or her National Practitioner Data Bank (NPDB) file.[52] The quality assurance program also should require periodic recredentialing and should provide for peer review. Finally, the vendor also should provide proof that the quality assurance program, in fact, is utilized.

When an employer establishes its own network, it must establish its own quality assurance program along the lines described in the FEHB program provision quoted above. The litigation risk to an employer is greater in this situation because no independent PPO sponsor is available to provide a tort buffer.

Employers also should assure themselves, through review of financial statements, etc., of the financial stability of their managed care vendors. This inquiry is most necessary because of the well-known financial instability of the health care industry over the last decade, particularly when, for example, an employer directs all of its employees to one HMO or EPO.

Obviously, employers will investigate the cost effectiveness of the managed care vendor's programs and the vendor's administrative capabilities. However, employers also may wish to inquire whether the managed care vendor offers incentives to its participating physicians that may impact adversely on the quality of care rendered to participants.

In addition, employers should ensure that the managed care vendor offers a timely and reasonable appeals procedure to plan participants. UR appeals procedures, in particular, should be easily accessible on short notice and should provide for physician-to-physician contact on order to nip potential liability issues in the bud. The trend among HMOs is to include an arbitration requirement in their contracts that may short-circuit malpractice litigation.

Finally, employers must thoroughly document their due diligence efforts. Memories, of course, fade overtime, and any legal challenge to the employer's managed care activities will occur many months, if not years, following the selection of the managed care vendor. Written proof of the exercise of due diligence will be invaluable evidence in any such legal proceeding.

Contracting With Managed Care Vendors

Managed care vendors and health care providers that engage in direct contracting generally have standard contracts that they expect employers to sign. Employers often do not pay much attention to these contracts, and that, quite simply, is a mistake. For the employer's protection, managed care vendor and health care vendor contracts must include provisions for the following purposes:

1. Recognition of the independent contractor relationship between the parties and a prohibition against the managed care vendor's using the employer's name, trademarks, etc., without advance written approval.
2. Adequate insurance indemnification provisions (even in the absence of a contract provision, the employer may utilize common law indemnity principles in the face of a vicarious liability claim). The vendor should have adequate insurance for itself and should require its participating hospitals and physicians to maintain such insurance. The employer also may request that the vendor add the employer as an additional insured on its insurance policies.
3. Termination provisions that permit the employer to cancel the contract when necessary to protect its interests.
4. Provisions that prohibit the managed care vendor from declining coverage based on contract terms that are inconsistent with the summary plan description (SPD) (or evidence of coverage) furnished to employees.
5. Provisions that require the managed care vendor to comply with its quality assurance obligations. The OPM contract provision quoted above provides a good model for employers to use.

Care should be taken to ensure that the contract meshes properly with the terms of the employer's benefit plan and that any necessary allocation of fiduciary responsibilities has been accomplished. For example, if a managed care vendor, such as an HMO or PPO, is responsible for adjudicating claims, then the employer contractually should delegate appropriate fiduciary responsibility to the vendor.

We also recommend that these managed care contracts include a "significant events" clause, a form of which is found in note 53 below, which requires the managed care vendor to alert the employer to matters that materially affect the vendor's ability to perform the contract and permit the employer to take appropriate remedial action. Many HMOs are familiar with this type of provision because OPM requires HMOs that participate in the Federal Employees Health Benefits program to accept a similar provision in their FEHB plan contracts.[53]

Finally, if an employer contracts with several HMOs or contracts directly with hospitals or physicians, it is sensible to retain an attorney for the purpose of drafting a standard contract that includes all necessary protective provisions.

Sensible Employee Communications
The final step is to ensure that the plan documents, particularly the SPD circulated to plan participants/employees, clearly disclose any obligations the participant has with respect to the managed care options:

- Notice of any precertification or preauthorization requirements.
- Procedures the enrollee must follow and any penalties for failure to do so.
- Explanation of differences in enrollee copayment obligations for selecting nonpreferred providers.

Those documents also should define important managed care terms such as *medically necessary, experimental/investigational* and *hospital.*

Careful drafting of plan documents is a key to avoiding ostensible agency liability, which, as discussed above, hinges on the conduct of the ostensible principal, here the employer. All such documents and other employee communications concerning the plan, such as PPO directories, must announce that an independent contractor relationship exists between the employer and the managed care vendor. In addition, if a buffer exists between the employer and the network physicians in the form of a PPO or EPO sponsor, the employee communications should identify the sponsor and explain that the sponsor created the network. The employer should not take credit for the network where such credit is not due because it also may receive the blame.

Employers should avoid the urge to boast in their communications about the quality of their network providers. Instead, they should stress that the purpose of managed care is to reduce health plan costs. Employee communications should disclaim employer involvement or interference in the doctor-patient relationship and stress that final decisions about health care matters are the sole responsibility of the doctor and the patient. The employee communications should explain that the employer's role is solely to pay for covered care.

The *Corcoran* case illustrates this point. Both the Corcorans and the United UR vendors relied on different sections of the Bell South plan documents to support their respective positions. Indeed, the court found substantial support in those documents for the Corcorans' position that United made medical decisions. The court pointed to passages such as these (id. at 1331):

> United "will discuss with your doctor the appropriateness of the treatments recommended and the availability of alternative types of treatments." Further, "United's staff includes doctors, nurses, and other medical professionals knowledgeable about the health care delivery system. Together with your doctor, they work to assure that you and your covered family members receive the most appropriate medical care."

Employers should avoid these types of statements in their plan documents and should instead emphasize the UR vendor's role in claim decision making and plan benefit cost containment.

Finally, when employers offer more than one managed care option, such as both an FFS plan and HMOs, in a cafeteria plan, the SPD should stress that the choice of a particular HMO is solely the employee's. The SPD also should disclaim any affiliation between the employer and the HMO and/or its network physicians.

A FINAL NOTE—ANTITRUST ISSUES FOR EMPLOYER COALITIONS

Although our focus here has been on managed care liability from the medical malpractice perspective, it is important to consider the federal antitrust implications of managed care, particularly employer coalitions. ERISA has no preemptive impact on other federal laws.[54]

Combinations or conspiracies that unreasonably limit competition in health care and other industries involved in interstate commerce are generally illegal under the federal antitrust laws.[55] The "interstate" commerce requirement of the antitrust laws is interpreted very broadly and is held to apply to any intrastate activity effect on interstate commerce. Thus, although managed care arrangements are designed to stimulate, not limit, competition, it is necessary to keep in mind that antitrust implications may arise from employer coalitions created to negotiate and administer such health services arrangements.

Generally speaking, employer coalitions organized to negotiate managed care arrangements should not be subject to antitrust liability. This is so because such coalitions seek to organize the purchasers rather than the sellers of the commodity or service at issue—i.e., health care.[56] Although the U.S. Department of Justice (DOJ) has not specifically ruled on the legality of employer coalitions that actually negotiate hospital rates, the DOJ has issued several favorable determination letters regarding the legality of employer coalitions that seek to hold down health care rates by jointly collecting and publishing rates charged for certain frequently used hospital services.[57] In so doing, the DOJ has opined that "making relevant price information available to purchasers of a product or service typically is procompetitive because it permits more informed purchasing decisions and thereby encourages competition among providers of the product or service."[58]

Although the DOJ has given its approval to the exertion of pressure upon sellers of health care through the collection of pricing and other data, the DOJ determination letters warn that employer coalitions must take steps to ensure that information collected by such coalitions is not used by sellers of health care services to facilitate price fixing and other anticompetitive practices.[59] The DOJ has indicated, however, that it views such risks as minimal because employer coalitions are "not provider controlled and [thus, have] a strong interest in ensuring that [coalition efforts] do not encourage such collusion."[60]

In sum, as a general rule, employer coalitions lawfully may negotiate with health care providers and then take the best deal among those providers, even if the resulting arrangement is an exclusive one.[61] This is so because such combinations constitute *buyers' coalitions,* which are generally permissible under the antitrust laws.[62] Care must be taken, however, to ensure (1) that pricing and other data gathered by the employer coalition are not permitted to be used by sellers of health care services for anticompetitive purposes and (2) that the negotiation of such arrangements is not done in a manner that drives certain providers out of business.

CONCLUSION

Managed care presents legal risks for unwary employers that are not present in the traditional FFS plan setting. Prudent employers should therefore engage in due diligence and take care to draft their ERISA plan documents, vendor contracts and employee communications carefully so as to avoid potential managed care liability. Doing so will permit employers to fully reap the rewards available to them and their employees from managed care.

1. 1991 Health Insurance Association of America (HIAA) *Health Trends Chart Book,* p. 10.

2. 2 *BNA Health Law Reporter* (January 7, 1993): 8-9; see generally U.S. General Accounting Office, *Employer Based Health Insurance: High Costs, Wide Variation Threaten System,* No. HRD-92-125 (September 1992).

3. 19 *BNA Pension Reporter* 790 (May 11, 1992).

4. Foster Higgins 1992 Health Care Benefits Survey, Report 1.

5. 19 *BNA Pension Reporter* 2049 (November 16, 1992).

6. 1991 HIAA *Sourcebook,* p. 33.

7. Ibid., p. 35.

8. See generally F. Sloan and R. Bovlojerg, "Medical Malpractice: Crises, Response and Effects," *HIAA Research Bulletin* (1989), pp. 7-8.

9. *Restatement (Second) of Agency,* § 219 (1958).

10. Id., § 2 and comment b.

11. Id., § 220; see generally F. Harper, F. James, and O. Gray, *The Law of Torts,* § 26.11 (2d ed. 1986).

12. See M. Mitka, "More Doctors Opt to Become Employees," 34 *American Medical News* 9 (March 25, 1991).

13. See, e.g., *Sloan v. Metropolitan Health Council,* 516 N.E.2d 1104 (Ind.App. 1987) (applying *respondeat superior* doctrine to the relationship between a staff model HMO and one of its physician employees); F. Harper et al., *supra* n. 11, § 26.11, at 63 and n. 9.

14. *Boyd v. Albert Einstein Medical Center,* 547 A.2d 1229 (Pa. Super. 1988); *Independence HMO v. Smith,* 733 F.Supp. 983 (E.D.Pa. 1990); *Kohn v. Delaware Valley HMO, Inc.* 14 EBC 2336, 2597 (E.D.Pa. 1992); *Elsesser v. Hospital of the Philadelphia College of Osteopathic Medicine,* 795 F.Supp. 142 and 802 F.Supp. 1286 (E.D.Pa. 1992).

15. E.g., *Johnson v. Misericordia Community Hospital,* 301 N.W.2d 156 (Wisc. 1981); see generally F. Harper et al., *supra* n. 11, § 2611 and n. 9, at 63-64.

16. *McClellan v. Health Maintenance Organization of Pennsylvania,* 604 A.2d 1053 (Pa. Super. 1992).

17. See 8 *BNA Civil Trial Manual* 134-137 (April 1, 1992).

18. See W. Chittenden, "Malpractice Liability and Managed Health Care: History and Prognosis," 26 *Tort and Insurance Law Journal* 451, 472 and n. 158 (1991).

19. See *Varol v. Blue Cross and Blue Shield,* 708 F.Supp. 832 (E.D.Mich. 1989); *Pulvers v. Kaiser Foundation Health Plan,* 160 Cal. Rptr. 392 (Cal.App. 1979).

20. For example, Connecticut, Florida, Georgia, Hawaii, Indiana, Louisiana, Maine, Maryland, Minnesota, Mississippi, Missouri, Montana, Nebraska, New Hampshire, North Carolina, North Dakota, Oklahoma, South Carolina, Tennessee, Texas and Virginia, all have adopted comprehensive regulation of the UR industry. California, Florida, Georgia, Illinois, Massachusetts, Montana, North Carolina, North Dakota, Utah, Virginia and Wyoming have enacted laws regulating PPOs, such as "any willing provider" and limitation on PPO differential provisions.

21. See, e.g., *Stuart Circle Hospital Corp. v. Aetna Health Management,* 800 F.Supp. 328 (E.D.Va. 1992) (holding that ERISA preempts Virginia's law requiring PPOs to accept any willing provider).

22. *Shaw v. Delta Airlines, Inc.* 463 U.S. 85, 90 (1983).

23. 29 U.S.C. §§ 1102, 1103, 1105, 1133.

24. 29 U.S.C. §§ 1161-1168.

25. See, e.g., *Nazay v. Miller,* 949 F.2d 1323 93d Cir. 1991) (upholding inclusion of preadmission certification penalty); *McGann v. H & H Music Co.,* 946 F.2d 401 (5th Cir. 1991), *cert. denied,* ____U.S.____, 113 S.Ct. 482 (1992) (upholding plan amendment to reduce AIDS coverage); *McGee v. Equicor-Equitable HCA Corp.* 953 F.2d 1192 (10th Cir. 1992) (giving effect to concurrent review provision for rehabilitation treatment); *Saah v. Contel Corp.,* 780 F.Supp. 311 (D.Md. 1991) (upholding requirement for pre-authorization of mental illness treatment).

Other federal laws, such as the Age Discrimination in Employment Act, 29 U.S.C. § 621 et seq., do impose plan design requirement. Employers should seek legal counsel on the impact the employment provisions of the Americans with Disabilities Act, 29 U.S.C. § 12,111 et seq., have on cost-containment measures targeted at specific disabling illnesses, such as AIDS, that fall within the scope of ADA coverage.

26. 29 U.S.C. § 1132.

27. *Massachusetts Mutual Life Insurance Co. v. Russell,* 473 U.S. 134 (1985); *Harsch v. Eisenberg,* 956 F.2d 651 (7th Cir.), *cert. denied,* ____U.S.____, 113 S.Ct. 61 (1992); *Novak v. Andersen Corp.,* 962 F.2d 757 (8th Cir. 1992), *petition for cert. filed,* 61 U.S.L.W. 3156 (Aug. 26, 1992) (no. 92-352); *McRae v. Seafarers' Welfare Plan,* 920 F.2d 819 (11th Cir. 1991); but see *Warren v. Society National Bank,* 905 F.2d 975 (6th Cir. 1990), *cert. denied,* ____U.S.____, 111 S.Ct. 2256 (1991) (holding that a plan beneficiary could recover breach-of-contract type damages under ERISA for the increased tax liability he incurred due to the plan administrator's failure to carry out his instructions in transferring his share of plan assets).

28. 29 U.S.C. § 1144.

29. 29 U.S.C. § 1144(b)(2)(A).

30. *Pilot Life Insurance Co. v. Dedeaux,* 481 U.S. 41 (1987) (holding that ERISA preempts state law-based actions for insurer bad faith).

31. 29 U.S.C. § 1144(b)(2)(A).

32. *Metropolitan Life Insurance Co. v Massachusetts,* 471 U.S. 724 (1985) (ERISA preempts application of state-mandated benefit laws to self-insured plans).

33. *FMC Corp. v. Holliday,* 498 U.S. 52 (1990).

34. *Rodriguez v. Pacificare of Texas, Inc.,* 980 F.2d 1014, 1017 (5th Cir. 1993).

35. *District of Columbia v. Greater Washington Board of Trade,* ____U.S.____ (Dec. 14, 1992). *Ingersoll-Rand Co. v. McClendon,* 498 U.S. 133 (1990).

36. Id.; *Pilot Life,* 481 U.S. 41; and *FMC Corp.,* 498 U.S. 52.

37. *International Resources v. New York Life Insurance Co.,* 950 F.2d 294, 298 (6th Cir. 1991) *(en banc), cert. denied,* ____U.S.____, 112 S.Ct. 2941 (1992).

38. See note 27 above.

39. *Firestone Tire & Rubber Co. v. Bruch,* 489 U.S. 101 (1989).

40. On September 23, 1992, the Corcorans petitioned the U.S. Supreme Court for review of the Fifth Circuit's decision (No. 92-547, reported at 61 U.S.L.W. 3287). On December 14, 1992, the Supreme Court denied the Corcorans' petition (____U.S.____, 61 U.S.L.W. 3433, 3435).

41. See *Altieri v. Cigna Dental Health, Inc.,* 753 F.Supp61 (D.Conn. 1990); *Holmes v. Pacific Mutual Life Insurance Co.,* 706 F.Supp. 733 (C.D.Cal. 1989); *Rollo v. Maxicare,* 695 F.Supp. 245 (E.D.La. 1988).

42. *Painters District Council No. 21 Welfare Fund v. Price Waterhouse,* 879 F.2d 1146, 1153, n. 7 (3d Cir. 1989) (holding that ERISA does not provide an implied cause of action for professional malpractice).

43. *Independence HMO v. Smith,* 733 F.Supp. 983 (E.D.Pa. 1990); *Kohn v. Delaware Valley HMO, Inc.,* 14 EBC 2336, 2597 (E.D.Pa. 1992); *Elsesser v. Hospital of the Philadelphia College of Osteopathic Medicine,* 795 F.Supp. 142 (E.D.Pa. 1992); and *McClellan v. Health Maintenance Organization of Pennsylvania,* 604 A.2d 1053 (Pa. Super. 1992).

44. See M. Langan, "Will Health Care Force Changes to ERISA?," *5 Benefits Law Journal* 619 (Winter 1992/1993); 19 *BNA Pension Reporter* 2512 (December 7, 1992).

45. ERISA's definition of *fiduciary* is found at 29 U.S.C. § 1002(21). ERISA's fiduciary responsibility provisions are found at 29 U.S.C. §§ 1104-1113.

46. See *Schulist v. Blue Cross of Iowa,* 717 F.2d 1127, 1121-32, n. 4 (7th Cir. 1983); *Brock v. Henderschott,* 8 EBC 1121 (S.D.Ohio 1987), *aff'd,* 840 F.2d 339 (6th Cir. 1988); *District 65 UAW v. Harper & Row,* 670 F.Supp. 550 (S.D.N.Y. 1987).

47. See *Brock v. Robbins,* 830 F.2d 640 (7th Cir. 1987); *Donovan v. Cunningham,* 716 F.2d 1455 (5th Cir. 1983); *Donovan v. Mazzola,* 2 EBC 2115, 2137 (N.D.Cal. 1981), *aff'd,* 716 F.2d 1226 (9th Cir. 1983), *cert. denied,* 464 U.S. 1040 (1984).

48. *Massachusetts Mutual Life Insurance Co. v. Russell,* 473 U.S. 134 (1985).

49. Of course, if the plan is funded, then the fiduciary is responsible for the loss plus a 20 percent civil penalty surcharge (29 U.S.C. §§ 1109, 1132). All collectively bargained plans are funded (29 U.S.C. § 186(c)(5)).

50. For example, federal law establishes the following quality assurance requirements for federally qualified HMOs:

    Federal HMO Act, 42 U.S.C. § 300e(c):

    Each health maintenance organization shall—

    (7) have organizational arrangements, established in accordance with regulations of the Secretary, for an *ongoing quality assurance program* for its health services which program (A) stresses health outcomes, and (B) provides review by physicians and other health professionals of the process followed in the provision of health services;....

    Federal HMO Act Implementing Regulations, 42 CFR § 417.107(h):

    (h) *Quality assurance program.* Each HMO shall have an ongoing quality assurance program for its health services which:

    (1) Stresses health outcomes to the extent consistent with the state of the art;

    (2) Provides review by physicians and other health professional of the process followed in the provision of health services;

    (3) Uses systematic data collection of performance and patient results, provides interpretation of these data to its practitioners, and institutes needed change; and

    (4) Includes written procedures for taking appropriate remedial action whenever, as determined under the quality assurance program, inappropriate or substandard service have been provided or services which should have been furnished have not been provided;....

    The National Association of Insurance Commissioners Model HMO Act, which most states have adopted, includes a similar quality assurance provision.

51. The American Association of Preferred Provider Organizations (AAPPO) has created voluntary accreditation standards for PPOs that include quality assurance requirements. The AAPPO's program is administered by the American Accreditation Program, Inc. (AAPI) in Reston, Virginia.

52. Federal law, 42 U.S.C. § 11,101 et seq. established the NPDB in 1990 to track malpractice judgments and limitations on privileges of physicians and other health care providers; employers, however, cannot directly access the NPDB.

53. 48 CFR § 1652.222-70. A standard "significant events" clause reads as follows:

Significant Events

    A. HMO agrees to notify Employer of any Significant Event within ten (10) working days after HMO becomes aware of it. In no event shall HMO notify Subscribers/Participants of a Significant Event before notifying Employer. HMO further agrees to allow Employer to review and approve any Significant Event notification that HMO intends to distribute to Subscribers/Participants.

    As used in this section, a Significant Event is any occurrence that does, or any anticipated occurrence that reasonably may be expected to, have a material effect upon the HMO's ability to meet its obligations under this Contract, including, but not limited to, any of the following:

    1. Disposal of major HMO assets;

    2. Loss of 15 percent or more of the HMO's total membership;

    3. Termination or modification of any contract or subcontract affecting HMO's performance of this Contract;

    4. Addition or termination of any Participating Provider agreement;

    5. Any changes in underwriters, reinsurers, or participating groups;

    6. The imposition of, or notice of the intent to impose, a receivership, conservatorship, or special regulatory monitoring;

     7. The withdrawal of, or notice of intent to withdraw, State licensing, U.S. Department of Health and Human Services qualification, or any other status under Federal or State law;

     8. Default on a loan or other financial obligation;

     9. Any actual or potential labor dispute that delays or threatens to delay timely performance or substantially impairs the functioning of the HMO's facilities or other facilities used by the HMO in the performance of the Contract;

    10. Any change in HMO's charter, constitution, or bylaws that affects any provision of this Contract;

    11. Any significant changes in policies and procedures or interpretations of the Contract or the Certificate of Coverage that affects the benefits available under the Contract; and

    12. any written exceptions, reservations or qualifications expressed by the independent accounting firm (which ascribes to the standards of the American Institute of Certified Public Accountants) with which HMO contracts to provide an opinion on its annual financial statements.

  B. Upon learning of a Significant Event, either upon notice form HMO or independently, Employer may take action as it deems necessary to protect the interests of Subscribers/Participants, including, but not limited to:

     1. Directing the HMO to take corrective action;

     2. Suspending new enrollments under this Contract;

     3. Advising Subscribers/Participants of the Significant Event and providing them with an opportunity to transfer to another HMO;

     4. Withholding payment of premiums;

     5. Terminating the enrollment of those Subscribers/Participants who, in the Employer's judgment, would be adversely affected by the Significant Event; or

     6. Terminating this Contract pursuant to Section ____.

54. 29 U.S.C. § 1144(d).

55. Sherman Anti-Trust Act, 15 U.S.C. §§ 1-7. Section 1 of the Sherman act prohibits contracts, conspiracies and combinations that restrain trade unreasonably, including schemes to fix prices. Section 2 of the Sherman Act generally prohibits monopolies and other concerted activities designed to monopolize a market.

56. *Hospital Building Co. v. Trustees of Rex Hospital,* 425 U.S. 738, 743 (1976). See also *Summit Health, Ltd. v. Pinhas,* ____U.S.____, 111 S.Ct. 1945 (1991); and William C. Holmes, *Antitrust Law Handbook,* § 8.01 at pp. 513-519 (1992 ed.).

57. See, e.g., *Webster County Memorial Hospital v. United Mine Workers of America Welfare and Retirement Fund,* 536 F.2d 419 (D.C.Cir. 1976).

58. See *St. Louis Area Business Coalition,* Dept. of Justice (DOJ) Business Review Letter (BRL) No. 88-4 (November 24, 1988); *Stark County Health Care Coalition,* BRL No. 85-19 (November 13, 1984).

59. *St. Louis Area Business Coalition,* BRL 88-4 at 2.

60. Id.; see also *Stark County Health Care Coalition,* BRL No. 85-19 at 2.

61. *St. Louis Area Business Coalition,* BRL 88-4 at 2.

62. Id.

8.   A Health Care Program Run by the Federal Government that Works

Walton Francis

Almost by accident, the federal government created a health care benefits program with a wide range of choices for its employees. Over the years, the program has increased benefits and kept costs lower than those of plans in the private sector. A look at what makes it so successful.

As the nation debates the merits of President Clinton's national health care proposal, a little-noticed but seminal health program should figure prominently in the discussions. Run by the federal government for its employees, annuitants, ex-employees, former spouses, and dependents, the Federal Employees Health Benefits Program (FEHBP) embraces many of the tenets economists believe are essential to a cost-effective health care program, and it is enjoying extraordinary success. Over the last decade, benefits have improved substantially and costs to the employee have risen much less than inflation. These impressive accomplishments were an *accident*. Still, the FEHBP was the original model for the "managed competition" proposals made by Stanford professor Alain Enthoven and endorsed by candidate Clinton. Under the managed competition idea, and in the FEHBP, a sponsor or manager arranges for a number of health plans to compete for enrollment on the basis of cost and quality.

Yet, as of this writing (mid-June), the informed expectation is that the Clinton administration will propose abolishing the FEHBP. How could this be? According to a health care task-force spokesman quoted in the *Washington Post,*

A longer and more complete version of the article appears in *Health Policy Reform: Competition & Controls,* edited by Robert B. Helms, The AEC Press, 1993. *The views expressed in this article are those of the author and not of the Health and Human Services Department.*

"We view the [federal employees' program] as a terrific system and we don't want to do anything that would hurt its effectiveness." Apparently, however, the desire to avoid the appearance of a special system for a privileged elite weighs heavily in the political calculus: "I think you're going to see federal employees treated like everyone else." Under the likely proposal, federal employees would be lumped into local health insurance purchasing cooperatives, along with the poor (Medicaid) and the uninsured. These cooperatives would provide a menu of health insurance choices similar to those offered under the FEHBP today. But large employers other than the federal government would be allowed to opt out and run their own managed competition systems.

Thus, in the ultimate paradox, the closest program to the managed competition ideal—the original inspiration for the Clinton proposals, and arguably the best performing health insurance program in America—would be abolished because it is too good to be allowed to exist. The federal government's own shining success would be terminated, while the antediluvian Medicare program would presumably continue unscathed so as to avoid offending the potent lobbies for the aged. Of course, the 3.5 million annuitants in the FEHBP might construct a different calculus. In that case, the impressive but accidental accomplishments of the FEHBP might well continue.

HOW IT STARTED

The federal government was a laggard in providing health benefits for its employees. Most large private employers added health benefits during World War II as a simple way of getting around wage controls to attract workers. Lacking employer help, unions and employee organizations representing federal workers set up group coverage for their members. In 1959, when the government proposed a single plan for its employees, unions and the employees resisted abandoning their own plans. A compromise was struck. The existing plans would be allowed to survive and to compete for members in an annual "Open Season." The government role would be limited to enforcing financial solvency safeguards, setting enrollment procedures, and creating minimal plan standards. The government would contribute a set amount for each employee, with the employee paying the difference between that amount and the cost of the plan he wanted to join. And so a system of choice was born.

Every year some 4 million Americans representing 9 million family members make a choice about their health care arrangements. During the month-long Open Season they decide which of two to three dozen health plans will best protect them against the cost of illness for the next year. Most people stick with the plan they chose the previous year. About 5 percent change plans during each Open Season. Although only one in 20 enrollees switches plans each year, some individual plans lose half or more of their enrollment, and some plans drop out each year.

Table 1. FEHBP Plans by Type of Plan

NATIONAL

Year	Fee-for-Service Plans	Health Maintenance Organizations	Total
1961	15	13	28
1970	18	21	39
1975	26	33	59
1976	24	41	65
1977	22	47	69
1978	19	65	84
1979	18	70	88
1980	24	86	110
1981	24	100	124
1982	24	101	125
1983	23	114	137
1984	23	162	185
1985	28	200	228
1986	31	294	325
1987	35	404	439
1988	33	478	511
1989	30	421	451
1990	26	378	404
1991	19	372	391

Note: Preferred Provider Option plans not shown. These were included in no-fee-for-service plans before 1990 but are now available in most. Each high and low option is counted as a separate plan.

Source: Annual Insurance Report of the Federal Employees Health Benefit Plan and other OPM documents.

Why has the program been so successful? A discussion of how it works, why it works, and how it compares to Medicare and to private-sector approaches in terms of costs, benefits, and equity follows.

HOW IT WORKS

The law creating the FEHBP was enacted in 1959. The program started with 28 plans; in 1991, there were 391 plans (see Table 1). Plans can compete for business if they offer group rates, provide reasonable policy coverage, and meet various requirements for financial solvency. Each plan must take any eligible employee *without regard to a preexisting condition.* The government generally allows new Health Maintenance Organizations (HMOs) to join without any barrier. An HMO is a groups of doctors who guarantee to provide all needed health care and share profits or losses. This "managed care" creates major incentives for efficiency. Today more than four-fifths of all of the nation's HMOs participate in the FEHBP. HMO enrollment took off in the 1980s, rising from 10 to 25 percent of total enrollment. Law and regulation generally prohibited new fee-for-service competitors (there were 15 in 1961), but that changed in the mid-1980s when unions demanded that new plans be included. For several years the number of fee-for-service—or traditional health insurance—plans increased, but most of the newcomers failed to succeed and have terminated their participation.

In practice, it is not a great exaggeration to think of the program as a voucher system—one in which the government simply pays part of the cost of privately selected health insurance—with all major decisions made by employees (purchasers) and plans (sellers).

WHAT IT COSTS

Table 2 shows how three archetypal systems—Medicare, the FEHBP, and private employer plans—have controlled costs in recent years. The data seem to show that Medicare and the FEHBP program do about equally well, and that both do substantially better than private employers in holding down costs. In fact, with the proper adjustments, the FEHBP would surge to the front leaving both Medicare and private employer plans to tie for a distant second.

Authoritative, published time series on private insurance costs are nonexistent. The best source may be a little-known series developed by the Hay/Huggins Company, a benefits consulting firm, for a major study of the FEHBP prepared by the Congressional Research Service several years ago. To extend the series, I added the 1992 increase (10 percent) estimated by another consulting firm, Foster Higgins. For a dollar estimate, I used the Foster Higgins estimate of about $3,965 average 1992 premium cost, which I then extrapolated backward using the Hay/Huggins factors. These data cover large corporate sponsors of health insurance.

Interestingly, the Foster Higgins estimate of $3,965 in per-employee premium costs is over 20 percent higher than the FEHBP figure of $3,197 for 1992. Some of this differential represents slightly better benefits. Most, however, imply that the Fortune 500 have not been able to figure out how to save the 20 percent which the federal government has been achieving without even trying vigorously.

The Medicare and FEHBP data are much more straightforward and utterly reliable. They simply reflect actual accounting data as to total costs incurred and total premiums paid. The idiosyncrasies in all of these series do not affect the main conclusions significantly, so long as one does not focus on a one-, two-, or three-year period.

Over time, these data show that Medicare and the FEHBP have been able to bring annual cost increases down from the double-digit levels of the 1970s to the single-digit range. Private employers once appeared to have achieved similar success but have lapsed in recent years. Cumulatively, the results of whatever forces and factors have been at work appear to have led to a compound annual growth rate in Medicare costs of around 8 percent to 9 percent a year, a growth rate for the FEHBP of about 9 percent a year, and a growth rate for private employers distinctly higher, at around 12 percent a year.

What explains these similarities and differences? There are myriad factors, most not susceptible to simple measurement. For example, the FEHBP has seen a distinct aging of the federal work force and annuitant pools that puts heavy pressure on costs. Starting in 1984, however, all new federal annuitants became eligible for Medicare once they reached age 65. Since Medicare pays first, this saves the FEHBP money. (Most annuitants, however, are not covered by Medicare, including all those age 55 to 64 and the several hundred thousand very old persons who retired before 1984 without Medicare coverage.) Considering that the model retirement age is 55, the first wave of these fully Medicare-covered annuitants is just about to benefit the FEHBP. On the Medicare side, these data dramatically show the effect of reductions in payments to hospitals through the "Prospective Payment System" in slowing growth in costs in the middle and late 1980s, and the attenuation of this source of savings in recent years.

Three factors, however, clearly stand out. First, Medicare has had the ability to exercise monopoly power. Medicare has by fiat set below-market prices for hospitals in the Prospective Payment System and in dozens of lesser initiatives. At present, according to the Congressional Budget Office (CBO) and the Prospective Payment Assessment Commission, Medicare is paying hospitals $10 billion a year below what it costs to serve Medicare clients. This translates into a saving of about $300 a year per enrollee, about 7 percent of total costs.

Second, the FEHBP runs a competitive program, and enrollees have been voting with their wallets for lower-cost plans. As stated previously, HMO enrollment rose from 10 percent to 25 percent of total enrollment in the 1980s and almost 30 percent today. Both today (1992) and ten years ago (1983)—the comparison points I use for Table 3—HMOs have had about a 20-percent cost advantage over fee-for-service plans. Therefore, simply shifting hundreds of thousands of people to a lower-cost set of plans was sure to save the program big money and lower the rate of cost increase. Likewise, enrollees have been shifting to lower-cost plans within the fee-for-service group, ameliorating cost increases there. Interestingly, HMO premiums have risen faster than fee-for-service premiums. Nonetheless, HMOs are so much less costly that the program has still done well. Total cost, an arguably better measure than premium cost because it

Table 2. Controlling Costs: Medicare, Private Employer Plans, and FEHBP

Year	MEDICARE BENEFITS PAID			PRIVATE BENEFITS PAID			FEHBP BENEFITS PAID		
	Total Cost Per Enrollee	Annual Increase	Ten Year Average Increase	Total Cost Per Enrollee	Annual Increase	Ten Year Average Increase	Total Cost Per Enrollee	Annual Increase	Ten Year Average Increase
1981	1,454	18%		1,053	17%		1,263	24%	
1982	1,670	15		1,232	17		1,384	10	
1983	1,887	13		1,562	27		1,485	7	
1984	2,103	11		1,676	7		1,548	4	
1985	2,320	10	17.1%	1,740	4		1,543	0	11.1%
1986	2,422	4	14.0	1,789	3		1,909	24	10.9
1987	2,561	6	11.9	1,942	9		2,029	6	10.2
1988	2,700	5	10.9	2,271	17		2,284	13	10.9
1989	2,923	8	10.3	2,725	20		2,472	8	10.8
1990	3,269	12	10.3	3,202	17	13.8%	2,801	13	10.9
1991	3,405	4	8.9	3,602	12	13.3	2,960	6	9.1
1992	3,793	11	8.6	3,965	10	12.6	3,197	8	8.9
1993	4,162	10	8.3	na	na	na	3,485	9	9.1

Note: Cost per enrollee is per person for Medicare and per employee (including family) for the other programs. Medicare data through 1991 *Green Book: An Overview of Entitlement Programs* (published annually by the House Ways and Means Committee), updated in 1992 and 1993 from the latest HHS budget. Some early years are interpolated.

Source: FEHBP data vary annually due not only to choice changes but also to changes in government financial reserves. Over time, these have no net effect. Date for private employer plans through 1991 from Hay/Huggins Benefits Survey, as reported in CRS and Lewin/ICF; 1992 data from Foster Higgins survey; total cost extrapolated back from 1992, FEHBP data from Annual Insurance Report and other OPM documents.

Table 3. Dissection of FEHBP Changes Over Last Decade for HMO and Fee-For-Service Plans

	Total Premium	Enrollee Premium	Enrollee Out-Of-Pocket	Total Cost to Enrollee (B+C)	Total Cost (A+C)	Out-Of-Pocket as a Percent of Total Cost
1983 HMO Self-Enrollment	$ 727	$224	$205	$429	$ 932	22%
1992 HMO Self-Enrollment	1,868	467	260	727	2,128	12%
Percent Increase in Decade	157%	108%	27%	69%	128%	
1983 Fee Self-Enrollment	$ 941	$426	$455	$ 881	$1,396	33%
1992 Fee Self-Enrollment	2,062	552	596	1,148	2,658	22%
Percent Increase in Decade	119%	30%	31%	30%	90%	
1983 Weighted (12% HMO)	$ 915	$402	$425	$ 827	$1,340	32%
1992 Weighted (28% HMO)	2,008	528	502	1,030	2,510	20%
Percent Increase in Decade	119%	31%	18%	25%	87%	

Note: These calculations average the five plans of each type with the largest enrollment in the indicated year. In all instances except 1992 HMO data this accounts for the majority of program costs.

Source: All data except enrollee out-of-pocket costs come from published OPM sources. Out-of-pocket costs are from the annual CHECKBOOK's *Guide to Health Insurance for Federal Employees*, by Walton Francis, published annually by the Washington Center for the Study of Services.

takes into account changes in out-of-pocket exposure, has risen far less rapidly than premium cost. It has also risen less rapidly than the cost of either type of plan, as is common when people shift from a high-cost system to a low-cost system (see Table 3).

Third, as a by-product of Medicare's payment rate controls, substantial costs have been shifted from Medicare to private plans: that is, to the FEHBP plans and other employer plans. The same CBO estimates show that private plans are paying some $25 billion a year more than the actual costs they incur due to the savings forced on hospitals by Medicare, Medicaid, and other programs. Taking into account cost shifting, the quasi-private FEHBP soundly outperforms Medicare in controlling costs, and the private plans probably match Medicare.

Taken together, these three factors suggest two obvious conclusions. First, absent coercive power, Medicare has done little or nothing effectively to control its costs. This is not merely a logical deduction. The very concept of managed care is alien to Medicare, despite much lip service. The percentage of Medicare clients in HMOs has remained stuck at 3 percent for years (fewer than one in five HMOs even bothers to do business with Medicare, in part because of bizarre reimbursement and enrollment systems). Medicare does not provide a Preferred Provider Organization (PPO) option to more than a handful of enrollees. (A PPO is an insurance plan which limits the choice of doctors more modestly than most HMOs do.) Medicare does not even use large case management. Instead, Medicare relies on those initiatives that command the support of congressional leaders and that someone argues will save money. Literally hundreds of large and small schemes aimed at saving money have been enacted in the last decade. A few of them (for example, mandatory second surgical opinions) have been repealed when it was found that they cost more than they saved. Most of the others remain on the books, monuments to the bean-counter school of budgeting, in a program whose structure creates a hothouse for growth in costs.

Second, competition works. The FEHBP has greatly outperformed the "one-size-fits-all" systems of *both* the private sector and Medicare. And it has done so with remarkably little management attention—far less than Medicare and not much more than most private employers.

BENEFITS

Over the last decade, the federal employee program has progressively improved its benefits coverage. For example, as recently as 1987 there were five fee-for-service plans with significant loopholes in their catastrophic guarantees. Today there are none. Almost all of the guarantees hold out-of-pocket costs to $3,000 or less. Medicare, of course, has catastrophic protection so gap-ridden that it has provoked an extensive supplemental market for "Medigap" policies. In contrast, the supplemental market for FEHBP plans is minor.

For routine coverage (including most but not all catastrophically large bills), Medicare has remained a consistently good but unchanged payer for decades. For the expenses it covers, enrollees paid 16 or 17 percent in 1975, 1980, 1985, and 1990. Of course, Medicare does not pay at all for outpatient prescription drugs or dental expenses (subject to minor exceptions, such as injectable cancer drugs administered by physicians). Calculated on a larger base, Medicare enrollees pay perhaps one-fourth of all health care bills.

The private sector is very diverse, but for the large employers covered in the major surveys, most plans have coverage slightly better than the FEHBP. A decade ago most of these private plans had significantly better coverage (for example, a $100 deductible when $200 was common in the FEHBP). Regardless, it appears that private employers have cut back coverage in recent years at a rate very slightly in excess of inflation, so that inflation-adjusted benefits have been modestly reduced.

What is surprising is that federal employee benefits have improved. Over the last decade, out-of-pocket costs have risen much less rapidly than inflation and have decreased from one-fifth to one-tenth of total costs of insurance for HMOs and from one-third to one-fifth for fee plans and for the program as a whole (see Table 3). Considering that the FEHBP covers major categories of expense excluded from Medicare coverage, and that these figures include dental expenses, it is clear that the federal employee program significantly betters Medicare in benefits.

EQUITY

All health insurance contains gaps and exclusions which are inequitable to some people. For example, virtually no plans pay for certain forms of dental surgery that are very expensive. But of the three programs under discussion here, Medicare has a surprising number of major exclusions, such as the gaps discussed above. Most large employer plans and all FEHBP plans have few consequential gaps. The most important of these, in an insurance sense, is that only a handful of FEHBP plans (and only one fee-for-service plan) covers more than 25 outpatient psychiatric visits.

An endemic problem for all kinds of insurance is "moral hazard," or "adverse selection." People who are worse risks will migrate to the best coverage and raise its cost. People who are better risks will in self-defense move to less attractive coverage to flee high costs. The FEHBP fails to manage adverse selection well, as discussed below. This creates, as a by-product, one unfortunate and arguably unfair program characteristic. Several plans now have a premium cost well in excess of actuarial value. The best known is Blue Cross High Option. This is because each plan must cover the costs of those enrolled, and this plan is used primarily by older persons without Medicare. In 1993, I calculated the Blue

Cross High Option and the Blue Cross Standard Option as having virtually equal actuarial value, yet the premium cost to single enrollees is $540 for the Standard Option as compared to $2,040 for the High Option. The $1,500 difference may be, in effect, an ignorance tax paid by those who do not understand, or who are afraid to leave, a plan that was once by far the largest in the program and still retains the strongest benefits for all services other than dental.

An economist could well argue that if consumers choose to buy a Mercedes plan at quadruple the cost of a Ford, that is a choice they are entitled to make. Peace of mind may be worth the premium difference to some. But many of the people involved are afraid or unwilling to change (about nine-tenths are annuitants) for no other reason than the erroneous belief that higher price means higher quality. Some do join, however, to get the best outpatient mental health benefits in the program. Regardless, the problem could be readily solved by simple premium adjustments that the government has been unwilling to consider seriously. This is a major but correctable flaw of the program.

EMPLOYEE COST AND BENEFITS

The analysis above assumes implicitly that total cost or total premium is the best measure of cost control. And so it is. But there is another dimension of cost: Who pays? From an economist's point of view, of course, this is a value question about which different people are entitled to hold diametrically opposite views. It may also be a moot question, since economic theory tells us that few things are more certain than that the employee pays both the "employer share" and the "employee share" of any fringe benefit—it is all labor compensation regardless of how the accountants and legislators label it.

Regardless, some would regard it as relevant that under the FEHBP the government pays distinctly less of the premium bill than is common in large corporations. The government pays slightly over 70 percent of total premium, on average, for both self and family coverage. This leads to the interesting result shown in Table 3. While the total premium for single enrollees has risen about 119 percent over the last decade, the enrollee share has risen only about 31 percent. As a result of this and of the improved benefit coverage, total cost to enrollees has risen only about 25 percent in ten years, far less than inflation.

These data have another implication. It turns out that about 15 percent of federal employees do not enroll in this program at all. Some are young, low-wage employees for whom feelings of immortality and having cash are more important than insurance, and who know perfectly well that they will get treatment if they need it (just like most of the 37 million uninsured). But most have spouses who get a better deal from their employers who pay, let's say, 90 percent of premium. There is some danger, however, that the FEHBP might improve to the point where fewer would elect the private employer option. If all government employees not now enrolled decided to enroll, the potential cost to the government in on the order of a half-billion dollars annually.

ADVERSE SELECTION

This program enrolls three distinctly different sets of people: employees, annuitants with Medicare, and annuitants without Medicare (this last is really two groups, one age 55 to 65, the other mostly in their 70s and 80s). Annuitants with Medicare cost the program about the same as employees because Medicare is primary insurer in almost all cases and this offsets, on average, Medicare recipients' much higher health bills. The other annuitants cost thousands of dollars more each year than employees.

The recent history of the FEHBP has been characterized by the first two groups fleeing the plans with disproportionate shares of annuitants without Medicare. This has had a number of unfortunate consequences, including the demise of well-managed, low-cost plans that suffered a death spiral from adverse selection. Many critics of the program have asserted (though with little evidence, even anecdotal) that the plans have subtly skewed benefits to attract the young and healthy rather than sick and old. This means, if true, that much of the advantage of competition has been lost. This is a criticism made by persons as wise as Alain Enthoven and as short-sighted as the benefit consultants hired by the government who fail to understand, let alone appreciate, the benefits of consumer choice and competition.

The adverse selection criticism is either wrong or misplaced. First, as an empirical matter, the plans have been improving benefits. Some of this has come at the prodding of OPM staff; but regardless of motive it has happened. Second, this program has been outperforming the competition quite handily. It is certainly conceivable that it could have performed even better, but that is a hypothetical gain compared to a real one. Third, the problem is readily correctable. The main reform needed is to have the high-cost annuitants carry an extra premium contribution with them as they move among plans.

To be sure, this correction raises political problems since a legislative change would be needed to implement it. In recent years, leadership at OPM, cognizant GAO staff, and some members of Congress have seemed more interested in abolishing this program than in reforming it. These abolitionists seems to share the view expressed by the chairman of the House Ways and Means health subcommittee (through which the Clinton proposal will pass) to the effect that "this is a dream of some people who say competition and free enterprise can do better than any government can do. That's not true. [The government] can run circles around [insurance companies]." The most common proposals would replace the present program with one modeled along the same lines as Medicare. Furthermore, to be budget neutral, a risk adjustment scheme would require paying a higher nominal contribution for some groups and a lower contribution for others. The net effect need be no real-world change at all in the government subsidy, but the appearances are to the contrary and therefore unsettling to unions and retiree groups.

As a technical matter, what is particularly interesting about the program is how slowly it responds to adverse-selection forces. Over the last decade profound enrollment shifts have occurred. Hundreds of plans have entered and left the program. Yet, only 5 percent of enrollees a year have changed plans. If all federal employees were the economists' hypothetical rational man, even more plans would have died a decade ago. Instead, evolution has been gradual. This has major implications for the health reformers worried about developing "risk adjustors" that would guarantee that every premium minimize adverse selection. In fact, the problem in insoluble. We can predict that an 80-year-old will cost five times as much as a 30-year-old, but among the 80-year-old group we will never be able to predict which will cost zero and which $50,000. The good news, from the FEHBP, is that perfect risk adjustors are not needed.

Another whole category of risk selection is involved in the FEHBP. People deliberately join particular plans to get particular benefits. For example, in the D.C. area all the plans with first-rate dental coverage are HMOs. The rational man will, nature permitting, save up his dental problems until he is ready to join an HMO with a high dental benefit for a year, get his teeth fixed, and perhaps then leave. Premiums reflect this excess usage. People with larger than average dental problems congregate in certain plans, pay the higher premiums, and let the rest enjoy a lower premium. I know of no economic argument against this arrangement. It does not lead to market instability or create any obvious administrative or other problem. There is a weak ethical line of argument against this practice, best answered by asking the critic: "Do you object, then, to charging different premiums for single people and families?"

Yet, presumably to prevent employee self-selection into plans they prefer (just as people choose the kind of car they prefer, even if it means spending more), the current theology of managed competition seems to insist that all plans have identical benefits. As discussed below, this has major adverse political consequences.

THE STRANGE POLITICS OF THE PROGRAM

The FEHBP is now so familiar and comfortable that few federal employees realize just how unusual it is to have an Open Season in which to make a choice among health plans. Ironically, this freedom exists under a federal government that sets all other pay and benefit policies by law and regulation. In sharp contrast to the FEHBP, the government treats the most minute details of health insurance for the elderly under Medicare as matters for only government decision. Similarly, in the large companies health insurance details are set by fiat, on a "take it or leave the company" basis. To persons from corporate America, used to the company plan, the FEHBP often seems beyond belief.

Every few years a small group of these private sector "experts" recommends that the present program be abandoned and replaced by a single fee-for-service plan and a few HMOs. Like most planners, they contrast the messy FEHBP with the neat single-plan world they know, and assume incorrectly that they can control costs better than competition can. Ironically, their single plan scheme could never work, even if it were otherwise desirable, because adverse selection would soon wipe out the single plan as healthy employees migrated into HMOs, leaving the oldest and sickest behind.

Another set of critics is the managed competition advocates. These advocates see the FEHBP as a primitive starting point. They rightly argue that the program could be better designed and more tightly managed. Management willing and able to make sensible mid-course reforms could and would improve the program. But in government as in life, the best can be the enemy of the good. In the context of Medicare and the Fortune 500, the FEHBP arguably deserves close to an "A" on performance alone, and the rest of the competition a "C."

Regardless of past performance, the FEHBP may also have some lessons for the brave new world of managed competition. The paradox of the program is that *it is successful because it is relatively unmanaged.* The riddle of the program is to understand how any government program can escape the endless tendency to create ever-expanding bureaucratic structures operating under ever more complex and rigid rules, dictated and driven by the political system's peculiar obsessions and logic. The paradoxical problem for advocates of health reform is how to improve management of health insurance while avoiding the seemingly inexorable tendencies of the American political system to redistribute wealth from the taxpayer at large into the congressional district or the lobbyist's salary. In the ideal world of managed care and managed competition hundreds of hospitals would be forced to close: will the preservation of these institutions replace the preservation of military bases as the next great preoccupation of American politicians?

The FEHBP is not entirely immune from political pressures aimed at fine-tuning the system. For example: a few years ago the statute was amended to require each plan to cover the services of clinical psychologists, clinical social workers, nurse-midwives, and nurse-practitioners through self-referral. The statute was recently modified to cover ex-spouses and some other new categories of eligibles. The Post Office planned, until OMB and Congress said no, to pull out of the system and finance benefits for current employees without the overhead of all those expensive annuitants. And so on. But the entire list of FEHBP changes made over the past decade would not equal a single year's business for the Medicare program.

LESSONS FROM THE CORPORATE EXPERIENCE

Is there any reason to think that a company expert in making and selling widgets is likely to be expert in administering anything as complex as health insurance? The question answers itself. Under the currently prevailing model, each Fortune 500 company hires directly or by contract a handful of experts who advise it on such matters as how to set the deductible, how to set the employer contribution toward an HMO, and whether and how to self-insure. The model that is taken for granted is a single contract with a large insurance company, with grudging acceptance of Preferred Provider Organization variations and an HMO or two on the side. The success of these experts can be measured not only by the dismal cost-control performance of private health managers over the last decade, but also by the knowledge that their recommendations were made largely in the context of labor-management relations and what is now called "human resources administration."

Private employers have responded to the costly trends of the 1970s and 1980s by greatly increasing their willingness to make large and small changes in insurance arrangements for their employees. For example, while the tendency toward ever-increasing use of the tax subsidy for health insurance as a means of increasing employee compensation has been halted and slightly reversed, self-insurance has enabled firms to escape costly state taxes on insurance premiums and state-mandated benefits. But these reforms have failed to come close to matching the performance of a competitive system.

In any event, even the largest corporations are hampered by the sheer size and complexity of the health insurance market. For example, even though the 150 employees running the FEHBP are a mere handful by government standards (Medicare uses over 3,000), it is hard to believe that any corporation could or would make a comparable investment to run its own system for consumer choice among competing plans. Multiemployer systems have not developed, due presumably to the utter disinterest of headquarters bureaucracy in competitive systems.

DESIGNING REFORMED PROGRAMS

The federal government and corporate America have many health reform choices. In evaluating these, how does one improve or maintain flexibility for prudent managerial decisions that improve program performance? Three factors seem to be important.

First, *decentralizing decisions* is preferable to centralizing decisions. On the surface, Medicare is a manager's delight because all important decisions are theoretically made centrally. But because they are centralized, the manager cannot make any important decisions unilaterally. Too many other people, from

OMB to the chairmen of key committees, have an interest and a voice. In the FEHBP, on the other hand, the initial responsibility for most decisions lies individually with hundreds of plans. The central manager seems impotent. But he can, if skillful, guide and steer by persuasion and pressure.

Second, a *menu of choices* is necessary. Quite apart from whether the decision is centralized or decentralized, are there options? The Medicare benefit package is detailed in law and regulation and presented to all enrollees on a "take it or leave it" basis. Therefore, in Medicare, a benefit change affects millions of people involuntarily. This brings into play the full panoply of bureaucratic and legislative forces that deal with issues of equity and fairness. In contrast, in the FEHBP choices are exercised by both carriers and clients. A change in benefits in one plan is not a decision automatically affecting millions of people in predictable and involuntary ways. After all, they can always change plans.

Third, a *neutral structural design* greatly improves flexibility and responsiveness. In Medicare, benefit and coverage details are set forth in law and regulation, and claims paid by bureaucracies that must follow those laws and regulations. Given this structure, every detail is subject to legislative, regulatory, budgetary, and contractual constraints. Medicare managers have the power to propose, but only subject to the rigidities, vetoes, and time delays imposed by bureaucratic and legislative processes. In the FEHBP, laws and regulations do not prescribe most benefit, coverage, and cost-containment details.

One simple example illustrates all these points. In Medicare, the plan deductible is set centrally, as a single number, by law. Changing the deductible is a major political act. In the FEHBP, there is no single deductible. Each plan has its own. As a result, changes in deductibles attract or discourage enrollment changes in Opens Season, rather than political wars (or, in the private sector context, strikes). Likewise, premium changes induce migrations into more economical plans. The search is for bargains, not for shop stewards, lobbyists, or votes in Congress.

CONCLUSION

This accidentally created program, scarcely managed by either government or private-sector standards, has actually outperformed in both benefits and costs the most tightly controlled health insurance program operated by the federal government. Medicare is a good program, and thousands of dedicated and skilled bureaucrats in both the executive and legislative branches continually seek to improve it. But Medicare operates under a crippling handicap—it is directly controlled by the meddlesome and creaky American political system.

Paradoxically, maintaining or improving management effectiveness requires diluting management authority. It is noteworthy that the FEHBP's greatest
failures have tended to arise in areas where the program is constrained by law.

*Author's Afterword: In 1994, FEHBP premiums rose an average of three
percent. Forty percent of the nine million enrollees received premium decreases
for 1994.*

9. Case Management: The Employer's Guide to Value

Sandra L. Lowery, RN, BS, CRRN, CCM

Employers have consistently had a strong interest in the health and wellness of their employees. Uniquely, case management has allowed them to offer a service that supports their employees' health while simultaneously serving as a highly effective cost containment tool.

Few employers are truly receiving the optimum benefits of case management. This is primarily due to the difficulty in distinguishing providers and evaluating the product. Given the high utilization and potential value of case management, it is remarkable that there has not been greater scrutiny of it. However, this is easily explained by the need for employers to simultaneously manage a multitude of cost containment strategies and the lack of accessible and effective evaluative criteria.

As managed care matures, however, further exploration of administrative expenditures for various services is indicated. For case management, a primary need is to identify the product. The extent of the great variance in application of case management is exemplified in this article.

Case. Mr. Smith, a 42-year-old married father of two, had been admitted to the hospital four times during the past three months for symptoms related to oral cancer. The recommended treatment plan was inpatient rehabilitation for four weeks. The case manager assigned, Marge, coordinated a transfer to a rehabilitation program two days earlier than the requested hospital length of stay. She closed the case after negotiating for a discounted rate for the rehabilitation program, reporting claims savings for the two days of avoided hospitalization and for the discount.

Case. Another case manager, David, met with the patient, Mr. Brown, his family, and treatment team, and learned that the underlying reason for multiple admissions was the patient's fear of terminality. David then worked with the physician, Mr. Brown, and his family to enable informed shared decisions, which resulted in a discharge plan for a home-based hospice plan. When there was no social worker available in the local hospice program, David recruited one so that the plan would work. He also collaborated with the hospice coordinator and Mr. Brown to identify possible contingency plans for likely medical complications and continued to provide ongoing assessments, coordination, and advocacy to ensure a successful plan. Most of all, he provided support and education to Mr. Brown and his family to promote their role as health care consumers. Mr. Brown remained at home until his death, despite medical complications, and claims savings were reported for a home plan in lieu of inpatient rehabilitation. The case manager wondered how to present further savings for avoiding re-hospitalizations, as these would be considered "soft" or intangible, yet it was clear there were further savings.

From the purchaser's perspective, it seems clear that David is a far more effective case manager, yet his model of case management is rarely practiced in the United States. Marge's model is the predominant model in the U.S. for the health product and is becoming increasingly popular for workers' compensation. Why is this the case? Where else would expenditures for such a costly service be misappropriated? The answers lie in the lack of awareness and the difficulty in evaluating the results.

UNDERSTANDING THE PRODUCT

There are many variables that can be indicative of an effective case management program. Before discussing these, it is important to define the product. The National Task Force on Case Management developed the following generic definition of case management:

> Case management is a collaborative process which assesses, plans, implements, coordinates, monitors, and evaluates options and services to meet an individual's health needs through communication and available resources to promote quality, cost-effective outcomes.

The philosophical premise of case management is that cost and quality outcomes will be achieved when the most effective and efficient care is delivered, as perceived by the recipient. Simplistically stated, case management's goal is to promote the right treatment at the right time in the right manner at the right cost.

It is the ultimate entity that is willing to be accountable for cost and quality outcomes.

Success Factors

It has often been said, and this cannot be understated, that the most critical factor for successful case management is the skill of the case manager. Would David have been effective if he had not shown compassion, collaboration, proactivity, comprehensiveness, and advocacy? On the other hand, he had to couple his ability with knowledge. If he had little or no knowledge of cancer, hospice care, service and funding resources, family dynamics, coping styles, or the principles of empowerment, he could not have achieved the same outcome.

As there are few health professionals who have knowledge in all clinical areas, the most successful case management programs have case managers who specialize.

David was effective because he was qualified, but also because he functioned consistently within his role as a case manager. His primary function was clear, that of a collaborative facilitator in promoting the best outcome for his client while simultaneously meeting the needs of the purchasers of his service.

Despite the best of skilled case managers, a program will be ineffective without adequate administrative support. A case manager cannot function optimally without a manageable case load, appropriate referrals, the ability to meet with individuals onsite when necessary, consistent programmatic policies, role clarity, and feedback via supervision and quality management. The following demonstrates this need:

> **Case.** Susan was required by her company to perform both utilization management and case management. In working with a young paraplegic client, John, she lost credibility and effectiveness as a case manager and advocate by informing John and his physician that she could no longer approve rehabilitation hospital days. In attempting to find an alternative plan that would meet John's needs, she met with resistance, as John and his physician assumed an adversarial posture. Susan realized that she could not make benefit decisions while serving as a facilitator.

Telephonic vs. Onsite

There is little disagreement by those who have practiced case management telephonically and onsite that onsite is more effective. However, in consideration of the higher costs, case management programs often try to develop criteria for onsite intervention (see Table 1).

Table 1. Evaluative Criteria for Case Management Programs

Program Criteria
- Dedicated CM Staff
- Case Manager Caseload of 20-40
- Specialty in Insurance Product
- Defined Product
  - —goals
  - —philosophy
  - —process
  - —role
- Case Management Specialists vs. Generalists
- Onsite Model 10%-100%

Case Manager Qualifications
- CCM or CCM-supervised plus:
- RN for Medical Case Management
- RN/LSW for Mental Health Case Management
- CRC for Vocational Case Management
- Clinical Experience with Population Served
- Minimum Five Years Prior Experience in Health Care
- Experience in Both Acute Care and Post-Acute Care
- Knowledge of Funding and Service Resources
- Effective Interpersonal Skills

Case Identification
- Comprehensive Assessment Process
- Screening: Not A Distinct Role
- Multiple Referral Sources and Settings

Measurement Criteria
- Aggregate Comparison Claim Data
- Employee Feedback Surveys
- Litigation Rates
- Hospital Re-Admission Rates
- Home Death Rates
- Wellness/Function Outcomes
- Return to Work Rates

Risk Factors
- Separate Medical Consent
- Treatment Decisions by Individual/Family
- Statement of Ethics/Client Rights
- Confidentiality Policy

The advantages of onsite case management are clear:

- Assessments are more comprehensive, avoiding surprises later on;
- Relationships with clients, families, and care providers are more trusting, collaborative, and credible and, therefore, productive;
- Coordination of services is more achievable, particularly when there are multiple providers in different locations;
- Empowerment and educational efforts are enhanced;
- Employer and insurer goodwill has a greater magnitude;
- Timeliness of care delivery is often accelerated due to greater flexibility in approaching obstacles;
- Knowledge of local resources; and
- Increased accountability by care providers.

The advantages of telephonic case management are twofold—decreased costs and a greater ability to have specialty staff.

Some of the best case management programs combine both models by restricting onsite activity to initial assessments, unless there is a clear indication for further onsite activity. Until research is conducted on this issue, there is no current validation of one model's effectiveness over the other. It is interesting to note that, historically, case management was never telephonic until recently. In looking at the earlier examples, it would be difficult for David to have the same level of effectiveness without meeting with the patient, family, and physician.

Case Selection

Since all health care consumers can benefit from case management because of the complexity of our health care delivery and reimbursements systems, there must be a screening process, unless all individuals are to be selected. The guiding principle should be that the effects must outweigh the costs; the effects, however, are difficult to quantify. More recently, some providers and purchasers of health care are case managing all individuals, and some are aligning this service with health promotion programs. The approach is proactive rather than reactive; in other words, it is micro-managing until individuals can self-manage as independent and competent health care consumers.

Those with a limited liability or scope are relying on various cost indicators such as high-cost ICD-9 codes and severity criteria. The screening should always include assessment of multiple factors, such as medical history, support systems, residential issues and, for workers' compensation, employment variables. For example, an individual with a mild stroke may not seem like a high risk until further research identified multiple underlying issues, including partial blindness, diabetes, heart disease, a residence in a two-story apartment building without elevator access, a distant family, and a history of poor medication compliance.

The most successful case management programs encourage referrals from all sources, including claims personnel, health care providers, individual

employees, family members, other payors, employers, and utilization management. They no longer rely on severity indicators retrieved from the precertification process. Sophisticated case management providers now include chronic
illness indicators and screen individuals who are receiving care at home or in a
nonhospital setting, realizing that they can have a significant impact on decreasing costs.

MEASURING RESULTS

Historically, case management has been evaluated by claims savings reports. Yet,
as we can see by the earlier case examples, this methodology is ineffective, as
the true value of case management is often in the prevention of unnecessary
claims. Additionally, with the trend of health care providers to inflate prices to
allow "discounts," or lengths of stay to avoid hassles, the credibility of some
savings reports are questionable. Further, with the emphasis of quantifiable
claims savings for demonstrating results, one could surmise that there is skewed
data reporting by case management providers.

The most effective methodology for evaluating case management is a
comparison of aggregate expenditures, from pre-case-management to post-case-
management, providing there are valid and comparable data. Some employers
have found that evaluative criteria can also include measurement of litigation
rates, employee and consumer satisfaction, return to work rates, rehospitalization
rates, home death rates (for terminal illness), and functional and wellness outcomes. There is a growing acceptance that achieving efficient and effective care
yields cost containment, but there is no scientific method of quantifying this yet.
Eventually, the outcome studies currently underway will be useful for this
purpose.

It is often credibly stated that there are tangential "hidden" benefits of case
management. For example, a decrease in employee lost time due to a more
manageable or less stressful illness of a spouse or child is usually not quantifiable;
nor is employee retention.

COST CONSIDERATIONS

There are three current pricing structures for case management: fee for service,
capitated, and per case. While the latter two involve risk-sharing, they have the
highest potential for compromised outcomes and adverse selection. Table 2
presents an outline of the current costs of case management in the United States.
Similar to other service costs in health care, the pricing of case management has
been allowed to fluctuate greatly, primarily due to uninformed purchasers, and
does not necessarily reflect a program's level of quality.

LEGAL FACTORS

Table 2. Costs of Case Management			
	Fee-for-Service	*Capitated*	*Case Rate*
Telephonic	$70–$130/hour	$0.45–$1.40/life	$300–$3,000/case
Onsite	$65–$130/hour	$0.50–$1.50/life	$500–$3,000/case

To date, there has been no litigation regarding the actions of a case manager. This is undoubtedly due to the primary advocacy role of the case manager. There are, however, some risk factors that a purchasers should be aware of.

The community standard (among case managers) is that a separate, signed authorization for case management is necessary. An insurance plan authorization is too limited for case management. Additionally, case management is generally a voluntary service and the authorization validates an individual's consent to service.

Even if a case manager is a treating clinician, there should be documentation of the consumer's role in treatment decisions. Similarly, there should be documentation relative to any benefit determinations by the benefit plan administrator. These activities allow the case manager to serve as a facilitator and not a decision maker, which would present a role conflict.

To clarify roles and responsibilities, a case management program should provide a consumer with a written statement. A code of ethics would further enhance that statement, and would also enhance the relationship of the case manager with the consumer, thereby promoting a more effective outcome.

CONCLUSION

Case management is frequently touted as the most effective strategy in providing qualitative and quantitative benefits for health and disability products. Additionally, it is consistently the one managed care service that is well received by employees and employers. Yet accountability for this product has been elusive due to an inadequate methodology for evaluating results. The purchaser guides in Tables 1 and 2 are designed to assist the employer by providing tools to become an informed consumer.

As case management develops at the national level, employers will soon have access to additional information to guide them. National standards of practice, developed by the Case Management Society of America (CMSA), will be completed by the end of 1994. Certification in Case Management (CCM) for practitioners has been available since 1993, and sets a standard for minimum competency. In 1995, it is likely that a national Code of Ethics will be available through the CMSA.

10. Utilization Management Within a Network Context: A Significant Enhancement over Traditional Utilization Review

Jonathan Stevens   Scott P. Smith, MD

The utilization review process has in recent years broadened its focus from attempting to avoid or shorten hospital stays to determining, the appropriateness of care and to managing utilization in the context of a network of providers. While it has run into problems in successfully determining appropriateness of treatment plans prospectively, it has become the mainstay of managed care plans that integrate utilization management and quality improvement with the management of provider networks. Utilization management produces a significantly greater impact when it is integrated with a provider network than when it stands alone.

As sponsors of health benefit plans look increasingly to networks of providers for cost management, they may overlook a significant contributor to their cost management goals: utilization review (UR). Utilization review has evolved from a narrowly focused, adversarial array of free-standing products to an increasingly sophisticated, scientifically based, integrated system that supports cost management and quality improvement goals within a network context. UR has evolved into what is commonly called utilization management (UM), although the extent of the development and integration of UM programs varies. The most effective UM programs are those that are directly tied to extensive provider networks and thus can capitalize on network agreements for the achievement of their goals.

TRADITIONAL UTILIZATION REVIEW PROGRAMS

For at least two decades, UR programs have assisted health benefit plans in their cost-containment efforts, most effectively by reducing expenditures for hospitalizations. The success of such programs, in precertifying elective hospital admissions and in reviewing requests for continued stays in hospital, has led to the development of additional, specialized review programs, including second surgical opinion, mental health review, ambulatory care review, dental utilization review, and other focused processes. Various competing programs have differentiated themselves by such means as on-site hospital review, physician-to-physician review, the use of computerized protocols, and applications of decision-support technology.

Traditional UR programs have focused on managing the setting of care and determining the appropriateness of that care. They have encouraged the transition of acute cases from the inpatient to the outpatient setting, and chronic cases from hospitals to long-term care facilities and home care. The appropriateness of particular treatments to particular conditions may be determined by proprietary appropriateness criteria packages. The effectiveness of these particular tools is a subject of considerable debate. In our experience, such tools can foster a climate of mistrust among providers, who see them as encroaching on their practice of medicine. This adversarial situation runs counter to the objectives of UM programs that are part of networks; these programs seek to foster a partnership arrangement with network providers.

CLINICAL GUIDELINES

In the past, UR programs have relied most heavily on medical judgments and consensus processes to determine what sorts of medical care not to certify; now various clinical guidelines are emerging that are based on scientific evidence of treatment efficacy and outcomes research. Studies are focusing on broadly defined and costly conditions which are subject to considerable variation in medical practice, such as angina, benign enlargement of the prostate, gallstones, arthritis of the hip, conditions of the uterus, and low back pain. As these guidelines are adopted, their dissemination will be aided by strong linkages between UM programs and provider networks. Provider education and ongoing dialogue will be aided by network contracts that establish the basis for the exchange.

Studies have upheld the assertions of these programs that they save money, although critics charge that they have outlived their effectiveness as physicians adapt to the new rules. However, newly adopted clinical guidelines require continual reinforcement by the UR program before they are integrated into providers' practices. Some sponsors of health benefit plans argue that utilization review has wrung all the readily available savings out of the system, and that the pervasiveness of UR has created a climate that makes it unnecessary for every plan to employ every aspect of UR. A prudent middle ground might hold that a medical benefit plan should keep basic UR in place (precertification, continued-stay review, case management), and should monitor utilization and cost data to determine which additional programs to keep, add, or drop. The UM approach would focus on clinical areas in which demonstrated quality and cost improvements are likely.

DISTINCTION BETWEEN MEDICAL NECESSITY AND BENEFIT COVERAGE DETERMINATIONS

It is important for sponsors of medical benefit plans to recognize that situations may arise in which determinations of medical necessity and benefit coverage come into conflict. A physician and patient may agree on a course of treatment that is covered by the plan but for which the medical necessity cannot be established. The benefit plan document should be crafted to recognize those conflicts and to spell out the procedures for determining coverage. The plan document will need to reserve the right to make benefit coverage determinations in the absence of clear rulings on medical necessity; coverage decisions based on medical necessity should cite the source or authority for the determination.

TOTAL COST EQUALS VOLUME TIMES PRICE

Traditional UR has focused on managing the volume side of the volume-times-price formula. However, UM programs that are integrated with networks of providers have found ways to optimize the price side of the formula as well.

Networks of providers are organized under various structures, ranging from individual practice association (IPA) model HMOs to open-ended HMOs (also known as point-of-service plans) to preferred provider organizations (PPOs). These structures vary primarily in the financial arrangements with providers, and less so in the contractual obligations of providers to comply with utilization management requirements. These contracts provide significant opportunities for UM programs to add value in a number of ways, over and above their traditional contributions in shifting to a less intensive site of care and in reduction of unnecessary services.

UTILIZATION MANAGEMENT SUPPORTS USE OF NETWORK

Utilization management programs can serve the plan's overall goals of managing care in networks, by supporting and encouraging the steering of patients into those networks. The most aggressive programs will offer little or no choice of going outside the network, as in closed-panel HMOs or carve-out programs such as transplant networks. Additionally, open-ended networks (PPOs and point-of-service plans) can expect their UM programs to steer patients into the networks, for good reasons. These reasons include the fact that the credentials of the network providers have been reviewed and approved; the practice patterns of these providers are monitored for quality; and the network provider contracts may (ideally) stipulate that providers will adhere to appropriate practice guidelines (as in the American College of Obstetrics and Gynecology guidelines for maternity care). Thus, there are good reasons for steering patients into networks that relate to quality, and not only to price.

Other mechanisms for channeling patients into the network can also be employed, including encouraging in-network referrals at the time of the UM encounter, making network referrals as part of the case management process, and providing ongoing access to up-to-date information about the make-up of the network to patients and providers to facilitate network use.

CASE MANAGEMENT ALSO SUPPORTS NETWORK USE

Case management is an important extension of utilization management. Case management is the intensive clinical support of specific types of cases that have historically proven to be susceptible to significant cost reductions and quality improvement. Criteria for acceptance of cases into a case management program will identify cases that are:

- Potentially high cost ;
- Amenable to significant savings as a result of active intervention;
- Treatable in cost-effective alternative modes of care (e.g., home care); and
- Subject to improvements in the quality of the patient's outcome.

Case management should focus on the early identification of potential cases for evaluation and should employ rigorous cost projection methodologies. By early intervention, in our experience, case management may return a savings of $8 or more for every dollar spent; a minimum prospective savings ratio can be set at, for example, 4:1. It is not enough to rely on a claims payment system to trigger high cost cases for case management attention; by the time the cost threshold is attained, much of the savings potential may have been lost. Claims data can be effectively deployed as a triggering mechanism in some cases, as, for example, in the occurrence of a single claim for AZT as a trigger for outpatient management of HIV, rather than waiting for hospitalization, as in the usual UM process. Nonetheless, the UM system should also be used as an effective early identifier of potential cases for case management.

Like utilization management, case management should also be viewed as a highly effective means of referring patients into networks. Oftentimes, case management support will be viewed favorably by the patient, family, and physician alike, for example, when case management is able to "stretch" the benefit plan on behalf of the patient. Case management clinicians can then be in a good position to recommend the use of more cost-effective network providers.

UTILIZATION MANAGEMENT AND NETWORKS: PARTNERS IN QUALITY IMPROVEMENT

Utilization management can support the quality improvement goals of the network in a variety of ways. Utilization management can provide key data for feedback to providers on ways to improve their practice patterns. In individual cases, UM can work with network providers in a consultative capacity, over and above the routine UM review functions. In our experience, physicians have from time to time expressed their appreciation for our expert consultation on particularly difficult or complex cases.

Utilization management can also set itself the goal of improving the quality of its own attention to network providers, and thus improving its processes as a whole. Utilization management can continually seek to improve its service statistics, for example, by reducing delays and by improving access to reviewers expert in the particular specialty in question. Network providers, by virtue of their contractual relationship, have a special interest in these UM processes, and can be called upon to give constructive feedback. Thus, the providers' perception of the UM process can become more favorable. This collaborative effort can help to counter the prevailing views among providers of UM as adversarial, or obstructive, or meddling in their practices.

CONCLUSION

Utilization management can contribute significant savings on its own. When integrated with network management, however, it can support the stabilization of cost trends and the continual improvement of quality and patient satisfaction.

11. Pay-Related Plans: The Latest Stage of Managed Care Evolution

Leonard E. Wood, III

Employers can realize significant savings and improve the quality of health care benefits if they are willing to redesign their benefit plans to take advantage of the latest plan options. Combining managed care choices with pay-related cost sharing is one particularly effective—and very equitable—way to control health care benefit costs.

Because insurers are not managers of financial resources but only payers of claims, it is largely up to employers to manage their own group health programs.[1] Employers seeking cost-savings should be willing to redesign their health care plans to take full advantage the many current plan designs and varieties of managed care available. Utilizing these new options can bring significant savings while allowing employers to be as equitable to their employees as possible.

Benefit plan redesign is usually the first step in reducing cost growth in health care benefit plans. Once redesign is completed, it should be communicated as a change in the delivery system rather than a reduction of benefits, because employees find this more acceptable.

Between 1986 and 1992, the Consumer Price Index rose 28 percent, while the medical cost component rose 93 percent. During the same period, the per employee cost of health maintenance organization (HMO) enrollment rose 55 percent.[2] While this HMO increase is substantially lower than that of traditional indemnity plans, it clearly shows that HMOs alone won't solve the nation's health care problems. To achieve the ultimate goal of reducing health care inflation, employers need to reevaluate and redesign their benefit plans.

HMOS

HMOs have played a key role in improving the cost-efficiency of the health care delivery system in the United States. However, had HMOs been as successful as predicted when Congress passed the HMO Act of 1973 we probably would not be discussing health care reform today. HMOs will continue to play a vital role in a reformed health care system, but their prospects for long-term savings are still not completely documented and proven.

Typically, HMO and preferred provider organization (PPO) plans have saved money compared to traditional indemnity plans. Average employee cost is about 20 percent lower for HMOs, and about 10 percent lower for PPOs.[3] Employers need to recognize the growing acceptance of managed care as an alternative to traditional health care delivery. Managed competition, in fact, will serve as the centerpiece of a reformed health care system, with a strong movement toward an HMO model where providers will go "at risk." These at-risk providers will be more directly accountable for the quality of their services, and will become more financially responsible for them as well.

HMOs vs. Indemnity Plans

HMOs have typically offered more comprehensive benefits than indemnity plans, especially preventative care, and fewer benefit plan restrictions. As an example, periodic physicals and well baby care benefits are usually covered by HMOs, yet only selected traditional indemnity plans have recently begun to cover these services. Indemnity plans also impose greater coverage restrictions than HMOs, such as not covering the costs of treating preexisting medical conditions (that is, conditions that were diagnosed before the employee joined the plan) for a stipulated time period. HMOs do not impose these types of restrictions.

Onset of PPOs

In the early 1980s, managed care organizations began to recognize these differences, as well as consumers' concerns with restricted HMO networks of providers, and set about redesigning the managed care model. They developed a middle ground health care system, the PPO, that maintains the option of providing covered benefits for both in and out-of-network services—an option neither HMOs nor indemnity plans could provide. PPOs offer many of the same benefits that both traditional HMOs and indemnity plans offer, while still preserving the patient's right to choose a health care provider. In a PPO, patients are free to choose a primary care physician, specialist, hospital, or other provider without any type of prior authorization. If the patient chooses a network provider, benefits are paid at a higher level than those payable for a service rendered by a non-network provider. This "spread" between network and non-network costs is usually about 20 percent.

POPULARITY OF MANAGED CARE

With the growing popularity of PPOs and HMOs, we have witnessed a massive increase in enrollment in managed care plans in recent years —to the point where approximately 40 percent of the population is enrolled in some sort of managed care plan. While this movement is encouraging, some employers have not yet redesigned their benefit plan away from the traditional indemnity plan model. The primary reason for this is a commitment to unrestricted choice of medical providers.

Consumer Choice of Health Care Provider

The American health care consumer generally does not choose a medical provider based on medical competence or financial attractiveness. Consumers generally use two criteria:

1. Recommendations of friends or coworkers; and
2. Convenience (how long will it take to get an appointment, and how long will I have to wait in the office before I see the doctor).

The quality of the care and its costs are rarely at the top of the selection process. Today's managed care organizations pride themselves on their ability to utilize only the most competent and financially attractive providers. They accomplish this by a provider selection and retention process that includes extensive professional credentialling. Employers should use the benefits of provider credentialling by managed care organizations, and should offer different managed care benefit plans to help employees and dependents select providers more effectively.

Plan Design Choices

Typically, financial incentives are used to channel patients to a managed care network of providers. We're all familiar with a traditional incentive plan where the managed care benefit is payable at 90 percent while the indemnity plan is payable at 80 percent (a 90/80 plan)—a benefit differential of only 10 percent. The current trend is toward increasing the benefit differential spreads to between 30 and 50 percent to further encourage utilization of network providers. These plans usually also have larger deductibles and coinsurance limits for out-of-network usage.

PAY-RELATED PLANS

While increasing cost sharing brings short-term cost relief to the employer, a pay-related benefit plan can make these changes more equitable to all employees. This type of plan recognizes that, as costs grow, the burden of paying a flat premium for family coverage falls more heavily on a $20,000 per year administrative assistant than a $200,000 per year executive. A pay-related plan makes employees' medical benefit contributions more equitable by having highly compensated employees bear a relatively larger share of the costs than lesser-paid workers. Under this type of plan, deductibles, out-of-pocket limits, and premiums are tied to a percentage of the employee's annual salary.

This type of plan design also has the advantage of automatically adjusting employees' premiums, deductibles, and out-of-pocket limits as salaries increase. If their annual salary increases, so do their medical plan contributions, and this helps control employer cost. Xerox Corporation did not reduce expenditures when it redesigned its indemnity plan; their pioneering pay-related plan worked for a long period of time without having to go back and tinker with cost sharing.[4]

PROVIDING PLAN CHOICES

Allowing employees to choose the best plan option within the medical plan helps employees to become better health care consumers. Offering plan options such as an HMO, PPO, and an indemnity plan—each with varying levels of employee contributions, within a pay-related structure—allows the employee true choice when it comes to health care. Most employees will recognize that pay-related plans are fair. Lesser-paid employees' costs will likely remain unchanged, while some of the highly compensated employees will see their costs increase. Generally, there are fewer highly compensated employees who will see their costs increase, and these are likely to be able to afford the higher premiums and deductibles. However, in many cases offering varying levels of managed care options may very well offset any higher employee contributions.

The main objective of a pay-related plan is to help an employee assume an appropriate amount of cost to bear. Employees become better health care consumers when they bear costs and cost increases. "Whenever you drive employees to less expensive options, there are savings."[5]

Typical pay-related plan designs vary from a 0.5 percent deductible and 3 percent out-of-pocket limit to a 5 percent deductible and 10 percent out-of-pocket limit. Placing caps on deductibles and out-of-pocket limits will help control some of the employees' medical expenditures.

CONCLUSION

Pay-related plans are not for everyone. They are usually more appropriate for larger employers that have many pay levels than for smaller employers with simpler pay structures. The more an employee makes, that is, the more the benefit costs vs. the more an employee makes, the more value that benefit becomes.

A final, important item: most employers need the professional advice and marketplace knowledge that a competent employee benefit broker or consultant can provide. By working with a competent professional you will usually achieve your objectives more readily and effectively.

1. *Employee Benefits J,* Mar 1994.

2. Foster Higgins, *Healthcare Benefits Survey 1992.*

3. *Business Insurance,* "Easing the Pain of Benefit Cost Shifting," Feb 21, 1994.

4. Supra note 2.

5. Supra note 3.

Part 3

EMPLOYERS' EMERGING ROLES

12. GTE Family Health Center: Reengineering the Health Care Delivery System Paradigm

Cindy A. Cline, MPH

Nearly two decades ago, America's employers stepped into the ring with a pretty tough opponent—rising health care costs. Many companies threw in the towel early on, cutting their benefits plans severely or eliminating them completely. GTE, on the other hand, continued to fight in the ring, avoiding severe cutbacks by making sound, strategic changes to its health care plans. Plans include the management of the health care payments system, the delivery of health care, and the measurement of health care costs and quality. These changes are designed to maintain high quality, affordable benefits for employees in years to come. One of the most notable of these changes in GTE's fight against rising health care costs is the concept of the GTE Family Health Centers.

Corporate sponsored medicine is a managed care strategy that monitors the quality of care that individuals receive, makes sure health care services are properly utilized, and manages the cost of health care. Moving people up the managed care continuum (see Figure 1) creates a more efficient and balanced approach to health care, and the logical end of the continuum is the direct provision of medical services by the corporation. GTE recognized this fact and in response created its Family Health Centers.

PRELIMINARY WORK

The Family Health Centers concept was the result of a study to examine the feasibility of GTE actually creating and operating a managed health care delivery system as an alternative strategy to purchasing care from existing providers. The

143

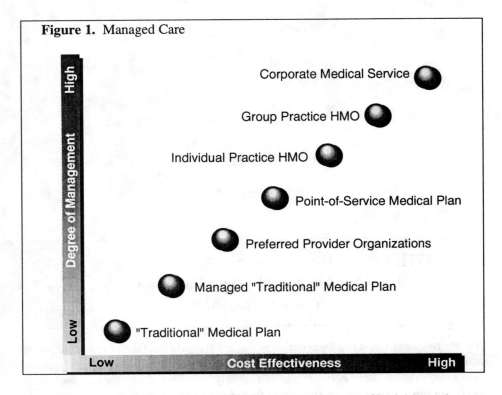

Figure 1. Managed Care

goal is to provide quality health care that is both more affordable and more accessible than traditional medical care. Key elements used to determine the potential for this concept included:

1. Sufficient employee, dependent, and retiree populations living within a "health care delivery service area";
2. Interest in a company sponsored medical facility by employee, dependents, and retirees;
3. Labor union/bargaining unit acceptance and active support;
4. Lack of an existing alternative such as a quality family or multi-specialty group medical practice; and
5. An opportunity for financial savings for employees and the company.

As a first step, a feasibility study was conducted to determine viable locations for one or more facilities. The Tampa Bay area, which encompasses Tampa and Clearwater, was selected based upon its dense population of active employees, dependents, and retirees—a total of approximately 35,000 covered lives. Once the locations had been selected, the next step was to query the eligible population about their potential interest in this new health care delivery system. Focus groups representing a cross section of GTE's population (management and union employees, retirees, HMO members and indemnity insurance members, etc.) were brought together to discuss and respond to questions about their interest in potential usage. The leadership of the IBEW Local Union # 824 was both helpful and supportive at this stage, ensuring the GTE Family Health Centers concept was widely understood by their membership. Concurrently, written surveys were mailed to additional employees to obtain similar information. The results of these focus groups and surveys indicated an overwhelming interest in this new health care delivery system, and so a detailed business plan for the concept was formulated.

THE HEALTH CENTERS

GTE selected PHP Healthcare Corporation of Alexandria, Virginia, to form a partnership to establish and manage the GTE Family Health Centers. PHP is a nationally recognized leader in the field of health care management.

Who Can Use the GTE Family Health Center?

The GTE Family Health Centers are designed to provide medical health care exclusively to all active employees, dependents, and retirees who participate in the GTE medical plan and health maintenance organizations (HMOs). HMO participants can choose a GTE Family Health Center doctor as their primary care physician (PCP).

Although the GTE Family Health Centers were originally designed to provide health care to only traditional indemnity plan members, in the initial phase, it became obvious that HMO members, whose ranks had grown to approximately 50 percent of all employees since 1993 enrollment, also had to be included. To ensure a smooth transition and a workable partnership with the selected HMOs, all GTE Family Health Center doctors have been credentialed to work within these HMO networks.

Scope of Services and Operations

The GTE Family Health Centers offer an array of services for adults and children. These services range from preventive care to the evaluation and treatment of most illnesses, both at the GTE Family Health Centers and in selected area hospitals. When the GTE Family Health Center is closed, a doctor is "on-call" by telephone to handle any medical problems that cannot wait until normal office hours. Services include:

- Treatment of minor illness and injuries such as bronchitis, colds and flu, earaches, muscle strains, and rashes

- Treatment of more serious and/or chronic medical problems such as high blood pressure, diabetes, pneumonia, and heart disease
- Minor surgical procedures such as suturing lacerations, removal of simple moles and cysts, and splinting and casting of uncomplicated fractures
- Treatment of emotional problems such as anxiety, depression, family or marital problems, and substance abuse
- Adult periodic physical
- Well-child examinations, including immunizations
- Camp and school sports physical
- Routine gynecologic examinations and treatments, and mammography screenings
- Routine laboratory tests and x-ray examinations ordered by the GTE Family Health Center doctors
- Pharmacy services covering medications prescribed by the GTE Family Health Center doctors and other doctors

Specialty care and sophisticated diagnostic tests are performed by community health care providers who have been selected to be a part of the GTE Family Health Centers referral network. The GTE Family Health Center doctors have admitting privileges in four Tampa Bay hospitals and admit patients as "attending physicians" to these hospitals, utilizing specialists as needed.

The hours of operation vary from one facility to the other. The Tampa office is open six days a week with office hours from 9:00 A.M. to 8:00 P.M. on Monday, Tuesday, and Thursday, 9:00 A.M. to 5:00 P.M. on Wednesday and Friday; and 9:00 A.M. to 12:00 P.M. on Saturday. The Clearwater office is opened from 9:00 A.M. to 8:00 P.M. on Monday and Wednesday; 9:00 A.M. to 5:00 P.M. on Tuesday and Thursday; and Friday from 9:00 A.M. to 1:00 P.M.

Office hours are by appointment only in order to provide quality time for the patient and doctor. Patients are encourage to choose one doctor as their PCP, although from time to time, when the PCP is not available, patients may see one of the other staff doctors. The GTE Family Health Centers are not meant to be used as a hospital emergency room or walk-in urgent care center (sometimes known as a "doc-in-the-box"). Open appointments are reserved each day to accommodate patients with urgent medical problems; however, patients are advised to call before walking in. This enables the medical staff to assess the medical situation over the phone and evaluate the patient in a timely fashion. There are no insurance forms to complete. A $5 fee is charged for an office visit at the time services is rendered. Pharmaceuticals vary in cost depending on what medical plan the patient belongs to, and prices can range from $5 for generic drugs up to $15 for brand name drugs.

The GTE Family Health Center will file claims for reimbursement from Medicare for patients over age 65, from any applicable carrier in workers' compensation cases, and from other insurance companies providing primary or secondary coverage for employees, dependents, and retirees. Because the GTE

Family Health Centers are committed to providing continuity of care and fostering a family practice environment, patients are encourage to establish a strong partnership with their PCP in order to share in the responsibility of their health care. GTE encourages and provides incentives to patients to receive all their primary care at the GTE Family Health Center or through its selected network of providers. However, patients may visit any other providers they wish to see in the community, subject to the deductibles and copayments of their medical plans.

The Staff

The staff consists of five board certified family physicians, a clinical psychologist, a licensed clinical social worker, a registered nurse practitioner, a physician assistant, nurses, lab technicians, x-ray technicians, medical assistants, pharmacists, pharmaceutical technicians, clerical staff, and a health educator.

The staff creates and provides an educational experience for every patient that receives care. A strong focus on health with more concentration on prevention and early intervention in addition to treating illness is the frame work by which the staff practices medicine.

COST CONTAINMENT EFFORTS

Applying some basic rules of sound management has enabled the GTE Family Health Center to provide services more efficiently. Operating under a staff model offers the GTE Family Health Center physicians a ready-made practice, with relatively fixed hours and a predictable income. This model also enjoys collaborative endeavors of medical knowledge and creates an environment that supports teamwork and attention to treating patients.

Using primary care physicians serves as a focal point for channeling patients to the most high quality and cost-efficient health care. Appropriate medical services for primary and preventive care and secondary and tertiary care can be monitored and managed through this approach. Some other examples include:

- The efficient use of laboratory services combined with services from a reference laboratory
- X-ray services that emphasize basic primary studies combined with the appropriate referral to more sophisticated means of diagnoses
- Pharmaceuticals that are purchased at below average wholesale prices (ALP) combined with the influence of a formulary, appropriate use of practice patterns, and educational intervention from the pharmacists
- Monitoring and managing the needs of specialty care beyond primary care services

- Making access to urgent care available for medical needs that would otherwise be treated at an emergency room or walk-in clinic

This approach enables health care to be delivered above the practiced standards and parameters; it encourages positive, measurable outcomes and avoids overtreatment and the use of marginal procedures; and it is economically prudent.

THE EVALUATION PROCESS

A project of this magnitude would not be complete without an evaluation process, and one is currently in progress. The goals of the evaluation are:

1. To measure the outcomes of services, patient satisfaction, and levels of functioning that are experienced by participants of the various plans in Tampa Bay, and thereby strengthen the determination of value received from health care delivery systems;
2. To determine if the costs of health care in the Tampa Bay area are reduced relative to what has been projected;
3. To determine the drivers of the change in costs and use patterns—for example, whether the practice patterns of the GTE Family Health Center physicians are significantly different from the community comparison;
4. To measure cost and quality issues of Tampa Bay HMOs by the use of the Health Plan/Employer Data and Information Set (HEDIS), a core set of health plan performance measures developed in response to employers' need to document and compare health plan value;
5. To evaluate the Employee Value Health Care Survey, which measures patient satisfaction, health status, and functional outcomes; and
6. To integrate a variety of measures of health care service cost-effectiveness, including: cost and use of services, worker's compensation and disability costs, patient satisfaction with service delivery systems, functional outcomes and health status, participants' health risk behavior, and modifiable lifestyles and their burden on health care costs.

The GTE Family Health Center concept brings health care full circle by integrating the delivery and financing of health care. This health care delivery system provides primary and preventive medicine as well as the ability to manage both the price and the use of hospitals and specialty medical care services. By contracting directly with primary care providers and the providers of ancillary services and pharmaceuticals, GTE can expect to reap significant savings.

Finally, the ability to identify potentially complicated illnesses and treat them early on will allow the centers to head off more expensive procedures. GTE will continue to monitor the performance of the centers and will consider additional sites as deemed appropriate. This may include opportunities to establish joint ventures with other employers in some of our areas with lower concentrations of employees, dependents, and retirees.

CHALLENGES

Managing success and the expectations of the employees, dependents, and retirees is a tall order. Traditionally, as consumers, we have not required from the medical profession what we have come to expect from other sellers of products and services we purchase. The first step in uncloaking health care is to be informed. GTE wants to educate employees, dependents, and retirees about the services received, quality of care, and alternatives available to them. In addition to this challenge, GTE wants to help everyone to become a more informed and responsible consumer of medical services.

THE FUTURE

The health care cost control fight is not over, but at this point managed care and the GTE Family Health Center look like winners. Studies continually exhibit that the major causes of morbidity and mortality in the United States are no longer viral and bacterial agents (excluding HIV), but rather are interactions of behavioral, environmental, and societal factors that strongly influence health. With that said, preventive health care, once considered a radical discipline at the fringes of conventional medicine, is gaining notoriety. Managing the health of individuals encompasses an array of measurable initiatives designed to encourage positive lifestyle changes. Managed health overlays the total quality continuous improvement process onto the philosophy of getting and keeping people well.

The GTE Family Health Centers are embracing an interdisciplinary approach to the delivery of health care. As primary care physicians, the GTE Family Health Center doctors can influence patient behaviors, satisfaction, and outcomes by emphasizing health instead of illness. As the GTE Family Health centers continue to broaden their scope of managed care to include a focus on managing health, they are building a long-term patient/provider partnership that places a high priority on preventing illness as well as treating it. This strategy will help foster a more quality driven, balanced, and efficient health care system for all.

13.   Controlling Health Costs in a Rural Community

Terry R. Tone

The usual thinking is that only employers and health insurers are truly interested in controlling health care cost, but the reality of the situation is that high costs negatively affect everyone, including consumers and providers. The people of rural Owatonna, Minnesota, recognized that fact and used the strong sense of community they shared to invent a new approach to driving down health care costs. They formed a partnership of providers, employers, and consumers and worked together creating a health care system designed for the greater good of the community.

Owatonna, Minnesota is a community located in southern Minnesota, approximately 55 miles from Minneapolis and its' surrounding suburbs. It has a population of approximately 22,000, and a highly developed employment base by which it draws employees from several other surrounding communities. Like most rural communities, there is pride in maintaining the vitality of the community itself. It is in that vein that the Owatonna Health Care Partnership was established in order to try to control the escalating costs of health care to its' population, while at the same time, maintaining and increasing the quality of the services rendered. Due to the size of Owatonna, good communications among employers, employees, and providers are easily facilitated. Providers have also shown a commitment to the whole population; they have not turned patients away from emergency room or the out-patient setting for a lack of insurance or inability to pay.

Approximately two years ago, several major Owatonna employers, representing approximately 8,000 enrollees, got together to discuss their concerns over the rising health care costs and where those dollars are being generated. It was decided that the Owatonna Clinic and Owatonna Hospital should be involved in these discussions to see if there was common ground in determining how to better control health care costs. At this time, all of the employers except one, were self-insured, thereby taking total financial risks for the health insurance of their employees. While they had not seen cost increases as severe as those seen by traditional indemnity products in town, they had seen enough of an impact on their bottom line to warrant the exploration of alternatives.

Over the course of the next six months, the employers and providers of the Owatonna Clinic sat down and looked at where the dollars were being spent for their populations. Interestingly enough, the dynamics of this expenditure were not unlike those other areas of the country. First, nearly 45 percent of the total health care dollars are being spent on the sickest 20 people in each organization. Second, about 25 percent of the total health care dollar was being spent locally with nearly 75 percent being spent outside of Owatonna community. Third, while many folks never received medical services during the year, 20 percent of the population accounted for nearly 80 percent of the total dollars expended. Additionally, there seemed to be little, if any, coordination of care due to the patient's ability to go where they chose, and the physicians' lack of responsibility outside of the walls of that particular institution. It became more and more evident as the discussion progressed that not only was there a concern over cost, but a true concern by providers and employers alike over the quality of the care being provided, due to the fragmentation of the community's health care system.

Employer concerns centered around quality, costs, and the lack of account-ability for services rendered on their behalf. Any other medical expenses incurred by the employers came with demonstrated quality and accountability assurances. Likewise, employers wanted the health care system to use similar parameters to determine the quality of services rendered. Employers wanted assurances that their money was well-spent. Therefore, a system needed to be provided by which employers felt they were getting the best value for the dollars expended. The employers were concerned that traditional metropolitan HMO packages seemed to be shadow pricing to the traditional indemnity products. Many employers are self-insured as a result of this particular situation. There was also concern about having metropolitan-based HMOs determining scope, quality, and access to services needed by a rural population.

While successful transplantation to a rural community of an existing metropolitan managed care plan would be difficult to achieve, that is not to say that managed care, per se, would be unwelcome. In rural communities such as Owatonna, local providers accept a deeply felt responsibility for patients of the community. Living and working within a small geographic location means providers and patients have to account to each other both personally and profes-sionally. It is through that relationship that the Owatonna Health Care Partnership was born.

From the provider perspective, there was obviously a concern about how HMOs would dictate the care provided in a location where tight relationships had been established between patients and physicians. The second concern related to the fragmentation of care once a patient left the Owatonna area, especially the lack of coordination by and to the primary care physician. It must be stressed that this fragmentation of the system was an inherent weakness for both providers and consumers. The final concern was about the amount of provider administrative overhead and consumer frustration created by prior authorization, pre-certification, usual-and-customary payments, and other cost control features of many of the self-insured plans.

Based on these concerns, the Owatonna employers, clinic, and hospital came up with a set of objectives by which they could redesign a new partnership arrangement. The mission of the Owatona Health Care Partnership was then defined. The mission is "to design and implement a managed care system which emphasizes delivery of quality health care services to consumers in the community." It is important to know that nowhere within the mission of the Owatonna Health Care Partnership is there a caveat that said it would provide the highest quality health care *unless* it cost too much. The issue and the focus of the partnership is quality, and ultimately, through better coordination, better quality, and better accountability, there will be lower costs and greater value for the local employers and their employees.

In order to better strengthen the mission of the partnership, several objectives needed to be established for future reference. The objectives were designed with the concerns of the employers, providers, and consumers in mind. The first objective was to strengthen the partnership among the employers, the health care providers in the network, and the consumers of the community of Owatonna. A major concern voiced by all stakeholders was that through past generations of health care cost control methods—such as prior authorization, pre-certification, etc.—consumers were exploited, and the results were little cost savings on the one hand and poor integration of system services on the other. Many of these prior authorization and pre-certifications actually became barriers or delays for care rather than a significant dollar saving mechanism. A review of the data revealed that, through this process of prior authorization and pre-certification, the employers of the Owatonna Health Care Partnership had authorized more in-patient days than were actually used by the Owatonna Clinic in 1992. Over the course of the same year, there also had been one documented incident where surgery was denied by a prior authorization process. Employers were paying a third party a substantial number of dollars for apparently useless precertification and prior authorization for services. The objective instead became for the Owatonna providers to be held accountable for services that they rendered, taking the third-party for-profit entities out of the picture.

The second objective was to modify the health care delivery system to provide quality care and manage long-term costs for the betterment of both the community and the employers. The partnership defined quality health care as that which "is necessary and appropriate, effective, delivered efficiently and the consumer is satisfied with the care received." This is an important definition in that many times providers provide what they perceive to be the best clinical outcome achievable given the circumstances of the patient. They assume all too often that because it's the best possible clinical outcome, the patient must be satisfied. Providers have tended to look at it more from a clinical perspective and less from the consumer's satisfaction side of the equation. While the technical expertise of the physician is extremely important within the care provided to the patient, the patient needs to be informed ahead of time what is reasonable to expect as an outcome of the services to be rendered, and the services must be rendered in a fashion that makes the patient satisfied with the care provided. That is truly a quality product as defined by the employers and providers to the population of the Owatonna community. By defining the term quality, the expectations of the patient, and the opportunities and obligations of both patients and providers, an integrated approach to providing care to the population will be obtained.

The third objective was to encourage consumers to use health care providers who demonstrate a commitment to quality-based management. This was done through plan design to financially encourage the patient to seek care from a network where providers have agreed to coordinate care and to provide account-ability statistics and information to the patient regarding the care they are about to receive. If someone would choose not to follow the plan of care or to opt out of the network established by the Owatonna Health Care Partnership, a substantial cost would be incurred by the individual for that decision; however, the option was available. The element of choice was the key to the whole process.

The fourth and final objective was to provide communication and education to consumers and ensure appropriate utilization of health care services, including preventative care. This is a critical piece of the partnership because it felt that the patient, over time, had been left out of the discussion of what type of care is to be provided and how. Unfortunately, patients have become used to having physicians make the decision as to where their care is to be provided, and having insurance companies make the decision as to how it will be provided. The patients have had little influence over these decisions. Providing outcomes information and discussing pathways with the physician helps empower the patient to par-ticipate more fully in their health care decisions. Lastly, the partnership firmly believes that pre-screening and preventive care can help identify major problems well before they become costly. The traditional health care system provides patients and providers incentives to treat conditions only once they are problems, as opposed to before they are problems. The partnership needed to change the paradigm so that people have incentives to take control and responsibility as consumers for the health and lifestyle that they lead, and physicians have incentives to educate people on the effects that such a lifestyle may have on them both physically and financially.

With the achievement of these objectives in mind, the Owatonna Health Care Partnership spent the next 12 months establishing a plan design, accountability requirements, and provider network. The process over the next 12 months was interesting from a sociological point of view as much as it was from a plan design perspective. There will of course be potential conflicts when providers, employers, and consumers—along with consultants—get around a table to try to establish a common goal and plan, but in Owatonna's care, despite differences of opinion, the commitment to maintain and operate a new paradigm whereby patients, providers, and employers have incentives aligned in the same direction was stronger than any one individual agenda. I believe this is not unique to Owatonna, but rather a strength of most rural communities due to the commitment of its inhabitants towards a focused goal. It was through this process that the evaluation of the data received by all providers and employers was used to determine where and how networks were to be set up.

Since the population preferred to use HealthSpan and Mayo Clinic as the two tertiary centers, the partnership focused its attention on these two centers from the beginning. The local hospital, being the only one in the county, was the obvious choice for secondary care, and they were brought in to the early discussions as well. At that point in time, primary care providers, secondary care providers, tertiary care providers, employers, and consumers were all at the table working together at defining quality health services for the community. This would be a tremendously difficult task if there was not commitment up front to do the right thing for the community.

Plan design took approximately six months. During that time it was decided that in order to meet the objectives three things had to occur: First, the patient had to be brought into the decision-making process *before* services were provided. In that respect, a considerable amount of patient education needed to be done by the employer to understand what type of design they were going to be utilizing. This plan had to encourage patients to receive necessary care, but discourage them from receiving care that is unnecessary or excessive. The partnership also felt it critical that a patient had the choice as to whether or not they wanted to enroll in the plan. It did not seem to be consistent with the values of the local community to force all employees into a limited network if they were unwilling to do so. Incentives were established within the plan whereby there would be no prior authorization/pre-certification required within the plan, that there would be a flat copayment for services rendered each time they visited the doctor (rather than having to meet a deductible), and that preventive care would be provided as a standard part of the package.

The second requirement was that information needed to be supplied to the consumers by both the employer and the provider with regard to outcomes measurement and patient satisfaction. The providers agreed to provide, on a per doctor basis, the level of satisfaction that the patient population has with the care given. This information is calculated on a semi-annual basis and, provided to the employers, will ultimately be available to the consuming public.

The third requirement was a streamlining of the administrative costs within the plan. It was decided that the patient would not be required to have prior authorization/pre-certification on the hospital admissions and procedures being ordered by the physicians. Instead, large-care review would take place on the top dollar cases annually to determine whether or not an integrated approach across tertiary lines was obtained. Finally, it was decided that through this integrated service process, cost could be expected to remain stable from 1993 to 1994. A global financial target was established whereby 1994 costs per member per month to the employers would not exceed the level obtained in 1993.

All providers are working within the same global target on a cost per member per month basis. Therefore, the incentive is the same for all primary, secondary, and tertiary care providers. That goal is to provide the highest quality of care to the patient, with accountability and financial responsibility for the overall population. In this vein, it will become critical for primary, secondary, and tertiary care centers to work as an integrated network, eliminating duplication and unnecessary testing. By better communication from physician to physician on the tertiary level, and physician to the hospital on the secondary level, fewer tests will be ordered in duplicate, and more appropriate documentation will be provided to the secondary and tertiary institutions by the primary care doctor (i.e., the results of the work up to the point of the referral).

Once the plan design was established, the process of employee communication was carried out prior to the enrollment process. The physicians of the Owatonna Clinic and representatives from the Owatonna Hospital went out and met with representatives of the employers to explain the new program and how it would be implemented. It was originally anticipated that an enrollment rate of 25 to 30 percent would qualify the program as a success. During these open employee meetings, many questions were raised regarding the quality of care, the type of referral required, and he process by which claims would be resolved. Following these employee meetings, open enrollment occurred for the next calendar year, 1994. By December 31, 1993, it became evident that this plan was well accepted by the community, receiving nearly 66 percent average acceptance within the employer networks. This represented approximately 1,300 employees and 4,000 enrollees out of a possible 8,000 for the first year.

The first three months of the new plan has seen a significant number of consumers change their decision-making process about health care services. Physicians are ordering fewer tests, and the number of surgeries in aggregate is down. While we will not have a true financial result until the end of the year, it appears that the combination of patient education, physician documentation, and explanation have had a significant impact on the cost of the care provided. There has also been a tremendous amount of employer-driven patient education to try to better explain to patients where costs are incurred and the importance of preventive care. Exercise initiatives, smoking cessation programs, and wellness screenings are being implemented at most of the companies, and these have been eagerly accepted by the employee populations.

There have been some operational issues with regard to referral authorization and the coordination of care across tertiary and primary care lines, but these problems have been met head on and resolved within a short period of time in order to make it as smooth a transition to the patient as possible.

The final issue was to establish a quality council whereby consumers, providers, and employers are meeting on a monthly basis in order to better enhance quality and access of the service provided in the Owatonna area. This is an important step, as it closes the loop within the quality improvement circle, which is important for patient satisfaction purposes as well.

Conclusion

Ultimately, I believe that the rural providers like myself, across the nation and in Minnesota in particular, are committed to do what is best for the populations they serve. We have intrinsic advantages in that we have commitment of purpose by the patient, employers, and providers of the community because we all live, work, and have to account for our actions to each other. This has made it easier for us to work as a group to change the paradigm, and to do so without becoming rigid and inflexible, and ultimately looking for outside help. A second issue that I believe is critical is the fact that ultimately we in Owatonna believe that health care reform is, indeed, a grassroots, local issue. It would be easy to reform the system and control costs by simply denying access to quality care to a population that needs it. It became important to us that we maintain access to quality and efficient services, and to establish better communication lines to tertiary centers for the care that cannot be performed locally. Ultimately, if the stakeholders are committed to resolving these issues, a solution will result.

Finally, there is a misconception that rural providers and employees are unwilling to take new and integrated steps towards reforming health care. The Owatonna Health Care Partnership represents a differing viewpoint; given the right set of circumstances, providers are willing to take an at-risk position that provides incentives rewarding efficient, appropriate, and high quality health care. If rural physicians are given the opportunity to work with employers to develop these systems, a more committed approach will be obtained by consumers, providers, and employers in obtaining quality health care services and controlling the costs of the services provided to the rural population.

14. Parker Hannifin's Health Benefits Program: Self-Management

Thomas S. Roos   Joyce M. Munsell   W. David Blake

During the early 1980s, most employers looked externally for assistance in controlling fast-rising health care costs, giving life to preferred provider organization (PPOs), utilization review, and patient case management. Within the same time period, Parker Hannifin, a Cleveland-based Fortune 200 company that produces manufacturing components and motion control systems, decided on a new path for its 20,000 employees: self-management.

On-site health care management nurses and direct relationships with medical providers are the heart of Parker's self-managed efforts. Parker's nurses, known as health care coordinators, monitor patient care and assist employees and family members with health care decisions such as physician selection. Preferred provider arrangements with hospitals and physicians are directly negotiated.

SELF-MANAGEMENT RESULTS

Self-management efforts have had a significant impact in lowering the rate of increase of annual employee health benefit costs. Before internal health management measures were introduced in 1985, Parker's cost increases for employee health benefits mirrored national trends. With self-management, yearly employee

Reprinted from Roos, T.S. Munsell, J.M., and Blake, W.D., Parker Hannifin's health benefits program: *Self-management, Managed Care Quarterly,* Vol. 1:4, pp. 1–11, with permission of Aspen Publishers, Inc. © 1993.

157

health benefit cost increases have averaged just 8.1 percent, substantially less than the national rise in employee health benefit costs (15 percent) during the same time period.

Per employee costs for Parker's self-managed program are less than its per enrollee health maintenance organization (HMO) costs. In each region where Parker offers HMO options to its employees, the HMO option is more costly. In southern California, about 20 percent of Parker Hannifin's employees are enrolled in one of three HMOs (most of Parker's southern California HMO enrollees are employees who joined an HMO while employed by a company that was subsequently acquired by Parker Hannifin). The remaining 80 percent of its southern California employees participate in the self-managed plan. This year, Parker's self-managed plan costs are running about 10 percent lower than the composite enrollee costs of the three southern California HMO plans.

Currently, annual administrative costs for Parker's program are approximately $30 per employee. This is half the fees that Parker would pay to outside organizations just to manage patient care and provide access to preferred medical providers. Administrative costs include the following:

- Nationwide contract negotiation with selected hospitals, physicians, and other medical providers such as hospices, home health nursing, and durable medical equipment;
- Employee health benefit communications costs (e.g., brochures, videos, and newsletters);
- All health care coordinator activities, including patient referrals to selected physicians, daily assistance with employee health needs, all facets of hospital utilization review and comprehensive patient case management, prevention and wellness activities, and coordination with disability, employee assistance program (EAP), and worker's compensation activities; and
- All equipment costs, utilization review software leasing, and licensing fees.

In contrast, fees to outside organizations for hospital and physician PPO access, patient utilization review, and catastrophic case management alone may typically average about $60 per employee. Table 1 compares Parker's self-management administrative costs to typical external costs for PPO network leasing, utilization review, and case management.

BENEFITS ENHANCEMENT

For the most part, Parker's low annual health care cost increases have not been achieved through cost shifting to employees. In fact, since self-management began in 1985, most changes to the company's health plan have focused on creating cost-effective alternatives that financially benefit the employees and the company. Parker Hannifin's most widely selected employee health benefits option is summarized below:

- Annual deductible for family: $250.
- Mandatory hospital utilization review: 10 percent penalty for not contacting the health care coordinator before elective hospitalization and outpatient surgery.
- Mandatory preauthorization for certain cases: 10 percent penalty for not contacting the health care coordinator before hospitalization or outpatient surgery for certain specified procedures.
- Inpatient care at a preferred hospital: annual $250 deductible waived; 100 percent coverage for the first $5,000, then 80 percent payment thereafter until patient reaches maximum out-of-pocket cost (at non-PPO hospital: 80 percent coverage, $250 annual deductible).
- Outpatient surgery: 100 percent coverage (both PPO and non-PPO) for the first $1,000; then 80 percent payment thereafter until patient reaches maximum out-of-pocket cost.
- Outpatient preoperative: 100 percent coverage for PPO, no limit; non-PPO: 100 percent coverage for the first $500, 80 percent payment thereafter.
- Outpatient laboratory and radiology: 100 percent coverage for the first $500, 80 percent payment thereafter.
- Centers of excellence: centers of excellence are identified for high-technology, costly procedures such as heart transplants; 100 percent paid benefits plus up to $10,000 paid travel expenses for patient and family.
- Hospice and home health: 100 percent coverage (both PPO and non-PPO).
- Low maximum out-of-pocket cost: $1,250 is the maximum amount that any employee is required to pay for annual health services, including employee coinsurance and the annual deductible.

Table 1. Annual Administrative Cost Comparison (Per Employee)

| | Total annual costs | |
Type of administration	Parker Hannifin	External vendor
	$4	$20
Preferred provider arrangements with hospitals and physicians	$3*	$18
Partnership development with preferred providers	$5	Not applicable
Utilization review (including precertification, concurrent, and retrospective)	$5	$27
Catastrophic patient case management	$4	$13
Routine case management for noncatastrophic cases	$4	Not applicable
Day-to-day assistance with specific employee health needs, including physician referrals	$4	Not applicable
Wellness activities	$2	Not applicable
Coordination with EAP, worker's compensation, and disability	$2	Not applicable

Based on 1993 numbers, Parker sought external bids for these services.
*Parker's own network of selected hospitals and physicians.

INTERNAL VERSUS EXTERNAL MANAGEMENT

The scope of Parker's self-managed health benefit activities is primarily confined to patient care management functions (e.g., preadmission review, utilization review, and case management) and direct relations with selected hospitals and physicians in regions of the nation. Prohibitive development costs and low concentrations of employees in specific geographic areas restrict the company from developing a fully self-managed benefits plan.

Nationwide, Parker cannot justify the costs and logistical requirements of on-site claims administration. Also, in certain regions Parker does not have enough employees to leverage meaningful financial and partner relationships with local hospitals and physicians. In spite of these restrictions to developing a fully self-managed, corporatewide health benefits system, Parker's relationship with external contractors (i.e., claims administrators and regional PPOs) represents a unique hybrid of internal/external management.

Claims Administration

Provident Life and Accident (Chattanooga, Tennessee) administers Parker's employee health claims nationwide. Provident has dedicated employee units that process health benefit claims solely for Parker Hannifin. Because Parker cannot currently justify the capital costs associated with on-site claims administration (e.g., personnel training and development; hardware and software development, integration, and revisions; and space requirements), Parker and Provident formed a business relationship that provides Parker with many of the advantages of on-site administration without most of the inconveniences. Two of the most important features of the Parker-Provident relationship are as follows:

- Provident's systems accommodate Parker's complex, detailed, and fast-changing contractual relationships with hospitals and physicians throughout the country.
- Provident and Parker have an on-line, two-way communication computer system allowing for full access to customized management reports, utilization review profiles, case management activities, and patient claim histories.

Regional Limitations

With 140 worksites nationwide, Parker recognizes regional limitations to self-management activities. In regions where the company's workforce concentration is fewer than 100 employees, the company typically leases a local PPO but retains full control of patient management activities (e.g., utilization review, case management, and precertification). Table 2 contrasts the control (internal or

Table 2. Internal Versus External Health Benefit Control

Type of administration	Traditional employer program	Parker Hannifin	
		< 100 employees per region	> 100 employees per region
Claims administration	External	External	External
PPOs	External	External	Internal
Precertification	External	Internal	Internal
Utilization review	External	Internal	Internal
Case management	External	Internal	Internal

external) of a traditional corporate health benefits program with Parker's self-managed programs.

CORPORATE HEALTH BENEFITS

Parker's health benefits program is directed by the corporate health benefits department, a division of corporate benefits and human resources. The two most important activities of the department are: program development and administration, and employee health care coordination. Exhibit 1 summarizes the key elements of each activity.

Program Development and Administration

Parker's self-management team, including the director of corporate benefits, the national health care coordinator, and the national coordinator of provider relations, develops and administers the corporate health benefits program. Key program development and administration elements are:

1. *Customized preferred provider arrangements.* Parker develops direct contractual relationships with its own network of preferred hospitals and physicians. In 1985, direct contracts were established with only 17 hospitals, all located in northern Ohio or southern California. Today's nationwide provider network includes 148 hospitals and several thousand physicians. This customized network of preferred providers is accessible to more than 80 percent of the domestic workforce. The network also includes regional centers of excellence (e.g., the Cleveland Clinic, the Mayo Clinic, and the University of California at Los Angeles Medical Center) for organ transplants.

Exhibit 1. Corporate Health Benefits

Program development and administration

- Customized preferred provider arrangements
  —Provider selection
  —Contract negotiation
  —Partnership development
- Traditional preferred provider arrangements
  —Provider selection
  —Contract negotiation
- Claims data analysis and monitoring
- Benefit plan design and modification
- Benefit plan promotion and employee communications

Employee health care coordination

- Early assistance with employee health needs
- Patient care management
  —Preadmission review
  —Utilization review
  —Case management
- Back-to-work assistance
  —Worker's compensation coordination
  —EAP coordination
- Prevention and wellness promotion
  —Personal fitness promotion
  —Health fairs
  —Early detection

Criteria used in selecting the preferred medical providers include historic employee utilization, cost of care, perceived quality, and willingness to work with Parker as a partner. The network of preferred physicians is selected in accordance with their affiliation with preferred hospitals. The majority of hospital contracts are based on per diems or discounts and are annually negotiated with the assistance of a health benefits consultant.

Parker expects the relationship with hospitals and physicians in its customized network to reach beyond a financial arrangement. Specific partnership agreements that are shared with each selected provider include the following:

- Develop a close, working relationship with a corporate officer (chief executive officer, chief financial officer, chief operating officer, or vice president) who can act on behalf of the hospital or physician group.

- Demonstrate high-quality, cost-efficient medical care with relevant statistics and reports.
- Provide financial arrangements for all services (deep discounts or per diems are not expected; likewise, shallow discounts and per diems are not acceptable).
- Develop a close, cooperative relationship with hospital and physician case managers in the day-to-day, case-by-case evaluation of appropriate patient treatment.
- Assist Parker in health education and promotion.
- Participate in problem-solving meetings, assisting Parker in identifying opportunities to control quality and cost.

2. *Traditional preferred provider arrangements.* In regions where the workforce concentration is fewer than 100 employees, traditional preferred provider arrangements are selected and negotiated.

3. *Claims data analysis and monitoring.* Parker works closely with its claims administrator and consultant to develop customized claims information that will identify opportunities to improve quality and increase cost efficiency. Such reports summarize utilization and costs of contracted and noncontracted medical providers, price and utilization summaries by diagnosis related groups and current procedural terminology, and employee utilization of health care services by region, department, and type of services received. On-line access with the claims administrator provides access to current patient records and report utilization review compliance.

4. *Benefit plan promotion and employee communications.* Employee sessions, videos, brochures, newsletters, health fairs, and ongoing health education classes are the primary sources of benefit plan promotion and employee communications.

Employee Health Care Coordination

Health care coordination is the most visible activity of the benefits program. Registered nurses and support staff assist employees and family members in making informed health care choices. As patient advocates and trusted, confidential advisors, the coordinators are personally available to employees and family members.

The health care coordinator is the central figure of the self-managed program. Promoted as a resource for employees, physicians, management, medical providers, and the claims administrator, the coordinator attempts to simplify, organize, and integrate care that may become complex and fragmented in the current health care system. Figures 1 and 2 contrast the role of the health care

Figure 1. Traditional Utilization Review and Case Management Focus

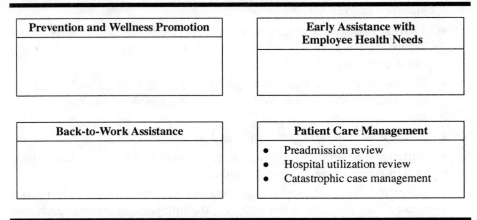

coordinator with the traditional role of utilization review and case management services.

Unlike the traditional utilization review nurse, who is unknown to employees and primarily focuses on patient care in hospitals and surgery centers, the health care coordinator helps employees and family members in these ways: early assistance with employee medical needs, patient care management and coordination, back-to-work assistance, and prevention and wellness promotion.

Figure 2. Health Care Coordinator Focus

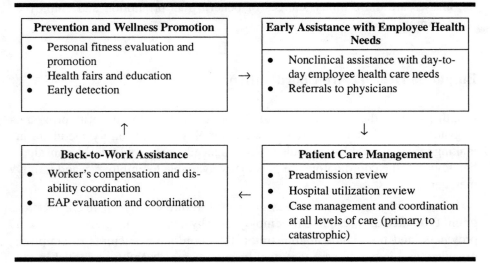

Early Assistance with Employee Medical Needs

Day-to-day assistance with employee health care needs provides health care coordinators with a singular advantage over utilization review coordinators, who traditionally do not manage care until hospitalization or surgery is required. Through day-to-day employee assistance, the health care coordinator has the opportunity to evaluate and manage patient care during the employee's initial phase of medical need. In most cases, coordinators can channel employees and families to medical providers long before hospitalization may ever be necessary.

The following example illustrates how the coordinator can provide service during the initial phase of medical need. An employee with chronic lower back pain needed medical attention but was not sure whether it would be better to see a chiropractor, a family physician, an orthopedic surgeon, or a physical therapist. The employee contacted the coordinator. After becoming familiar with the patient's case, the coordinator referred the patient to a nearby medical center's back clinic. The coordinator contacted the clinic to discuss the referral and kept in contact with the clinic and the employee during the next few weeks to monitor progress.

Coordinators dedicate approximately one third of their average workday to assisting employees and family members with individual health care needs. On a voluntary basis, employees and family members contact the health care coordinator to discuss personal, current health needs. Such discussions mostly focus on what to do for a recent illness or health problem. Many employees also contact the coordinators for other health-related needs, such as understanding a medical bill. The majority of inquiries are initiated through telephone calls or personal visits to the coordinator's office.

In 1992, the coordinators received more than 12,000 requests for day-to-day health care assistance. About 90 percent of patients seeking assistance from the health care coordinators want to know what to do or where to go to take care of specific health problems. Patients also ask about the care they are currently receiving from local medical professionals. Typical employee inquiries of health care coordinators include the following:

- Do you know a physician who specializes in . . .?
- My physician recommends that I have surgery for. . . . Will my health plan cover the surgery?
- If I have the surgery, about how many days will I miss from work?
- My physician seems to be charging too much for my last office visit. What can I do?
- Is there a lower cost alternative?
- Can you help me understand my physician's bill?
- My cholesterol is high. What should I do?

The health care coordinator is a resource, not a medical provider. Rather than prescribe medicine or suggest treatment patterns, the coordinator's primary objective is to help employees make informed health care consumer decisions.

Common questions asked of employees seeking medical assistance are "How long have you had this problem?" "What are the symptoms?" and "What forms of treatment have you considered or received?" Based on these contacts with employees, the health care coordinator is able to help employees better understand their medical concerns and, if warranted, to direct them to an appropriate medical provider.

Physician Referral Services. Through daily voluntary contacts with employees and family members, the health care coordinator has opportunities to refer patients to primary care physicians and physician specialists. In some cases, employees and family members ask coordinators to assist them in finding a physician with certain characteristics (e.g., a female obstetrician/gynecologist who has an office near the employee's home). Employee participation in physician referral services has grown significantly, from a few hundred referrals in 1985 to more than several thousand physician referrals in 1992.

Where preferred provider arrangements are developed, employees have access to a directory of physicians. Some employees, however, seek assistance from the coordinator in narrowing the physician directory list of many physicians to a few. The coordinator always provides patients with a minimum of three physician names when making any referrals. The coordinator considers the following in referring patients to physicians and other medical providers:

- Location: patients generally prefer seeing physicians whose offices are located within a 20- to 30-minute drive from home.
- Patient preferences: employees frequently look for a physician with a specific profile, such as a physician who has extensive, successful experience performing a certain procedure or a physician who is warm and caring.
- Patient health history: the coordinator also refers patients to physicians based on patient health history and medical need; where appropriate, patient referrals are made directly to specialists rather than to primary care physicians.

Sources Used for Selecting Effective Physicians. Whenever possible, the health care coordinator refers patients to primary care physicians and physician specialists who are considered effective in their specialty.

Although measuring physician effectiveness has significant limitations, the coordinators use a number of resources to develop a list of preferred physicians. These resources may include the following:

- Patient surveys: focusing on individual perceptions of outcomes, patient surveys are helpful tools in identifying individual physician effectiveness; on occasion, patients are asked to share perceptions regarding care provided by their physicians.
- Patient care management experience: because health care coordinators perform patient utilization review, case management, and other managed care activities, they work closely with physicians and physician office staffs in reviewing decisions regarding patient treatment.

- Claims data analysis: Parker's claims administrator analyzes claims data to identify physicians who game the payment system (e.g., those who use surgical unbundling, office visit code creep, and excessive tests and procedures); Parker is able to use this claims data analysis information to identify physicians who are not cost effective.
- Regional experience: as professional registered nurses with years of local patient care experience, Parker's coordinators have a unique advantage in managing patient care through their knowledge of local medical resources.

Patient Care Management and Coordination

The patient care management and coordination role of the health care coordinator is better known throughout the health benefits industry as utilization review and case management. Yet the coordinator's patient care management duties and responsibilities extend beyond traditional utilization review and case management. The basic mechanics of utilization review and case management are similar, but Parker differs from the traditional approach in six key facets:

1. Continuity of patient care: A principal difference is continuity of patient care. Traditional approaches are typically fragmented. For each patient, one nurse conducts precertification, another conducts concurrent review, another conducts retrospective review, and yet another conducts catastrophic case management activities (if necessary). Typically, no one nurse will coordinate precertification through case management activities from beginning to end. If the same patient is hospitalized frequently, it is possible that the patient's care would be reviewed by an entirely different set of nurses for each admission.

   The health care coordinator fully integrates all patient care management activities from precertification to case management. The same coordinator who conducts preadmission and utilization review activities is also responsible for conducting or coordinating case management activities for all patients in a specific geographic region.

2. Timing: Under normal, nonemergency circumstances, utilization review nurses do not learn of a pending hospitalization or surgery until just a few days before the scheduled event. At Parker Hannifin, however, patient care management can begin long before hospitalization or surgery is ever necessary. Health care coordinators are available to help patients make informed health care choices. Through accessing appropriate medical providers and making informed decisions, coordinators, patients, and medical providers work together to minimize unnecessary hospitalizations and surgeries.

3. Linking physician referrals with patient care management activities: Physicians who cooperate with Parker's health care coordinators during utilization review and case management activities are more likely to receive patient referrals than physicians who do not cooperate.

4. Personal relationships: Parker's patient care management program centers on building personal relationships between the health care coordinators and employees, family members, physicians, and hospital management. The coordinator is available to answer questions and concerns regarding hospitalization, surgery, and recuperation. Also, in many cases the coordinators are personally acquainted with area physicians caring for employees and family members. On occasion, physicians may be asked to participate in employee health fairs and employee health education classes and seminars. Through periodic meetings, personal relationships are also formed with hospital utilization review and case management departments and hospital management.

5. Utilization review activities: Health care coordinators follow standard utilization review procedures for patient hospitalization and surgery, including precertification and concurrent patient review, the coordinators use nationally recognized computer software programs (e.g., *Erisco*) and published medical protocols (e.g., Value Health Sciences) for patient management and discharge planning. In response to physicians who do not cooperate with the nurse and standard utilization review protocols, Parker Hannifin and traditional utilization review organizations both pursue many similar steps: initiating conversations between the uncooperative physician and a utilization review physician advisor or medical director, soliciting the assistance of hospital utilization review departments, and requesting assistance from physician leadership of the respective physician contracting group.

6. Case management activities: A significant departure from traditional patient care management, where individual case management is conducted for only high-cost, catastrophic cases, a coordinator manages and coordinates care for all hospital and surgical patients. These include patients who are not hospitalized but have long-lasting illnesses or are in need of costly procedures. Traditionally, certain criteria are applied to activate or trigger the need for case management. Such criteria may include a diagnosis [such as acquired immunodeficiency syndrome (AIDS) or cancer] or when the patient's medical bill exceeds a predetermined amount (e.g., $15,000 or higher). The health care coordinator does not wait for such criteria to activate case management but manages each patient case in an effort to integrate and balance patient and family needs and resources with community health resources such as hospice care, home health nursing, and durable medical equipment.

   Case management efforts are categorized as follows:

   • Episodic: these cases are usually self-resolving and have a beginning and an end (e.g., high-risk pregnancy);

   • Evolving and ongoing: these cases typically are managed for an extended period (e.g., AIDS, cancer, or diabetes);

   • Sudden: these cases have massive complications, and it is difficult to predict when they will end (e.g., sever accident or stroke);

- Costly and/or illusive: these cases are often difficult to identify because patients may not have been hospitalized or had surgery (e.g., organ transplants or growth hormone treatments);
- All other patients as needed: these cases can be a simple as helping a patient order a wheelchair or as cost-effective as transferring a patient to a lower-cost care setting.

Back-to-Work Assistance

Another role of the health care coordinator is to assist employees to return to productive employment as soon as possible after an injury, illness, or hospitalization. Where appropriate, the coordinator provides back-to-work assistance for long-term and short-term disability patients. On request of management, and with patient cooperation and consent, the coordinator reviews the medical record and makes an assessment of the patient's work abilities. If an employee is unable to return to normal job assignments, the coordinator is available to assist the patient and management in identifying other potential job activities that the employee could successfully perform permanently or until the employee is able to return to the job held before the disability.

Worker's Compensation Coordination. Worker's compensation costs, including associated legal expenses, represent the company's fastest rising health care cost components, increasing as much as 80 percent in 1 year. Studies to determine key factors for high annual cost increases indicate that employees receiving worker's compensation benefits often feel misguided and confused about selecting physicians. Recent statutory changes in many states allow employers to coordinate worker's compensation care during the first 2 months after the initial injury.

In 1992, health care coordinators began assisting employees with work-related injuries in terms of coordinating and accessing medical care. Health care coordinators focus on coordinating care for patients with work-related injuries from the initial assessment to back-to-work assistance.

EAP Coordination. Many employees have access to EAPs for emotional health and substance abuse. Some employees also have direct access to a social worker who specializes in helping employees and family members access EAPs. In nearly all cases, the company contracts with external organizations for EAP services to maximize patient confidentiality. The majority of employees and family members who need EAP services directly contact the EAP. Twenty percent of those seeking services first contact the coordinator, who immediately provides referrals to the EAP for individual assessment and evaluation.

If inpatient hospitalization is required, the EAP is encouraged to work with the coordinator to refer patients to preferred hospitals. The coordinators conduct and coordinate all patient care management services for inpatient behavioral medicine needs. In some regions, the EAP and a psychologist are available to assist the coordinator in conducting concurrent medical reviews as needed.

Prevention and Wellness Promotion

Employee physical fitness and wellness activities are organized and coordinated by health care coordinators. In addition to promoting physical fitness and illness or injury prevention, the coordination of wellness activities enhances employee awareness of health care coordinator services.

In southern California, coordinators recently initiated a needs-driven wellness program at each employee location. Personal physical fitness risk appraisals are now conducted among employees. Patient medical claims data are reviewed to identify health needs. After this initial analysis, a series of site-specific health education programs will be offered to employees and family members. Current employee wellness and physical fitness activities coordinated by the health care coordinator include the following:

- Mammography screening: In some cases, preferred providers offer mammography screenings to employees and family members. The screenings, offered at no cost to the patient, are occasionally conducted on-site through mobile units.
- Employee health fairs: Employees and family members participate in on-site health fairs, which are conducted every 18 months. Tests and screenings conducted at health fairs include comprehensive blood work, pulmonary function, cardiac assessment, cholesterol, and hypertension screening. Approximately 50 percent of employees participate in company-sponsored health fairs.
- Newsletters health message: The health care coordinator contributes health and nutrition articles to in-house newsletters.
- Organized athletic competition: Employees participate in many organized athletic teams, including baseball, basketball, volleyball, golf, tennis, and bowling.
- Stop-smoking classes: Smoking-cessation classes are periodically offered to employees and family members. Most employee worksites have a smoke-free policy.
- Brown-bag health education lunches: Preferred physicians and hospital representatives offer employee health education at brown-bag lunches, discussing topics such as cancer, mammography, nutrition, stress management, and physical fitness.
- Health club discounts: In some regions, local gyms and health clubs offer special discounts to employees.

HEALTH CARE COORDINATOR CHARACTERISTICS

Parker Hannifin employs seven full-time health care coordinators, one for every 2,850 employees, and three managed care clerical assistants, one for every 6,660 employees (external utilization review companies typically employ one nurse for every 6,000 to 10,000 employees). The ratio of health care coordinators to employees is largely a function of the following three factors: the scope of duties and responsibilities assigned to the coordinators, the degree to which local providers willingly cooperate with the coordinator in utilization review and case management activities (high cooperation requires less coordinator time for patient management), and the level of employee participation in various program components such as wellness and health fairs. In some circumstances, a case could be made to have one health care coordinator for every 1,000 employees.

The following examples illustrate how regional circumstances affect health care coordinator activities and requirements. In regions where physicians customarily challenge managed care efforts, additional resources are required to monitor utilization review and to manage individual patient cases. Also, in states such as California, where employees have higher healthy lifestyle consciousness, employees contact coordinators more frequently than employees in other states to discuss health information needs such as nutrition and wellness, physician selection, and cost of care.

Health Care Coordinator Qualifications

Parker attributes much of its program's success to the individual health care coordinators, who work closely with employees and family members. In addition to being licensed as registered nurses who have extensive hospital patient care backgrounds (mostly in critical care units and emergency departments), they are more effective at analyzing situations and assisting patients in recognizing treatment options than nurses whose professional experience is focused in utilization review or case management.

The following are general qualifications and characteristics of health care coordinator candidates:

- Approximately 10 years of local emergency care and critical care nursing (intensive care, critical care, and emergency department training);
- A personal style that can effectively communicate with senior management, employees, family members, physicians, hospital representatives, and claim administrators;
- An ability to balance and integrate management priorities with personal employee needs; and
- A strong business acumen marked by the ability to interpret and generate management data effectively to identify opportunities, contain costs, and demonstrate program effectiveness.

Patient Confidentiality

Strictly followed guidelines protect patient privacy and confidentiality. The coordinator's ability to maintain employee trust is essential. Consequently, confidentiality is a mandatory requirement of the coordinator and anyone who works in the coordinator's office, including data processing personnel who have access to health-care-related documents and information.

All employees who have access to confidential health care information are required to read and sign a corporate policy statement regarding confidentiality. Corporate confidentiality policies cover the following information:

- Individual employees' right to privacy,
- Compliance with statutory laws regarding privacy of information,
- Proper patient authorization before medical information is received from physicians,
- Privacy of employee personal identification codes (e.g., name, address, and social security number),
- Third party requests for patient medical records,
- Computer system security measures, and
- Unauthorized reading of confidentiality documents.

On review of the various corporate policies regarding confidentiality, Parker employees are required to sign and date the following confidentiality statement:

I have read the policy and standards regarding confidentiality and security regarding health care claims information and agree that I will not discuss confidential (i.e., personal) information with anyone not involved in the normal processing of our work. I will refer any third party requests for such information to the corporate director of employee benefits.

I also agree that I will not discuss confidential information outside the company or in settings not appropriate for the maintenance of confidentiality.

I further understand that passwords are confidential and should not be disclosed to anyone. Only terminals assigned by management should be used, and these should be signed off when I leave them unattended.

I acknowledge my understanding of the information covered in the memorandum, and any violation of the standards outlines therein can be cause for disciplinary action, which could lead to termination of employment.

Additional safeguards for maintaining confidentiality of employee medical records are as follows:

- EAP referrals: mental health and substance abuse cases are referred to an outside EAP;
- Locked file cabinets: medical records and confidential patient information are kept in double-lock file cabinets;
- Document shredder: rather than being discarded in wastebaskets, confidential information is shredded;

- Floor-to-ceiling-walls with a door: the coordinator's office has a confidential environment for talking on the phone and visiting with employees; doors are closed and locked at all times when the coordinator is not in the office; and
- Computer system with password protection: computers that are used for confidential medical records, utilization review, or other coordinator activities have password protection and are accessible only to coordinators.

Office Location

To maximize personal contact between employees and the health care coordinators, coordinator offices are located in areas that are easy to find, accessible, permanent, and private. Regionally, all coordinator offices are located in the buildings that have the largest number of employees per building and are near areas that attract high employee foot traffic (e.g., near building entrances or cafeterias).

LESSONS LEARNED

The key lessons learned during the past eight years of self-management include the following:

- *The development of self-management is an evolutionary process.* Senior management has supported a gradual, step-by-step development of Parker's internally driven health benefits program. In 1985, coordinators initially focused on conducting precertification, hospital utilization review, and catastrophic case management. Over time, other key components of self-management were added (e.g., Parker's own network of direct contracts with selected hospitals and physicians, routine case management for all patients, worker's compensation coordination, and wellness activities).
- *Hospitals and physicians have become increasingly responsive to Parker Hannifin.* During the first few years of self-management, the relationship between Parker and hospitals and physicians was primarily driven by Parker. Gradually, many hospitals and physician groups in Parker's network expressed more interest in developing closer ties. Consequently, Parker and its selected network of medical providers have become more team oriented, working closer together to identify and meet each other's objectives. For example, before 1990, the relationship between Parker and its network providers generally could be characterized as financial, based on annually negotiated reimbursement rates. Starting in the 1990s, network providers began to seek opportunities to work together in activities such as health fairs, mammography screenings, primary care physician capitation rates, and global fees for open heart surgery and obstetrics.

- *Employees seem to appreciate having access to the health care coordinators.* An early concern of management was the issue of patient confidentiality associated with employee willingness to discuss health care needs with a fellow employee. Experience, however, has clearly shown that employees are appreciative of being able to talk with coordinators. Employee compliance with self-managed activities is as high as 80 percent in some regions. The number of phone calls and patient visits to the coordinators' offices has increased each year since the inception of the program.

- *Health care coordinators recognize opportunities to manage care and costs before claims administration reports identify a need for case management.* Parker receives a monthly report from the claims administrator identifying patients who should be receiving catastrophic care management. In nearly all cases, health care coordinators have already been coordinating patient care long before the claims administrator identifies case management prospects. Parker's early awareness and patient care coordination provide opportunities to help employees use medical resources appropriately.

15. Teaming Up to Cut Health Care Costs
Shari Caudron

HR executives are banding together in communities throughout the U.S. to form health care coalitions. Through their combined purchasing power, these coalitions are changing the way that health care is purchased and delivered in this country.

Instead of waiting for federal health care reform to address the critical issue of soaring costs, employers in many communities are joining forces to reform the system on their own. The health care coalitions that they're creating have the potential to fundamentally change the way health care is purchased and delivered in this country. More often than not, in the companies involved, it's the human resources department that's leading the way.

In Minneapolis, for example, the HR executives of several large, self-insured companies have pressured local providers to put greater emphasis on the quality and cost-effectiveness of care. A major aim of the coalition is to cut back on the care delivered by expensive cardiologists, orthopedists and other specialists, and instead to rely more heavily on primary-care doctors. According to Paula Roe, vice president and director of compensation and benefits for Norwest Corp. in Minneapolis, it was natural for the HR professionals in that community to join forces because they shared the same "compelling interests."

"Our main interest was in how we could collaborate in the whole area of health care reform," says Roe. "The kind of reform work we're doing has tremendous potential to reduce costs because we're focusing on the delivery of necessary, effective and efficient care."

The Minneapolis coalition, known as the Business Health Care Action group, has been instrumental in changing the way that providers deliver health care in the Twin Cities area because the group will do business only with providers that show a commitment to high-quality treatment. Like other coalitions, it's working to make the system more accountable to those who are picking up the tab.

"For a long time, employers have sat back passively and accepted their role as a major financier of health care, but they have been unable or unwilling to proactively manage those costs other than through traditional benefits means," explains Bryan Bushick, a consultant in the Minneapolis office of Towers Perrin.

But cost-shifting and managed care—the two primary avenues of cost containment—aren't working because there has been no accountability in the U.S. health care system. Providers are paid based on the number of services that they provide, not on how well they provide them. Patients aren't the primary purchasers, so they have no incentive to shop around. And, lacking information on treatment effectiveness, purchasers have sought price discounts based on quantity, not quality.

Community-based health care coalitions like the one in Minneapolis represent a grass-roots effort by employers to change this expensive paradigm. How? By using their combined purchasing power to make demands on the system. At last count, there were close to 100 of these employer-driven coalitions, according to the National Business Coalition Forum on Health in Washington, D.C.

Health care coalitions aren't a new idea. Many of them have been around for more than a decade, explains George Morrow, principal and health-practice leader for William M. Mercer Inc. in Minneapolis. However, the focus of coalitions has changed during the years. "They originally were designed for the purpose of exerting raw economic leverage and achieving some significant discounts in the cost of care," says Morrow.

But in the late 1980's, employers began to realize that cost by itself wasn't the problem. They caught on to the idea that cost and quality don't necessarily go hand-in-hand; that a higher price for health services doesn't always mean that care is more effective. Today, as the coalition movement spreads, employers—both large and small—are demanding quality and cost-effectiveness from the health care system.

The way this is done varies greatly from community to community. Some coalitions put their energy into lobbying for local health care reform. Others offer managed-care services to their members. Still others say that the only way to get the attention of providers is by putting financial pressure on them. For all their differences, however, employer-led coalitions share a common belief that because health care is a local industry, reform must be community-based.

As Catherine Kunkle, vice president of operations and information services for the National Business Coalition Forum on Health, explains, "State and federal reform efforts are an attempt to look at the global picture and legislate from the top down how health care will be delivered and paid for. In reality, it's done at the local level. Every health care market is somewhat different in terms of the number and capacity of providers available, the demands on the system and the complexion of employers who pay for benefits for people in the community."

The Memphis Business Group on Health provides just one example of how this works.

PURCHASING POWER HELPS MEMPHIS EMPLOYER REDUCE HEALTH CARE COSTS

In 1985, a coalition of 11 self-insured employers in Tennessee, including Federal Express, Holiday Inn and First Tennessee Bank, started the Memphis Business Group on Health. Like many coalitions, its original focus was on health-cost control.

Soon after forming, the group commissioned a study that revealed that some local hospitals charged up to 80% more than others for the same health services. The members publicly released the results of the study and sought a competitive bid for the hospital care of their combined 25,000 employees. "We didn't want to start an open war," explains Fred Bowman, chief financial officer of Seessel's Supermarkets, "but most companies felt that they had been on the outside looking in at the health-cost issue. We wanted the medical community to acknowledge that we were important and that we needed to have input."

Baptist Memorial, the only hospital that responded to the bid, got the contract. By making employees pay more out-of-pocket if they went elsewhere, coalition members were able to steer their workers and dependents to Baptist and its affiliated network of doctors. Two years later, during a new bidding cycle, all four Memphis-area hospitals bid on the contract. The coalition stayed with Baptist, and in recent years, members have received about a 20% discount in hospital prices.

According to Robert Ellis, vice president and manger of employee benefits at First Tennessee Bank, the coalition was the result of HR executives joining forces in search of a solution to rising health care costs. "Our objective was to have a moderating influence on cost by establishing greater efficiency and a price-competitive hospital market," he says. In doing so, the employers recruited other members, used membership dues to create an annual budget and hired a staff to give guidance to the new coalition.

Today, in addition to influencing competitive prices through open bidding, the business group runs a utilization review program for members that has reduced the use of inappropriate services by their employees. The coalition also established a resource library, and full-time specialists manage employee cases involving home care, substance abuse, psychiatric services and workers' compensation claims. Members purchase these managed-care services from the coalition for an additional fee.

"For every dollar spent in medical costs, First Tennessee Bank has saved between $7 and $9 by using the managed-care services of the coalition," explains Ellis. "And when we save money, our employees save money because they're required to pay a portion of their own health costs."

The Memphis group's success in demanding cost concessions from providers is typical of how coalitions have operated. But the group's focus is changing. As the coalition has grown—there now are 46 companies representing more than 100,000 employees and dependents—members say that their improved purchasing power will lead to a restructuring of the local health care market. More than gaining price reductions, members hope to encourage providers to deliver efficient, high-quality health care to the local community.

There are early indications that this is happening. For example, during the hospital bidding process, Methodist Hospital—Baptist's chief rival—discovered that its costs were 15% to 20% higher than Baptist's. This prompted a productivity drive that included use of a computer program to show doctors how their use of resources varied, even on similar cases. At another local hospital, everything from heart surgery to admissions procedures is undergoing quality review.

COALITIONS CAN INFLUENCE A VARIETY OF HEALTH CARE ISSUES

The results achieved by the Memphis Business Group on Health illustrate the influence that the employers can have when they become involved in activities related to health care at the local level. In fact, many of today's coalitions were formed for the express purpose of influencing local health planning and policy issues.

The Health Care Purchasers Association (HCPA) in Seattle, for example, was established to support health care legislation that's beneficial to employers, and to resist public policy that's detrimental to business interests. More than 100 companies belong to HCPA, and members purchase health benefits for more than 1 million covered lives. This includes companies that are self-insured as well as those that purchase insurance.

"Our objectives are to influence the political process associated with health care and to speak with a more unified voice in the marketplace," says Steve Hill, senior vice president of HR for Weyerhaeuser Co. in Tacoma, Washington. "We believe that the people paying for health care ought to have a larger say in the process."

As a result of the coalition's efforts, state legislation was passed in April that will require all providers of health care services to make data on these services available. These data eventually will become part of a state-wide health-information network that will, among other things, allow employers to gain access to cost and quality information that, in turn, will help them make better-informed benefits and purchasing decisions.

"Imagine what business would be like if it didn't have the latest computer systems to track customers, inventory or quality," says Dorothy Graham, director of HR for Puget Sound Power and Light Co. in Bellevue, Washington. "The health care and insurance industries still operate that way. This information system finally will give employers a basis to judge the value of health care received. That's the only way to get a handle on what we're paying and to work with providers on cost-containment."

Another coalition that has been actively involved in health planning and policy issues is the Greater Detroit Area Health Council. Now 37 years old, it's one of the oldest employer-led health coalitions in the country. Its members include HR representatives from such corporate heavyweights as Ford, Chrysler and General Motors. The organization was established in the 1950s to guide the growth of health care services during that decade's hospital boom. But 10 years ago, faced with a quite different health care market, the council changed its mission to address cost-and-access issues.

Last year, for example, the coalition was extremely vocal in its opposition to a proposed new open-heart-surgery program. Although there were already 28 such programs in Michigan, the chief executive of a Detroit hospital said that his facility needed one to compete. The coalition disagreed. Why? Because heart treatment is expensive, especially in Michigan, which ranks number one in deaths from heart disease. At Detroit Edison, for instance, as much as 25% of benefits costs goes to heart cure.

Believing that runaway replication of medical services drives up costs, the coalition lobbied hard to defeat the hospital's proposal, John Smith Jr., chief executive of General Motors, went so far as to tell Michigan's governor that one of GM's top priorities was to block new heart surgery units. Thanks to the coalition's lobbying efforts, the state's certificate-of-need commission denied the hospital's request.

"If coalitions didn't exists," says James Kenney, president and CEO of the Detroit Coalition, "the business community would be fragmented and inarticulate on the most-important human resources issue of the day."

INTRODUCING COMPETITION INTO THE MARKETPLACE CAN IMPROVE THE QUALITY OF HEALTH CARE

In addition to influencing local health policy, many coalitions are using their members' collective purchasing power to introduce competition in the marketplace—that is, competition based on the quality of health care services delivered, rather than on the quantity. For example, HR professionals who were frustrated with managed care and other ineffective cost-containment techniques founded the Business Health Care Action Group in Minneapolis.

"All of us had used a confrontational approach to managing costs—beat the hell out of the doctors, that kind of thing—which never works in the long term," explains Fred Hamacher, vice president of compensation and benefits for Dayton Hudson Corp, in Minneapolis. "We decided as a group of employers that we needed a system that focused more on quality, because if you buy quality, then cost takes care of itself. We brainstormed ways to get competition into the marketplace and to put some efficiency into the delivery system."

In doing so, Hamacher and his HR colleagues from 13 other local companies spent four hours each week for several months hashing out a common benefit-plan design. The group—which includes large, self-insured employers, such as Norwest, Honeywell Inc., Ceridian Corp. and General Mills—then put its employee health care out to bid, choosing providers not on the basis of cost, but on whether they could demonstrate a commitment to continuous quality improvement. Members were determined not to impose rules on doctors, but instead to purchase care only from an organization that developed and followed its own practice standards and worked to improve overall performance.

Providers were happy about the opportunity to bid on the contract—which currently represents about 6% of the local health care market—because the coalition was asking providers to improve the quality of care on their own. "We didn't want to shoot the bad guy," Hamacher says. "We wanted the physicians to come up with their own best-practice guidelines."

The coalition's combined benefit plan is an option offered to employees in addition to the members' existing benefit plans. Financial incentives make the new plan more attractive, however. Currently, more than 50,000 employees and dependents are participating, but total sign-up could reach 200,000.

At some companies, the new plan is more generous than existing plans, whereas at others, it's more restrictive. At Dayton Hudson, for example, provider choices are more limited under the combined plan, but the amount of covered services has increased. At Norwest, however, employees who choose the new plan now face exclusions based on preexisting conditions, a restriction that isn't part of the company's standard health plan.

But Norwest's Roe emphasizes that plan design is less important than the overall goals of the coalition. "Plan design is an old paradigm," she explains. "In an indemnity world, we focused on deductibles and whether a person was eligible or ineligible for certain treatment services. We're trying to shift a new paradigm in which we can deliver all that's necessary and effective. To do this, we need practice guidelines and outcomes data.

"The most interesting element to me," Roe adds, "is that 14 corporations with different cultures have been able to agree on the importance of collaboration between payers and providers to deliver effective and efficient care."

The coalition's combined benefit plan has been in place only since the first of the year, so it's too early to tell what kind of quality improvements providers will make, and how those improvements, will impact benefit costs. "There was a one-time initial savings of 10% to 14% because of the increased administrative efficiency created by a common plan design," says Bushick. "The real savings remain to be seen. Proof will be borne out over multiple years." (Providers passed on the cost savings of having one plan to employers.)

Another effort to influence the quality and cost of local health care is underway in Cleveland. There, through the Greater Cleveland Health Quality Choice Program, all local hospitals are collecting data on intensive care, acute care and patient satisfaction. Results are soon to be released to local corporate benefits officers. Based on these data, employers will provide incentives to steer employees to the highest-quality hospitals.

The effort was initiated by the Health Action Council of Northeast Ohio. A study in the late 1980s found that employers could fly patients to Minnesota for care at the Mayo Clinic for far less money than it would cost to buy care locally.

According to Tom Roos, director of employee benefits and HRIS for Parker Hannifin Corp. in Cleveland, members of the Health Action Council eventually will use the provider data to make health care purchasing decisions. "In the meantime, a lot of us HR folks are meeting with our peers at local hospitals to learn about the provider side of business, and to teach our hospital friends about the purchasing side. Working together, we're coming up with long-term solutions based on quality." says Roos.

DATA COLLECTION HELPS COALITIONS SELECT THE MOST COST-EFFICIENT HEALTH PLANS

It makes sense that for employers to make purchasing decisions based on quality, they need better information about treatment outcomes. That's why many coalitions place such strong emphasis on data and data collection. Information is one of the keys to reforming the health care system. Without it, health care purchasing will remain a costly guessing game. With it, employers can give their business to physicians, hospitals and health plans that truly offer the best quality at the best price.

HCPA in Seattle is leading the effort to develop an electronic data network that will provide this kind of important information. The coalition received a grant from the Hartford Foundation to prepare the design specifications for a statewide community health management information system (CHMIS). Based on the technology behind ATM bankcards and credit-card validations, the system would track the costs and services of health care providers in the state. A similar system is under development in Memphis.

The cards would give physicians, hospitals, and other providers access to an on-line communications network that could verify benefits eligibility, speed claims and payments and reduce paperwork. With the patient's permission, a physician would have on-line access to the patient's history of illness and to the care given by other providers. Because information on diagnoses, treatment and results would be transmitted through the system, purchasers would be able, over time, to analyze provider performances, as well as other data covering cost, utilization and public health.

"The goal of CHMIS is to have an electronic medical record of sorts," Kunkle explains. "It's an exciting concept in that it will create a paperless trail, which is more efficient and less expensive to administer. The system will promote quality because there will be less confusion, less duplication of services and more information to compare on actual treatment results."

For community health care reform to take root, consumers have to make changes right along with purchasers and providers. That's why, in addition to gathering data to aid in purchasing decision, coalition members throughout the country are using available market data to help employees understand important health care issues.

Members of the Business Health Care Action Group in Minneapolis held focus groups to determine their employee's expectations of the health care system. "At Norwest, the employees' perception was that the more services they utilized, the better their care would be," explains Roe. "This revealed a significant opportunity and challenge to educate consumers on how to use the health care system appropriately."

Similar information was uncovered at Honeywell Inc. in Minneapolis, and it prompted the company to create an employee health-education program that includes courses on health care consumerism. According to John Burns, vice president of health management, Honeywell wanted its employees to understand the complexity of the health care system and their ability to play an active role in receiving necessary, appropriate and affordable care.

"The main points we try to cover are 1) that the health care system is extremely complex, and 2) that there's wide variation in practice styles among providers," Burns explains. "We want employees to understand the need to request services on the basis of quality and effectiveness." Honeywell's consumer-education courses are voluntary, but the company offers cash incentives for employees to participate. At last count, about 65% of its work force had participated in the program.

As quality data become available in Minneapolis, Honeywell will share the information with employees, so that they can choose providers who offer the most-effective treatment. "Employee communication is a critical part of our health care strategy," Burns says.

HR HAS TWO ROLES IN MAKING HEALTH CARE COALITIONS WORK

In the final analysis, HR professionals are influencing community-based health care reform in two ways. The first is by joining with HR representatives from other companies to form health care coalitions. "Coalitions are broad and flexible," says Morrow of William M. Mercer. "All you need is a de facto coalition, meaning that you don't need to incorporate or even hire a staff. You just get a bunch of employers together in a room and get them to agree on common objectives. Announce those objectives to the world in some sort of manifesto, and then sit back and wait for the world to beat a path to your door."

Forming a coalition is relatively easy, agrees Roos. All it takes is HR people and others who are concerned about health care issues to get together and talk about their common interest. Chances are, HR people in many communities have been doing this for years, he says.

In the early stages of coalition-building, members will be concerned primarily with recruiting other businesses, and with identifying goals for the group. Is the coalition going to focus on legislative issues, for example, or are members interested in forming a collective purchasing association? These questions need to be answered before an action plan can be developed. Once this occurs, most coalition find it necessary to organize as nonprofit corporations, and hire a staff to perform administrative duties and to represent the coalition at public meetings.

For those coalitions in which a staff and incorporation become necessary, the budget usually is made up of dues charged to coalition members based on the number of employees they have. Dues typically range from $1.50 to $5.00 per employee, putting the total membership costs for a given company at anywhere between $500 and $18,000 per year.

In an incorporated coalition that has staff members, HR professionals continue to provide guidance by sitting on the organization's board of directors. In most coalitions, board members are nominated and elected by their peers. The top-ranking HR professional in a member company is most likely to be nominated, along with chief financial officers, and in some cases, the CEO. Board members, on average, spend five hours a month on routine coalition meetings.

In most coalitions, there are also ongoing committees that perform specific duties, such as developing a common benefit plan, preparing a request for proposal for employee health care services or monitoring state legislation related to health reform. Because the time needed for participation on these committees is much greater than that required for board meetings—up to half day each week as found in Minneapolis—it's typically junior-level HR staffers from member companies who serve on the committees.

For HR professionals who are interested in pursuing coalition activities in their communities, Ellis has this advice: "Just do it!" Visit other coalitions to see how they operate, and make the commitment to spend time on developing the coalition's objectives," he says. "Health care issues are extremely complex, and we don't need to pretend to understand all of them."

The second way that HR is influencing the community delivery of health care is by taking the information it gains from coalition efforts, educating employees about their role in purchasing decisions, and giving them incentives through the benefits system to use only the most-effective providers. In the long run, it's the consumers using the health care system who will determine whether reform efforts at the community level will succeed.

What impact will federal health care reform have on the coalition movement? Not much, at least not at any time soon. But don't throw up your hands prematurely, Kunkle cautions. "HR professionals have been negotiating benefits on behalf of their employees for years, and are therefore in the best position to create models for reform that work. From a federal standpoint, no legislation will be passed quickly. The more coalitions that get started and the more they accomplish, the greater the likelihood that we may see a local, community-driven solution evolve over time."

Adds Morrow, "I would say that if the government acts prematurely or overregulates the delivery system of the insurance industry in an attempt to solve problems that are solvable through other means, they will kill the developing coalition movement. The private sector, with very little fanfare, is solving the health care problem for government. The greatest fear we have is that government will intervene prematurely, in its usual clumsy, heavy-handed way, in an attempt to solve problems that already are in the process of being solved.

"For HR professionals, my advice would be to hang in there," he adds. "The private sector, working together with providers and managed-care organizations, is in the process of providing this country with a solution to all the things we've been frustrated about."

Part 4

FLEXIBLE BENEFITS

16.   Quaker Oats' Employees Shape New Plan

The best way to create a benefits package that will appeal to employees is to have the employees create it themselves. Chicago-based Quaker Oats Company found this to be true when they involved employees in the development of the company's new flexible benefits program.

According to Melanie Pheatt, Quaker Oats' benefits manager, the company set out to design the new package to improve benefits value to employees, to facilitate costs containment for the company, and to promote an employee ownership philosophy that would encourage employees to buy into the program. Ms. Pheatt discussed the company's efforts at the annual meeting of the Employers' Council on Flexible Compensation in Washington, D.C.

To begin the process of designing the new program, Quaker conducted a survey of employees' perceptions of how important it is to receive benefits versus cash payments. According to the survey, a total of 3 percent of the respondents felt that receiving benefits was much more important than receiving cash, 13 percent said benefits were somewhat more important, 64 percent said they were as important, 17 percent said benefits were somewhat less important, and 1 percent said they were much less important.

Survey participants also were asked to convey their perceptions of the quality and competitiveness of the benefits offered by Quaker. Most respondents gave the company's existing benefits packages average to above-average rankings; however, many also indicated that they desired added flexibility.

SOURCE: CHARLES D. SPENSER & ASSOCIATES, INC., PUBLISHERS.

EMPLOYEE DESIGN TEAM

The company embarked on the task of creating its new flex plan by forming, through a "job posting" effort, an employee design team, according to Ms. Pheatt. "We wanted employees who were aware of other employees' needs, and we had to let them know how big of a job they were in for," she said. The benefits department ultimately received 40 applications from employees who wanted to participate on the team; 15 individuals were selected, including only two benefits department representatives.

The team, composed of employees recruited from different work units, pay levels, family backgrounds, and age groups, met for ten full-day meetings to develop a vision statement and process guidelines. "We got a diverse group, with a nice demographic mix," Ms. Pheatt said.

To begin the design process, the team looked at the results of a survey on benefits preferences of those employees eligible for enrollment in a flex plan, as well as a survey on work and family concerns.

To identify employee needs, Ms. Pheatt said, the team used a role-playing exercise, wherein an employee would play the part of another employee seeking something specific from the benefits plan that is different than that sought by his or her coworkers.

The team also held a brainstorming session during which, according to Ms. Pheatt, members papered meeting room walls with plan ideas ranging from "pet insurance to dating services."

Next, the group honed its options to a few designs that "we knew we could pay for," Ms. Pheatt said. After previewing the designs to management and to focus groups, the team's product was refined to a final design and resubmitted to management for review and approval. The process, Ms. Pheatt said, began in February of 1992, an the plan received management approval in July of that year.

The tougher issues the team faced were whether to base benefits on need or on total compensation; how to reallocate current benefit spending to provide equity to employees, such as those with single coverage; how to identify waste and improve value; how to create a plan that was simple, understandable, and usable; and how to deal with adverse selection, tax and legal limitations, and administrative concerns.

NEW PLAN

Under the new plan, employees can accumulate flex credits in a number of ways. Universal credits provide each employee with a flat allocation; medical and dental credits are based on the coverage category an employee selects; and health life-style credits can be earned when employees pledge to cease activities that may be health-adverse, such as smoking and/or drinking to excess.

Among other changes Quaker made to its flex plan were greater discounts on vision care, more choice in its life insurance and long term disability options, and a 25 percent company match for employee contributions to dependent care spending accounts.

To gauge the success of the effort, Quaker surveyed employees on their perceptions of the new program. Figure 1 below shows how employees compared the new plan, prior to implementation, with their current benefits. As to the flexibility presented by the plan, nearly nine out of ten employees responded that they were in favor of the additional choicemaking allowed under the program, and three-fifths said that choice was the most appealing feature to them about the program.

To communicate facets of the program, Quaker asked members of the design team to "star" in informational videos that would be shown to employees. Also, 250 employees were trained as enrollment counselors and leaders of informational sessions. "Watching those people was one of the most exciting things for me in this project. Their peers felt very comfortable asking them questions and their enthusiasm was contagious," Ms. Pheatt said.

For Quaker, developing the new program served several purposes—it responded to the diverse needs of its employee population, provided industry- and market-competitive benefits, increased employees' awareness of benefits costs, provided tax-effective benefits, and helped manage costs effectively.

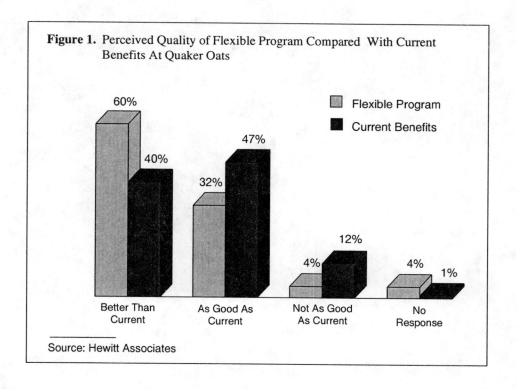

Figure 1. Perceived Quality of Flexible Program Compared With Current Benefits At Quaker Oats

Source: Hewitt Associates

"Employees are able to look at the price tag of everything they're interested in buying," Ms. Pheatt said.

Overall, the program increased employees' perceptions of the value of their benefits and established a new role for them in shaping their own and the company's benefits plan.

17. Optional Flex:
How Southwest Wooed its Union Workers to Join
Rebecca Morrow

Like virtually all companies, Southwest Airlines (Dallas) has seen its workforce become more diversified and its health care benefits costs rise alarmingly in recent years. After analyzing what to do, Southwest became convinced that introducing a flex plan made sense.

Southwest has taken the unique approach of making its flexible benefits plan optional—yet it still boasts a participation rate of more than 68 percent. Moreover, the company has thus far avoided the need for any significant cost sharing with employees.

The optional plan was a good idea in many respects. If the company had not structured its flex plan this way, it would have had to reopen contract negotiations with the eight unions that represent about 90 percent of its workforce, which in 1989, the year flex was introduced, numbered 8,272.

And the airline's flexible benefits plan, which is known as BenefitsPlus, had to be alluring enough to attract union members away from their existing medical plan. That, notes Libby Sartain, director of benefits and compensation, was crucial for generating the savings the company needed.

Thanks to a well-designed plan—and an aggressive communications campaign—enrollment in Southwest's flex plan reached 40 percent in September 1991, only 18 months after it was implemented. By April 30, 1992, enrollment had reached 55 percent, and by April 1993, it had jumped to 66 percent. Southwest now has about 12,000 employees.

Reprinted with permission from IOMA, Institute of Management & Administration, Inc., IOMA's Report on *Managing Benefit Plans*, "Optional Flex: How Southwest Wooed its Union Workers to Join," by Rebecca Morrow, October 1993, pages 6, 12–15.

PLAN DESIGN

In a nutshell, Southwest's medical coverage consists of five options: its regular medical plan—which has a $200/$300 individual/family deductible and 80/20 coverage—and the four plans available through its flex program (Table 1):

- Plan A offers a low deductible ($150/$300) with network coverage at 90/10 and out-of-network coverage at 75/25. The out-of-pocket maximum is $1,150 for in-network coverage and $2,875 for out-of-network coverage. The plan also includes preventive care (physical exams costing up to $150 annually and a mammogram and Pap smear for employees and/or spouses) and new- and well-baby care.
- Plan B, with the same deductible and out-of-network coverage as Plan A, pays 85 percent of in-network provider visits. The out-of-pocket maximum, while the same for out-of-network care, is somewhat higher for in-network care: $1,725. Preventive care is only offered for employees and spouses.
- Plans C and D both allow employees to select their physicians (no network providers are offered) but, beyond that, differ markedly.

Plan C has a deductible of $500/$1,000, 80/20 coverage, and employee/spouse preventive coverage. The out-of-pocket maximum is $5,500.

Plan D has a lower deductible ($200/$300), but only covers 20 percent of all medical costs and has no out-of-pocket maximum. Nor does it offer any preventive care. (For a breakout of how many employees enroll in each type of medical plan, see Table 1 below).

Other Flex Offerings

The company's BenefitsPlus plan also offers dental care, vision care, dependent life insurance, two long-term disability plans, multiple life insurance, accidental death and disability pay, and two pre-tax spending accounts.

Table 1. Employee Enrollment in Southwest Airlines' Flexible Benefits Plans

Plan	Enrollment
Plan A	1,277
Plan B	6,171
Plan C	224
Plan D	539
Plan R*	4,123
	12,334 (w/o COBRA)
	135 (COBRA)
Total	12,469

*Regular medical plan

Communication

Although design was critical to the plan's success, it was not the only reason the majority of Southwest's workers selected flex as their benefits delivery system. Communication was also key.

"Our challenge was to attract the employees to the BenefitsPlus plan voluntarily," notes Sartain. "And because our workforce is, literally, on the move, we had to come up with an effective way to communicate."

Southwest Airline's flex information blitz consisted of five parts:

1. A newspaper called BenefitsPlus Today, modeled after USA Today, contained news and feature articles about the new plan.
2. A 35-minute video, formatted like a talk show, also included Southwest Airlines commercials.
3. Training sessions at the company's various U.S. locations.
4. Updates about the flex program in the airline's newsletter.
5. Postcards mailed to employee's homes.

According to Sartain, Southwest's efforts to educate staff about the flex plan, and benefits in general, resulted in an initial plan enrollment of 25 percent. And she believes it would have exceeded that had the program not begun mid-year, when many of Southwest's employees had already met their deductible under the old program and didn't want to switch.

Cost Savings

The average medical claim cost per employee was 8.7 percent lower in flex than in the regular medical plan in 1990, 18.2 percent lower in 1991, and 29 percent lower in 1992. Flex costs are estimated to be 34 percent lower for 1993.

New Employees.

Persuading new workers to join BenefitsPlus is getting easier, according to Sartain. Because many come from companies with considerable flexibility in their benefits, they appreciate the choice afforded by Southwest's plan.

Continuing Communications

To keep health care costs in line, Southwest looks for ways to make employees savvy health care consumers. During the last quarter of 1992, the airline launched an education program designed to get employees to use their health plans—flex or otherwise—more wisely.

"We wanted our employees to recognize that it isn't some insurance company paying for their health care benefits—Southwest is paying for them," Sartain explains.

A team at Southwest designed the campaign, then turned it over to a consultant for execution. Each quarter, the airline's facilities are decorated with a new poster that makes a salient point about the value of their health care benefits. Reinforcing the message, a small reproduction of the poster—with more detailed information on the back—is sent to each employee.

The posters are engaging and lighthearted—but each delivers a serious message:

"We could buy 37,041 six-packs of beer with what we pay for one day of health care. The plane fact: health care costs are attacking Southwest," declares one poster.

Another poster alerts employees to simple actions they can take to help save the company money without hurting themselves:

"We spend nearly $2 million a year on health care paperwork. And we pay $7.77 every time a claim is processed—no matter the amount of your medical claim. That's the same $7.77 to file for a $10 or a $100 claim. So it makes sense to cut the paperwork and cost by sending several claims at once, such as all the claims for one illness or to meet your deductible."

While definitive numbers from Southwest's year-end 1992 communication campaign are not yet in, Sartain has already noticed a drop in utilization. "So far we're spending less than we budgeted this year for health care. We thought we'd be up about 14 percent, but right now, after half a year's data, we're only up about 10 percent.

"While I can't be conclusive about it yet," she says, "the trend is that utilization is down."

Part 5

SELF INSURANCE

18.   Trends Toward Self-Insurance and Stop-Loss Coverage

Steven Schoen, FSA, CEBS   Marie Klinkmueller

Smaller companies are saving money through self-insurance, but the risks are greater because they lack the deep pockets of their bigger business brothers.

In the early 1970s, employers typically provided health benefits to their employees by purchasing fully insured group health coverage from an insurance carrier. Today, more than half of all employers providing health benefits to employees self-insure, according to the Health Insurance Association of America.

This self-insurance trend has been apparent since the passage of the Employee Retirement Income Security Act in 1974. And in recent years, there was rapid growth in the number of firms self-insuring their medical plans as more employers looked for ways to control skyrocketing medical costs and to meet the demands of the economic slowdown.

The move toward self-insurance began with the country's largest employers, and today the vast majority of employers with over 5,000 employees self-insure their group medical coverage. While the market for self-insurance may be reaching saturation, growth continues to be largely attributable to smaller firms making the move to self-insurance, since most large employers already self-fund. This was especially clear in 1991 when the percentage of self-insured employers with fewer than 1,000 employees grew from 44 percent to 48 percent, according to Foster Higgins.

New Foster Higgins data for 1992 indicate that growth in the number of firms that self-insure reached only 3 percent between 1991 and 1992. In comparison, the number of firms choosing self-insurance grew at about 6.5 percent a year on average over the six-year period between 1987 and 1992. At its peak in 1990, this growth rate reached 13 percent, according to the Foster Higgins 1991 Health Care Benefits Survey. This recent slowdown in the number of firms moving to self-funding may be an indication that the market is reaching saturation because most employers that can successfully self-insure have already done so.

In addition, the success of many managed care programs in controlling benefit costs has created a viable alternative for employers whose main reason for self-funding is cost control. Finally, ERISA protection for self-funded plans has come under fire both in the name of health reform at the state and federal level and in response to the highly publicized H&H Music Company case, in which the employer reduced a $1 million lifetime cap on health care benefits to $5,000 after an employee with AIDS had already filed a claim. This perceived weakening of the law that protects one of the primary benefits of self-insurance— freedom from state benefit mandates—may also be a concern for employers considering self-funding.

STOP-LOSS INSURANCE TRENDS

This shift to self-insurance has brought about a significant increase in the use of stop-loss insurance to protect these businesses from unexpected claims.

The trend toward self-insurance among smaller employers has also resulted in many stop-loss carriers making coverage available to smaller and smaller firms. For example, while many carriers used to market only to firms with 200 or more employees, now many offer coverage to firms with as few as 100 employees. Some companies now even target firms with as few as 25 to 50 employees, a market that was virtually nonexistent only a few years ago.

And while some types of businesses are more likely to self-insure their medical plans, the concept has penetrated virtually all industries. According to Foster Higgins, the energy/petroleum and consumer products industries are the largest users with 83 percent and 78 percent of firms, respectively self-insuring. The average percentage of firms self-insuring in all industries in 1992 is estimated to be 67 percent.

Similarly, self-insurance has not been limited to specific geographical locations. The funding method has been chosen by employers in all regions of the country, although companies in the country's mid-section are more likely to self-insure than those located on either coast, according to the 1991 Foster Higgins Benefit Survey.

WHY SELF-INSURE?

The primary reason employers are choosing to self-insure their group medical benefits is that they can save money. Annual medical expenses per employee averaged $3,469 in 1991 for self-insured plans, compared with $3,736 for insured plans, according to Foster Higgins.

With an increase of just over 12 percent from 1990 to 1991, self-insured plans have also experienced a slightly slower cost increase than fully insured plans, which averaged over 13.5 percent.

In addition to cutting benefit costs, self-insurance also allows employers to retain control over the plan benefits they offer, since self-insured plans are not subject to state benefit mandates. Here's a breakdown of some of the reasons businesses are moving in increasing numbers to self-insure their group medical coverage:

- *Control plan design and cost.* Many states mandate that medical insurance must cover certain specified services, but self-insured plans are exempt from these mandates. This is especially important to employers with locations in several states. Freedom from the packaged products of insurers and state regulation allows employers to customize benefit plans to meet the unique needs of their workforce.
- *Avoid insurance costs by retaining risk.* Rather than paying out premium to an insurer, which includes a profit margin as well as a fee for taking the risk, employers can budget for anticipated medical claims, taking on the risk that claims will exceed the amount budgeted.
- *Retain financial control.* By funding at the time of the claim rather than in anticipation of the claim through premium payments, employers gain the "float" on funds budgeted for medical claims payment, and increase their financial control.
- *Avoid premium tax.* In most states insurers pay a premium tax of several percentage points. This cost is passed on to employers. Self-insured plans are not subject to these premium taxes.
- *Reduce administrative costs.* By using third-party administrative services or retaining administrative services in-house, employers generally realize substantial cost savings because they will more closely analyze their administrative needs and pay for only the services they believe they truly need.

TYPES OF STOP-LOSS COVERAGE

Stop-loss coverage helps protect self-insured employers from the financial burden of large, unexpected claims. Self-insured employers face two types of risk: higher than expected claims from an individual plan participant, and higher than expected overall plan utilization.

The two corresponding types of stop-loss coverage handle these risks. "Specific" or "individual" coverage provides protection against a large medical claim for any one individual. "Aggregate" coverage protects against excessive total claims against the employer's self-insured medical plan.

Specific coverage is more commonly purchased by employers than aggregate coverage. In 1991, while 85 percent of the self-insured employers surveyed for the 1991 Foster Higgins Health Care Benefits Survey purchased specific stop-loss coverage, 65 percent purchased aggregate coverage. This is due in part to the fact that most employers' plans offer medical benefits with lifetime maximums of $1 million per individual. Catastrophic claims resulting form organ transplants, cancer and heart disease, premature births, and head injuries from accidents can easily exceed $100,000 and may have the potential to reach the $1 million level. Specific coverage helps limit the large dollar payments and keeps the employers' annual payments more manageable.

However, smaller employers—those with fewer than 1,000 employees—are more likely to purchase both specific and aggregate coverage since they do not normally have the funds available to pay larger than expected claims against their plan, either from an individual employee or dependent, or from the total of all participants in the plan.

Specific Coverage

Specific stop-loss coverage features include:

- A range of deductibles for employees and dependents;
- A lifetime maximum of $1 million (higher limits are occasionally available); and
- Flexible plan reimbursement options.

Typically, carriers offer four types of reimbursement options:

1. An incurred and paid basis;
2. An incurred and paid basis with a run-in;
3. A paid basis; and
4. An incurred and paid basis with an extension period.

The incurred and paid basis only recognizes claims both incurred and paid within a benefit year. Since medical benefits are typically paid two to three months after the date of incurral, this reimbursement option excludes claims that were incurred before the start of the benefit year. A paid basis contract recognizes all claims paid in a benefit year, even if they were incurred before the start of the benefit year. Therefore, a paid basis contract is more expensive than an incurred and paid basis contract.

Run-in options of one, two, or three months recognize claims incurred one, two, or three months prior to a benefit year if they are paid in the benefit year. Thus, an incurred and paid basis with a run-in costs less than a pure paid basis but greater than an incurred and paid basis contract. Finally, the extension period, typically three months, covers claims incurred in a benefit year but paid within the three-month period after the end of the benefit year. Carriers rarely offer a paid basis contract in the first year of specific coverage. In renewal years, however, a paid basis is very common. Depending on the employer's situation, any of these four options may best suit their needs.

Aggregate Coverage

Aggregate coverage features can include:

- A monthly or annual premium payment;
- Corridors of about 20 percent or 25 percent; and
- Flexible claims reimbursement options.

The corridor is the amount of claims above the expected claim level paid by the employer before the aggregate coverage reimbursements are made. The aggregate reimbursement options are similar to the specific options except a paid-basis is often offered in the first year of coverage (i.e., all claims paid in a benefit year are recognized no matter when the claims were incurred). Some carriers modify the pure paid basis in the first year by limiting the amount of claims incurred prior to the effective date of the coverage.

Another type of coverage offered by some stop-loss carriers is a medical conversion privilege, which allows employers to make health insurance available to individuals who are no longer covered under their self-insured plan. With this feature, employees and their dependents are offered an individual medical conversion policy. This conversion privilege is less common today because the need is satisfied by continuation rights now available under the federal COBRA regulation. COBRA provides continuation rights to employees and their dependents for 18 to 36 months, depending on the circumstances involved.

Some stop-loss carriers can also offer employers the option of packaging their stop-loss insurance with group life or long-term disability insurance products, with the benefit of discounted rates for consolidating their group insurance coverage.

THIRD PARTY ADMINISTRATOR'S ROLE

While the combination of self-insurance and stop-loss insurance can help employers save a significant amount of money, there are risks involved. And since each business is unique, there are few set rules about the amount or type of stop-loss coverage a particular employer should purchase.

A third party administrator (TPA) or stop-loss insurance broker has the expertise to help the employer assess both the carrier offering the stop-loss coverage and the insurance contract itself. With regards to the carrier, the employer and TPA should check, among other things, the company's reputation,

history, financial standing, and ratings from industry analysts such as Standard
& Poor's and the A.M. Best Company.

With regard to the contract, the carrier can place limits on the claims covered
under various contract provisions. So it is important that the employer review the
contract carefully with its TPA before purchasing the coverage. Some of the facts
to check include what type of claim reimbursement option is involved, what the
dollar limits of the coverage are, what the carrier's pricing philosophy is, and
what types of discounts are available.

Self-insurance and stop-loss coverage have become the rule rather than the
exception, and use of these cost-saving tools is becoming common among smaller
and smaller companies. However, the risks of self-insurance can be particularly
high for a small business with less of a financial cushion to protect company
assets. That's why employers considering a move to self-insurance must do their
homework to determine the right self-insurance/stop-loss package for their
particular operations.

19.   Retrospective Insurance Premiums: The Law Favors the Policyholder

Eugene R. Anderson   Glenn F. Fields

If a company buys insurance policies with a retrospective premium feature, its risk manager should be aware that the law protects the policyholder's interests. Do not hesitate to question the insurer about settlement of claims, its reserves, or any other problems with "retro" adjustments and bills for added premiums.

Insurance policies, particularly workers' compensation insurance policies, frequently require the policyholder to pay additional premiums based upon the insurer's outlay to claimants. Even more significant, many of the policies base these additional or retrospective premiums on reserves—the amount the insurance company estimates in advance of any actual payment that will ultimately be paid to the claimant. The insurer thus has the use of the policyholder's money for the years the claim is pending. Such insurance policies are called "loss sensitive" and have "retrospective premium adjustments." These adjustments can be made on either a "paid-loss" basis or on an "incurred-loss" (reserve) basis, the latter of which risk managers should be particularly concerned about.

The premium adjustments, or requests for further premium, often come as a severe jolt to policyholders. The anomaly is that the bigger the reserves and losses, the bigger the premium and the bigger the insurance company's profits. Since the insurer has exclusive control over loss payments and reserves, it can control the amount and timing of additional premiums.

Some, but not all, insurance policies with retro premiums have "stop-loss" or loss limitation provisions that limit the policyholder's additional premiums should a particular loss or its aggregate losses go above the "stop-loss."

Reprinted with permission from *Risk Management,* Eugene R. Anderson and Glenn F. Fields, Nov. 1993.

The courts recognize the fact that the insurer is paying every claim below the retro loss limitation (if there is one) with the policyholder's money. Indeed, a Kansas court (in Transit Casualty Co. vs. Topeka Transportation Co., 1983) stated that, in a retrospective premium context, "when the insurer settled a claim it did so with the insured's money." The courts in recent years have said much more than this in favor of the policyholder who is asked to pay a retrospective premium.

DUTIES TOWARD THE POLICYHOLDER

The key aspect of recent court decisions regarding retrospective premiums is that the insurance company has certain duties toward the policyholder who is paying the additional premium. These duties stem mainly from the fact that the retrospective premium feature involves a possible conflict of interest between the insurer and the policyholder. The Delaware Supreme Court, in Corrado Brothers Inc. vs. Twin City Fire Insurance Co., 1989, noted that there is a potential for conflict between the insurance company and the policyholder if the settlement of a claim imposes consequences, such as an additional premium payment, upon the policyholder. If a company's policy has a retro premium, that company is, in reality, paying for most settlements made by the insurer. Therefore, the policyholder is better off having claims paid at a low figure.

All retro premium formulas have "add-ons" to "compensate" the insurer. These add-ons can be as much as 40 percent of the insurance company's reserve or payment on a claim. Given that the policyholder pays these add-ons in addition to the amount of the actual paid losses and reserves, the insurer has an incentive to settle higher so it can charge that policyholder more add-ons. At the very least, the insurer lacks the usual incentive to minimize loss payments. The conflict is obvious.

If the additional premium charged to the policyholder was dollar for dollar the amount the insurer paid to the claimant, the problems would be minimized. However, this is not the case. Insurance companies benefit from higher losses in three ways. First, there are the add-ons—if the insurer pays a claimant one dollar, the insurer will charge a retro premium of as much as $1.40. Second, incurred loss retrospective premiums are based upon the amount the insurer "reserves" for future payment. Thus, an insurance company charging $1.40 for a $1.00 reserve has the present use of $1.40 to cover a claim it may not pay for several years. Third, the same reserves also go into the policyholder's experience rating. This fact usually leads to an increase in premium at renewal time for the policy. Thus, overreserving gives the insurer a "double dip"—more of the policyholder's money to use in the present and a higher "standard" premium in the future.

This conflict of interest is the reason the insurance company has duties toward its policyholders. For example, insurers have a duty to exercise good faith when paying claims under retro policies. The Illinois Court of Appeals in National Surety Corp. vs. Fast Motor Service, 1991, has ruled in this regard. Other courts have echoed the Illinois decision. A key aspect of the duty of good faith—as it relates to retro policies—is that the economic decisions of the insurer have economic ramifications for the policyholder. In other words, the insurer should be responsible to its policyholders since it is spending their money. And this is particularly important in situations where the more the insurer spends of this money, the greater its profits.

Courts have also ruled that insurers have a duty to investigate claims paid under retro policies. The Supreme Court of Minnesota, in Transport Indemnity Co. vs. Dahlen Transport Inc., 1968, noted that the policyholder with a retrospective premium has delegated the duty to investigate claims to the insurance company. An important element of the duty to investigate is that the insurer alone has the information to determine the soundness and validity of the reserves, the claims and the settlements. The insurer must act in good faith because the policyholder simply lacks the legal right, the facts and the resources needed to investigate and evaluate claims.

THE BURDEN OF PROOF

Insurance companies must meet a "reasonableness test" when they settle claims under policies having a retrospective premium feature. Indeed, the burden of proof is on the insurer, not the policyholder, to show that settlements are reasonable. In this regard, the Delaware Supreme Court (in the Corrado decision) stated that the burden is on the insurance company to demonstrate "that it acted reasonably and in good faith." At least some of the insurers some of the time are aware of their duties. In one of its briefs in the Corrado case, Twin City (a member of the ITT Hartford Insurance Group) stated: "It is admitted, however, that Hartford's right to recover is conditioned upon a showing that it acted in good faith in settling the claim and that the settlement of the claim was reasonable." Here we have an insurer admitting to its duty of good faith, to its burden of proof and to the reasonableness test.

WHAT THE RISK MANAGER SHOULD KNOW

Knowing that the law is on the policyholder's side, risk managers may next wonder what they should be aware of regarding retrospective premiums. What problems could arise? First of all, watch out for the insurance company settling claims just at, or close to, the loss limitation within the retro. If your company's policy has a $200,000 loss limitation, the insurer gets more premium dollars and more add-ons by reserving or settling a claim at $200,000 rather than at $100,000.

Insurance companies may make generous settlements to avoid risking their exposure for amounts in excess of the loss limitation. An insurer knows that there is a risk that a larger payment may have to be made to the claimant if a case is contested. Also, it knows that larger payments in excess of the loss limitation would be made with the insurance company's money, not the policyholder's. It is a gamble, since the claimant might lose his or her case, resulting in a savings both to the policyholder and to the insurer. However, the insurance company might decide not to gamble with its money and pay the claimant a "beefed-up" settlement with the policyholder's money to close the claim. Risk managers should be cautious about this scenario. Risk managers should check their company's loss runs to determine whether too many claims are being reserved or settled at or just below the loss limitation. Risk managers have a right to demand information from their insurance company!

Risk managers should also look at the "names" of all the newly opened claims, and investigate those claims involving the names of claimants they do not recognize. Do not accept claims with the name "Unknown." Once again, request supporting documentation from the insurance company.

Beware of reserves set at a figure larger than the average for a similar type of claim. This situation may occur if, for example, a company has a number of back injury claims. There is an average figure that the insurer tends to use for newly opened back injury cases in a given geographic area at a given point in time. Risk managers who are concerned about the size of the reserves for newly opened claims should speak first with their colleagues in the industry, brokers or risk management consultants—then with the insurance company.

THE INCREASED LIMITS PROBLEM

Everyone has received holiday or birthday gifts he or she did not like. Remember the purple necktie covered with green fish? Policyholders may receive unwanted gifts, too. Risk managers should check their companies' records on older and current liability policies. Suppose an older general liability policy had per occurrence limits of $250,000, an aggregate of $2 million and a retro (still open) with no loss limitation. Make sure that the policy limits were not suddenly, inadvertently "increased" to, say, $500,000 per occurrence. If this policy had to cover (for example) only three large occurrences, without ever being exhausted, then the retro premium would be higher than it would have been before the "gift." In other words, $1,500,000 \times 1.4$ is larger than $750,000 \times 1.4$.

Watch out for the assignment of a claim (especially a paid loss) to an improper line of insurance. Was a workers' compensation claim assigned as a general liability claim or vice versa? Was a premises-operations bodily injury claim wrongly assigned as a products bodily injury claim? Improper assignment of claims can adversely affect a risk manager's ability to access his or her excess insurance coverage. In other words, the company's underlying coverage, due to error, may not be exhausted. So, review the firm's loss runs—for older policy years as well as for the present period.

Also watch out for the assignment of a claim to a policy year in which the retro is still open. Insurers are inclined to assign claims—particularly multi-year losses—to years that have an open retro rather than to a year with a closed retro or no retro.

SETTLING DISPUTES

When a policyholder is settling a dispute with an insurance company, it is always better to settle net of the retro. Policyholders have been surprised to find that after reaching an agreement with an insurance company pursuant to which the policyholder is to receive $1.00, the insurer then sends a bill for up to $1.40 (the settlement amount plus the retro-adjustment). if your company cannot settle net of retro, then agree in advance on the amount and method of retro chargeback. If the company is not in litigation with its insurer, then the risk manager should speak with the insurer about the retro. Giving an insurance company complete freedom on a retro chargeback could mean that the settlement could ultimately cost your company more than it receives from the insurer.

ADDITIONAL CONCERNS

Beware of retro chargebacks of a "one occurrence" loss being classified by the insurer as multiple occurrences. Once again the law is on the policyholder's side. Certain groups of claims, such as asbestos cases, are usually viewed by the courts as a single occurrence. This results in a single retro charge and the policyholder immediately reaching the loss limitation. if, on the other hand, such claims are treated as multiple occurrences, then the loss limitation for each of the many claims would probably not be exceeded. Instead of receiving any "real" indemnity after a single loss limitation has been reached, the policyholder would pay for all of the claims when it pays its retro premium. If multiple claims result from one common cause, it is usually better to have these treated as a single occurrence. This will reach a single loss limit and result in a larger amount of indemnity flowing to the policyholder, with a much reduced retro chargeback.

Furthermore, risk managers need to be wary of sets of loss runs from the same insurance company prepared within a few months of one another, covering the same policies but giving highly conflicting data. Perhaps the conflicting reports came from different insurance company data centers. Check into it. The policyholder has a right to get an accurate report.

Also, beware of routine mathematical errors. This may seem obvious, but remember that errors in calculations are common. Do not assume every retro adjustment is accurate. In fact, make certain the actual adjustment was done and that the "adjustment" is not merely a bill. Check the math on the losses, and always check the figures to make certain that the appropriate return premium has been collected. One number out of place could cost a policyholder thousands of dollars.

Retrospective premium agreements involve complex formulas. Risk managers should make certain they understand whether, for example, defense costs are to be included in both the premium calculations and the loss limitation for each occurrence. Check with an insurance consultant or attorney before putting a retro program into place. He or she might be able to negotiate a claim-size agreement with the insurer. Such an agreement states the maximum amount at which an insurer can settle any claim without the policyholder's authority. Indeed, risk managers may wish to check with these professionals in later years about monitoring claims handling. These consultants may, for example, be able to negotiate for a reduction of certain reserves that the risk manager believes to be too high. Additionally, risk managers are advised to meet with their insurers periodically to review retro calculations and claims data.

If a company has an insurance policy with a retrospective premium feature, the law is on the policyholder's side—the insurance company has certain duties toward you, the policyholder. So stop, look and crunch those numbers. It's your money!

20. Flex and Self-Insurance: Third Party Administrator Issues

John Haslinger   Donna Sheerin

Hiring the right TPA is the key to successfully combining two of the major cost-cutting trends in benefits design today, self-insurance and flexible benefits programs. A flex TPA must be capable of the more complex tasks involved in handling flex benefits, as well as providing the normal services required by self-insured plans. Employers implementing self-insured flex plans need to understand the necessary requirements so they choose their flex TPA wisely.

This article addresses an important decision facing any employer that has decided to self-insure its health and welfare program and administer its flexible benefits plan via a third party administrator (TPA). If handled correctly, that decision—selecting a flex TPA—involves a number of important issues that must be considered and decided upon within the context of the self-insured firm's objectives, plan provisions, and budget.

Following a background section on the increasing use of self-insurance, the article discusses the following issues that employers should consider when choosing a flexible benefits TPA:

- TPA services available
- Administrative considerations
- System requirements
- Legal/regulatory requirements
- Implementation

John A. Haslinger is a Principal and serves as Director of Health and Welfare Administrative Consulting Services and **Donna Sheerin** is an Assistant Benefit Consultant at Buck Consultants, Secaucus, NJ. (201) 902-2300.

209

A short conclusion then summarizes the most crucial aspects of this important decision.

THE MOVE TO SELF-INSURANCE

Health and welfare benefits long ago ceased to be a "fringe." Today, they are clearly a significant portion of an employee's total compensation and of an employer's human resources (HR) budget. It is not surprising, therefore, that employers have focused increased attention on better managing the costs associated with these benefits.

Over time, it has become clear that self-insuring presents an opportunity to reduce costs, improve administrative efficiency, and customize administrative services to each employer's needs. Increasingly, employers of all sizes have moved toward self-insuring the risk associated with their benefit plans, especially their health care plans.

The move toward self-insurance was initially fueled by two factors:

1. **Lower costs.** A number of the elements that comprise the cost of health and welfare benefits may be reduced or eliminated by self-insuring a plan.
2. **ERISA preemption of state regulations.** State regulations are preempted when an employer makes the choice to insure its own benefits. For employers that are operating in several states with regulated mandated benefits, self-insuring their benefits eases the extra administrative burden of adhering to the various state regulations.

In the broadest terms, there are three elements that comprise the cost of employee benefits:

1. **Paid claims.** Paid claims make up the greatest component of costs and are typically not impacted by funding changes. The size of an employer's population generally determines the predictability of the paid claims. The larger the population, the more predictable the claims.
2. **Reserves.** Reserves are funds set aside to cover a range of contingencies such as:
   - Incurred but unreported claims
   - Catastrophic claims fluctuation
   - Actuarially projected liability

   In an insured arrangement, reserves are normally held by the insurance carrier. In a self-insured arrangement, the reserves are held by the employer. This gives the employer some flexibility in the use of the funds.
3. **Retention and administrative fees.** These fees are basically the cost of administering the benefits. They include the cost of such items as:
   - Claim processing
   - Recordkeeping and reporting

- Employee and provider communications
- State premium taxes
- Risk charges
- Carrier profits

Reducing administrative fees is key in the move to self-insuring benefits. By self-insuring, plans can eliminate all or most of the state premium taxes, the risk charges, and the carrier profit. The main difference between an insured plan and a self-insured plan is who is taking the risk. In an insured arrangement, the carrier takes some or all of the risk; in a fully self-insured arrangement, the employer takes all the risk. (See Exhibit 1.)

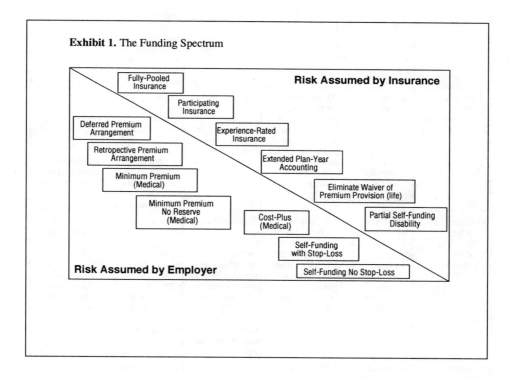

Exhibit 1. The Funding Spectrum

By comparing various health and welfare plan funding alternatives, Chart 1 illustrates the areas of cost savings possible through self-funding.

Chart 1. Cost Impact of Alternate Funding Methods

	Normal Cost/Cash Flow Impact			Cost/Cash Flow Impact After Implementing	
	Risk Charge	State Premium Taxes	Earnings on Reserves	Retrospective Agreements	Premium/ Claim Lag
Experience Rated Fully Insured	Maximum "book" charge • Direct cost to company • Limited annual liability • Carrier recoups losses in future years	All premiums fully taxed • Average cost = 2%	Retained by carrier • Offset administrative expenses to some degree	Reduce ongoing premium payments • Improved cash flow • Potential for slight savings in premium taxes • Provides protection for carrier by allowing reduction to be "called in" at year end if needed	Delays premium payment 60 to 90 days • Improves cash flow • Savings if earnings exceed carrier's cash flow charge
Minimum Premium —Reserves Held by Carrier	Maximum "book" charge • Direct cost to company • Limited annual liability • Carrier recoups losses in future years	"Premium" reduced to about 10% of fully insured cost, and taxed • Tax liability reduced • Some states disagree	Retained by carrier • Offset administrative expenses to some degree	Reduce estimated liability • Little impact on cost or cash flow • Provides protection for carrier if retro is in addition to anticipated costs	Delays claim payment 30 to 90 days • Improves cash flow • Savings if earnings exceed carrier's cash flow charge
Minimum Premium —Reserves Held by Company	Maximum "book" charge • Direct cost to company • Limited annual liability • Carrier recoups losses in future years	"Premium" reduced to about 10% of fully insured cost, and taxed • Tax liability reduced • Some states disagree	Retained by company • Slight increase in carrier charge for interest it loses on reserve • Earnings will generally exceed any increase in administrative expenses	Reduce estimated liability • Little impact on cost or cash flow • Provides protection for carrier if retro is in addition to anticipated costs	Delays claim payment 30 to 90 days • Improves cash flow • Savings if earnings exceed carrier's cash flow charge
Fully Self-Insured • Life Insured • ASO or TPA	No risk charge • Immediate cost reduction • No limit on company's annual liability • Stop-loss coverage can be purchased	No premium taxes are paid except for life insurance • Premium tax liability is eliminated (except for life insurance)	Retained by company • Earnings will generally exceed any increase in administrative expenses (Note: administrative costs may actually decline)	Not applicable except for life insurance	Not applicable except for life insurance

Note: Depending on design, retrospective agreements can be used to reduce or minimize risk charges. However, there is a tradeoff resulting in an increase in employer liability.

THE IMPACT OF FLEXIBLE BENEFITS

The rapid spread of flexible benefits plans throughout the 1980s created a growing need by employers to have administrative services customized to their specific needs. Because a flexible benefits program offers choice and addresses the varied needs of today's diversified workforce, it requires greater administrative capabilities. Therefore, many employers use the services of a TPA to supplement or even replace internal capabilities.

A well-designed flexible benefits program recognizes that one size does not fit all. Unlike the package that was designed for the "traditional" employee, a flex program can avoid duplicating coverage for an employee whose spouse works outside the home and receives employee benefits. It can also respond to the varying needs of an increasingly diverse workforce. For example, a single parent might need additional dependent care assistance, life insurance, or time off, while an older employee might prefer to increase contributions to a 401(k) plan or purchase group universal life insurance. Moreover, if designed properly, a flexible benefits program can also be an effective tool in controlling benefit costs.

SELECTING A FLEX TPA

There are several important issues for employers to consider in choosing a TPA to handle the administration of a self-insured flexible benefits plan, since administration encompasses more than just a software package. As the possibility of health care reform increases, so too does the need to analyze current administrative processes with an eye toward simplifying and streamlining procedures. This is because national health care reform is likely to increase the complexity of health and welfare benefit administration.

The administration selection process can be quite cumbersome. With numerous vendors providing a wide variety of health and welfare benefit administration services, it can be difficult to choose the most appropriate vendors. Consulting firms, insurance carriers, and other third party administrators all offer administration systems (mainframe and PC) and related services. The employer's objectives, needs, and budget should drive the approach taken.

The first thing to consider is what benefits are part of the program offered to employees. Self-insured flexible benefits administration systems and services typically incorporate a wide variety of benefits. The most common are:

- Medical
- Dental
- Long-term disability (LTD)
- Short-term disability (STD)
- Health care spending accounts
- Dependent care spending accounts

Due to unfavorable tax laws, most employers do not self-insure life insurance but instead continue to provide life insurance on a fully insured basis.

The next thing to consider is what level of external support is necessary. Assuming the company has decided that internal staff needs to be supported by an outside vendor, the basic options include:

- **Systems only.** The internal staff can handle all administration but systems and/or procedures need to be upgraded.
- **Hybrid.** The internal staff works with one or more outside vendors, with the outside vendors providing support only in the areas where internal staff cannot respond as efficiently.
- **Outsourcing.** The internal staff is virtually eliminated and one or more outside vendors provides the full range of HR administrative support including ongoing, direct interaction with employees.

Generally, employers do not use a single administration vendor. While many employers would find it cost-efficient to use one vendor—for example, an insurance carrier—to handle all administration in order to take advantage of economies of scale, it is still rare that one vendor can provide the full range of services needed, especially when the company offers a flex plan.

A flexible benefits plan requires: claim administration, to verify eligibility and process claims; and enrollment administration, to produce customized forms, track an employee's eligibility for benefits, and maintain records of dependent information, coverage elections, salary deduction/reduction amounts, etc.

TPA Services

Most of the major insurance companies provide limited flexible benefits enrollment administration services. Several will provide these services regardless of whether or not they are providing claims administration.

There are also numerous other third parties that will handle enrollment administration. These include benefit consultants, TPAs, and accounting firms. Some of these utilize a mainframe system while others use a PC-based system. For example, at Buck Consultants, the flexible benefits system runs on both an IBM system AS/400 (which is faster and more flexible than a PC-based system) and a PC platform (for clients that wish to do their own administration).

System costs can vary significantly. Depending on the vendor selected, costs for third party enrollment administration can range from $75,000 to $225,000 or more. First year costs will vary depending on system requirements, with reduced costs for ongoing administration after the initial plan year.

In choosing a third party administrator, several requirements should be considered in order to select a system that best suits the needs of the employer.

System Setup

When an employer decides to use a TPA or PC-based system, the system setup is crucial to a successful administration program. The employer should begin by documenting current procedures and practices that the new administration system needs to accommodate. For example, the system must be able to handle plan components such as the following:

- Eligibility rules
- Scope of benefits/options
- Flexible dollar formula(s)
- Benefit cost bases
- Benefit limits/restrictions (e.g., adverse selection, evidence of insurability, etc.)
- Existing reimbursement accounts
- Demographic/location variations (e.g., benefit options, costs, reporting, etc.)

Flexible Benefit Forms

The forms necessary for the flex plan need to be designed and then produced. The employer should have the option to either customize its forms or use preprinted forms offered by the third party administrator. The employer should consider, when choosing a TPA, how much customization is necessary to accommodate its needs. Among the key forms a self-insured flex plan needs are enrollment forms, confirmation statements, flexible spending account explanation of benefits forms (EOBs), and reimbursement account statements.

The flexible benefits enrollment form is one of the most important aspects of the entire implementation process. An enrollment form can be a key tool in the communication of flex and can help improve the efficiency of the implementation process. Only on the enrollment form do all the elements of the plan come together for the employee, because the form does the following:

1. It summarizes plan design in understandable terms;
2. It aids implementation and administration by personalizing the various flexible elements to the particular employee; and
3. It supplements communications, since the art and layout supporting the flex theme and concepts are used on the form as well as throughout the flex program.

The employer should strive for several goals in designing the enrollment form. These include allowing employees to make informed enrollment decisions and making the enrollment process quick and relatively easy. The most important goal is that the design of the form should reflect the way people in the real world actually behave and how they are likely to use the form. For example, a significant portion of any employee group does not read the implementation communication material. The enrollment form therefore needs to "walk" employees through the process.

A confirmation statement is also a key form for a flexible benefits program. A confirmation statement should always show detailed election information including:

- Employee information (e.g., name, social security number)
- Dependent information (e.g., names, social security numbers)
- Beneficiary information
- Benefit elections including levels of coverage
- Payroll deduction information for both per cycle and annual deductions
- Additional required information (e.g., evidence of insurability)

Data Output Requirements

A key function of a TPA is to maintain and report data. Automated premium report production by location or corporation (as necessary) for all benefit options should be a standard feature of any TPA being considered. The reports should include volume of coverage and rates used for calculations. In addition, various types of standard reports should also be available as follows:

- Benefit election statistical reports
- Employee election summary/status reports
- Benefit eligibility/coverage reports
- Payroll reports
- General ledger reports
- Other financial, statistical, and management reports that are required

System Capabilities

The employer needs to ensure that the TPA's benefit administration system can interface with the sponsor's HR and payroll systems. This includes the capability to download specific benefit administration data from the HR system on a scheduled daily basis.

Also the employer needs to meet with all carriers and TPAs to determine the initial automated interface requirements. This should include file layouts, data descriptions/values, information to be used (such as group designations), reconciliation reporting capabilities, eligibility structure, and scheduling of updates.

Pretax contributions are used to fund the health care and dependent care spending accounts. The interface between the benefit administration system and the company's payroll system provides the ongoing information flow to allocate employee funding for benefits. Information should be fed from the benefit system to the payroll system, detailing the employees' elections of pretax deductions. The first payroll cycle at the beginning of the plan year will establish payroll deductions for all employees during the new plan year. Subsequently, the benefit system will, on an ongoing basis, feed payroll deductions to the payroll system for new hires, family status changes, or employee terminations.

Information detailing the actual deductions taken should be fed from the payroll system to the benefits system to verify the accuracy of payroll actions and for the accruals to the flexible spending accounts. The reconciliation process should be able to produce a report based on each pay cycle as well as the year to date. The system should give the company the ability to differentiate and track causes of deduction differences by a code established by the company.

Data should be able to be downloaded to an internal system at the company (PC, minicomputer, or mainframe) or maintained by the third party with direct on-line access by the company.

Legal/Regulatory Requirements

The TPA should be capable of complying with various legal/regulatory requirements. These include:

- Nondiscrimination testing
- OBRA '93 dependent Social Security number reporting requirements
- Health care reform requirements

Nondiscrimination testing for dependent care spending accounts should be automated. Also, although health care reform is still being formulated, the system should have the flexibility to track the type of data that many experts feel will be required by whatever health care reform legislation passes.

IMPLEMENTATION

Once a TPA is chosen, the employer begins the implementation stage, which typically lasts six to eight months. Implementation involves establishing procedures and modifying the system decided upon to handle all enrollment information, payroll interfaces and provider interfaces. It also involves an extensive communication campaign designed to educate employees about the concept of choice and to enable employees to make intelligent choices among the available benefit options.

CONCLUSION

When selecting a TPA to provide services for a self-insured flexible benefits plan, careful planning and consideration must be given to the specific requirements of the employer's plan. Consulting firms, insurance carriers, and other TPAs all offer a wide range of systems with varying strengths and weaknesses. The final system chosen should be based on the objectives, needs and budget of the employer.

Part 6

ELEMENTS OF EFFECTIVE PLAN DESIGN

21. Reducing Medical Costs with Employee Claims Data
James A. Dadonna

This article discusses the use of claims data from the perspectives of managing the process, organizing data, developing issues and programs, and measuring the impact of programs put in place.

Companies and institutions committed to maintaining indemnity medical plans find it increasingly necessary to provide proactive management to reduce medical costs. Why? There is a train of facts and studies that runs as follows:

- The United States spent $890 billion on health care in 1993, up from $666 billion as recently as 1990;
- Of all medical expenditures, employer-sponsored programs provided 63 percent of all coverage for those under age 65, while 16 percent of expenses were uninsured; and
- A study by a highly reputable consulting firm indicated that 30 percent of health care cost is driven by cost shifting.

The result is a keen interest in sufficient plan management to assure that due value is received for growing medical plan expenditures. Management means more than just cutting costs, or the company could simply and inexpensively cut medical plan coverage and call it a day. The objective should be minimizing expenditures for inappropriate and ineffective treatment and not paying more than you need to for medical goods and services; that is, optimizing value for the dollars spent. The basic tool in accomplishing this objective is analyzing employee health claims data.

ASSUMPTIONS

To discuss what to do and how to do it, we need to make some assumptions about context. For our purposes, assume that the medical plan is self-insured, serves between 1,000 and 10,000 employees, and spends up to $40 million dollars annually. This scale assures that efforts to manage the plan will easily have sufficient payback to warrant management efforts, even at the lower end. If the plan is larger than these assumptions, more in-company analytical capability may be justified than is assumed in this article. The size of the plan and the ambitiousness of the management objectives should determine how elaborate (and expensive) the efforts at medical plan management will be. Many alternatives exist, but like any other business expenditure, substantial payback should be expected. While that payback is not predictable until well into the process, we also need to assume that the company is willing to actually manage this major area of expenditures by making appropriate resources available to do the necessary data gathering, analysis, program development, implementation, and communications.

The presumption that there is a genuine need to manage a medical plan should be tested on one point before we proceed. There are certain geographic areas where on-going medical care management can be provided by extremely strong and mature managed health care organizations (e.g., HMOs and buyers' co-ops), to which it may not be necessary to offer alternatives. Where regional opportunities exist, the best and least-cost management alternative may be to outsource the management of medical care to such an organization, particularly when there are solid indications that utilization, price controls, and community rating of risk are in place. Even then, however, it is the initial analysis of your plan's medical claim experience that provides evidence that these regional opportunities are genuine.

MEASURE WHAT YOU CARE ABOUT: SETTING OBJECTIVES

Start by articulating the impact of the medical care plan on the organization that supports it. The first component is to identify why the business spends money on the medical plan. Business direction (strategy) determines whether and how the organization is expanding or contracting its workforce and, in turn, how the organization chooses to compete in the labor market (total compensation). From those decisions, the realistic role of the medical plan as an element of employee retention and recruiting must be derived. The relative importance of the medical plan's impact on these business needs must be contrasted with the second impact of the medical plan, that is, the company's costs. The plan manager has to identify the organization's need for, and tolerance of, cost controls in the medical plan.

An organization's internal priorities often further define perspectives from which to identify meaningful measurements from employee claims data. For example, organizations concerned with substance abuse among employees (or other employee wellness issues) may be highly dependent on medical claims data in identifying the incidence of substance abuse treatment as well as the frequency of medical treatment that may have been substance related but was not formally diagnosed as such.

Knowing how you intend to use the information that you develop is key in organizing the analytical effort.

WHO WILL DO THE ANALYSIS AND WHAT MUST THEY DO?

For most employers, an in-depth look at medical claims data every two to three years provides the information needed to identify needs and opportunities, develop and implement programs, and identify progress (or lack thereof) on the issues chosen. The capability to provide claims data manipulation and analysis is most economically sought through an outside consultant. A good reason for not manipulating medical claims data in-house is to protect against the appearance of compromising the confidentially of employee medical history.

Standard good purchasing practices need to be applied to the task of selecting an outside consultant. Find out what companies have have engaged in similar projects, who did the work, and whether the customer was satisfied. Provide the alternative vendor candidates identified with a bid request describing your organization, locations, basic demographics, the project goals and objectives, the information sought, and the basis on which you intend to make the selection. Make the competitive process scrupulously clean, with all vendor candidates getting the same information and hearing the same words. Because of the desirability of a long term relationship with the consultant—measure movement in data over periods of years—take the time needed to make a good decision the first time. Changing vendors means recreating data bases and data points to preserve the continuity of data, all of which is expensive and usually only partially successful.

Selecting the vendor to provide analysis of medical plan claims data can be based on some of the following capabilities and characteristics:

- Adjustment of raw claims data for case mix and severity and arrangement into episodes of treatment data are key to the analysis;
- A large client data base from which to draw relative comparisons in plan utilization and health care costs;
- Ability to adjust claims experience for demographic factors such as age and sex; and
- Access to other large data bases of various types of medical experience against which to compare your plan's experience.

Having made a decision on a consultant, and come to agreement on objectives and price, the next step is to develop the schedule in coordination with other players. Generally, there will be two streams of data that must be provided to the consultant for merger and further manipulation. First, a payroll or personnel data base must provide demographic data on plan participants for the same years for which claims data will be provided. Second, claims data must be requested from the claims administrator for the initial two to three year period that will be used to establish the data base. Bear in mind that some of the analysis required can be performed at little or no additional cost by the claims payor as part of the contracted services provided, rather than as part of the outside consulting work.

WHAT DID THE MEDICAL PLAN PAY FOR ORGANIZING DATA AND DEVELOPING ISSUES

To save dollars on re-work, care needs to be taken to assure that the analyst has a clear understanding of how the information being developed must be structured to address issues arising from the data. Consider the structure of risk pooling and funding in the medical plan; segration by employees, dependents, and retirees; and breakdown by location.

The first level of analysis is to:

- Compare claims experience against norms of other relevant populations, and
- Compare changes in utilization over time.

Data are gathered and developed into issues around some of the following key points.

Admissions per thousand covered lives. These baseline data are best interpreted in the light of the other data points below, but they are often useful in helping to decide that your population is more or less healthy than other groups, or that the plan may have a problem with the excessive inpatient care being delivered; a pre-admission certification program may be the prescription for the latter malady.

Inpatient versus outpatient care mix. Identifying cases by diagnostic type that are normally appropriate for outpatient care, and the percentage of those cases in which such treatment was actually given, is often helpful. Breaking down these data by geographic area helps in arriving at action plans such as provider education, pre-admission certification, or direct contracting, and in deciding the priorities among various locations for such actions.

Average length of stay (ALOS) per inpatient admission. Comparison against the norms derived from larger data bases will initially describe whether and to what extent this is a problem area. Since this is one of the key drivers of cost, comparison over time is an important element in scoring any cost control progress. As admissions go down due to better case management (pre-certification of admissions, case review, discharge planning, and outpatient utilization), look for this number to begin to rise again, since those being admitted may be only the sickest of the plan population.

Inpatient days per thousand covered lives. This may be one of the most important indicators of how sick or healthy the plan population is relative to other similar populations, particularly if pre-certification brings the number of inpatient admissions within reason. This measurement may have implications on business issues such as the fitness of a workforce for work, and can provide valuable informational input for companies and organizations looking at the justification for safety training, medical assessment, health management, and employee assistance programs.

Mental health utilization. Because of the importance of this area as a cost driver in the medical plan and in employee performance, many companies have broken this area out into special subsets of data on all of the points discussed above. The results of those data have also caused many companies to break out mental health for managed care programs by specialists. Inpatient versus out-patient utilization and average length of stay are critical measures of progress in mental health management. A word of caution—separating mental health versus substance abuse treatment is helpful, but the lines between the two diagnoses have been known to be blurred at times because of physicians' "chicken and egg" problem in deciding whether mental or substance problem came first, sometimes, out of concern for labelling a patient. Breaking the treatment into episodes of care rather than isolated claims will enable the analyst to more accurately identify the duration of related treatments and to include cases, and dollars, in the analysis that may not have been otherwise diagnosed as substance abuse, but are highly suspect because of the type of treatment and pattern of recurrence. Additionally, the analyst can identify the total care and dollars being consumed by those employees and families who also receive mental health and substance abuse treatment.

Employee, dependent and retiree usage. Many of the data points discussed above will yield more action-oriented information if broken out by user group within the plan. Depending upon how contribution rates are structured—single, family, single parent—it may be critical to look at utilization patterns by user group to understand how to fairly set employee and company contribution rates. Specialized problems in prescription drug consumption by retirees, however, may lead you to change plan design.

Having more information than ever before means that you are likely to then have more questions and issues to address than ever before. Most of the data points above are intended to identify fundamental medical plan utilization issues, and to suggest the magnitude of those issues, for further investigation. Having done that, we are in a position to rationally establish priorities and to decide how much additional information may be needed to construct and sell the medical plan programs. The budget may be key in effectively addressing opportunities.

Measuring these same data points in the future years provides a fair report card for the programs installed.

The types of data below are focused on narrower issues and are good on-going comparison points with which to gage the true price movement for goods and services within the plan. Since dollar pricing within defined categories is substantially simpler than utilization studies, much of this information is available from claims payors at reduced expense. Some of these data points are as follows.

Per diem payments to hospitals. While case mix in any given year may vary widely, the major hospitals that provide services to plan participants tend to be stable. The movement of prices paid to these hospitals tends to be a most reliable indicator of the actual cost inflation occurring to the hospital expense portion of the plan.

Physician per case payment by diagnostic category. A breakdown by major category, such as medical, surgical, psychiatric, substance abuse, and childbirth, will elimlinate some the price changes due to changes in case mix. Substantial price movement may warrant data by location to pinpoint the source. Close inquiry of the more aggressive providers by the claims payor may be helpful in better understanding the reasons for such increases.

Maternity average length of stay and payment per case. Wide regional variations in treatment practices (frequency of C-sections) make this information difficult to react to, but utilization reviewers will attempt provider communication programs. Longer-term action plans, such as education and counselling of expectant mothers, may present the best opportunity for improvement in the experience of the plan.

CONCLUSION

For an organization determined to have an impact on medical costs, the basic process described above provides a means of continuous improvement. It would be hard to overstate the power of using factual data developed from the actual medical health care experience of people in your medical plan in determining whether the task at hand is to design medical plan programs or to sell the programs to management or employees. Solid analysis of employee health claims data provides a fact-based approach in a medical plan management arena fraught with large expenditures, larger potential legal liabilities and, often, serious personal issues for plan participants and their families.

22.   Drug Formularies

Richard A. Levy, PhD

A formulary is an approved list of medicines from which a physician may choose and for which a program will pay. Although the primary objective of the formulary should be to promote the rational use of medicines, many managed care organizations are using it mainly to control drug budget costs. Using the formulary to channel reimbursement for only selected medicines may produce savings through inventory simplification and volume purchasing.

Restrictive formularies were first introduced in hospitals, which are closed medical environments in which reliance on a relatively small number of drugs can be justified. In this environment constant monitoring of the patient can detect any problems that occur, and there is immediate access to alternative therapies. The hospital formulary represents a continually revised compilation of medicines that reflects the current clinical judgments of the medical staff. Items on the formulary may differ from hospital to hospital based on such factors as the patient mix, the medical "culture," the training of the staff, and leadership.

The American Society of Hospital Pharmacists distinguishes between the formulary and the formulary system. The hospital formulary system contains four elements:

1. The formulary;
2. The systematic process by which drugs are admitted to and deleted from the list;
3. The monitoring of drug use, interactions, and adverse effects; and
4. Ongoing education of providers regarding listed agents.

An effective hospital formulary system meets these criteria:[1]

- Medical staff support for the formulary system concept;
- Informed and timely review of drugs for formulary admission and deletion;
- Continuous involvement of informed professional staff in the operation of the formulary system;
- Flexibility in the use of nonformulary drugs when reasonable; and
- Perception of the formulary as a vehicle for provider education and evaluation of drug therapy.

These criteria reflect a vision of the formulary as a "dynamic tool, sensitive to the needs of prescribers and patients while preventing waste" (see note 1).

Although originating in the controlled hospital environment, use of the formulary soon expanded into the community (outpatient) setting of state Medicaid programs and, more recently, into private managed care organizations. Most staff and group model HMOs now use formularies. But in transplanting the formulary idea to managed care, the formulary *system* concept is often forgotten—and it is the system that is crucial in balancing the medical needs of doctors and patients with the cost containment goals of managed care organizations and insurance plans.

DO FORMULARIES SAVE COSTS?

Although the primary objective of the formulary should be to promote the rational use of medicines, many managed care organizations are using it mainly to contain drug budget costs. Ironically, strong evidence indicates that restrictive formularies are actually associated with higher overall treatment costs. Some studies have shown that formularies can reduce drug program budgets, but no studies have shown that overall treatment costs are reduced through the formulary process.

There are many reasons formularies may be counterproductive.[2] For example, costs associated with the implementation and management of formularies may offset anticipated economic and therapeutic gains. In addition, restrictive formularies may lead to undesirable effects on the physician prescribing; to increased use of other, more expensive services; and to increased drug use, all with attendant increases in expenditures. Lastly, drug switching may occur when a patient enters a managed care plan and finds that the drug he or she is already taking is excluded from the formulary. In such cases, dosage adjustment may be necessary or additional expenses (laboratory tests, office visits) may be incurred when stabilized patients are switched from one drug to another.

ADMINISTRATIVE COSTS

The costs of administering the formulary can be substantial. The formulary is a dynamic tool that demands regular review and updating by the organization's pharmacy and therapeutics (P&T) committee.[3] These committees often comprise 10 to 20 persons who meet monthly for an average of one hour.[4] Committee members and support personnel spend additional time preparing materials and presentations. These and other administrative costs may quickly negate potential savings, particularly when the cost differential between therapeutic alternatives is small.

Factors that must be considered when evaluating formulary decisions include the impact on usage patterns of other products, the effect on hospitalizations, and the side-effect profiles of alternative therapies. Inappropriate use of recommended therapeutic alternatives and the cost of adverse drug reactions should also be weighed in the economic analysis.[5]

Formulary implementation has, in some cases, been shown to shift prescribing toward more toxic agents, such as gentamicin when cephalosporin antibiotics are restricted, or codeine when other pain medications are restricted.[6] Formulary restriction can also result in "diagnosis drift"; in other words, an increase in those diagnoses for which prescription reimbursement is available. For example, following the introduction of a restrictive formulary, one study showed a 27 percent reduction in the diagnosis of uncomplicated bronchitis, for which prescriptions were no longer reimbursable, but a 21 percent and 61 percent increase in the diagnosis of chronic bronchitis and acute bronchitis, for which reimbursement was available. Overall treatment expenditures for bronchitis increased by 5 percent.[7]

Formulary restriction may cause patients to terminate drug therapy or switch to other, more expensive drugs. For example, following restriction of the Michigan Medicaid formulary, 46 percent of the patients discontinued drug therapy, with unknown effects on total treatment costs. Another 24 percent of the patients had alternative drugs prescribed from the formulary. The average cost of these alternative drugs was nearly double that of those originally prescribed.[8] Service substitution following implementation of a drug formulary is illustrated by a study of Louisiana Medicaid expenditures that showed a 34 percent increase in hospitalized patients and a 10.7 percent increase in length of stay.[9]

VULNERABLE POPULATIONS

Indigent

Strong evidence exists that, when formulary restrictions are introduced for Medicaid patients, other drugs and services are often substituted, and this is associated with an increase in total Medicaid expenditures. A series of studies examining the effects of restrictions on Medicaid programs revealed a reduction in prescription expenditures, but at the expense of increases in other areas, such as hospital admissions or readmissions, physician visits, emergency department visits, and surgery (see note 9). In one study, savings of $5.6 million were realized from reduced spending on prescription medicines, but total program expenditures rose $15.1 million because of service substitution by elderly and totally disabled patients and because of increases in the frequency and duration of hospitalizations. Perhaps most telling was a significant increase in the number of diagnoses of central nervous system, heart, and circulatory system diseases related to the removal of specific drugs from the formulary. For example, removal of benzodiazepines from the formulary was correlated with an increase in anxiety-related cardiovascular admissions. This study concluded that a restrictive formulary had an adverse impact on the health status of the Medicaid population and that the savings the program hoped to achieve were overwhelmingly offset by the trade-off for other services.

Elderly

In an elderly population, the abrupt elimination of a frequently used blood pressure medication (nadolol) as a cost containment measure caused large increases in the use of other drugs and increased overall costs. Discontinuation of nadolol therapy resulted in a considerable decline in the percentage of patients able to achieve blood pressure control with one agent alone—from 28.6 percent down to 16.3 percent. The study found that money expended to achieve optimal blood pressure control in this aged population increased sharply, suggesting that switching medicines in patients already on a well-established drug regimen was not advisable. Ramirez *et al.* suggest that, because forgetfulness is a major cause of hospitalization of the elderly, the number of blood pressure medications used by persons in this age group should be kept to a minimum. Changes in a drug regimen in a geriatric population may also lead to compliance problems and, as these findings suggest, necessitate additional office visits.[10]

Ethnic and Racial Groups

Ethnic and racial minority groups, like the elderly, should also receive special consideration with regard to formularies that restrict access to the full range of drugs within a class. Pharmacogenetic research over the last 15 years has uncovered significant differences in the ways people of different racial and ethnic groups respond to medicines. Although genetic factors are the major determinants of the normal variability in response to medicines, the factors involved in determining drug responses in ethnic and racial groups are complex. Environmental factors (diet, alcohol consumption, smoking) may have profound effects on drug metabolism and disposition in the body. Cultural or psychological factors may also affect the efficacy of, or compliance with, drug therapy.[11]

Available information suggests that ethnic and racial minority patients may be subject to greater risks if they are prescribed, or are switched to, an "equivalent" drug, because the agent may not be as effective or because substantial dosage adjustments may be necessary to avoid overdosing or underdosing (see note 11). Drugs with varying effects among different ethnic and racial populations include those used to treat common illnesses; e.g., heart conditions, high blood pressure, depression, schizophrenia, and allergies.

These findings indicate that it is very important to individualize therapy for special population groups. Specifically, formularies should be broad and flexible enough to enable rational choices of drugs and dosages for all patients, regardless of age, race, or ethnic heritage.

DISCLOSURE AND LIABILITY

The existence and details of service limitations, such as restrictive formularies, are generally poorly communicated to members of indemnity and managed care health plans. A study by the National Association of Employers on Health Care Action (NAEHCA) revealed that, of those HMOs using a formulary, the existence of the formulary was mentioned in only 56 percent of all HMO/employer contracts, and less than 54 percent of employers discussed this limitation with their workers.[12] The results of a 1990 Gallup poll revealed that only 17 percent of benefits managers were familiar with the operation of formularies.[13]

Since formularies and other restrictive drug policies govern the level of medical care, they result in some liability exposure in malpractice cases for managed care organizations, physicians, insurance companies, and in theory, employers and unions.[14] Liability could result from negligent selection or substitution of drugs, in conjunction with economic pressure or actual direction of physicians or patients to use formulary drugs. The NAEHCA has warned that, the use of restrictive drug mechanisms by managed care organizations may compromise quality of care and expose employers to increased liability, unless enrollees are made aware of restrictions in advance.[15]

QUALITY OUTCOMES AND FORMULARIES OF THE FUTURE

Restrictive policies often deny access to the latest advances in drug therapy and, as a result, may cause increases in overall treatment costs. One study reported that the availability of new drugs in HMOs was negatively associated with the existence of a formulary system. The study further suggested that few new drugs representing important therapeutic gains were available without restriction, compared with new agents with modest therapeutic advantage.[16] Similar results have been found in Medicaid programs.[17] Since newer agents can often reduce overall treatment costs, the potential savings are not realized when programs restrict access to these agents.

Formulary modifications often result in a ballooning of costs in other service sectors and in altered patterns of prescribing, diagnosis, and drug consumption. Additional data and research on the true costs of formularies are required. Moreover, as improved quality of care and treatment outcomes continue to assume greater importance in health care management, we need to focus on these more global objectives and not allow decisions and policies to be driven predominantly by the most obvious economic impacts. A simple economic analysis based on the cost of a medication per day of therapy is an inadequate perspective for achieving these important goals.

These five criteria, derived from issues discussed above, may be helpful in identifying or constructing a formulary program compatible with quality care:

1. Selection of products for the formulary should be made by a team of pharmacists and physicians representing various medical specialties.
2. Physicians should be allowed to override the formulary and select a nonformulary drug when it is necessary for an individual patient.
3. Patients entering the program who are stabilized on a nonformulary drug should be allowed to continue with that agent and not be switched to a formulary drug.
4. The formulary should be broad enough to accommodate the individual needs of special populations.
5. Provisions of the restrictive formulary program should be fully disclosed and clearly explained to workers.

Notwithstanding these characteristics of a quality program, even well designed restrictive formularies can only exert a positive economic influence on the drug budget, a small component (less than 10 percent) of overall health plan costs. Another approach to managing pharmaceuticals, however, has considerably more potential in reducing costs. That approach, the converse of restricting pharmaceuticals, is the optimal use of medicines. This can have a highly leveraged effect in lowering overall costs by decreasing utilization of other, more expensive services.

Some health care organizations are aware that formulary and other component management approaches are not working to bring overall costs under control and that we must begin to focus on "systems management" organized around particular diseases. A systems approach emphasizes management with clinical and economic logic, as well as tactics customized for each disease and for each patient. Leading managed care systems are beginning to adopt this approach.[18]

Formulary programs of the future will be driven primarily by the goals of quality therapeutic outcomes and overall disease management and not by the more narrow objective of containing drug budget costs. In some cases, this may even mean an expanded use of drugs and higher drug costs, as newer, more powerful agents are selected. But if treatment is optimized, overall costs will be lower.

1. Jang, R, "US Formularies: Distortions in Therapeutics and Its Economic Effects," in Towse, A, ed., *Not What the Doctor Ordered* (Northern Ireland: W. & G. Baird Ltd.; 1993).

2. Colligen, BH, and Levy, RA, "The Formulary Process in Managede Care: Hidden Costs and Doubtful Benefits," *P&T,* August 1992; 1290-1293.

3. Hinnant, JT, and Grapes, ZT, "Formulary Management Activities in Georgia," *P&T,* 1992; 17: 475-488.

4. Green, JA, "Point: The Formulary System and the Emperor's New Clothes," *Am J Hosp Pharm* 1986; 43: 2830-2834.

5. Thornton, JP, Brown, D, Stonich, TL, and Hutchinson, RA, "Pharmacy Managers Should Evaluate the Full Impact of Formulary Decisions," *Am J Hosp Pharm* 1989; 46: 1131-1132 (Letter).

6. Plumridge, RJ, Stoelwinder, JU, and Berbatis, CG, "Improving Patient Care and Pharmacy Management: The Effect of Hospital Formularies," *Drug Intell Clin Pharm* 1984; 18: 652-656.

7. Smith, T, "Limited Lists of Drugs: Lessons from Abroad," *Br Med J.,* 1985; 290: 532-534.

8. Smith, DM, and McKercher, PL, "The Elimination of Selected Drug Products From the Michigan Medicaid Formulary: A Case Study, *Hosp Form* 1984; 19: 366.

9. Hefner, DL, "A Study to Determine the Cost-Effectiveness of a Restrictive Formulary; The Louisiana Experience" (Washington, DC: National Pharmaceutical Council; 1979).

10. Ramirez G, Ayers-Chastain, CW, Bittle PA, and Straumfjord JV, "Formulary Restrictions on Antihypertensive Drugs," *Hosp Ther* 1990; 15(2): 205-221.

11. Levy, RA, "Ethnic and Racial Differences in Response to Medicines: Preserving Individualized Therapy in Managed Pharmaceutical Programmes," *Pharmaceutical Medicine.* 1993; 7: 139-165.

12. National Association of Employers on Health Care Action, "Drug Benefit Programs and Disclosure Policies: A National Survey of HMOs," 1990.

13. Benson, S, and Marshall, D, "How Employee Benefit Managers Choose Health Plans," *Medical Interface* August 1990; 10-22.

14. Levy, RA, "Liability Issues Resulting from Nondisclosure of Restrictive Policies in Managed Care Pharmacy Programs," *Drug Benefit Trends* 1992; 4(4): 10-14.

15. Kenkel, PJ, "Liability at Issue as Firms Target Drug Costs," *Modern Healthcare* August 27, 1990; 20(34): 41.

16. Chinburapa, V, and Larson, LN, "The Availability of New Drugs in Health Maintenance Organizations," *J Res Pharm Econ* 1991; 3(1) 91-110.

17. Grabowski, H, "Medicaid Patients' Access to New Drugs," *Health Aff* 1988; 7: 102-114.

18. Levy, RA, "A Systems Approach to Cost Management," *Drug Benefit Trends* January/February 1994; 6(1): 4-8.

23. Using the Resource-Based Relative Value Scale (RBRVS) to Help Control Physician Costs

Zachary Dyckman, PhD

In January 1992, Medicare began implementation of a new physician services payment methodology: the Medicare Fee Schedule, with fees based on the resource-based relative value scale (RBRVS). Until now, virtually all private and publicly sponsored health benefit programs had been paying for physicians' services based on physician charge patterns. Under RBRVS payment systems, physician fees are based on the estimated costs of the resources used by the physician to provide the specific service.

Within the past three years, many HMOs, PPOs, and other payers that use contracted provider networks have started using RBRVS-based payment approaches for physician services. All these payers hope to achieve long-term savings in physician claims costs, but a number of payers have implemented RBRVS payment approaches in ways intended to achieve immediate claims cost savings as well. This article first briefly describes the development of RBRVS and how it is being used under the Medicare program. Then it examines several of the different RBRVS implementation approaches being used by private payers and assesses the feasibility advantages and disadvantages of their being used in employer-administered health benefit programs.

In 1976, the Health Care Financing Administration (HCFA), which administers the Medicare program, awarded a contract to two researchers at Harvard University to conduct initial research on resource costs of providing selected physician services. Drs. William Hsiao and William Stason hypothesized that certain so called cognitive services, such as physician office visits, were reimbursed at much lower rates (per unit of time) than were procedural services, primarily surgery. Hsiao and Stason developed a methodology to estimate the relative resource costs of performing different physician services and estimated these relative values for a small number of specific procedures. Among the resource costs identified by Hsiao and Stason are physician time required to perform the service, specialty training costs, intensity of effort, physician practice overhead expense, and malpractice risk. After publication of the initial study findings in 1979, Hsiao led further studies that, with the assistance of the American Medical Association (AMA) and various physician specialty societies, refined the methodology of what now had become known as the resource-based relative value scale or RBVS and estimated relative values for more than 2,000 procedure codes.[1]

Starting in 1986, Congress began using the results of the RBRVS analysis to identify "overpriced procedures," such as cataract surgery, and to reduce Medicare fees for them. In 1989, Congress enacted legislation that called for replacing the existing charge-based Medicare physician payment system with a new Medicare Fee Schedule based on RBRVS values. The new Medicare Fee Schedule was implemented in 1992.

Congress had several objectives in changing Medicare fees from charge-based fees to resource-based fees. The primary objectives were:

- To remove inequities from the existing payment system. Physicians should not receive higher fees (relative to resource costs) than other physicians do for performing certain services.
- To eliminate financial incentives to perform surgery and costly diagnostic procedures relative to other services. This should help reduce the cost of physician care as well as the cost of other medical care associated with unnecessary physician services.
- To eliminate inappropriate financial incentives for new physicians to train in procedure-oriented specialties that, as a result of existing inappropriate fee disparities, produce considerably higher earnings than non-procedure-oriented specialties. (In 1992, average earnings for an orthopedic surgeon were $284.000. This compares to $137,000 for a general internist and $122,000 for a pediatrician.)[2]

It is important to note that the RBRVS is not a fee schedule but a set of relative procedure values that are defined in terms of units, not dollars. In order to use the RBRVS to develop a fee schedule, one must develop a dollar conversion factor to be multiplied by RBRVS unit values to determine fees for specific procedures. The congressional intent was to use a conversion factor for the Medicare Fee Schedule that would be budget neutral. That is, the existing Medicare payment pie for physician services was to be redivided into pieces that reflects RBRVS values but leave the size of the pie unchanged. However, the Medicare Fee Schedule was implemented in a way that actually shrank the size of the Medicare physician payment pie instead of simply changing the relative size of the pieces.

THE MEDICARE FEE SCHEDULE

The basic Medicare Fee Schedule (MFS) system has three components: a national conversion factor to be used with all services; an RBRVS value for each service measured in relative value units (RVUs); and geographic adjustment factors to be calculated for each locality. Total RVUs for each service are composed of the sum of:

- physician work effort RVUs
- practice expense RVUs
- malpractice RVUs

The RVUs for each of the three components of the physician service are multiplied by its respective geographic practice cost index (GPCI) and summed to arrive at the GPCI-adjusted total RVUs for the service. This figure is multiplied by the dollar conversion factor to compute the Medicare Fee Schedule fee for a specific physician procedure in a specific locality.

A five year transition approach is being used by HCFA to implement the Medicare Fee Schedule. This is being done to limit the magnitude of fee changes from current maximum allowances; for some procedure codes, the new fees are less than 50 percent of the existing fees.

Implementation of the RBRVS fees under Medicare continues to be gradual. In the three years prior to formal implementation of the Medicare Fee Schedule, HCFA reduced fees for selected identified "overpriced" physician procedures and hospital-based physician services. HCFA also either froze or limited increases in fees for other services to levels below those that would have prevailed with no modification to the Medicare physician payment system. In addition, in setting the budget-neutral Medicare Fee Schedule conversion factor for 1992, HCFA assumed that physicians who experience a reduction of revenue under the Medicare Fee Schedule would make up 50 percent of the revenue reduction through aggressive billing practices (such as upcoding or unbundling services) or by providing additional services. The budget-neutral Medicare conversion factor, covering all physician services, was set at $31.00 for 1992. For 1993, two conversion factors were used, one for surgery and one for all other physician services. These are:

- Surgery: $31.96
- Other medical services: $31.25

The Medicare conversion factors were increased for 1994, based primarily on the previous year's increase in volume of physician services under Medicare relative to target rates set by the Federal government. Actual volume changes were below predicted increases, particularly for surgery. For 1994, three conversion factors are being used under the Medicare Fee Schedule. These are:

- Surgery: $35.16
- Primary care (physician office visits): $33.72
- All other physician services: $32.91

A recent analysis of Medicare charge and fee data indicates that Medicare fees (payment levels inclusive of required enrollee cost sharing) are generally 40 percent to 50 percent below usual physician charge levels.[3] Despite this large discount from charges, in 1993, approximately two-thirds of U.S. physicians are Medicare participating providers, i.e., agree to accept assignment for all Medicare claims and agree not to "balance bill" enrollees for charges above the Medicare fee. In excess of 90 percent of Medicare-allowed charges are assigned from participating physicians and from nonparticipating physicians who may except assignment on a case-by-case basis.

A primary reason for the high physician participation and assignment rates, despite the relatively low Medicare fee levels, is the substantial amount of leverage Medicare has with physicians. Under Medicare rules (which have been upheld after physician legal challenges), physicians are not permitted to bill patients more than 9.25 percent above the Medicare maximum allowance, even if the physician does not submit the claim to Medicare for payment. Private payers generally do not have as much leverage with physicians as Medicare does. For this reason, most private payers will not be able simply to adopt the Medicare Fee Schedule as they seek to implement an RBRVS payment approach. Instead, they will have to develop a different, somewhat more generous payment methodology.

PRIVATE PAYER ADOPTION OF RBRVS PAYMENT APPROACHES

Until 1993, managed care programs and other payers that use provider networks were for the most part slow and hesitant in implementing RBRVS payment systems. One reason for this was a concern that physicians who experienced fee reductions would withdraw from the payers' networks. A related concern was the negative reaction most physicians had towards the way Medicare implemented RBRVS, which some believed was a disguised approach to cutting fees. Consultants who conducted RBRVS cost-impact modeling and RBRVS fee schedule development for numerous payers during 1991 and 1992 found that in most cases, payers either postponed the implementation decision or only marginally adjusted their fees in implementing what they called an RBRVS payment system.

Then, during 1993, accounts were publicized of aggressive and successful RBRVS implementation efforts without large numbers of physician resignations from provider networks. This emboldened other payers who, reacting to competitive pressures, customer requests, or simply the perceived opportunity to reduce their physician claims costs, decided to implement RBRVS in a real and meaningful way. Reliable information is not available on the extent, timing, and nature of subsequent RBRVS implementation, but it appears that during 1993, a large proportion of network-based payers began serious RBRVS implementation efforts. As of mid-1994, it appears that the majority of managed care and other network-based payers have either implemented RBRVS-inspired changes in their physician payment systems or are in the process of doing so.

RBRVS Implementation Strategies

A wide variety of RBRVS-inspired payment system designs and implementation strategies are available to payers. Most of those outlined below have been implemented by one or more private payers:

- Allowances set at fixed percents above area Medicare fees (RBRVS Strategy 1)
- Allowances set at RBRVS fees using the budget-neutral conversion factor (RBRVS Strategy 2)
- Allowances set at the average of existing allowance and percent (usually 100%) of area Medicare fees (RBRVS target fee)—blending the approaches of existing allowances and RBRVS target fees (RBRVS Strategy 3)
- Use of the Medicare transition formula approach—use of RBRVS target fee if existing allowance is within 15 percent of target fee; if above range, use of existing allowance less 15 percent of target fee; if below range, use of existing allowance plus 15 percent of target fee (RBRVS Strategy 4)
- Selectively increased allowances with no reduction in allowances; increased allowances only if below RBRVS target fee—increased to RBRVS target fee; use of a formula to increase fees in proportion to deviation from RBRVS target fee (RBRVS Strategy 5)
- Selectively reduced allowances—reduced to RBRVS target fee; use of a formula to decrease fees in proportion to deviation from RBRVS target fee (RBRVS Strategy 6)
- Fee adjustment differentially within "fee corridors," developing 5 to 7 corridors of ratios of existing fees to RBRVS target fees: Greatest changes to procedure fees in corridors furthest away from RBRVS target fees; little to no change to fees in the target range. Sample fee corridors:
  —Fees $\geq$ 200 percent of Medicare RBRVS fee
  —Fees 150 percent to 200 percent of Medicare RBRVS fee
  —Fees 115 percent to 150 percent of Medicare RBRVS fee (target fee range)
  —Fees 100 percent to 115 percent of Medicare RBRVS fee
  —Fees < 100 percent of Medicare RBRVS fee (RBRVS Strategy 7)

   Payers may consider RBRVS Strategy 1, either as an implementation option or as an initial starting point in the assessment of alternative RBRVS payment systems. That is, they may develop a fee schedule that incorporates RBRVS relativities as a basis for comparison with existing allowances. An examination of fee schedules based on budget-neutral conversion factors (RBRVS Strategy 2) is also useful as part of the RBRVS development and selection process. Several of the early RBRVS payment systems were intended to achieve budget neutrality; now, most seek to reduce average fees. Blended RBRVS fees and existing allowances (RBRVS Strategy 3) can be considered as a viable transition strategy to full RBRVS implementation over a three to four year period. The Medicare first-year transition approach (RBRVS Strategy 4), or a variation in which the percentage limits are applied to existing allowances rather than RBRVS fees, may also be considered a feasible and attractive transition approach by some payers. (This approach was adopted by the State of Washington for its PPO program for state employees, as well as for other state-administered benefit programs.)

RBRVS Strategy 5 is a conservative approach when compared to the other RBRVS strategies. However, it may not seem conservative to payers which are accustomed to increasing allowances on an annual basis and to not systematically limiting fee increases. Several of the early movers to RBRVS used this strategy during the system's initial year.

The sixth RBRVS strategy, selective reduction of allowances, may be appropriate in the short run in a highly competitive physician services market and/or for a payer with generally higher fees than its competitors. Under this approach, allowances are not increased but are selectively reduced based on comparison with defined RBRVS target fees. Such a strategy is not likely to be sustainable over the long run in an inflationary economic environment. Blue Cross & Blue Shield plans in Illinois and California recently used this approach to help reduce physician fees and claims costs.

RBRVS strategy 7 is one we are increasingly recommending to payers. It very quickly narrows the spread of fees relative to the RBRVS target fee while leaving a sizable number of fees unchanged in an acceptable target range.

In all the RBRVS modeling and payment system fee development where Medicare RBRVS fees are used, the final Medicare RBRVS fees should be used rather than Medicare transition fees, which are based on some combination of pre-1992 Medicare allowances and final Medicare RBRVS fees.

Comparing RBRVS Fees with Area-Existing Fees

In considering adopting an RBRVS payment approach, and before selecting a specific fee development strategy, it is useful to obtain some feel for how Medicare RBRVS fees compare to area existing fees or maximum allowances. Shown in the first two columns of Exhibit 1, for a sample of high-dollar-volume procedure codes, are national (not geographic area-adjusted) RBRVS relative value units (RVUs) and 1994 Medicare RBRVS fees (1994 Medicare conversion factors multiplied by RVUs). The next two columns show what can be considered "typical" fees used by a PPO or a Blue Cross & Blue Shield plan in a moderate-fee and a relatively high-fee environment. (These are actual 1992 fees developed as part of a study of physician fees in various local market areas.) Fees used by indemnity carriers based on usual, customary, and reasonable payment methodologies would tend to be higher, whereas HMO fees would tend to be lower than those shown in Exhibit 1. Note how the private payer fees compare with Medicare fees. For every procedure code, the moderate private payer fee is substantially above the Medicare RBRVS fee. For surgical fees, private fees tend to be more than double Medicare RBRVS fees.

The last three columns in Exhibit 1 show sample RBRVS fees that may be considered by a private payer. (It is assumed that the existing fees for each of the three payers are those shown in the moderate private payer fee column.) The aggressive implementation approach (RBRVS Strategy 1) sets the new fees at 1.25 of Medicare RBRVS fees. Note that all fees are reduced but one, most by sizable percentages. The moderate implementation 1 approach is a highly simplified version of the "fee adjustment within fee corridor" approach (RBRVS Strategy 7). More than half the fees are unchanged, and all but one of the remaining fees are reduced. The moderate implementation 2 model is a blending of existing fees with a RBRVS target fee (RBRVS Strategy 3). All fees are changed, but generally by moderate percentages. Most payers will want to do a substantial amount of RBRVS fee modeling, using different models and parameters, before they decide on an approach that meets their objectives and their comfort level.

Each of the three RBRVS strategies illustrated in Exhibit 1 would result in reduced average fees and reduced physician claims costs in most environments. The few exceptions to this outcome would be for payers in relatively low-charge environments whose existing fees are already low relative to physician charge patterns.

FEASIBILITY AND ATTRACTIVENESS OF RBRVS IMPLEMENTATION FOR EMPLOYERS

Feasibility

In assessing feasibility for employers who self-administer their health benefit plans, as well as for other private payers, three important preconditions for successful implementation have been identified:

- A contracted participating provider (PAR) network
- A corporate commitment to RBRVS
- Adequate and appropriate resources

Exhibit 1. RBRVS Fees and "Typical" Existing Private Payer Fees for Selected High-Dollar-Volume Procedure Codes

Procedure CPT Code		1994 Medicare		Private Payer Fees		RBRVS-Inspired Fees		
		RVUs	RBRVS Fee	Moderate	High	Aggressive* Implementation	Moderate** Implementation 1	Moderate*** Implementation 2
99213	Mid-level office visit	.97	$33	$40	$50	$41+	$41+	$42+
59400	Obstetrics, vaginal delivery	39.89	1,403	1,800	2,500	1,753–	1,800NC	1,833+
59510	Obstetrics, cesarean delivery	44.98	1,581	2,300	2,730	1,976–	2,300NC	2,201–
90844	Psychotherapy, 45–50 min.	2.37	78	107	125	98–	107NC	105–
99232	Mid-level subseq. hospital visit	1.38	45	70	73	56–	70NC	65–
99244	Consultation, office	3.60	118	160	180	148–	160NC	158–
66984	Cataract remov., insert lens	27.07	952	2,600	2,760	1,190–	1,904–	1,933–
58260	Vaginal hysterectomy	23.10	812	1,980	3,070	1,015–	1,624–	1,530–
33512	Coronary art. bypass, 3 veins	70.16	2,467	6,400	7,785	3,084–	4,934–	4,841–
29881	Knee arthroscopy	19.81	697	2,000	2,625	871–	1,394–	1,464–
71020	Chest x-ray	.97	32	59	71	40–	59NC	51–
70551	MRI, brain, prof. comp only	2.27	75	130	155	94–	130NC	115–
49505	Repair inguinal hernia	11.75	413	1,065	1,500	516–	826–	807–
43235	Upper GI endoscopy, diag.	6.09	200	475	520	250–	400–	371–
93307	Echo exam of heart	5.97	196	315	450	245–	315NC	288–

*1.25 Medicare RBRVS Fee

**Set floor at 1.25 Medicare RBRVS fee; set ceiling at 2.0 Medicare RBRVS fee; maintain existing fees if between 1.25 and 2.0 RBRVS Medicare fee.

***Set fee at average of existing fee and 1.33 of Medicare RBRVS fee.

+ indicates upward change in fee.

– indicates downward change in fee.

NC indicates no change in fee.

Contracted PAR Network

Implementation of an RBRVS payment approach involves fee reductions for at least some and possibly for most procedure codes. In the absence of a contracted provider network, most physicians who are paid fees below their charges will likely balance-bill the patient. For most employers, frequent balance-billing of covered employees and dependents, unless it occurs for non-PAR providers under a PPO or POS program, is not tolerable. Because of employers' perceived need to provide balance-billing protection for their covered workers and dependents, use of an RBRVS payment approach is generally not recommended other than with a contracted provider network where physicians have agreed to accept the payer's fees as payment in full.

In addition to having a contracted provider network, it is important to have strong provider commitment to the program. Without strong physician commitment, the employer may feel excessively constrained in implementing fee control on other cost-containment programs for fear of provider withdrawal from the network. Physicians should not be expected to participate merely because of tradition or community service, however, but because it is in their best professional/financial interest to do so. It has been the author's experience in working with managed care programs that the ability of the program to steer patients to or (especially) away from specific physicians is a critical means of obtaining physician commitment to PAR programs. For the RBRVS program as well as other cost-containment programs to be effective, employers must convince physicians that they will likely lose patients if they withdraw from the network.

We have been approached by one large employer regarding the feasibility of implementing an RBRVS payment methodology under an indemnity program having no contracted provider network. Although not generally recommended, this may be feasible under a program that uses a claim-based assignment form, where enrollees are trained to discuss claim assignment and physician acceptance of the employer's fee prior to the provision of the service. Such an approach is consistent with an effort to enhance patient empowerment and consumer purchasing of cost-effective medical care.

Corporate Commitment

As noted, implementation of RBRVS involves fee reductions for some services and possibly for a large number of services. Announcement and implementation of an RBRVS-based payment approach may bring complaints from individual physicians (who may have social relationships with employer board members or executives) and possibly from local medical societies if the employer has a large presence in the area. Employees may also complain about higher balance-billing as a result of reduced RBRVS fees when they use non-PAR physicians. To manage these complaints effectively, senior management must be both well informed about the RBRVS implementation plans (before they are finalized) and strongly committed to seeing the process through. Absent that commitment, the mere implied threat of physician withdrawal from network participation may thwart the implementation plans.

Adequate Resources

Depending on the scope of payment system changes to be made, implementation of an RBRVS payment methodology may require significant financial resources and major system changes. There are more than 10,000 procedure codes, so adopting a new methodology for setting fees is a highly complex process.

In discussing causes for plan departication with provider relations staff, and in assessing results of surveys indicating reasons for withdrawal from PAR programs, the conclusion is reached that claims processing problems, payment errors, and payment delays are more significant than fees that are perceived as too high. Thus, prior to final RBRVS implementation decisions, it is important to ensure that adequate financial, administrative staff, and systems resources will be available for a smooth and successful transition to the new RBRVS payment system.

Attractiveness

If RBRVS implementation is feasible, is it worth the effort? Some of the pros and cons related to changing from a charge-based to an RBRVS physician payment system will be examined in this section.

Listed below are goals and objectives typically cited by payers (including employers) for changing to an RBRVS payment system:

- Improved rationality of the physician payment structure
  - improved payment system equity for physician services
  - improved incentive structure relating to specific services
  - help in achieving long-term cost savings
- Prevention of adverse cost shifting from Medicare and other payers implementing RBRVS
- Reduced physician claims costs—reduced pie size as well as recut pieces

Improved Rationality of Payment System

The desire to improve the rationality and incentive structure under the existing physician charge-based payment system was the primary rationale for Medicare implementing an RBRVS payment system. It may also be very important to other publicly financed health benefit programs, such as state Medicaid or public employee benefit programs, or to private payers that have a strong public interest perspective. However, the potential for improving long-term cost-effectiveness of the medical care system (even if it holds promise of producing savings in the long run to the payer) may not be sufficient incentive to overcome the expected RBRVS implementation cost and potential risk of physician withdrawal from the payer's PAR network.

Most employers that self-administer health benefit programs and other health care payers will require the expectation of short-term (e.g., one to two years) or at least intermediate-term (e.g., two to four years) benefits in order to justify development and implementation of a new, radically different physician payment system. In addition, unless the employer or other payer considering adopting a RBRVS payment system is a dominant payer in a specific medical service market area, changing to a RBRVS payment system will likely have little impact on most physicians' practice patterns.

Preventing Adverse Cost Shifting

In discussions with payers immediately prior to and during the first year after Medicare implementation of its RBRVS fee schedule, preventing adverse cost shifting was often mentioned as the primary reason for adopting RBRVS. Even now, it remains an important rationale for many payers. Cost shifting can occur in different ways: Physicians who experience fee reductions as a result of implementation of RBRVS payment systems by Medicare and other payers could increase their charges for the procedures for which fees were reduced, or for other procedures; perform additional services and charge for them; unbundle services into separately billable services; or upcode selective services (e.g., use a level 4 office visit code instead of a lower-fee level 2 office visit code).

The evidence for such cost shifting is ambiguous, however. Evidence exists of aggressive physician billing behavior, such as procedure unbundling and upcoding for several types of services, but this appears to be a continuation of previous trends. Initial assessments of procedure volume changes during 1992 and 1993 suggest no unusual increases, either under Medicare or under privately sponsored health benefit programs.[4] In fact, volume trends appear to be either down or stable compared to trends over the previous several years. There is also little evidence of cost shifting in terms of physicians' increasing their prices. Shown below are annual percent changes in the physician services component of the Consumer Price Index (December over December) over the 1989-1993 period.[5]

- 1989–1990: 7.4 percent
- 1990–1991: 5.5 percent
- 1991–1992: 6.3 percent
- 1992–1993: 5.1 percent

Although there may have been a larger-than-expected increase in 1992, this appears to be related to a change in procedure coding for office and hospital visits and associated increases in charges for those services, rather than to a general increase in physician charge levels.

It is useful to recognize that even if physicians in specific specialties or localities did seek to cost-shift as a result of fee reductions related to RBRVS payment systems, implementation by employers and other private payers of RBRVS-inspired fees would be only a partial and possibly not a very effective remedy. To respond to the various types of cost shifting behavior noted above, payers should use a variety of cost-containment tools including enhanced utilization review, provider profiling, and procedure rebundling software, as well as fee control mechanisms.

Reducing Physician Claims Costs

The third primary objective for implementing an RBRVS payment approach is that it can help reduce physician claims costs. Over the past four decades, primarily as a result of increased prevalence of health insurance coverage and little effort by health insurers to control growth in physician fees (as well as prices paid for other medical care services), physician fees increased much more rapidly than other consumer prices. This is particularly true for surgery and hospital-based services, for which insurance coverage has traditionally been more complete than for medical office visits. As a result of these insurance and price trends, physician charge levels in most localities for surgery, procedure-oriented diagnostic tests and many hospital-based services are substantially higher than charge levels that would prevail under competitive market conditions. Although physician charges are generally disproportionately high compared to would-be competitive prices for the above cited services, there is little indication that charge levels in most localities are too low for physician office visits and for other "evaluation and management" services, as they have come to be called. Thus, efforts to improve the structure of physician fees may include reductions for a sizable proportion of procedure fees but need not include increases for more than a small proportion of them. Furthermore, an RBRVS payment system can be used as a tool both to improve the structure of physician fees and to reduce average physician fees—as noted earlier—to reduce the size of the pie as well as to change the relative sizes of the pieces. In addition, managed care growth and the increasing popularity of IPA and POS plans (which use primary care gatekeepers) have focused specialist physicians' concern on being included in the managed care networks and on obtaining satisfactory levels of referrals, rather than on receiving their full charges.[6]

POTENTIAL PROBLEMS

There are several disadvantages to implementing an RBRVS payment system. The most obvious are the implementation resource requirements. RBRVS implementation is more complex than selecting a fee-setting formula and loading the new fees onto the claims processing system. Alternative RBRVS models will have to be developed and evaluated in terms of the reasonableness and appropriateness of fees and the projected impact on physician claims costs. Most employers will want to examine very carefully RBRVS fee changes for the most common procedures, such as physician office visits and maternity cases. Manual adjustments to the RBRVS fees may be required to help ensure adequate enrollee access for these services as well as to ensure that fees are not substantially higher than average physician charges for these services in their area or average fee levels being used by most other payers.

A commonly encountered problem in the RBRVS implementation process relates to differences between how procedures are defined in the RBRVS schedule and in the employer's payment system. These differences, which are most common for diagnostic procedures that include a professional and a technical component, have to be identified and resolved for the new fees to be applied correctly. Also, although private payers do not have to adopt all the Medicare payment policy rules associated with the Medicare RBRVS fee schedule—such as multiple procedure rules, global surgery definitions, and anesthesia coding and payment rules—most should at least be examined and considered for adoption.

What about the possibility, touched upon earlier, that physicians who are upset about the new fees will resign from the employer's network, possibly hampering enrollee access to care? Some payers that have implemented an RBRVS payment system have been surprised by the minimal number of physician complaints and withdrawals from their networks, but there is a real risk of physician withdrawal. This risk can be minimized, however, by developing and appropriately using information on fees being paid in the employer's market area as well as on the recent experience of other payers that have implemented RBRVS payment systems.

If physicians do threaten to withdraw from the payer's PAR network or actually provide notice of withdrawal as a result of fee reductions under a newly implemented RBRVS payment system, the payer may consider several options for responding. These options include:

1. Offer to meet with those physicians considered vital to the network to explain the need to cut medical care claims cost and how some fees are reduced and others increased under the new system. As a last resort, the payer may offer to consider selective fee adjustments to the new fee schedule.
2. Advise the physicians in writing that physicians who withdraw from the network will not be eligible for payment by the payer, will likely lose as patients most of those covered under the benefit program, and may not have the opportunity to rejoin the PAR network any time in the future.
3. Accept a limited number of physician withdrawals from the PAR network as the price of implementing a reduced fee RBRVS payment system which will result in reduced medical care claims cost.

While physician reaction to reduced fee levels may not be accurately predictable, we are unaware of any payer experiencing significant withdrawals from a PAR network as a result of a wall conceived RBRVS fee schedule and implementation plan.

CONCLUSION

For employers, the primary advantage to changing from a charge-based payment system is that it can help them reduce physician claims costs, both immediately and over time. Most employers will be able to use an RBRVS-inspired fee-setting formula that results in many more fee reductions than fee increases as well as in a reduction in average fees. The magnitude of the average fee reduction will depend on existing fee levels relative to physician charges; on the confidence the employer has in its contracted provider network (assuming it has one); and on the extent of its willingness to accept the possibility of negative reactions from physicians and (if a provider network is not in place) from some employees. Employers who are using fees or maximum allowances defined at the 80th to 90th percentile of physician charges, as is common under usual, customary, and reasonable payment approaches, will be able to achieve greater reductions in average fees than will employers who currently use lower fee levels.

The fee reductions shown under the three hypothetical private payer implementation approaches in Exhibit 1 are comparable to fee changes which have actually achieved by some payers. In future years, further fee changes can be made to narrow the range of fees relative to target RBRVS fees. In most cases, additional average fee reductions are likely. Perhaps equally as important as the fee reductions is the break in the tie between physician payment levels and physician charges. No longer will payment levels increase simply because physicians increase their charges.

In summary, employers who self-administer their benefit plans as well as other private payers should be considering adopting an RBRVS payment system for physician services. Most will find it both feasible and cost-effective to do so if they use a contracted provider network and if their current fees are near or above the average charge levels in their market areas.

1. Hsiao, W., and Stason,W., Toward developing a relative value scale for medical and surgical services. *Health Care Financing Review*, Fall 1979, pp. 23–38.

2. American Medical Association. *Physician Marketplace Statistics.* 1993, Table 58.

3. Dyckman, Z., *Analysis of Private Insurance and Medicare Physician Claims Experience Before and After Implementation of the Medicare RBRVS Fee Schedule*, Report to the Physician Payment Review Commission, Center for Health Policy Studies, 1994.

4. Physician Payment Review Commission, *Annual Report to Congress*, 1993, pp. 99–108.

5. Bureau of Labor Statistics. *Consumer Price Index*, 1989–1993.

6. See for example, Pase, L., "Early Signs of Shakeout," *American Medical News,* October 3, 1994.

24. Dental Coverage: This Benefit Hasn't Lost Its Bite
Paul Lombino

Despite soaring health care costs and corporate cutbacks, dental plans are still going strong. At some companies, even part-timers participate.

While health care benefits at most U.S. businesses have come under increasing scrutiny by red-ink-weary CFOs, dental benefits have remained remarkably intact. Long considered a minor perk along with life insurance, disability, prescriptions, and vision care, dental coverage is gaining visibility—albeit by default, as medical benefits are reduced or yanked from employee-benefits packages.

"In recent years, my clients have been so caught up in trying to slow down the medical problems that there has been very little movement toward cutting back dental benefits," says Mark Straus, a consultant in the Sherman Oaks, California, office of the Wyatt Co. The employee-benefits consulting firm reports that 92 percent of corporations provide some form of dental coverage, a 19 percent gain since 1982.

Dental represents less than 10 percent of a typical benefits portfolio, making it the most affordable and most utilized benefit companies can offer to keep workers happy. "Some employers are using dental plans to help attract and retain vital employees," says Edward Fox, a benefits consultant for Buck Consultants Inc., in Secaucus, New Jersey. "That's not to say inflation and increased utilization have not taken their toll."

Still, that toll is relatively mild. Dental trend (which indicates the annual rate of cost increases) is running about 9 percent, half the annual rate of medical. Furthermore, experts say managed care can help some companies effectively

Reprinted with permission from the April 1993 issue of *CFO*, The Magazine for Senior Financial Executives.

reduce trend—which is influenced by inflation, technological advances, and supply and demand—another 2 points a year.

MANAGED CARE CATCHES ON—SLOWLY

Managed care has been the most significant addition to the field of dental benefits over the past few years. Today, employers use dental health maintenance organizations and preferred provider organizations 26 percent and 11 percent of the time, respectively. Traditional indemnity plans still rank as the number one delivery system, used by 60 percent of companies carrying dental, according to benefits and compensation consultants Hewitt Associates.

"Managed dental plans make a lot of sense," says Tom Beauregard, a health care consultant in Hewitt's Rowayton, Connecticut, office. "They're just a low priority for employers these days." Over the next few years, as employers will perhaps find more time to review their dental programs, managed care could play a larger role. Dental HMOs, similar to models used for medical, allow employers to choose at a discounted rate a primary care dentist, or gatekeeper, who directs treatment during the course of a year.

"Some plans are structured so that the dentist is actually at risk," says Beauregard. Capitation programs pay dentists a fixed monthly amount per employee or family member. "In the first year, the dentist may actually lose money while he brings a claimant to a healthy status."

For employers, dental HMOs provide a high degree of control, since they restrict an employee's choices. This may be particularly important when trying to manage care for a senior population. "Up to 40 percent of cost comes from major restorative work, which is done on older people," says Beauregard. "Children are less expensive."

In contrast, PPOs offer employees a list of discounted providers from which to choose. "In regions where there is an oversupply of providers, you can get discounts as high as 30 percent," says Beauregard. However, such freedom also limits an employer's control.

PREVENTION IS EMPHASIZED

Taking a hard look at benefits distribution doesn't necessarily have to hurt the quality of dental care. At Starbucks Coffee Co., in Seattle, both full- and part-time employees can have their teeth cleaned twice a year, including a set of X rays, for less than the price of a cup of caffe latte.

Starbucks provides coverage for its 1,900 insured employees through an indemnity plan with Blue Cross. "The way our dental plan is structured, we encourage our people to get care proactively," says Bradley Honeycutt,

Starbucks's compensation and benefits manager. "They have 100 percent coverage and no deductibles for checkups. We want to catch the small problems before they get bigger."

Starbucks's aggressive approach is typical of a growing number of corporations nationwide, which have bolstered coverage and waived deductibles for early-preventive treatment. Today, the American Dental Association estimates the average per capita dental bill is $136 a year, while health expenditures come to about $2,255 per person.

MOST PLANS ARE FREESTANDING

Since the late 1980s, three out of every four companies with combined plans have separated their dental and medical coverages into two distinct, or freestanding,

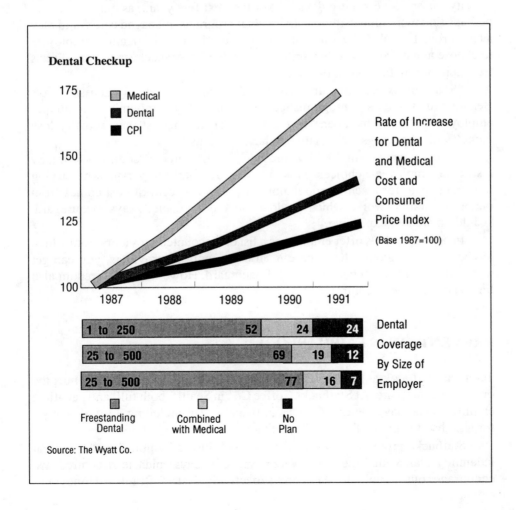

formats. "A common deductible was popular five years ago, but it was a killer in terms of claims cost," says Wyatt's Straus, "Employers got whipsawed, and it really had a significant impact on benefits paid." Combined plans may carry some advantages, but these can only be determined by a careful review of a company's past experiences and current objectives.

Another trend has been a shift toward the exclusive use of "usual, customary, and reasonable" (UCR) schedules rather than the once-popular fee schedules. According to Wyatt, fully 96 percent of companies use UCR schedules because of their sensitivity to changing price conditions. UCR schedules indicate "maximum allowable expenses" by region or zip code, while a fee schedule limits procedures to a fixed-dollar amount.

"Fee schedules are going the way of the Saber-toothed tiger," says Fox of Buck Consultants. While fee schedules are apparently less expensive to implement, they must be periodically updated to keep pace with changing market rates. For a growing company like Starbucks, which has operations in 13 cities and plans for expansion, a fee schedule would be an accounting nightmare. "If we had a fee schedule, we'd probably have to set a different schedule for every zip code we operated in," says Honeycutt.

SHARING COSTS

Like the 75 percent of companies that make workers chip in for medical insurance, more than two-thirds of companies that offer coverage are now asking employees to share dental premiums. Companies requiring employee contributions have jumped 18 percent since 1987, according to Wyatt. In 1991, workers paid for 35 percent of their plan's total cost (40 percent for family plans). Although the percentage that employees contribute is twice the percent they have to ante up for medical benefits, employees still pay only about $6 per month for single dental coverage and $18 for family plans.

In addition to worker contributions, employers are placing more emphasis on deductibles and maximum limits—usually $1,000 to $1,500 per year—as tools to influence utilization patterns. Straus says a typical corporate dental plan includes four components: 100 percent coverage for preventive care; 80 coverage for basic dentistry—extractions, fillings, root canal (after a $50 deductible); 50 percent reimbursement for major work—crowns, bridges, dentures (again, after a $50 deductible); and 50 percent coverage for orthodontia, with a $1,000 to $1,500 lifetime maximum.

"This type of plan creates an incentive for people to use their coverage early without giving away the store for major work later," comments Straus. Eligibility is typically based on length of service: 53 percent of all plans report immediate eligibility, 32 percent provide coverage after 90 days, and the remaining 15 percent require more than three months of employment.

According to Wyatt, about 60 percent of companies now offer flexible spending accounts (FSAs), which give employees the option to set aside up to $2,000 of pretax salaries for anticipated health care expenses. If an employer offers, say, 50 percent reimbursement for major dental work, employees may draw on their FSAs to make up the difference.

What about self-insurance? Generally, dental is less risky to self-fund than medical because costs are more predictable. "There's no such thing as a catastrophic dental expense," explains Fox. Still, because potential savings are marginal—maybe 4 or 5 percent—self-insurance is most likely to make sense for large employers.

Most industry observers don't see much change in dental benefits over the next few years. "Other than raising deductibles and maximums because of inflation, and possibly a slight trend toward prepaid plans," says Straus, "I think there will be a static state in terms of the type of dental benefits provided."

25.   Cost-Effective AIDS Workplace Programs
Patrick May

A significant minority of U.S. businesses have taken action to address AIDS and HIV, the virus that causes AIDS, in their workplaces. The constructive initiatives they have undertaken include: (1) developing workplace HIV/AIDS policies, (2) training managers and supervisors, (3) conducting employee education programs, and (4) supporting community prevention and care efforts including volunteerism.

The majority of U.S. businesses continue to ignore the need to integrate AIDS-focused workplace training, policies, and prevention initiatives into their overall management practices. For all employers, but especially for those who neglect to incorporate HIV- and AIDS-related concerns into their long-term business plans and strategies, the HIV/AIDS epidemic poses complex management, cost, and legal problems.

This article explores the impact of the AIDS epidemic on U.S. business, and sets forth business guidelines for developing cost-effective HIV/AIDS policies and prevention programs in the workplace.

THE IMPACT OF HIV/AIDS ON U.S. BUSINESS

As the HIV/AIDS epidemic worsens, increasing numbers of U.S. workplaces, employers, and employees will be affected. More than two-thirds of large businesses, and nearly one in 10 small businesses, have already encountered employees with HIV infection or AIDS.

The majority (more than 60 percent) of America's 122 million working people are between 25 and 44 years old. According to the Center of Disease

253

Control and Prevention, AIDS is currently the leading cause of death among men and the fourth leading cause of death among women in this age group. Currently, an estimated one in 250 Americans is infected with HIV; the vast majority of them are unaware that they are HIV positive.

Americans who are employed and in their prime working years also make up an estimated 90 percent of all Americans with HIV infection. People in this age range also are likely to be sexually active and thus at heightened risk of exposure to HIV.

Furthermore, as the nation's labor force comes to reflect more accurately the nation's population diversity, employers will increasingly encounter HIV among their employees. Greater numbers of women, teenagers, and people from ethnic and racial minority groups are becoming infected with HIV. Women are the fastest growing group of Americans infected with HIV, and the rates of infection among racial and ethnic minority groups are double their percentage of the population.

Meanwhile, the AIDS epidemic has moved steadily beyond the metropolitan areas and into smaller cities, towns, and rural communities, affecting businesses throughout the nation.

LEGAL RESPONSIBILITIES OF EMPLOYERS

The Americans with Disabilities Act of 1990 (ADA), which took effect in July 1992, includes HIV infection and AIDS in its definition of disability. Under the employment provisions (Title I) of this law, companies with more than 25 employees are prohibited from discriminating against employees with HIV infection or AIDS, including firing, refusing to hire, or failing to make "reasonable accommodations" for those individuals based solely on their disease.

Significantly, the law also prohibits discrimination against people "perceived or regarded as having HIV" because of their status in a group perceived as being at high risk. Also covered under this provision of the law are relatives and associates of people with HIV, since their association with infected individuals, "particularly as caregivers for family members and loved ones with HIV or AIDS," may result in their being discriminated against in the workplace.

As the epidemic into the nation's smaller cities, towns, and rural areas, AIDS increasingly affects smaller businesses. In July 1994, when the employment provisions of the ADA expand to include businesses with 15 or more employees, by then, an estimated 500,000 additional small businesses will be required to comply with the ADA and its HIV/AIDS provisions.

THE SIGNIFICANCE OF EMPLOYEE ATTITUDES AND OPINIONS ABOUT HIV/AIDS

The attitudes and opinions of working Americans about AIDS might not at first seem relevant to employers. But employee ignorance and misinformation can place an employer at risk in a variety of ways.

"AIDS has generated more individual lawsuits across a broad range of health issues than any other disease in history," notes Lawrence Gostin of the HIV Litigation Project.

A 1993 national survey of employee attitudes about AIDS by the National Leadership Coalition on AIDS reports that large numbers of Americans hold negative and potentially discriminatory attitudes toward their HIV-infected co-workers. Significantly, the survey finds that most employees either do not know how their employers would react to HIV or AIDS-related situations in their workplace or think their employers would act illegally.

For example, 32 percent of working Americans surveyed thought an employee with HIV infection would be fired or placed on disability at the first sign of illness. Clearly, if an employer moved to dismiss an employee with HIV infection solely on the basis of the disease, that employer would be breaking the law. Such widespread employee ignorance of an employer's legal responsibilities clearly makes an employer—and by extension, his managers and employees— vulnerable to potentially costly discrimination lawsuits, work disruptions, and employee morale and productivity problems.

Discriminatory attitudes and behaviors among managers and employees can place an employer at unnecessary risk. For example, 67 percent of workers surveyed thought their colleagues would be uncomfortable working with some-one with HIV infection. Managers who acceept such employee attitudes may erroneously assume that discriminatory treatment of those with HIV infection or AIDS, or those perceived as being infected, is also acceptable.

THE COST OF HIV/AIDS TO EMPLOYERS

One of the most common misperceptions about AIDS is that it represents a "bottomless pit" of costs to employers. In fact, AIDS-related health costs are declining. For example, AIDS has changed from being an acute illness leading rapidly to death to a long-term disease characterized by long periods of good health interrupted by intermittent episodes of illness. The average cost of treating a person with AIDS from the time of diagnosis until death is currently $69,100, down from the $102,000 estimated in 1992. The main reasons: earlier diagnosis and intervention, improved treatment options, and fewer and shorter hospital stays.

The most commonly cited costs of AIDS to business are direct costs associated with health, life, and disability insurance and pension plan payouts. Additional indirect costs include those associated with employee replacement and training, workplace disruption, litigation, and lost productivity, as well as costs associated with employees who care for HIV-infected family members and loved ones.

An April 1994 economic study called "Costs to Business for an HIV-infected worker," by Paul G. Farnham and Robin D. Gorsky, found that large and midsize U.S. businesses can expect to pay an average of $17,000 and a maximum of $32,000 for an HIV-positive employee over a five-year period (between 1990 and 1995)—a typical time frame for business decision-making. These new estimates of the cost of caring for HIV-infected employees to business are considerably less than the lifetime medical costs to society of a case of AIDS, previously estimated at more than $100,000.

"Businesses can now see what portion of the $100,000 medical costs they will actually bear," Farnham says. "Because information on the business costs of the epidemic is not readily available, companies may use data on the overall medical costs inappropriately and assume that these costs will be borne entirely by the firm. The overall AIDS costs to business are not out of line with other types of illness that an employer could encounter," he adds.

The study also notes that businesses may realize significant economic advantages by retaining and accommodating HIV-positive employees. The business cost estimates apply to companies with more than 100 workers—companies that employ about 65 percent of the private sector labor force. Further, the study asserts that businesses do not have a great economic incentive to attempt to dismiss HIV-infected employees or force them to resign.

"This relatively low expected business cost, combined with the intangible aspects of an employee's knowledge and experience, suggest that there are significant benefits for an employer to retain HIV-infected workers on the job as long as their health permits," Farnham concludes.

HIV/AIDS MANAGEMENT CHALLENGES

The medical, legal, financial, and workplace developments that have arisen out of the HIV/AIDS epidemic pose a host of challenges for people with HIV infection and AIDS, for their families, and for their employers. Business executives, human resource professionals, and front-line managers face increasingly complicated duties, including controlling costs, providing "reasonable accommodations" for employees with HIV infection and AIDS, and protecting employee confidentiality.

"Businesses must have foresight, must be prepared, and must know that managing HIV disease is not only feasible, but essential," says Lee C. Smith, former president of Levi Strauss International. "It is a question of demonstrating exemplary management practices."

As people with HIV infection remain at work longer, employers are challenged to manage HIV infected employees fairly and effectively, often with little or no training or guidance on the issue. Effectively managing employees with HIV and AIDS requires keeping abreast of emerging health care options, health insurance and health care costs, and legal and regulatory requirements, shaping effective "reasonable accommodations" and managing concerns about confidentiality and privacy, discrimination issues, employee fears, harassment of infected workers, customer concerns, work disruptions, lawsuits, and declines in worker productivity and morale—all while maintaining a productive and profitable workplace and meeting business goals.

"You can't wait until an employee walks into your office and says, 'I have AIDS. What are we going to do?'," says Smith. "By then, you're managing a crisis when you could have been managing an employee with a fatal disease."

Amid the barrage of questions and concerns about the epidemic and ways to manage its impact on the workplace, employers can take constructive and cost-effective steps to minimize risk, reduce health care costs by protecting the health of their workers, protect their companies' future, and, most importantly, save lives.

STEP ONE: ESTABLISH A WORKPLACE HIV/AIDS POLICY

The first step a business should take to prepare for managing workplace issues arising from the HIV/AIDS epidemic is drafting a workplace policy. It should clearly set forth the ways the business will deal with the host of complex but manageable challenges generated by HIV/AIDS.

"Developing and reinforcing a sound policy that accounts for the legal duties to both the infected and affected employees will help a business to keep from becoming a test case," says management labor lawyer Peter Petesch.

It would be facile and misleading to assert that a workplace policy itself will remove the difficulties inherent in managing an employee with a fatal and often stigmatized illness. A written workplace policy, however, goes a long way toward preparing a company to manage HIV/AIDS issues by minimizing risk and protecting the company's workforce.

An effective written HIV/AIDS workplace policy:

- Sets standards for a company's entire HIV/AIDS program;
- Sets standards for a company's position and communications about HIV/AIDS;
- Sets standards for employee behavior;
- Informs all employees where they can go for information and assistance; and
- Instructs supervisors how to manage HIV/AIDS issues in their work groups.

Policy Provisions

Effective HIV/AIDS workplace policies should cover, and provide guidance, on the following: compliance with the law; nondiscrimination; confidentiality and privacy; safety; performance standards; reasonable accommodation; co-worker concerns; and employee education. To be effective, the policy must be communicated to employees at every level of the organization. Moreover, it is crucial to have the outspoken, highly visible support of upper level management and executives, including the CEO, in reinforcing the urgency and importance of the policy's messages. Without this level of leadership, a paper policy runs the risk of becoming like a lion with no teeth.

Approaches to Policy Developement

There are two general approaches to developing HIV/AIDS policies.

Life-Threatening Illness Approach: Some employers choose to develop their HIV/AIDS policies as part of the continuum of all life-threatening illnesses or disabilities. These policies usually state that HIV/AIDS will be handled as are other long-term illnesses—compassionately, sensibly, and without discrimination.

The HIV/AIDS-Specific Approach: This approach to workplace policy development specifically acknowledges and addresses HIV/AIDS as a major health issue with potential impact on the workplace. In addition to the policy statement itself, this approach often includes an educational component asserting (1) that HIV/AIDS is not transmitted through casual workplace contact and (2) that employees with HIV infection or AIDS do not pose any health risk to their co-workers.

STEP TWO: TRAIN MANAGERS AND SUPERVISORS

Effective workplace policy implementation requires managers and supervisors to become thoroughly familiar with the company's HIV/AIDS policy guidelines for the workplace. It is vital to ensure that every level of management be informed with clear and consistent guidance about the medical facts and the minimal risk of transmission of HIV/AIDS in the general workplace; about compliance with the Americans with Disabilities Act and its "reasonable accommodation" requirements; and about nondiscrimination; confidentiality and privacy; workplace safety; and employee performance standards.

In addition, all managers must be educated so they can be prepared to respond to questions and concerns from employees about HIV/AIDS and the workplace. Often the frontline managers are the first ones called on to provide information and referrals to other sources of information and in-depth answers to employee questions about why they should be concerned about HIV infection and AIDS and how they are expected to behave. In terms of priorities, management training should be completed *before* employee education programs are instituted.

STEP THREE: EDUCATE EMPLOYEES

Workplace-based education programs are inexpensive and cost-effective ways to minimize company risk, protect workers' lives, and save money on health care costs. MacAllister Booth, CEO at Polaroid, recently said that AIDS education and training for all Polaroid employees cost less than the treatment costs of one case of AIDS.

Workplace wellness programs are already established as a cost-effective and appropriate venue for communicating health information to employees. Particularly in larger companies, HIV/AIDS education programs can be readily integrated into these ongoing health promotion efforts; in fact, studies have shown that employees trust their employers to provide accurate information about a broad range of topics, including health education, and want to learn more about HIV/AIDS.

Furthermore, according to a study by the New York Business Group on Health, employees generally have a positive opinion of employers that provide information about AIDS, and are likely to consider employers more credible as a source of such information than either the media or the government. According to the National Leadership Coalition on AIDS' survey of working Americans' attitudes about the disease, 96 percent of employees who received AIDS education at work supported workplace-based HIV/AIDS education.

Ideally, attendance at employee education sessions should be mandatory, and the program should last at least 90 minutes. The session should be conducted by a trained educator and should present materials in an objective and nonjudgmental way. The program should also allow for a question-and-answer period and provide referrals for confidential assistance. "HIV/AIDS in the workplace" initiatives should be ongoing, not one-shot events, and are even more effective when linked with World AIDS Day observances, AIDS Awareness Month events, or workplace displays of the Names Project Memorial Quilt. Finally, one of the most effective methods for discussing AIDS with employees is to invite a person living with HIV infection or AIDS to address a session. Hearing first-hand how someone lives and works with HIV infection or AIDs has been shown to have a positive impact on employee attitudes.

Topics to Cover

An effective HIV/AIDS education program in the workplace should include the following:

- The medical facts—for example, discussion of how HIV is and is not transmitted, emphasizing that it cannot be spread through casual contact and is virtually impossible to contract in the general workplace;
- The legal facts, including employers' responsibilities—especially regarding the importance of confidentiality and privacy and of providing reasonable accommodations;
- The psycho-social issues—including how to respond to a co-worker with HIV/AIDS and what it is like to live and work with HIV/AIDS;
- Guidelines on HIV/AIDS-related company policies and benefits;
- Information for employees to take home to their families—to teach them how to protect themselves from HIV/AIDS; and
- Information on community resources—for example, places to go for anonymous HIV/AIDS testing.

Pitfalls to Avoid

Studies caution that attitudes about HIV/AIDS can be negatively reinforced if an education or training session is too brief, or is not sufficiently thorough and interactive. (Similarly, simply handing out a brochure has been shown to increase anxiety about AIDS.) Attendees at such a session have been found to absorb some of the facts but to leave with unresolved anxieties about transmission of HIV—anxieties that have actually been aroused by introduction of the subject. Thus, it is important to allow sufficient time in a training session for in-depth discussion, for questions and answers, and for referrals to other sources of confidential information. As noted earlier, attendance at a training session should be compulsory because the stigma still associated with HIV infection and AIDS may undermine attendance.

The resources section at the end of this chapter provides guidance and referrals to inexpensive and cost-effective sources of workplace education programs.

STEP FOUR: ENCOURAGE EMPLOYEE COMMUNITY INVOLVEMENT AND VOLUNTEERISM

Employees are more likely to retain, use, and share their knowledge and educated attitudes about HIV/AIDS when they are encouraged by their employers to volunteer for community AIDS efforts, services, and fundraisers. They are more likely to support their employer's commitment to community AIDS prevention and care programs. In fact, there is a strong correlation between employees who have received HIV/AIDS education in the workplace and those who participate in community-based AIDS-related activities.

CONCLUSION

Despite the increasingly common incidence of HIV infection among working Americans, only about one-fourth of America's largest private-sector employers have policies and programs to guide their employees' response to HIV and AIDS. The number of smaller businesses that are prepared to deal with HIV-infected employees is unknown and therefore more difficult to measure.

In the American Management Association's 1993 HIV and AIDS-related policies survey of 630 companies, it was reported, "Experience is driving policy, which means that companies are reacting to instances of HIV infection or AIDS rather than proactively developing policies before the fact. Few are ahead of the curve with policy provisions and workplace initiatives in place before the first instance strikes."

Although companies responding constructively to the day-to-day workplace challenges of HIV/AIDS are in the minority, such companies are providing leadership and generating educational models as well as a growing body of knowledge to help employers effectively address HIV/AIDS as a workplace concern. Experience gained over the past 10 years demonstrates that well-planned HIV/AIDS policies, ongoing management training and employee education concerning HIV/AIDS, establishment of appropriate workplace standards and practices, and strong executive leadership are effective methods for addressing these challenges.

Resources

Business Reponds to AIDS

The Centers for Disease Control and Prevention's *Business Reponds to AIDS* program provides a "Manager's Kit," a "Labor Leader's Kit" and a special business resource service and referral network at the CDC National AIDS Clearinghouse to help businesses develop policies, practices and education programs. 1-800-458-5231; 1-800-243-7012 (TDD).

National Leadership Coalition on AIDS

National Leadership Coalition on AIDS can help businesses develop specific workplace strategies, policies, and workplace initiatives. 202-429-0930.

Part 7

RETIREES AND HEALTH CARE

26. Is There Good News About Retiree Health Benefits?

Lance D. Tane

Employers have generally viewed FAS 106 as bad news for their benefits programs since it forces them to account for future liabilities right now, and therefore affects their bottom line. However, FAS 106 has focused much necessary attention on the issues of retiree health benefits, and in the long run, this focus will be positive for employers and employees alike. This article outlines the current state of retiree health care planning, provides practical, step-by-step guidance on how to handle the important issues facing employers, and supplies useful insights to the future of retiree health benefits.

Few recent benefit issues have caused more headaches than retiree medical care. While the amount of popular attention this benefit has received from employees and the press has increased significantly over the last year, it took a new accounting rule—Financial Accounting Statement 106 (FAS)—to make it an issue for CEOs and the rest of the country.

FAS 106 requires that companies recognize the expense for retiree health benefits on an accrual rather than cash basis, which means that employers must recognize as a current expense the portion of the future benefit that each employee earns each year. Employers are given a period of time over which to recognize the benefits that had been earned before the adoption of the FAS 106. What the new rule means is that benefit funding problems, previously ignored because they were in the future, must now be dealt with in the present. Under FAS 106 the future is now.

As companies come to grips with the implications of their retiree medical commitments, it becomes clear that the status quo is not acceptable. Many

Reprinted from *Compensation & Benefits Management,* Vol 10, No 1, Winter 1994. A Panel Publication. Aspen Publishers, Inc.

companies cannot afford the plans they have in place; moreover, traditional plan designs do not support business objectives. Companies that have researched the issue have found that retirees may be ready for a change, too, since retirees are frequently frustrated and confused in their attempt to understand and use their benefits.

Many companies initially focus on the negative accounting implications of FAS 106 and make their objective the reduction of this new expense item, rather than coming to grips with the real issue: providing medical benefits to retirees. However, as more and more managers recover from the shock of the initial numbers, they are beginning to think about viable long-term solutions to this continuing cost problem. It is in this evolution in thinking about solutions that the good news about retiree medical benefits may lie. As the limitations and inequities of traditional plan designs are more fully understood, totally new approaches to providing these benefits are developing. These new ideas hold the promise of being more meaningful to employees and more sustainable for employers.

To best understand the good news about retiree health benefits, it is important to understand first the problems and limitations of traditional plans. From that understanding can come a better perspective from which a framework for a more effective retiree medical program, as well as some specific plan design alternatives, may become clear.

PROBLEMS WITH TRADITIONAL RETIREE MEDICAL PROGRAMS

With or without FAS 106, retiree medical programs are going to have to change. Two major problems have become increasingly clear—cost and equity.

Escalating and Uncontrollable Costs

While FAS 106 accelerates the recognition of the fact, the cost of existing retiree medical plans is spiraling out of control. It is clear that the rate of cost increase is on the rise, and employers have few tools for controlling these escalating costs.

The cost increases for retiree medical benefits are being driven by two powerful and essentially uncontrollable engines. The first is the increase in health care costs in general, and the second is the aging demographics of the workforce combined with increased life expectancy.

Health Care Cost Inflation
Because of the current national debate on health care reform, widespread awareness of the level of health care inflation has been heightened. Health care costs consume an increasing portion of our nation's gross domestic product, having grown from 7.4 percent in 1970 to 12.2 percent in 1990 (and projected to exceed

18 percent by the year 2000). The rate of increase for employer-sponsored health care plans has been even greater because of cost shifting associated with government programs and the cost of providing health care for the uninsured.

Aging Workforce and Growing Number of Retirees

Basic cost inflation, as troubling as it has been, is further compounded in the population of retirees. The aging demographics of the workforce mean that the ratio of retirees to active employees is growing. This means that the cost of retiree medical benefits as a percentage of the cost of active employee medical benefits is growing, too. Increased life expectancy, attributable to advances in health care, means two things: Not only is there an increasing proportion of retirees to active employees, but the people who retire remain alive for a longer period of time. Moreover, the health care cost for older retirees is especially high, since health care expenditures are directly related to age.

Unpredictable Costs

Almost as troubling for plan sponsors as the level of costs is the difficulty in predicting what they are going to be in the future. Retiree medical benefits are paid in the future, after the employee has retired. But the money to pay for those benefits must be earned now, when the employee is working. The cost of paying future benefits must be included in current labor costs. But what are those costs going to be? Changes in technology, patterns of medical practice, and disease patterns make predicting these costs very problematic.

Predictability is further limited because employer retiree medical costs are so dependent on government policy. For retirees eligible for Medicare, the employer plan is the secondary payer. This means that the employer's cost of providing the promised plan is offset by the payments the retiree receives from Medicare. But any curtailment in Medicare benefits is absorbed by the employer. A change in the reimbursement percentage or a change in the age at which an individual is eligible for Medicare significantly affects employer costs. The possibility of government mandates concerning retiree medical programs further exacerbates the difficulty of predicting future costs associated with retiree health care.

From a planning perspective, the inability to predict the costs is made even more troublesome by the fact that, even if the costs were predictable, there is little way for the employer to control them.

Limited Ability to Change Existing Plans

Limits on the employer's ability to change the plan to achieve cost savings further compound the problem. Employers have become increasingly aware of the legal constraints that may be imposed on future plan changes and, therefore, employers attempt to clearly and explicitly retain the right to do so;

however, most employers find themselves with few options for existing retirees. Even with explicit language reserving the right to modify or terminate the plan, employers who attempt such changes still may find themselves in a legal quagmire, as plaintiffs' lawyers develop increasingly convoluted legal theories to bring suit. The costs of defending lawsuits alone has deterred many employers from making changes.

Concerns over negative employee relations and community relations, as well as a real sense of obligation to fulfill promises made to retirees, also keep many employers from making changes. For many reasons, most companies think long and hard before proceeding with changes to their retiree medical plan.

Cost containment strategies other than plan redesign are also difficult to implement. The strong relationships retirees tend to have with their doctors makes the implementation of network managed care programs potentially as traumatic as plan reductions. Other types of changes are difficult to implement. Once an employee has retired, contact with the employer is minimal, limiting opportunities to promote initiatives designed to change patterns of health care utilization or to increase wellness. Realistically, it is difficult if not impossible to persuade retirees to change patterns and habits developed over the course of a lifetime.

DESIGNED FOR INEQUITY

If you were designing a benefit plan for retirees, would you design it so that someone who became an employee at age 45 and retired at age 55 received a benefit that was five or ten times more valuable than an employee who gave you a full career of 30 or 35 years and retired at age 65? Probably not. Yet that is the way most retiree medical plans have been designed.

Unlike other retirement plans, such as pensions or profit-sharing plans, retiree medical plans have not recognized service and have not been adjusted for early retirement. Furthermore, a married retiree typically receives twice the benefit of an employee without a spouse. Because each of these factors affects the others, the difference in the value of the benefits provided to retirees can be significant—and unfair.

Traditionally, retiree medical benefits, if offered, are an all-or-nothing entitlement. Generally, if an employee retires and is eligible to receive a pension, he or she receives a lifetime of retiree medical benefits. This means that someone who has worked for a company for as few as ten, and in some cases five, years and leaves the company after age 55 is entitled to the benefit. Another employee who might have worked for the company for 25 or more years, but leaves before retirement eligibility, gets nothing. In any event, everyone receiving the benefit is generally entitled to the same plan, regardless of service.

Another typical plan feature is that, when an employee retires, coverage continues for life. This causes disparities far greater than the obvious fact that the expected cost of lifetime medical care for someone at age 55 is greater than for someone at 65. The fact that at age 65 retirees become eligible for Medicare, and Medicare becomes the primary payer, means that a year of pre-65 coverage might cost three to five times as much as a year of post-65 coverage. So, not only are early retirees not having their benefits adjusted for the greater expected duration of coverage, but no adjustment is made of the significantly higher cost of coverage for each of their pre-65 years.

The final factor that contributes to the inequity in benefit values is the fact that, if an employee has a spouse, spousal coverage is provided at little or no cost. Coverage for the spouse continues not only while the employee is alive but for the life of the spouse as well.

All of this might not have been too bad 20 years ago when the cost of medical care was much lower and a full career with one employer more the norm. But in the current environment, it makes no sense at all.

The contrast with other retirement benefit plans could hardly be greater. Pension benefits are directly related to service. The benefit is accrued for each year of service. Vesting is required after a specified period of service, with the employee ultimately entitled to a benefit whether he or she retires from the company or leaves before retirement. If the benefit is expressed as an annuity, it is defined as the benefit payable at the normal retirement age, which is then adjusted for early retirement. Lump-sum payments are not increased if the employee retires early. Not only is the pension not increased if the retiree has a spouse but, if it is provided in a lifetime annuity form—which takes into account the spouse's life as well—it is actuarially adjusted to reflect this.

DEVELOPING A NEW FRAMEWORK FOR RETIREE MEDICAL

Most companies have focused on reducing the impact of FAS 106 on their financial statements. Increasingly, however, they have acknowledged that the real solution lies not in a quick fix but in a total redesign based on a solid conceptual framework. The process of retiree medical redesign is most effective if it is a comprehensive process of retirement program assessment and redesign, rather than a fragmented effort focusing solely on retiree medical.

While most plans have been implemented to continue the active medical plan into retirement (another nice "fringe benefit"), under scrutiny it becomes clear that they have evolved into major components of the retirement program.

Finding a long-term solution to the problem requires developing a set of principles and objectives for the retirement program as a whole.

HEALTH CARE AS A RETIREMENT INCOME NEED

Viewed objectively, it is difficult to see a difference between health care and all of the other financial needs of retirees. Retirement is that period of time when financial needs must be met from previously accumulated resources. This is true for housing, clothing, and shelter, and it is true for health care.

One of the first issues a plan sponsor must address is the amount of responsibility the company wants to assume for the individual. In the past, many employers assumed a paternalistic role, in effect saying to the employee, "Don't worry about it—if you take care of us during your working career we will take care of you during retirement." This approach to retirement plans is becoming less prevalent. The changing economic environment of the 1990s, as well as changing employee expectations and needs, are leading an increasing number of employers to discard the paternalistic model for one characterized as a partnership.

Under the partnership model the employee is recognized as having the ultimate responsibility for his or her financial affairs. This transfer of responsibility redefines the role of the employer. Under the paternalistic model, the employer decided how much income the employee would consume while working and how much would be deferred in the form of benefits. While an employer providing rich retirement benefits might believe that it was taking care of its employee, the employee might be better taken care of if he or she had access to the money earlier. The partnership approach more appropriately recognizes the unique needs of each individual and allows employees greater control over the income they earn.

Recognizing retiree health care as a retiree income need, and recognizing the employee as having ultimate responsibility for planning for retirement, can form the basis for restructuring the retiree medical plan in the best interest of the employee and the employer. It is not in the long-term interest of the employee to have the employer distribute as compensation, either current or retirement, more than the market will allow. The result of such continued action would be the failure of the employer. Undoubtedly the employee would prefer more to less, but given a limit on the ultimate amount that can be spent on total compensation, the employee is best served when he or she is provided with the most control over how and when to use compensation dollars.

This is not to say that the employer should abandon all retirement plans and distribute the value annually in cash. Retirement plans are in existence to meet the needs of the employer, as well as the employee. In addition, the tax code and the current retirement and health care delivery infrastructure create opportunities for the employer to leverage the compensation that they are able to provide. An effective retirement program maximizes the value of compensation by providing employees with the greatest control possible over their compensation while still ensuring that the needs of the employer are met.

KEYS TO AN EFFECTIVE RETIREMENT PROGRAM

If the current retiree medical crisis prompts companies to implement more efficient and effective total retirement programs it will be good news for employees and employers alike. While the specific plan structures may vary based on a number of factors, there are certain key elements of an effective plan that apply to every employer.

Communicating Employee Responsibility

First, it is essential that employees understand that they are responsible for their financial circumstances during retirement. Giving employees the opportunity to shape their financial condition during retirement can enable each employee to make decisions that best meet individual needs both now, while active, and later, when he or she retires. However, the success of the approach depends on the employee becoming an active participant in the process.

It's important to begin any transition with an assessment of your employees' current sense of responsibility for retirement planning. Employees need to understand that, at some point, they will want or need to retire, that they have choices, and that what they do now will affect their situation when they do retire. The recent period of financial uncertainty, concerns about the federal deficit and the implications it has for future payments under government programs, and all the publicity about health care costs have all served to heighten employee awareness about retirement income and security issues. Even so, most people have not fully accepted the necessity of taking responsibility for their retirement.

Retirement Planning Assistance

Employers should provide assistance to employees in determining their needs. The first step in retirement planning is for each employee to identify and quantify their expected financial needs during retirement. While different employees will have different expectations, employers can be helpful in making employees aware of the different types of expenses they are likely to have, and in encouraging employees to begin to estimate what they might be. It is at this point in the process that health care can be established as one of the financial needs an employee will have.

The differences in financial needs before and after retirement, as well as the way in which needs change over the course of retirement, should be explained. Providing employees with examples of typical expense patterns and illustrating different scenarios will help employees to begin to think about their own retirement plans in a meaningful way.

It is also important to assist the employee in understanding the resources they will have to meet their needs. Most employees will meet their retirement needs through a number of different sources. Social Security, Medicare, a pension, money from company-sponsored profit-sharing and 401(k) plans, individual savings, part-time employment, and the proceeds from the sale of a home are some of the possibilities. Valuing each of these and understanding when each becomes available is a complicated task. The company can be helpful in providing tools employees can use to help to understand what these resources are likely to be. Benefits plan designs that are easier to understand will also help employees.

Making Commitments

Employers should make reasonable commitments and keep them. Employees need to determine what their needs will be, what their income will be, and what decisions they need to make about current consumption and savings while they are working. In most cases, company-provided benefits will be a key component of retirement income. An employer who makes a commitment to provide a reasonable benefit, who gives employees a clear understanding of the value of the benefit, and provides employees with the time to accumulate additional resources, serves employees much better than one who makes a more generous commitment but is later forced to abruptly curtail the benefit without providing the employees with time to adapt. If financial circumstances require the curtailment of a benefit, the redesign should consider the amount of time employees have before retirement to adjust to the change.

Core Benefits

Providing a core level of retirement benefits is another important principle in effective retirement benefit design. While the goal is to maximize the value of the total compensation package by giving the employee greater control over the timing of the receipt of income, it is necessary to ensure that all employees have some minimum level of resources accumulated for retirement. It is important not to lose sight of the fact that the retirement program is there to benefit the employer, too.

A change in organizational needs—for example, restructuring or downsizing—may mean that the employer wants to encourage employees to retire. However, it is illegal to require that older people retire, and generally, if individuals do not have the necessary economic resources—i.e., a core set of retirement benefits—they will be reluctant to retire. Similarly, abrupt cancellation of retiree medical plans may discourage people from retiring. If individuals who are not as productive as desired stay on the job as a result of not having resources to cover anticipated retiree medical costs, the ultimate cost to the employer may be greater than what the cost of the retiree coverage would have been.

In addition, retirees have contact with active employees and the community in general. If long service employees find themselves with inadequate resources during retirement, their ill will could affect perceptions about the company by active employees and by the public.

Providing the Means

Employers should also provide employees with effective wealth accumulation vehicles. Incentives in the tax code—as well as the employer's purchasing power and financial acumen—enable the employer to provide opportunities for productive wealth accumulation that employees would not have on their own. If an employer provides employees the means to accumulate wealth on a tax-deferred basis, or to accumulate money to pay for retiree medical with pretax dollars, the employees will be better off and the employer will leverage compensation expenditures.

Medicare Integration

At the current time there are no effective ways for retirees who are not yet age 65 (when they reach Medicare eligibility) to secure health care coverage. For this reason, employers should provide sources for securing medical coverage during this period. Generally, this means giving retirees the opportunity to purchase coverage through the company plan until they reach age 65, although the employer may want to structure the financial commitment this involves to a dollar amount.

It is not necessary for the employer to provide retirees age 65 or older the opportunity to secure coverage through the employer's plan because such retirees are eligible for Medicare. While there are some gaps in Medicare—most significantly, no limitation on the 20 percent copayment amount for doctor expenses, no prescription drugs, and limited protection for hospital stays over 90 days—the retiree is fully able to buy coverage at competitive costs. Now there are ten standard Medigap policies, each providing different degrees of additional protection, which are available without proof of insurability from a variety of sources including the AARP, Blue Cross/Blue Shield, and a number of commercial carriers. The standardized plan design means that comparison shopping is easy, while ten different types of protection means that a retiree can select the plan that best meets his or her needs and resources.

PLAN DESIGN POSSIBILITIES FOR AN INTEGRATED RETIREMENT PROGRAM

The key to creating an integrated retirement program is changing the medical component from a defined benefit—that is, a specific health care plan—to a defined contribution plan, where an employer contribution is made to the employee (or the employee's account), who then uses it to purchase medical care. This approach is attractive to the employer because it eliminates the uncertainty associated with health care inflation as well as possible changes in Medicare.

Under this approach, the employer-provided retiree medical benefit becomes a dollar allowance to be used by the employee to purchase the level of care he or she needs. The advantage to the retiree under this approach is that he or she gets to use the money that the employer is willing to spend in the way that best meets personal needs during retirement, and to adapt spending patterns as those needs change. At different times during retirement, different levels of coverage may be available. For example, if a retiree has a spouse who is working and the retiree can initially get coverage through the spouse, he or she can "save" the employer's dollars until they are really needed.

While perhaps to implement this approach would be to eliminate the retiree medical program and replace it with an increase in pension plan benefits, differences in the taxation of pension benefits as compared with retiree medical benefits, as well as differences in vesting, make this approach less attractive. Under current law, pension payments are taxable to the recipient when paid, while employer-provided retiree health care is nontaxable. If a pension payment is substituted for a retiree medical plan, the retiree would have to pay taxes on the amount before being able to use the money to purchase health care. The result of this approach is that the employer would have to provide significantly greater pension benefits to enable the employee to secure the same level of protection, or else the employee would be able to buy less medical coverage.

Secondly, while ERISA requires that pension benefits become vested, there is no such requirement for retiree medical plans. These plans almost never vest. If the employee leaves before being eligible for retirement, medical benefits are forfeited. While the appropriateness of this practice could be questioned, changing it would significantly increase employer cost, a consequence that is unacceptable for most employers. Two specific plan designs have emerged to address this issue: the account balance retiree medical plan and the qualified-plan/cafeteria-plan hybrid. These designs can be used separately or combined.

ACCOUNT BALANCE RETIREE MEDICAL PLAN

In this plan, a national account is established for each employee. Each year the company credits each active employee with an allocation of dollars. The account can also be credited with interest. At retirement, employees draw on the account to buy coverage for themselves and their spouses, either from the employer or from any of the other available retiree medicare supplement plans.

Because the money in this account can only be used for medical coverage, it is not taxable. The fact that it grows each year based on service means that employees receive an equitable allocation of employer contributions based on service. Employees receive their account whenever they retire. This eliminates the disproportionate employer subsidy for early retirement.

A more complicated variation on this design allows active employees to trade nontaxable current benefits for greater employer contributions to the account. Because of constructive receipt and Section 125 limitations, it is not possible to trade off any taxable benefits for retiree medical credits.

QUALIFIED-PLAN/CAFETERIA-PLAN HYBRID

Under this type of plan, the employee has the ability to make a cafeteria plan election for the pension benefit to which he or she is entitled. If the employee chooses, he or she could trade taxable pension benefits for nontaxable medical benefits. The dollars converted would be used to purchase medical benefits. While there is not explicit authority to implement this type of program, a detailed analysis of both the applicable cafeteria plan law and regulations and applicable pension laws and regulations appears to support its viability. By combining the two plans, the employer can provide a core level of coverage in the form of a base medical allowance and the employee could use converted pension dollars to pay for supplemental levels of coverage.

CONCLUSION

No doubt everyone would prefer it if health care costs weren't increasing as rapidly as they are, but at least we are getting something for our money. Much of the increase in cost is due to increases in medical knowledge and improvements in technology that mean better treatments and better protection from illness and disease. However, employers do not have the ability to absorb all of these cost increases and still remain competitive. FAS 106 did not create the problem of increased retiree medical costs, it merely focused attention on it. In forcing us to address this problem sooner rather than later it has given us more time to adapt.

As employers wrestle with this problem, it is becoming clear that the plan designs of the future need to respond to the needs of individual employees, but must also be economically sustainable. While employees may have preferred more to less, they may find that the results of FAS 106 are worthwhile in the long run. For employees, the good news about retiree medical benefits may be the ability to use the resources available as they choose, an increased ability to depend on the coverage provided, and increased competitiveness for their employers, with greater job security as a consequence.

27. Easing Pressure with Medicare-Risk HMOs

David W. Barr

Do you worry about paying too much for retiree health benefits? About meeting your funding obligations under FAS 106? Medicare-risk HMOs may give you and your retirees a break.

Gone are the days when American companies could reward their retirees with a gold plaque and a cornucopia of health-care benefits. Today, soaring health-care costs, a steadily growing pool of retirees, the burgeoning health-care reform debate and Financial Accounting Standard 106 have clouded the retiree health-care picture. American companies are in a quandary. Many can no longer afford to pay for these benefits and have been forced to eliminate them, even in the face of threatened lawsuits. Other companies are shifting benefits costs to retirees, paying them a fixed monthly amount, charging higher deductibles, eliminating ancillary benefits or laying off workers.

Medicare-risk plans can help relieve the pressure. For seniors who have Medicare, these plans provide comprehensive health-care benefits through a health maintenance organization at a very low employer cost. First approved and implemented in 1985, Medicare risk plans have grown steadily from 950,000 members in 1987 to more than 1.6 million people currently enrolled in 96 plans nationwide.

Under Medicare risk, the federal government, through the Health Care Financing Administration, estimates its cost to cover an average Medicare beneficiary in a geographic area. The numbers are based on the cost for beneficiaries who are not in an HMO, also known as fee-for-service cost. The government then contracts with an HMO that has met certain eligibility requirements, agreeing to pay it 95 percent of the estimated fee-for-service amount for each enrollee. Each enrollee assigns his or her Medicare benefits to the HMO.

In return, the HMO agrees to provide comprehensive health care benefits to the Medicare recipient under an annually renewable contract. These benefits, which surpass traditional Medicare coverage, do not require deductibles, coinsurance payments or time-consuming paperwork. A typical plan includes hospitalization (100 percent coverage for an unlimited number of days); physician visits ($5 to $10 copayment charge); annual physical exams; hearing and vision exams ($5 to $10 copayment charge); and prescription drug benefits.

For the employer, cost is the biggest draw of a Medicare-risk HMO. Because the government is already paying the HMO for basic services, you can offer a Medicare-risk plan for as little as $30 to $45 per month per person. This lets you customize the plan by offering benefit upgrades or enhancements to meet retirees' special needs or to match the company's regular indemnity plan. You could adopt lower or no copayments; additional benefits, such as hearing aids, chiropractic care, or dental care; and expanded prescription-drug coverage.

Medicare-risk plans also reduce liability under FAS 106. You can decrease the amount of money you need to set aside for Financial Accounting Standards Board compliance by more than 50 percent, depending on the coverage and the employee contribution you select. In fact, a 1992 Ernst & Young study, which compares a company's FAS 106 liability under a Medicare-risk HMO with that of a typical indemnity plan, clearly demonstrates the potential savings, as shown in Table 1.

Table 1. Indemnity Plans Meet Medicare-Risk HMOs

Intrigued by Medicare-risk HMOs? To demonstrate how they can help you save money, take a hypothetical company with this breakdown of employees:

Total beneficiaries (including dependents)	34,107
Active employees	14,386
Retirees	2,197
Early retirees	446
Medicare-eligible beneficiaries	2,870

Here's how the costs and liabilities stack up:

	Indemnity Plan (in Millions)	Medicare-Risk HMO (in Millions)
Accumulated post-retirement benefit obligation	$190.0	$49.0
Net periodic post-retirement benefit cost:		
• 20-year amortization	32.0	8.0
• Immediate recognition	212.0	55.0
• First-year cash payments	5.1	2.7

WHAT WILL RETIREES THINK?

A Medicare-risk plan can be a good deal for the retiree. Although the government pays for Medicare Part A, a retiree faces additional fees under conventional Medicare coverage, including Medicare Part B, currently $36.60 per month; a $652 deductible fee for the first 60 days of hospitalization; a $100 annual deductible for medical care; and a 20-percent coinsurance charge on all covered costs. In addition, to safeguard against conditions and charges that Medicare doesn't cover, retirees often purchase supplemental policies, commonly known as Medigap, to the tune of $50 to $300 per month.

Not all employers, however, are sold on Medicare-risk HMOs for their retirees. In most cases, the number one drawback is availability. While Medicare-risk plans are expanding at a fast clip—and will probably figure significantly in health care reform—they simply are not yet operating in many regions. (See "Look Before You Leap" beginning on page 280, for some other considerations.)

Also, many employers are reluctant to encourage their retirees to join a Medicare-risk HMO. They sense their retirees' apprehension about HMOs, which stems from unfamiliarity and fear of change. Once retirees get better acquainted with HMOs, they often change their minds. In fact, a 1991 Gallup Poll survey reports that more seniors are "very or somewhat satisfied" with their managed-care plans than with traditional indemnity plans.

To help you determine whether a Medicare-risk HMO is right for your retirees, here are some guidelines:

- The HMO should be federally qualified and financially stable. The Health Maintenance Organization Act of 1973 and subsequent amendments established federal qualifications for HMOs. Has it been accredited by the National Committee for Quality Assurance, an independent, nonprofit organization that evaluates the quality of HMO care?
- For how long has the HMO provided Medicare-risk programs? Ask how many members are enrolled and whether the providers and administrators are experts in understanding and meeting seniors' needs.
- Find out how large the plan's provider network is and which physicians and hospitals belong to it. The physician roster should encompass all specialties, and all physicians should be credentialed and board-certified. Are the provider hospitals well-established? Consider the geographic area the Medicare-risk plan covers and whether it will be convenient for most of your retirees.
- How easily can you and your retirees participate? What administrative work is required? Does the plan offer benefit flexibility and comprehensive administrative assistance? Check the disenrollment rate and member satisfaction surveys, which are often revealing.

KNOWLEDGE IS POWER

To save money with Medicare-risk HMOs, you must be committed to educating your retirees about all aspects of the program and to working actively to enroll them. You should work closely with the HMO to inform potential members about the advantages of the plan. Be particularly sensitive to the requirements and adjustments that may be necessary for retirees whose past experience has been with indemnity plans rather than managed care. Video presentations, discussions and printed materials have all been used successfully to educate retirees.

Also, financial incentives often increase retiree enrollment. Many companies pay 100 percent of the least expensive plan, which is usually a Medicare-risk HMO, requiring the retiree to pay the difference between that and a more costly option. This method steers retirees to the most cost-effective plan.

The selection of the Medicare-risk plan plays a large part in overcoming retiree doubts. A Medicare-risk plan with a large network of physician and hospital providers helps increase membership because it offers retirees the choice and convenience they want. In fact, they may not even have to change doctors. Once the plan is in place, you should continue responding to members' needs by ensuring immediate and helpful customer assistance, prompt answers to inquiries, periodic telephone follow-up calls, formal satisfaction surveys and member education.

If you like what you're reading about these plans, the next question is where to find one. The states with the highest enrollment (15 percent or more) are Arizona, California, Colorado, Minnesota, Nevada, New Mexico and Oregon. States with 5 percent to 10 percent of the total Medicare population in risk plans are Alabama, Florida, Kentucky, Massachusetts, New York, Washington and Wisconsin. California or Florida, which both have large numbers of Medicare beneficiaries, will probably grow the fastest.

Medicare-risk HMOs are not a panacea for the retiree benefits crisis, but as they become increasingly widespread, employers and retirees may find they're just what the doctor ordered.

LOOK BEFORE YOU LEAP

Although Medicare-risk HMOs can be a good benefits strategy, they won't solve all your retiree benefits problems, so proceed with caution. Just ask Janine Devera-Amico, senior benefit analyst at Florida Power & Light Co. in Juno Beach, Florida. She says the company intends to eventually adopt a Medicare-risk HMO as part of its gradual shift to managed care, provided it can iron out the wrinkles in the plan.

Until 1991, FP&L's 15,000 employees had a traditional indemnity plan. Then astronomic health-care costs forced the company to re-examine its benefits. After adopting a flexible benefits plan for active employees in 1992, the company installed a point-of-service plan for active and retired employees last March, which had a 73-percent enrollment rate, she reports.

FP&L hopes to implement Medicare-risk HMOs in 1995. Why the delay? "We needed to keep things simple this year—to offer the same plan to everyone," Devera-Amico explains. Before it makes any more health-care moves, the company wants all of its employees and especially its retirees to adjust to the idea of managed care, she says.

Once retirees become more comfortable with HMO concepts and processes, the company will begin educating them about the Medicare-risk plan. Fortunately, FP&L already has well-established communications channels. Retirees are organized into nine chapters, each with its own lead coordinator. And each of the company's five regional offices has a human resources representative whose job, among other things, is to work with retirees to answer benefits questions.

Although cost savings are an advantage of Medicare-risk HMOs, it's not a major consideration for FP&L. "The over-65 people don't cost much, because Medicare is the primary coverage for them," Devera-Amico explains. And the company had already reduced its FAS 106 liability through other means. The real problem was public relations. Retirees believed the company was reneging on their benefits. "We've got a lot of retirees who devoted 25 or 30 years of their lives to this company. Their attitude is 'I did for you; now you take care of me,'" she says. So the company's interest in a Medicare-risk HMO stemmed from a need to demonstrate its commitment to its retirees rather than to save money, she says.

Nevertheless, she concedes the biggest problem will be overcoming retirees' dislike of managed care. "Retirees are a skeptical group," Devera-Amico observes. They often believe the quality of HMOs is low and balk at being limited to a set pool of physicians. To ease the transition, the company will search hard for a good Medicare-risk HMO plan. "It would have to be a quality program with a lot of doctors and locations," she stipulates.

If retirees still aren't convinced, they will be able to choose one of several other plans the company will offer, Devera-Amico notes. But this could open yet another can of worms for FP&L. Most healthy retirees probably would opt for the cheaper Medicare-risk plan, while the retirees with the biggest medical bills would stick to traditional indemnity.

Despite the risk of adverse selection, some element of choice is necessary, because Medicare-risk HMOs are unavailable in North Carolina and Georgia, two of the company's major locations. And although the plans are much more common in Florida than in other states, many retirees live in the northern, more rural parts of the state, where HMOs haven't yet penetrated.

The plans have some other drawbacks. Under federal law, patients enrolled in a Medicare-risk HMO must be permitted to opt in and out of the plan. But some retirees travel for months at a time or stay with family in other states. According to Devera-Amico, FP&L is concerned that allowing such individuals to move in and out of the plan several times a year would create a huge administrative burden.

Also, retirees may have spouses who are under age 65 and therefore ineligible for Medicare benefits. Devera-Amico says the company may solve that problem by permitting the spouse to enroll in the HMO as a regular patient. The individual would have the same benefits as the retiree, and the HMO would bill FP&L for the spousal coverage.

Although Florida Power & Light has yet to resolve all of its concerns, it's moving ahead with its plans. Devera-Amico believes the debate on national health-care reform will help broaden retiree awareness and defuse any lingering resistance. "People hear about it all the time," she says. "Eventually, they'll begin to accept it."

—Rona L. Ferling

28. Group and Executive Long-Term Care Insurance: A New Essential Retirement Benefit

Alfred C. Clapp, Jr.

In these days of corporate belt tightening, particularly in the employee benefit arena, it is important to recognize that there is a meaningful benefit that can be provided at little or no cost to the employer and yet provide significant assistance to the employee and retiree population. This article focuses on how group long-term care insurance benefits both employer and employee.

The possible need for long-term care represents a very large financial risk for employees, one that will have an impact on not only older employees and retirees but also the younger caregiver-employee population. Can your aging workforce—as well as your own personal future needs—be affected by long-term care insurance (LTCI)?

With the high costs of existing benefit plans today, interested employees (not employers) are usually paying for this benefit themselves, although executives may have LTCI paid in a carve-out plan or bonus. LTCI plans also are available for employees' spouses, parents, and even parents-in-law.

Imagine being faced with both college tuition bills and nursing home care bills simultaneously. Several years of these expenditures can and often do upset the financial planning of most members of a workforce. The effects go beyond the finances of the employee; the company may face losses in employee productivity.

A NEW BENEFIT: EXPECTED GROWTH IN LTCI

While employee assistance programs including elder support services have been accepted and adopted by some pioneering larger companies, as of the end 1992 only 506 diverse size companies offered LTCI, according to the Health Insurance Association of America (HIAA) 1993 National Long-Term Care Insurance Conference. (HIAA is the source for valuable materials and charts included in this article.)

Today, while waiting for national health care reform, companies continue to reduce benefit packages as well as other expenses. LTCI is in a gray area since its tax deductibility is not clear; it is not fully understood as a new benefit. Therefore, LTCI may be given lower priority and implementation may be delayed. However, there are even more fundamental reasons why LTCI plans are delayed, such as the long-term care aging denial syndrome, underestimating the catastrophic risk of long-term care, and failing to understand how LTCI benefits both employers and employees.

In 1992 group plans grew at a faster pace from a small base of acceptance than did solely individual policies. As of that year's end, there were about 200,000 group-sponsored individual policyholders. This trend is expected to continue. By the year 2000, the number of group policyholders should exceed one million, and may possibly approach 1.5 million. Many companies sponsoring group LTCI are concerned with the fact that initially only 5 to 10 percent of eligible employees sign up. However, it's important to recognize that as more employees enroll, the number of LTCI policyholders will increase considerably, making for more viable plans, representation, and actuarial acceptability.

The Conference Board's report "Long-Term Care: A New Employee Benefit?" has indicated that nearly all large corporation are considering long-term care insurance as a natural and crucial extension of their current benefit plans—a complement to their health, disability, and retirement policies. Employers recognize that with employees paying premiums there is only modest out-of-pocket cost, and survival could depend on long-term care. Therefore the issue of employer LTCI responsibility will not disappear. It deserves management's serious consideration for the 21st century.

Offering LTCI decreases workers' anxiety over caring for their parents, and increased worker productivity is the result. By sponsoring a group, generally the employer can offer better coverage, more control, and a much-valued group discount. Given the need for LTCI and an increasing acceptance and understanding of this new type of insurance, a sizable growth of group plans is expected. To understand the value (cost/benefit) of LTCI, consider this strategy and its alternatives.

Long-Term Care and Activities of Daily Living Defined

Long-term care may be defined as a set of ongoing custodial assistance services delivered daily over a sustained period of time to persons who have lost some

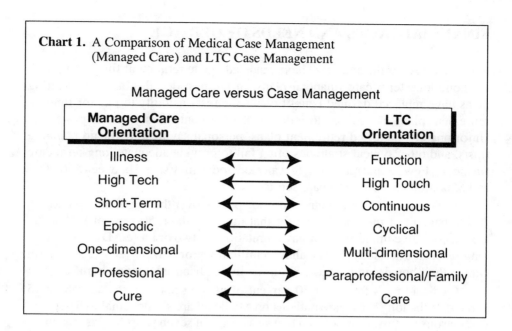

Chart 1. A Comparison of Medical Case Management (Managed Care) and LTC Case Management

Managed Care versus Case Management

Managed Care Orientation		LTC Orientation
Illness	⟷	Function
High Tech	⟷	High Touch
Short-Term	⟷	Continuous
Episodic	⟷	Cyclical
One-dimensional	⟷	Multi-dimensional
Professional	⟷	Paraprofessional/Family
Cure	⟷	Care

degree of physical or cognitive capacity. The confusion that sometimes exists between medical and long-term care case management is clarified by the comparison of differences highlighted by Chart 1.

It is common for the elderly to suffer from a variety of illnesses that prevent them from performing activities for daily living (ADLs). Any chronic or disabling condition that requires either non-skilled, custodial care in the home or placement in a nursing home may trigger a need for costly long-term care services.

Many long-term care causes are recognized. In the United States there are about 4 million persons with Alzheimer's disease. This is classified as a cognitive impairment and may qualify for LTCI coverage. Other important causes include accidents, blindness, cancer, diabetes, dialysis, emphysema, osteoporosis, Parkinson's disease, rheumatism, strokes and heart disease, old age frailties, or a combination of any of these conditions. Many of these causes are associated with long-term care—i.e., what happens after the patient is released from the hospital?

The inability to perform two out of the five or six ADLs is recognized as a claim trigger in most LTCI contracts. Bathing is the first ADL that may require assistance, and because this may be scheduled on an occasional, not regular basis, the other five ADLs (dressing, transferring, toileting, continence, and feeding) are the principal capabilities or functions used to qualify for claim payments. In many cases, assistance is needed for a number of the ADLs, not merely one or two. Under many circumstances this may necessitate full-time live-in assistance, not just occasional care visits by health care personnel.

FINANCIAL FACTS AND NEEDS OF OLD AGE

Few persons over the age of 50 have made adequate retirement financing plans, let alone long-term care financial plans. In the past decades, as profit sharing plans have replaced defined benefit plans, the responsibility to pay for funding retirement plans has shifted to individuals on a contributory or full-pay basis. Unfortunately, qualified retirement plans, personal savings, Medicaid planning trusts, and other typical strategies often fail to provide adequate long-term care financing. Few people recognize that an elder today may spend between $200,000 and $500,000 for long-term care services.

Today, there are more than 31 million people over the age of 65, accounting for 12 percent of the population. Of that number, about 50 percent will suffer from a cognitive impairment or have limitations in two or more ADLs, requiring long-term care services. Today, about 4 million senior citizens receive long-term care in their homes, and about 1.8 million live in licensed nursing homes.

Medicaid pays for about 70 percent of nursing home costs, and about 75 percent of the long-term care patients on Medicaid are single females. There are two reasons for this: first, women live an average of seven years longer than men; and second, for many married couples the husband is the first to become ill, and the couple's resources are depleted by the cost of his care.

By 2020, those over 65 will number 51 million and represent 17 percent of the population. The number of people potentially requiring long-term care is projected to continue increasing, as will the "dependency ratio," which is the ratio of retired and non-working people to FICA-taxpaying workers. By 2020, over 9 million elders will need long-term care services.

Quantifying the cost of long-term care is a difficult task. Statistics are limited, especially for home care, and those that are available are usually only estimates. A high percentage of home care services for the elderly are provided by unpaid family, friends, or volunteer agencies. However, some trends can be projected for the future. For example, we can anticipate fewer available care givers; the cost of building new facilities will continue to climb; and it will be difficult, if not impossible, to curtail Medicaid expenditures for those receiving public assistance.

Most elders prefer home care, viewing a nursing home as a last resort. The average duration of home care that might be eligible for LTCI payments is an estimated three years, while the average stay in a nursing home is an estimated two years.

In 1993, the nationwide average annual cost for nursing home care was about $36,000. In the New York area, the annual cost averages $70,000. Nursing home charges increased 8 percent a year in the past decade and are expected to continue to climb at about a 5 percent rate in future years.

Assuming home care and other supportive services cost as much as nursing home care, today's "real" current annual cost of long-term care nationwide is about $200 billion. By 2020, given the projected growth in the elderly population and an annual 5 percent increase in costs, the real annual cost could be as large as total health care costs today, or $900 billion. In 25 years, annual long-term care costs per person might amount to $100,000, or over triple today's average costs.

Myths, Hopes, and Excuses

Resistance to long-term care planning is common. The human resource manager has to recognize the underlying reasons why employees avoid making practical plans. The decision process is often difficult, frustrating, time-consuming, and sometimes only as effective as a manager's experience with the complex issues in elder care. Many half-truths, myths, and misperceptions persist about long-term care and its financing; following are some of the more common of these:

- The belief that the person will never need long-term care services
- The highly questionable generalization that home care costs much less than nursing home care
- The fear that all nursing homes are terrible and abuse the residents
- The myth that there is no difference in quality among nursing homes
- The hope that retirement income, savings, and real estate assets will be adequate, and will not be depleted by long-term care costs
- The myth that Medicare and Medicare supplementary (Medigap) insurance are significant long-term care payers
- Failure to recognize that uncovered long-term care costs often exceed the costs of acute medical care
- The hope that the government will pay for long-term care, whether through Medicaid or through creation of some new comprehensive program
- The myth that private LTCI is not affordable and the related assumption that, since it is not affordable, it offers poor value

FINANCING LONG-TERM CARE: ALTERNATIVE STRATEGIES

Medicaid

Medicaid was created in the mid-1960s as a Great Society program for the poor. Today, it functions as a program not only for the poor, but also for the middle class who cannot afford to pay the high cost of nursing home care. This is because Medicaid pays for nursing home custodial care. Consequently, legal strategies have been devised to help people who are not poor by conventional definitions to qualify for Medicaid by spending down assets, transferring funds to family, or establishing trusts.

Medicaid expenditures are increasing dramatically. In 1993, total Medicaid expenditures amounted to $166 billion for the states and $76 billion for the federal government. New York, the state with the most generous Medicaid payments, pays $20 billion a year for Medicaid benefits to its residents, half of which goes to nursing homes. As Medicaid reimbursement rates to nursing homes are far below the rates of private payers, Medicaid patients may not be accepted in more attractive nursing homes, or may face a longer waiting period. New York State also provides better Medicaid home-care benefits than most other states. Total Medicaid expenditures have been increasing at an annual compound growth rate of about 13 percent.

The Omnibus Budget Reconciliation Act of 1993 (OBRA '93) also has adversely impacted long-term care Medicaid planning and use of trusts. OBRA '93 extended the general look-back period from 30 to 36 months and, for certain trusts, to 60 months. The recoupment of assets has become a greater Medicaid trust risk, and as of mid-1994, federal and state regulations were being implemented. For those with limited income and assets, Medicaid may remain the most viable nursing home long-term care strategy.

OBRA '93 also greatly slowed Medicaid planning and trusts by elder lawyers during the time federal and state regulations were being implemented. OBRA '93 also created the need for a longer planning time period and reinforced the value of LTCI as a bridge before Medicaid eligibility. Medicaid and future proposed home care programs are always subject to major government cutbacks.

The Clinton Health Reform Proposal

The Clinton plan, which proposed to launch a new home and community based program, raised the hope that the federal government will pay for limited (not comprehensive or full) long-term care custodial services. The Clinton plan would offer a phased-in, coinsured custodial long-term care program for all qualified elder or disabled persons who prefer to remain at home rather than enter a Medicaid paid nursing home.

As proposed, the plan would be designed and administered by each state, but funded mostly by the federal government and individual coinsurance. States also may pay for long-term home care, as is done in New York, which has a generous Medicaid program.

About 3 million persons (not on Medicaid) might initially benefit from such a program if it were fully phased in by 2005. With the overemphasis on health care, the Clinton long-term care program is less understood, less debated, much larger in scope than recognized, and appealing under the guise that today's budget impact is tolerable. It is expected to be a 1995 Congressional focus.

The main concern is the cost of such a program. The Clinton plan estimates annual total costs to be $38 billion by 2005. However, this assumes an unrealistically low cost per person to provide long-term care services. At the outset of the program, costs may be more than double the estimate and amount to as much as $90 billion. After 2005, costs could double every 15 years due to the increasingly large older population and inflation. A generous, federally paid program that is not means-tested is too expensive, as well as a major new unknown. Employers also have been caught up in Congressional debates, and because of the uncertainties have slowed down their own LTCI implementation.

The Clinton plan also has recognized the importance of private LTCI. It and other bills in Congress advocate federal regulation and standardization of all private LTCI contracts. The National Association of Insurance Commissioners (NAIC) promulgated standards would be the basis for any future standardized policies. The proposals with provisions including a required nonforfeiture rider may be expensive and limit benefits. Long-term care insurance may follow the Medigap contract precedent. This could help minimize the difficulty that currently exists in evaluating these policies, and might encourage many to purchase LTCI.

The Clinton plan proposed favorable tax treatment of LTCI premiums to permit employees deducting these premiums. Unfortunately, this may not be approved, and so remains a major reason for employers not offering LTCI coverage, even though coverage is not paid by employers and is portable.

LTCI BACKGROUND AND MARKET

The history of LTCI goes back about 15 years when this coverage was introduced. The first generation contracts were inexpensive but restrictive, with an emphasis on nursing home care and little, if any, home care coverage. Many of these contracts have since been withdrawn from the market. Purchasers were often given the right to convert to an improved policy.

LTCI is a product with a significant, but not unlimited, potential for growth. Currently, only 3.4 million persons—in comparison with a total elder population of over 31 million—own LTCI. The average age of those who have individually purchased LTCI to date is 68. However, with group LTCI the average participant age is 42. This favorable trend should encourage employers to sponsor plans. However, LTCI as an employer benefit will always be purchased by a much smaller percentage of employees in comparison with other plans, as summarized in Table 1.

Table 1. Participation Percentages	
Life Insurance	92%
Medical Insurance	90%
Standard Disability	46%
Long Term Disability	42%
Long-Term Care Insurance	.04%

However, the amount of coverage actually needed by employees may exceed other benefit packages, as Chart 2 indicates. It is also clear that the real need for LTCI is after retirement and not before.

In the future, many persons age 40 and older will purchase LTCI either individually or through group policies sponsored by businesses or associations, but coverage will still never become universal. Many of the recent second generation of policies have been greatly improved with standard provisions, home care benefits, and valuable, affordable coverage. However, possibly less than 30 percent of elders may qualify or be able to afford more than a minimum level for Medicaid strategy purposes. After the age of 79, LTCI policies, if available, are so limited and restricted that the coverage is often not cost effective. Many senior citizens also have serious health problems that may result in LTCI policies with high premiums, or simply being declined any LTCI. Nevertheless the potential for growth in LTCI individual and group markets is very strong.

Four States' Public-Private LTCI Partnerships

The Robert Wood Johnson Foundation successfully sponsored public-private long-term care partnerships to encourage LTCI planning and financing and to reduce state Medicaid expenditures in four states (Connecticut, New York, Indiana, Iowa, and California). The projects link insurance coverage and Medicaid eligibility. The first LTCI partnership was implemented in Connecticut in 1991. An individual who purchases one of the LTCI policies that is precertified under the Connecticut Partnership can protect one dollar in assets for every one dollar of coverage purchased. Under this Medicaid protection, there is no protection for income, only assets. There is no minimum specified period for the coverage, and purchase of inflation protection riders (an expensive feature) is discretionary with the purchaser. The plans later adopted in Indiana and California also followed the Dollar Model of Connecticut.

The New York State Partnership, implemented in early 1993, has the same goals as the Connecticut program, but has a different philosophy. The precertified New York State policies require a minimum purchase—$100 daily benefit for

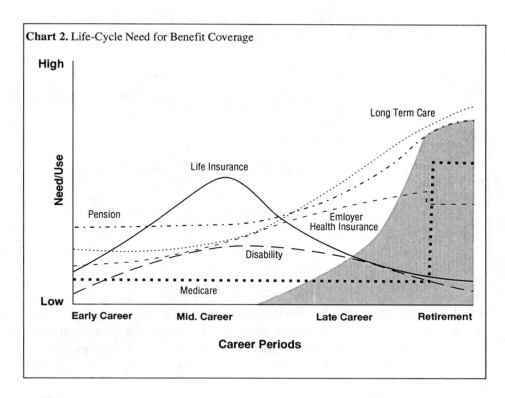

Chart 2. Life-Cycle Need for Benefit Coverage

three years of nursing home treatment, plus a $50 daily benefit for six years of home care. If this level of coverage is maintained, the insured person will qualify for Medicaid after the private insurance is exhausted, irrespective of his or her level of assets. The New York plan includes a mandatory 5 percent inflation rider.

State partnerships are only effective if the insured continues to live in the state of insurance origination. While other states are considering Robert Wood Johnson projects to reduce both federal and state Medicaid payments, OBRA '93 discouraged future partnerships by protecting assets during life, but not after death in an estate. However, the Medicaid cost reduction resulting from these positive efforts endorsing LTCI may be ten to 20 years into the future, when precertified and other LTCI coverage becomes more widely accepted by middle-income elders as a primary way to avoid Medicaid dependency. In Connecticut, the partnership products are more expensive than nonpartnership policies. In New York State, the requirement to purchase a 5 percent annual compound growth rate rider increased policy costs.

LTCI Design Standard Provisions

LTCI has been described as a new, hybrid insurance product with aspects that appear to be derived from other standard products but also have considerable differences. Some of these similarities and differences are illustrated in Table 2.

Table 2. LTCI Compared to Other Insurance Products

Insurance Type	Similarities	Differences
Life	Age rated as term insurance. Costly if purchased at an old age. Long-term payment commitment	No cash value as permanent life insurance
Health	Indemnity/reimbursement model	Not reasonable, but fixed benefit.
Disability	Disability income model	Benefits older, not younger persons.
	Inflation rider is available.	

While the comparisons in Table 2 are helpful for understanding certain aspects of LTCI, it is equally important to understand the specific new areas LTCI contracts have introduced. LTCI is a genuine new product, not just a rebundled set of old ones. Great confusion exists on the part of all persons who review LTCI contracts about what parts of a contract are substantively different, let alone how to evaluate different plan choices.

LTCI contracts may be customized for larger groups with over 5,000 employees, but even these are usually based on almost identical contracts for individuals or groups. Employees select company sponsored LTCI plans after considering the possible alternative long-term care strategies. Those employees who decide to purchase a group LTCI policy also have to select a level of LTCI benefit coverage from a single company recommended by an employer. Employees are effectively encouraged to project their ability to pay premiums as a commitment both while they are employed and after retirement.

A company may offer a better, less expensive, payroll deduction plan, which may be guaranteed issued for larger groups or individually underwritten for smaller groups. Most important, by encouraging employees to purchase group LTCI at much younger ages, premiums will be much less expensive, both initially and over the long term. In contrast, the average age of individuals purchasing LTCI today is 68. Waiting to older ages increases the risk the coverage will not be affordable, or that the person will be considered uninsurable.

Today, major companies offer LTCI policies with many standard contractual terms and a few provisions that differ between contracts. While there is no uniform nationwide standard for LTCI policies, the NAIC has promulgated standards that have influenced most state regulators. Common features of LTCI policies include:

- *Coverage for a fixed purchased benefit and number of years.* This approach contrasts with the "reasonable and customary" full coverage philosophy of health insurance.
- *Guaranteed renewability.* The insurer does not have the right to cancel an individual's policy because that person's health has deteriorated. However, insurers do have the right to seek state approval for a premium increase for an entire class, and probably will after claims experience justifies some rate increase. While the risk of class-wide increases is an important one to disclose to everyone considering an LTCI purchase, states mandate minimum loss reserves, reasonable actuarial assumptions, specific product designs, and so are reluctant to allow rate increases without ample justification.
- *Benefits are payable without a prior hospitalization requirements.*
- *Daily benefits available in varying amounts.* The amounts of daily benefits available generally range up to $250 a day ($91,250 annually).
- *Coverage usually begins after a waiting period.* Typical waiting periods might be 20 to 30 days or 90 to 100 days.
- *Premiums are level and paid until an insured dies or a benefit is paid and a waiver of premium triggered.* The annual amount of premium paid depends on the age at which the policy was purchased and the level/type of coverage.
- *Inflation riders.* These are common, but options to purchase additional coverage are not.
- *Home care custodial benefits.* These are available as a percentage of the coverage for nursing home costs.
- *Nonforfeiture features.* Nonforfeiture features are usually available as riders, albeit at a significant additional cost. However, most policies now available do not include a return-of-premium feature, nor the ability to fund a policy on an abbreviated payment basis similar to the life insurance policies that are fully paid up after several years.

Most companies have adopted underwriting guidelines similar to those required for life insurance. LTCI also is concerned about mobility, serious arthritis, and blindness. While attending physician statements often are ordered, medical examinations are seldom required. Older persons are often interviewed by a social worker personally or by phone, primarily to determine possible Alzheimer's, degree of mobility, or other observations prior to underwriting approval.

Problems caused by alcohol, drugs, or mental illnesses are excluded from coverage. Most LTCI contracts only cover U.S. residents and not persons residing overseas. Alzheimer's disease and other dementias are covered by LTCI.

Individual and Group LTCI Terms and Exceptions

The group and individual contracts for this portable benefit are quite similar. Larger groups plans may be custom made and issued on a guarantee basis. Smaller ones for under 500 employees are based upon individual contracts, individually underwritten, deducted from payroll, and often afford a group discount as an incentive.

For larger companies, a LTCI contract may be customized. However, usually insurance company contracts follow the pricing and provisions of individual contracts in force on a state-by-state basis. On an overall basis, as the NAIC 1990 Long-Term Care Model and 1992 Regulations prevail, there are fewer variations in contract terms than sometimes exists in the pricing of policies. An educated buyer must review contracts to understand these differences before making a LTCI commitment, in particular the following:

1. The amount of daily/annual benefit coverage, years of coverage, amount of home care coverage, waiting period before benefit begins, and inflation rider options vary by contract.

2. Home care coverage is usually available at the 50 percent, 80 percent, or 100 percent level of the base nursing home care coverage. This is the most important variable area. If home care is a priority, it is important to factor the different level of home care coverage into any comparison of premiums between different company proposals. A home care rider has an incremental cost for the extra years purchased, which amounts to about 30 percent of the base nursing home cost.

3. Contract provisions also vary in the following other respects, but these differences are less substantive:

    •   Claims can be paid on either an indemnity or a reimbursement basis. In an indemnity policy, an insurance company reimburses a licensed agency for custodial aid services or a nursing home up to, but not more than, a policy benefit limit. In a reimbursement policy, the full coverage is paid directly to the insured. While a disability income approach recently introduced allows the insured to use the benefits paid for any purpose, this approach is relatively expensive. Disability policies also include long-term care riders. As long-term care costs are likely to be greater than the amount of coverage purchased, the three different payment approaches are not an important contractual or financial issue.

    •   The definition of activities of daily living varies, but inability to perform two or more ADLs is the usual qualification for LTCI benefit payments.

    •   Contracts also vary slightly on extra areas such as respite care or day care, reimbursement for certain home equipment, starting time period for a waiver of premium payments, and waiting time periods after an interruption in long-term care services.

Long-Term Care Alternative Retiree Housing Strategies

Development and expansion of innovative long-term care housing alternatives for seniors nationally has to be recognized in any review of an LTCI contract. Continuing care retirement communities' (CCRC) financing of LTCI vary. Most employ LTCI nursing home coverage. While CCRCs are a promising long-term care strategy, there are today only about 250,000 CCRC residents (about 1 percent of the senior citizen population). Don't count on being admitted if you are not on a short waiting list and ready to move. Because it is difficult to finance new CCRCs, it is unlikely that the number of CCRCs will increase sufficiently to satisfy the long-term care needs of the growing elder population. CCRCs may be too expensive unless sponsored by a nonprofit organization.

Hospital programs offer another solution. With their client base, access to medical professionals, and space for health and long-term care programs, hospitals are starting to consider offering programs, including LTCI coverage at association discount rates. These programs will expand a hospital's patient community.

Further alternatives (some of which can be covered by LTCI) include:

- Congregate assisted living housing that does not include nursing home capabilities
- Respite programs that take care of the elderly for short periods of time to relieve care givers
- Home modification and installation of special equipment to meet long-term care needs at home
- Adult day-care programs

Many of the above programs depend upon some kind of private financing. Since these types of housing plans and arrangements are made—if they are made at all—at older ages, it is better to have LTCI plans in force at earlier ages.

AFFORDABILITY

Affordability is often cited as an important issue and a reason not to buy LTCI. This argument is often made in a political context to advocate universal LTCI coverage. However, it also has to be acknowledged that LTCI often costs less than private medical insurance. The amount of coverage may be geared to a person's budget and strategy. The younger a person is, the more affordable the coverage. One guideline is that medical and LTCI should not cost more than 10 percent of after-tax income. Of course, an elder's children might also decide to pay LTCI premiums.

At year end 1992, the HIAA published the survey results of the average annual premiums for leading individual and group association LTCI sellers. Table 3 shows these results, which are based on the following assumptions: $80/$40 a day nursing home/home health coverage after a 20-day elimination period and four years of coverage.

Table 3. Average Premiums, 1992

Age	Base Plan	Base Plan with 5% Inflation Rider
50	$ 435	$ 705
65	983	1,597
79	3,998	5,334

The survey results indicate that premiums increase at a much faster rate at older ages. The plans in the survey only offer home care at 50 percent of the nursing home base. Many association LTCI plans only offer up to this percentage of home care coverage. Association insurance companies have not adequately emphasized the importance and costs of home care.

There is also a concern among employers who sponsor plans that premiums may not remain level. This concern is well recognized by each state insurance department. LTCI policies state that rate increases as a class may be approved by a state. However, the approval will be limited to minimize overlapping. The review of actuarial considerations also helps explain the basic way LTCI has been priced. Remember as well that the benefits offered by this relatively new type of coverage are not based on a reasonable-and-customary fee determination but rather on a fixed level of payment.

Inflation

Purchasing an inflation rider increases the cost of the coverage by over 80 percent for a younger person, though it is much less for older individuals. For a younger person, an inflation rider is a greater value and a more essential feature; Table 3 provides some indication of the age differentials in potential costs for a 5 percent rider. The amount of this financial risk should be recognized. At the same time, other financial planning options that will serve as a hedge against inflation risk should be considered, including the following techniques:

- Purchase more than the estimated coverage required initially
- Consider using a less expensive long-term care service or moving to a less expensive area
- Be prepared and able to cover inflation either with investments or sale of a residence or less liquid assets
- Consider Medicaid strategies after an initial coverage time period

Cost/Benefit Value

The main reason to purchase LTCI is the expectation that premium costs will be much less expensive than the potential outlays for long-term care services. The following example highlights why LTCI is valuable.

Example. Assume that a person aged 50 buys an LTCI policy with an inflation rider, paying a level annual premium of $705 for 30 years (the 1992 average; see Table 3). At age 80, which is the average age at which long-term care services are required, the purchaser will have paid $21,150 in premiums. A $60 daily benefit, which at 5 percent inflation compounded annually for 30 years would be worth $259.32 per day, paid for four years would total $378,607. This results in a 18 to 1 value ratio.

Of course, a person may purchase as much or as little coverage for as many years as are deemed at risk. However, the financial risk is greater for long-term care services above the average required time, and it is made economically attractive to purchase more coverage rather than a lesser amount on a conservative basis. No one will be disappointed if, because of good health at the age of 80, long-term care services were not yet required and the ratio ended up being lower.

FLEXIBLE BENEFIT PLANS AND THE LIFE CYCLE APPROACH TO BENEFITS

Flexible benefit plans, which were initially only implemented by larger companies, now are available for smaller companies. In terms of administration, they are one of the best ways for employers to sponsor LTCI benefits. However, pending national health care reform has probably stopped some companies from adopting these plans. With the possibility that some health insurance premium costs may no longer be fully deductible—and health costs have been the underlying benefit package and stimulus for flexible benefit plans—flex plans may no longer be as useful or worthwhile. Section 125 of the Internal Revenue Code (IRC), which governs these plans, does not address whether LTCI may be included or excluded. Different employers have interpreted this omission in different ways, and included or excluded LTCI plans within their flex plans.

As an extension of flexible benefits, a new life cycle concept has been proposed, but so far employers have not implemented such designs. Life cycle plans are enhanced benefit plans with possible additional services offered, such as child and elder care, discounted LTCI, and work site convenience buying.

ACTUARIAL ASSUMPTIONS IN LTCI PRICING

LTCI offers a fixed benefit over a long time period, not a benefit based on whatever fees may be customary and reasonable at a future time period, as health insurance does. The pricing of LTCI products also takes into account the following actuarial assumptions:

1. Mortality;
2. Persistency (the length of time a policy remains in force without lapsing);
3. Investment return earned by the insurance company;
4. Expenses of marketing, compliance with government regulations, and operations;
5. Morbidity (i.e., the length of time benefits are paid);
6. State required minimum loss reserve ratios;
7. The company's underwriting standards and experience; and
8. Product profitability.

Considering the above actuarial factors, it is possible to understand the favorable cost benefit values and pricing of LTCI. A high percentage of individuals will either die or lapse their policies. With long-term care services required, on average, at about the age of 80, and with an estimated payment period of three years at home and two years in a nursing home, it is understandable that the premiums paid increase with age.

TAXATION OF LTCI AND EXECUTIVE PLANS

A strong case can be made for treating many LTCI policies as health insurance under IRC Sections 104(a)(3) and 213. Traditionally, the IRS has allowed a broad interpretation of the definition of "medical expenses," and the full cost of a nursing home stay (including meals and lodging) can be treated as a medical expense as long as the primary reason for institutionalization is a need for medical care, not the convenience of the patient or family. Given this treatment of nursing home expenses, it seems plausible that the insurance covering such expenses should also be entitled to favorable tax treatment, and that premiums should be included with the medical expenses that are deductible above a floor of 7.5 percent of adjusted gross income.

However, the IRS has not pronounced on the status of LTCI, and it is impossible to promise favorable tax treatment to a client who wishes to purchase LTCI. One reason employers are reluctant to add LTCI to the benefit package is the uncertainty of whether premium costs are deductible. Nor has Congress legislated on the LTCI tax issue, perhaps as a ploy to exchange favorable tax treatment for strict federal regulation.

LTCI premiums may be paid out of executive bonuses. A company also may establish an LTCI carve-out plan for its executives, similar to the way more favorable disability plans are often offered to executives. While it may be possible to pay for premiums as a dependent care tax deductible expense under IRC Section 129, this is a gray area that should be carefully reviewed with tax advisors before serious consideration and implementation.

LIVING BENEFITS, DISABILITY LONG-TERM CARE RIDERS, AND OTHER FINANCING STRATEGIES

Senior citizens who own whole or universal life insurance policies and are expected to die in less than a year may be able to turn to two related financial strategies: living benefits (LB) and viatication. Under LB, a life insurance policy that contains an accelerated benefit rider can be accessed during lifetime with part of the death benefit paid out to the insured. New York State has regulations permitting insurers to add accelerated benefit riders to new and existing life insurance policies. Usually, there is no charge for the rider.

However, LB riders added to life insurance policies are not an attractive way to guarantee long-term care coverage. The riders are restrictive and provide limited benefits. Life insurance and long-term care insurance serve very different needs and purposes, and acceleration of benefits should not be viewed as a LTCI substitute.

In December 1992, the IRS proposed regulations that would permit the proceeds from LB to be considered nontaxable.

Under viatication, a third party (not the insurance company issuing the life insurance policy) purchases the insurance policy from the insured outright, at a discount. The insured now has cash for use during a health crisis, but no longer has life insurance coverage.

A few companies are offering disability income (DI) policies with a long-term care rider so that an employee may convert their DI policies into LTCI. Such policies may require that an employee convert before reaching age 55.

LTCI BENEFIT ADMINISTRATION

Enrollment in LTCI plans so far has been small, amounting typically to less than 10 percent of employees. Even with the inclusion of spouses, parents, and parents-in-law, only a small number of employees may originally enroll. Some companies with younger employee or lower income profiles may not give as high priority to LTCI as those with contrasting profiles. What's important to recognize is that the numbers enrolled may grow along with the ages of employees or a growing understanding awareness of LTCI's value, or the jolt that often comes when visited by a long-term care crisis.

Working with and educating employees on the importance of LTCI is a part of the process of introducing any plan. There is a greater need to introduce LTCI in early retirement planning programs, to provide employees with a simple computer generated model to project their retirement income, and have a commitment to be in contact with employees, and even, to a limited extent, to represent them in terms of possible plan changes and claims submitted. LTCI plans should be integrated with other employee/retiree programs to ensure service responsiveness and effective communications. A company should encourage employees to project their income, assets, family legacy considerations, and most important, should encourage them to think about the importance of dignity and self-respect in retirement. The goal is to have employees understand the possible retirement choices and have some freedom to choose, with appropriate value assigned to factors such as independence, choice, and income.

Selecting a stronger company with a commitment to LTCI is another requirement. The plans are portable. If you lose confidence in the insurer originally selected, it may be difficult to convert a group to a new carrier on acceptable terms and prices.

Part 8

MENTAL HEALTH

29. Mental Health: A High-Return Investment

Mental health coverage can be one of the most cost-effective benefits you can offer. Employers who try to control costs by limiting type or duration of treatment can undermine their chances for achieving either cure or savings.

Cutting corners on mental health benefits may be more expensive than you think. Leading mental health supporters, including former first lady Rosalynn Carter, are advocating a new approach: that mental health benefits should provide for appropriate care, continued as long as necessary, instead of the fixed limits now provided in most benefit plans. They believe the long term benefits will outweigh the initial expense. Many mental health organizations are now concentrating on having their views included in any forthcoming plan for national health care reform.

"Appropriate mental health care doesn't cost too much," says Mrs. Carter. "Investing in early intervention, treatment and follow-up care will prevent far more costly disability and even death." She advocates mental health coverage "subject to no greater limitations than other health care benefits."

Most health insurance packages do include some form of mental health coverage. According to the Mental Health Liaison Group, a coalition of national mental health organizations, 98 percent of the people who have private health insurance also are covered for outpatient mental health treatment. Only 3 percent, however, have mental health coverage that is equivalent to their coverage for other illnesses. Typical mental health plans limit the number of visits covered, the maximum reimbursable cost, or the percentage of charges they will pay.

THE COST QUESTION

The cost of mental health benefits is rising even more rapidly than the cost of health insurance in general. In 1988, the New York-based benefits consultant A. Foster Higgins & Co. surveyed 1,633 employers nationwide on their health care costs. The survey found that average health benefit costs per employee had risen nearly 19 percent during the previous year. The rise in mental-health and substance-abuse costs was 27 percent. Individual employers reported financial horror stories that seemed to bear out these findings.

A more recent study (Table 1) has challenged conventional wisdom. The Washington-based Hay/Huggins Company, in a 1992 research report for the National Association of Private Psychiatric Hospitals, strongly suggested that traditional cost controls are self-defeating. This report advocates a continuum of care approach as an alternative to the traditional mental health benefits package. Each patient should have access to an appropriate course of treatment. The limits of most conventional plans often cut treatment short of success. That leaves employers to shoulder the problems of stress, absenteeism and misbehavior that might otherwise have been solved.

Hay/Huggins surveyed 1,048 employers about their mental health benefit policies. These employers required copayments in the form of deductibles, coinsurance or coverage limits, in 90 percent of all psychiatric inpatient treatments. For other types of illness, these employers required copayments in 69 percent of cases. Most employers also limited the number of days their plans would pay for inpatient care. More than half cut off coverage at 30 days.

There was an even greater discrepancy in the benefits for outpatient mental health care. For non-psychiatric cases, the typical employer surveyed covered 80 percent of the allowed charges after an average deductible of $250 a year. A full 99 percent of the mental health plans had greater restrictions. About 25 percent

Table 1. Treatment of Psychiatric and Non-psychiatric Admissions		
Plan Provision	*Psychiatric Inpatient Services*	*Non-psychiatric Inpatient Expenses*
Covered in full	10%	31%
Copayments required but limited by maximum out-of-pocket provisions	0%	58%
Covered in full but no coverage after a specified number of days	28%	0%
Copayments required on all days but no limit on days	38%	11%
Copayments required on all days and no coverage after a specified number of days	24%	0%

limited the covered fee per visit, typically to $50 or less. A third of the plans limited the number of visits covered per year (typically 50 visits, but often lower). One third also limited annual expenses for outpatient mental health care, and two thirds required larger coinsurance payments than for non-psychiatric care.

These efforts to save money can actually cost money, Hay/Huggins says. A traditional plan usually offers an either-or choice between inpatient and outpatient treatment. The patients have few opportunities to pursue "middle ground" options like partial hospitalization and residential treatment centers that might be less costly and more effective.

Furthermore, says the report, "hospital services traditionally have been covered at a much higher percentage than office visits. As a result, patients have had financial incentives to use hospitalization rather than office therapy."

Concerned about these same questions, McDonnell Douglas commissioned an intensive study a few years ago of its mental health costs. According to Daniel Smith, director of the firm's employee assistance program (EAP) the company now "is heading in a dramatically different direction than that which many other companies seem to be taking."

The objective was to determine exactly what the McDonnell Douglas EAP has contributed to the company in objective financial terms. Researchers compared such data as health care costs and absence rates. Smith says early results persuaded the company to exert stronger management over its mental health and substance abuse costs.

The experience also provided a new focus. "Our study shows that long-term case management has the best effect," says Smith. This is true "not only during the treatment years, but post-treatment."

The Hay/Huggins report recommends a similar approach, with two major elements:

- Access to all appropriate types of care, with middle ground options.
- A case management system which "directs the patient to the appropriate level of care throughout an entire treatment program." The intent: to provide no more intensive care than is medically necessary as the patient recovers, and to remove financial incentives to seek more intensive treatment than necessary.

There is "clear evidence" that this approach can reduce costs, Hay/Huggins says, though there are no definitive studies to say exactly how much. Some organizations report savings of 25 to 40 percent. Hay/Huggins believes 15 percent is a realistic figure for most employers.

Those cost savings won't necessarily mean short term premium reductions. Hay/Huggins estimates that a typical employer who decides to get rid of arbitrary limits and covers all illnesses equally would pay additional premiums of $3 to $8 per person per month. That cost is minimal, says the report, and the payoff in improved health care is worth it (Figure 1).

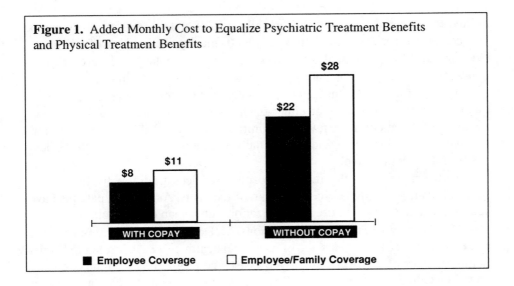

Figure 1. Added Monthly Cost to Equalize Psychiatric Treatment Benefits and Physical Treatment Benefits

LONG-TERM SAVINGS

A more comprehensive approach can also bring intangible but important long term savings. The Mental Health Liaison Group cites one estimate that the indirect costs of failing to provide a complete and appropriate treatment program can be three times the cost of the treatment itself. Michael A. Freeman, M.D., president of the Institute for Behavioral Healthcare in San Francisco, says restricting or eliminating benefits is exactly the wrong way to go. Freeman says behavioral health problems, as he prefers to refer to mental health problems, can produce many indirect costs including:

- Excessive medical claims
- Absenteeism
- Higher worker compensation expenses, particularly for stress
- Reduced productivity
- Higher accident and injury rates
- Wasted management time
- Excessive employee turnover

MEASURING RESULTS

A managed system of mental health care can have three important results for employers. That is one finding of a research project by Northwestern University and Integra Inc., a healthcare management company based in Radnor, PA. These outcomes are:

- Fewer symptoms of distress
- Improved functioning
- Enhanced sense of well-being

This finding is based on focus group sessions with corporate benefit managers. "Alleviating the symptoms makes subsequent illness less likely," says Grant Grissom, Ph.D., Integra's vice president of research and development. This "reduces overall medical expenses as well as absenteeism. The improved functioning translates into better productivity on the job and. . . a sense of well-being contributes to a positive attitude, job satisfaction and higher morale in the workplace."

These results are not just important to the individuals involved. They also are useful yardsticks for measuring a program's effectiveness. They relate both to employers' needs and to the major goals set by mental health professionals. If the program produces any or all of these results, an employer can generally consider the treatment a sound investment. If not, the program produces no results that are of any value to the organization.

Though costs and benefits vary with individuals and employers, Lee Wenzel, president of Managed Care Systems, Eden Prairie, MN, offers these general rules:

- For about $40 a year per employee, you can provide basic mental health care.
- For about $100, you can expect enough return benefits to pay back the cost.
- For about $200, you can offset indirect costs like absenteeism, turnover and lost time due to employee problems.
- For any higher figure, you are offering added compensation, not mental health benefits.
- Beware of false measurements.

Smith of McDonnell Douglas warns that high use is not itself a measure of how well the program performs. The volume of use depends primarily on how many problems employees have, he points out, not on how effectively the program deals with them. High use may mean you are performing an effective social service, but it does not necessarily mean you are meeting your goals or providing a good return on your investment.

MANAGEMENT ALTERNATIVES

Employers are naturally concerned with managing the cost of mental health care. They have many options, including these:

Benefit redesign. Various limits, restrictions, exclusions and incentives are built into the program. These are the traditional controls that may produce initial cost savings but can leave long term problems unsolved.

Stand-alone utilization review. This is easy to administer and can reduce costs while maintaining higher benefit levels. In practice, though, the review process tends to be confrontational. There are no accepted standards for these reviews. Providers have often complained that reviewers use arbitrary standards, which they sometimes create on the spot.

Demand side cost sharing. These are coinsurance plans that impose deductibles and copayments to moderate demand.

Supply side cost sharing. HMOs and other managed care plans often include mental health care. The costs are lower, but so are the benefits. In an experience familiar to many employers, the Chevron Corporation examined its HMO relationships and concluded that employees with mental health problems were "getting restricted access or poor care." Chevron switched to a separate provider and found it could handle twice as many patients for the same cost.

The carve-out approach. This approach takes mental health benefits out of the health insurance program. The employer contracts with a separate vendor to treat a particular case. Wenzel suggest that you think of it as issuing a purchase order, not buying insurance.

Management though an EAP. An EAP is often the starting point for mental health treatment. This approach places mental health care completely under the EAP, which handles an initial assessment and manages the continuing care. This approach often produces positive results, Freeman says, but the start-up cost can be high. Employers should also beware of legal liability for the results of programs they manage in-house.

Continuous managed care. This is the approach recommended in the Hay/Huggins report and by many mental health advocates and providers. It calls for a managed program of continuing care designed to provide necessary treatment without fixed limits.

TAKING ACTION

Though some of the values of improved mental health benefits are indefinite and long term, you can make a reasonable cost/benefit analysis. Start by examining your present benefits. Look for:

- Provisions that grant less coverage than you provide for other types of illness.
- Limits that might curtail treatment before it is completed.
- Working with carriers and providers, determine how the premiums would change were you to offer improved coverage. You can use the Hay/Huggins estimate that a continuous, managed program would cut costs by 15 percent.
- Identify the costs you now incur for mental health-related problems. Check attendance records, health and worker's compensation claims and EAP statistics. This should give you a good idea of the costs you can reduce in return for any added premium costs.

MORE KEYS TO SUCCESS

There are many other things you can do to control costs and ensure results:

- Set goals and objectives. Visualize what an optimum program should do for your employees and the company. Design your plan to meet those objectives. The basic goal should be to achieve health, not just to get rid of the specific ailment.
- Be prepared to exercise judgment. There is no formula to determine the right course of treatment for an individual employee. Employees have different needs, and practitioners have different methods. Use objective criteria when they are available, but recognize that most judgments about a course of treatment must be subjective, based on the circumstances of the case.
- Use the methods of total quality. Build quality into the system; don't depend on after-the-fact audits and inspections. Seek continuous improvement; don't settle for a statistical norm.
- Get benefits and EAP administrators together. What seems like rational cost-cutting to a benefits administrator may strike an EAP worker as excessive zeal that interferes with the goal of returning a productive worker to the job. Better communication can relieve this problem.

30. Psychiatric Treatment Programs: The Continuous Services Model

William M. Glazer

With the inclusion of behavioral managed care in the design of many benefit plans, the delivery of psychiatric care has changed. The continuous services model offers advantages for both employers and employees who utilize mental health benefits.

Research is beginning to make it clear that individuals with mental health and substance abuse disorders can often be treated more effectively and at less cost in settings other than hospitals. Because indemnity-oriented benefit plans favored costly inpatient services over treatments in "less restrictive environments," it is no wonder that psychiatric programs followed suit. Now, with behavioral managed care, psychiatric programming is changing in fundamental ways. The purpose of this article is to describe the components of the *continuous services model* that is emerging in behavioral managed care environments.

Partial hospitalizations, residential treatment and other alternatives to inpatient care are crucial components of the continuous services model, producing more positive patient outcomes with fewer relapses at lower cost to employers and beneficiaries. The alternative treatment approach generally costs between 50 percent and 65 percent less than traditional hospital treatment.[1] Fifteen studies conducted in the 1970s and 1980s comparing percentage of relapse, number of hospital readmissions and suicides found that outpatient alternatives to hospitalization worked well and often better than the traditional inpatient approach.[2]

Ideally, patients with psychiatric and chemical dependency disorders should have access to a coordinated continuum of services in their community. Unfortunately, such programs are still somewhat difficult to find in a single location. Insurance companies are currently attempting to develop such systems of care, often referred to as *networks,* on a nationwide basis. Dr. John Montgomery of Human Affairs International (HAI), a subsidiary of the Aetna Life Insurance Company devoted to behavioral managed care, predicts that the two or three companies that successfully create national managed care networks will dominate the health care industry of the future.

Until now, private sector service delivery systems have offered only *parts* of a continuum rather than the whole. For example, it is easy to find a psychiatric inpatient unit but more difficult to find a "stepdown" program such as partial hospitalization into which the patient can move smoothly and quickly when inpatient level care is no longer necessary. Our prediction is that eventually there will be an emergence of total systems of care in private sector mental health. How rapidly this change occurs will depend on factors such as payer expectations and demands, health policy and local economic factors. With this vision in mind, then, following is a description of standard psychiatric services in the context of a comprehensive continuum of services.

TRIAGE AND EVALUATION

The first step in the treatment of the psychiatric patient is called *triage.* Triage, which in a medical context means to prioritize patients for treatment, commonly occurs in busy emergency rooms of hospitals and mental health centers. The triage function should be rapidly responsive and precise, focusing on separating (triaging) patients who need crisis intervention or inpatient (acute) care from those who require treatment in less restrictive settings. With the emergence of managed care, the triage function has expanded to the point where it also takes place in employee assistance plans (EAPs) and utilization review (UR) programs where trained mental health professionals screen, call or interview prospective patients requesting help. Since this screening is the first step in the treatment process, it has enormous potential for controlling the subsequent treatment that the person will receive.

Role of Triage

When triage assessment is conducted skillfully, it is possible to accomplish a number of tasks at one time: Evaluate the patient directly, establish benefits eligibility, initiate the claims process and perform a precertification review. Therefore, its utilization management *as well as* its clinical application is now the source of considerable interest among managed care service vendors. Clinicians accustomed to working in traditional EAP settings often express discomfort and role conflict when they are asked to assume a utilization management role, but we predict that successful EAP programs will eventually incorporate this new approach.

The psychiatric evaluation that takes place at this time is limited by an important fact: There is no objective, valid test available to diagnose a condition. Without such a test, a clinician must make a subjective judgment that is vulnerable to numerous sources of bias. For example, if you are a psychiatric nurse performing utilization review and your company is pressuring you to keep your log of inpatient days down, you are more likely than not to perceive the severity of the patient's condition as "mild" and assign him or her to a treatment setting less restrictive than inpatient care. On the other hand, if you are employed by a psychiatric inpatient unit that requires a minimum bed occupancy of 80 percent at all times (or else layoffs will occur), you are more likely to see the same patient's condition as "severe" and assign him or her to inpatient level care. Or, if you are a psychiatrist in private practice and you believe that you will lose valuable office time tending to a patient in crisis, or if you feel that you are likely to receive more income with your patient in the hospital than in outpatient crisis treatment, you are likely to admit your patient. We are not claiming that all mental health professionals operate consciously under such biases. We *do* suggest, however, that the power of such biases is both subtle and strong. Although these biases are rarely discussed in training programs and during crisis situations, it can be difficult to operate without being influenced by them. In defense of the providers, however, it is important to remember that until recently, mental health insurance benefits were written to *favor* inpatient treatment by covering those costs more completely or by *not* covering less expensive alternatives at all.

Ways to Deal with Biases

There *are* a few solutions for dealing with these potential biases. First, it is best to avoid scenarios in which the evaluation is performed by a staff person of an inpatient facility that might subsequently admit the patient. Second, it is usually not clinically logical to support the idea of employees traveling long distances for assessments by specialty inpatient hospitals that are devoted to conditions such as chemical dependency, eating disorders or multiple personality. Although such facilities may have good intentions, we believe that their motivation to carry out their tasks might lead to overtreatment (i.e., unnecessary inpatient care) in many circumstances. The treatment of such conditions should occur (ideally) in the community in which the patient lives.

When it *is* necessary for the employee to travel a long distance for treatment, before the trip is approved, there should be an evaluation by a "neutral" clinician in the community (one who has no vested interest in the hospitalization of the patient). Under such circumstances, it should be assumed that the employee's condition will not be totally "cured" in the distant facility and will require continuing treatment back in the local community. The evaluation by the neutral psychiatrist should include an assessment of the proposed facility's ability and willingness to bridge the employee's treatment in the home community.

To this end, benefit plans could specify that employees pay more out of pocket if, without a local psychiatric evaluation, they receive inpatient treatment from a facility located more than 100 miles from their home.

A third solution to the inpatient bias described above is to employ utilization review administrators who use objective and clinically sound precertification UR scales. The UR administrator should be asked to explain the company's criteria and its efforts to determine the reliability[3] and validity of its scales.

There are two reasons to justify inpatient care in an out-of-town facility:

1. The privacy of the employee might be jeopardized because he or she is known in the community or the local facility.
2. The employee may need a distant specialty facility if he or she has failed to improve during treatment from available resources at home.

Traditional indemnity mental health benefits set fairly arbitrary limits on both inpatient care and outpatient visits, with little or no coverage for anything in between. Until recent years, many of today's multilevel options simply were not available. Mental health treatment and cost options were far more appropriate for medical than psychiatric care or substance abuse rehabilitation.

Widening Range of Alternative

Fortunately, that situation has changed to some extent. We now recognize the importance of treating psychiatric disorders differently and have developed a constantly widening range of alternative treatments that do a far better job of meeting patient needs as well as providing cost-effective alternatives to inpatient care. While hospitalization will always be appropriate and necessary for some patients, many of these people can be phased quickly into alternative care after a brief inpatient stay, or else referred to an alternative setting from the beginning, with advantages for everyone.

This is called the *alternative/intermediate/continuous services/stepdown* approach to managed mental health service delivery. The idea, in terms of benefit design, is not only to make alternatives to inpatient care available to appropriate patients, but also to provide as part of the plan design financial incentives for beneficiaries to access these other levels that are not only less expensive than full hospitalization but more appropriate and effective for patients.

The essence of managed mental health care involves thinking about benefit plan design, provider networks and utilization review as a single system. Traditional benefit designs fostered fragmentation of mental health services, with inpatient services predominating. Under managed care, however, the delivery system is conceptualized as a whole, with inpatient services no longer dominating the picture. With greater availability of alternatives to inpatient care, inpatient services become a smaller part of the total system.

CRISIS INTERVENTION (DIVERSION)

The psychiatric inpatient industry is now facing an interesting reality. For about 20 years, research with severely ill patients has repeatedly demonstrated that most patients can be maintained safely and effectively outside of hospital environments. Yet, in spite of such research knowledge, private sector psychiatric practice has emphasized the development of inpatient services. As mentioned above, since the old indemnity benefits structure emphasized inpatient more than outpatient care, it is no wonder that we witnessed such an emphasis on hospitalization. With the growth of managed care, the interesting reality is that providers are going to have to listen to what past research tells them and change their style of practice.

The term *diversion* refers to the avoidance of inpatient treatment. However, many diversion programs can also serve a *stepdown* function, i.e., they can allow a shortening of an inpatient stay by providing an effective but less restrictive (and less costly) setting to meet the patient's needs. In this section, we will describe the diversion programs available in some parts of the country.

Assertive Community Treatment (ACT)

This is an innovative treatment model developed by Stein and Test.[4] In this approach, a comprehensive list of outpatient services is made available by a multidisciplinary team on a 24-hour-a-day basis. Therapists take a *proactive*, assertive and continuous treatment stance in order to avoid utilization of costly inpatient services. They met patients in *their own setting* rather than insisting that patients come to the facility. For instance, therapists might supervise and support patients over coffee at the local donut store or accompany patients for job interviews. This model has been tested numerous times since its inception, and the results indicate that it reduces inpatient utilization while improving functioning in spite of persistent psychiatric symptoms.

ACT contrasts sharply with the typical private psychiatric inpatient program that focuses only on the immediate crisis, then discharges the patient to another program in another setting that may or may not be effective for that individual.

The ACT model has served as a powerful prototype for many public sector agencies around the country. We believe that the time has come for the application of ACT principles in private settings as well.

Traditional Crisis Intervention Programs

These are found in most hospitals and mental health centers. As part of the outpatient clinic, trained clinicians treat patients in crisis via intensive (three to seven days a week) meetings that include key persons in the patient's life. The more advanced clinics (still in a minority) employ "mobile crisis" techniques in which clinicians go to the home of the patient when necessary.

Home Care

This approach involves a home care clinician who supports relapsing patients in their own homes instead of in an inpatient setting. Home care can be utilized to avoid hospitalization altogether or to shorten a necessary inpatient hospital stay. The clinical principle followed in this strategy is to stabilize patients in their home settings in order to preserve their social support system. We predict an increase in the psychiatric home care industry in response to the influence of managed care programs. Such home care programs typically will be nurse run and will offer services including predischarge hospital assessment for after-care planning; comprehensive home-based assessment; programs for individuals, couples and families; and crisis intervention treatment, case management and home-based educational programs to assure accurate compliance with treatment recommendations. When psychiatric crises result from family dysfunction, home care must include family treatment to improve functioning and divert inpatient hospitalization. Such an approach will not only manage the immediate crisis but will also contribute to the prevention of future disruption. The potential for cost savings with such programs is enormous.

Case Example
A 54-year-old woman has been depressed since her husband of 30 years died suddenly of a heart attack six months ago. She has been crying daily and missing work (she serves as an administrative assistant.) Three days ago she went to a private psychiatrist who started her on antidepressant medication. Two days later, she called the psychiatrist and reported that she "couldn't hold on" and was afraid that she might decide to kill herself. The psychiatrist sent her to the emergency room where she was assessed by the ER physician. The ER physician called the HMO to which she belonged and discussed the possibility of admitting her to the inpatient unit. The HMO utilization reviewer offered instead a home care intervention in which a nurse's aid (at $7.50/hour) would stay with the patient at home

on a 24-hour-a-day basis and report any difficulties to the patient's treating psychiatrist. The patient and the ER physician agreed with the plan, and the nurse's aide stayed with the patient, reporting daily to the psychiatrist for the next five days. By that time, the patient's depression began to lift (the antidepressant medication finally took effect), and the patient stated that she no longer felt suicidal. Home care in this case cost $900 in charges for the nurse's aide and $150 for the psychiatrist's supervision. Had this patient been admitted, the hospital charge would have been $750 per day for five days, or $3,750, and it is not certain that the hospital would have discharged her in as few as five days.

Noninstitutional Acute Sites

In comparison to the home care treatment model described above, *noninstitutional acute sites,* also called *residential treatment centers (RTCs)* are another diversion option. This strategy is closer to inpatient psychiatric care but offers an informal (and less costly) noninstitutional setting. Here, an apartment site might serve as an informal unit, staffed by a nurse or social worker and supervised by a part-time psychiatrist. In such settings, medications can be administered and the patient can be monitored closely but without the use of restraints or locked units. Research has also focused on the "crisis hostel," volunteer private homes, respite care and other nonhospital treatment settings with low staff-to-patient ratios. Interestingly, studies have indicated that these noninstitutional sites are not only successful for the acute episode but also may reduce subsequent episodes of illness more than institutional settings because they deemphasize institutional dependence. Residential treatment is far less expensive than traditional institutionalization: $6,000 to $9,000 per month versus approximately $20,000 per month.[5]

Partial Hospitalization

Partial hospitalization or *day hospitalization* programs are designed as a substitute for acute inpatient admission and consequently have lengths of stay measured in days or weeks. As private inpatient facilities adjust to the demands of managed care, this treatment modality is increasingly covered by insurance benefits and consequently is rapidly emerging as a favored method of "stepping down" from inpatient treatment. It remains to be seen if day hospitalization truly offers an effective alternative to inpatient care in managed care settings.

In the typical private sector "partial" program, patients participate in individual, family and group therapies six to eight hours per day for a fixed time period, usually about 30 days. Even patients who are quite ill are able to live at home or in inexpensive, supervised apartments. These apartments are sometimes affiliated with the sponsor of the partial program, with staff consisting of medical professionals, including a psychiatrist.

If a hospital has developed these programs thoughtfully, they can serve as a viable alternate to inpatient care, thus reducing inpatient lengths of stay substantially. There is currently a concern that an increase in these programs, which often charge 50-75 percent the daily rate associated with an inpatient unit, will offset the reduction in inpatient days brought about by managed care and therefore the cost savings.[6] This concern is heightened by a finding by the National Association of Private Practice Hospitals (NAPPH) that the proportion of inpatients treated in partial hospitalization doubled between 1990 and 1991 from 3.1 percent to 6.4 percent.[7] It is clear that managed care companies will need to develop strategies to contain costs and maintain high-quality care if these programs are to offer a solution to the overall increase in mental health care costs. Assuming that the partial hospitalization approach will be managed effectively, it is well worth including such treatments in benefit plans.

Case Example

A 34-year-old married woman with a history of bipolar disorder became hypomanic, i.e., she exhibited mild signs of mania including rapid speech, reduced need for sleep and irritability. Because she had become manic in the past, her treating psychiatrist admitted her to an inpatient unit to allow 24-hour monitoring of her behavior and to allow time to adjust her lithium treatment. By the third day of hospitalization, she appeared to have settled down, although she was not back to her usual status. The psychiatrist decided to "step her down" to the hospital's partial program, where he continued to see her for a half hour every other day while she participated in structured activities eight hours a day with the program staff, living at home with her family the rest of the time. After ten days of this treatment, her behavior returned to "baseline," allowing the psychiatrist to discharge her to his outpatient practice.

Before partial hospitalization programs were common, this patient would have spent at least 14 days on the inpatient unit; the savings of the approach amounted to 57 percent of that cost.

Case Management

Comprehensive diversion strategies employ *case management,* which is defined differently depending on the program using the term. Generally speaking, the term *case management* refers to the linking and coordination of services for an individual patient. In managed care settings such as HMOs or PPOs, case managers will identify high-risk/ high-cost cases, assess these patients to identify their needs, work with the health care providers to develop a comprehensive treatment plan, implement services and evaluate the total process. For example, they might meet with patients, take them to the welfare office for their checks, call them to be sure that they keep a doctor's appointment, advocate for legislation to help with their care and sometimes provide psychotherapy or psychoeducational services.

Patients living in the community with chronic illnesses like schizophrenia often require care management services because their needs are complex. They require services extending beyond the therapist-patient relation such as rehabilitation, crisis intervention, housing and medication monitoring. Since the funding of these services usually comes from multiple sources such as the federal, state and local government as well as private insurance, and since many professionals and administrators are involved with the patient, a single case manager is designated to coordinate all of the services so that the patient does not "fall through the cracks" of multiple treatment systems and payers. Case management may be performed by mental health professionals of different backgrounds, and it can also be carried out by nonprofessional advocates working outside the medical system of care. Recently, the Certification of Insurance Rehabilitation Specialists Commission has developed a voluntary credentialing process for medical professionals working as managers.

In contrast to the type of case management described above, in UR companies case management involves the administrative oversight and coordination of treatment services as distinguished from the direct delivery of care. The goal is similar, however, and is directed at coordinating services so that the patient is treated effectively. Often case management in a managed care company will be provided to the complex cases, i.e., the ones that are utilizing a lot of services or have diagnoses such as schizophrenia, borderline personality, multiple personality or bipolar disorder.

It is important to note how comprehensive the case management services are that are offered by managed care companies. In some instances, the term *case management* simply means UR. If the company is only performing UR, its ability to manage cases may be quite limited, particularly if the contract is only for inpatient services. Ideally, case management should cut across systems of care.

Studies indicate that case management increases accessibility to and utilization of existing services, but the outcome is more a function of the services that are in place than case management. It is also apparent that hospital use is diminished when case management connects patients to appropriate social services provided in the community.

INPATIENT TREATMENT

Inpatient treatment occurs in medical settings where trained medical professionals are able to monitor the care of the patient on a 24-hour-a-day basis. Inpatient treatment occurs in units and beds (scatterbeds) within general hospitals and in freestanding not-for-profit and for-profit psychiatric facilities. Specific methods unique to inpatient settings include 24-hour monitoring by trained medical staff; daily examination by a psychiatrist; immediate access to laboratory tests, CAT scan, magnetic resonance imaging, EEG, etc. (it is a rare patient who requires these tests immediately; most patients can be tested electively as out-patients); and restraint facilities, e.g., two- and four-point restraint, locked rooms (and units), "quiet" rooms, etc. The frequent group meetings (three to six a day with different rehabilitative themes) and individual therapy (usually three times per week) are not necessarily unique to inpatient milieus; the partial hospital programs mentioned above provide such services as well.

Principles Driving Change

It is in this setting that we are witnessing the most radical change in the culture of practice in response to managed care trends. There are three driving principles that are fostering this change. The first principle is that treatment must be cost effective yet high quality. If research has shown that the quality of care delivered from inpatient venues is equal to that delivered in less expensive settings such as those listed above, then it stands to reason that inpatient care is less preferable in most cases. Inpatient care should be used only for patients whose psychiatric illness has rendered them so dangerous to themselves or others, or so unable to negotiate their hour-to-hour existence, that the highly intensive (and costly) inpatient approach is necessary.

The second principle is that confinement in an inpatient unit must be medically necessary. Although more will be said about this them later, suffice it to say that medical necessity implies that the treatment is both *effective* and *appropriate,* i.e., delivered in the correct setting.

The third principle is that all patients should be treated in the least restrictive setting. The theme of *least restrictive setting* emerged following class action suits against state hospitals that were providing substandard treatment. The courts acknowledged that the treatment was poor and referred to the principle that patients should not be held in hospitals that are not able to provide appropriate levels of care. Ironically, hospitals in the private sector have been well equipped to treat their patients; the problem is that many are *too* willing to treat patients who could be treated effectively in less costly settings. Thus, if a patient's condition is such that he or she could be treated in a setting other than an inpatient unit, it is ethically and legally appropriate to do so.

As a result of these three themes, many "habits"—not standards of care—require alteration. The psychiatric profession is now mourning the loss of the old ways,[8] but the ambitious and astute providers are getting the point as evidenced by a 1991 survey from NAPPH that found a substantial reduction in inpatient utilization rates in 1991 compared to 1990.[9] Here are some of the changes they are experiencing.

Inpatient Care a Means

Inpatient care is a means, not an end. In the indemnity days, when it was common to see unlimited benefits allocated to hospital treatment, psychiatrists envisioned hospital treatment as a comprehensive strategy, with a beginning, middle and end. A "treated" patient was one who was almost "cured" when he or she walked out the door. Consequently, it was not uncommon to see lengths of stay measured in years. When less generous benefits were available, the *still* specified 30, 60 or 90 or more days per confinement and, consequently, the "30-day" or "60-day" unit was a common administrative entity. With the emergence of managed care, and in the absence of scientific data to support fixed length-of-stay programs, inpatient level care becomes a small, though important, aspect of the total treatment approach, as a specialized service for the dangerous or seriously dysfunctional patient who, once improved, can and should move on to a less restrictive setting.

Length-of-Stay Issues

Fixed length-of-stay inpatient programs are not synonymous with high-quality, cost-effective care. Fixed length-of-stay policies allow providers to behave as though a treatment is like a novel or a play, with a crisis at the beginning, a working through process in the middle and a resolution at the end. When you look at cost, however, the obvious question becomes: Why pay these rates for the middle and the end? Inpatient treatment does not have to be a neatly wrapped package with a bow on it. It needs instead to be a high-intensity stabilization environment where patients can benefit from expensive but necessary medical monitoring until they are ready to face their problems in a less structured setting. Usually, such monitoring requires days, not weeks; then patients can continue the process in a "stepdown" program, which may have a longer duration. Many chemical dependency and eating disorder programs are still reluctant to adapt to this theme (not coincidentally, there has been an explosion in the development of such programs in the 1980s). Many insist that 28 days are necessary to get patients to the point where they will not relapse into substance abuse if discharged. Such reasoning is difficult to accept when (1) research mentioned above does not justify such programming and (2) all chemically dependent people are and will be at risk for relapse for the rest of their lives. What is so special about 28 days relative to the enormous time that the person must struggle with recovery following discharge? In fairness, it is important to say that there are *some* patients who *may* need extra inpatient time to prepare them for the road to sobriety. It behooves us to develop valid methods to identify such patients, but fixed, 28-day programs, we feel, are not the solution.

Importance of Continuity

Programs should provide continuity between the inpatient unit and the "step-down." In mourning the loss of the old ways, inpatient providers are disturbed the most by a perception that they must lose the experience of aligning with their patient. Therapists choose their specialty in part because of the rewards they experience with successful therapeutic alliances. If the therapist works only on an inpatient unit, he or she will have the unfortunate task of learning to develop alliances in ten to 14 days. Administrators should see the logic in allowing these clinicians to stay with their patients as they move through stepdowns. Under such a scenario, we predict that the alliance will be saved, the patient will be satisfied and the costs will be less.

Importance of Timeliness

If inpatient care is for stabilization, providers must respond in timely ways. In the old days, when inpatient confinements were long, providers reacted in a slower, more leisurely way than they must in today's managed care environment. Here are a few tips to help spot providers who are still trying to cling to the past. Beware of the facility that:

- Cannot present (in writing) a comprehensive treatment plan within 72 hours after admission.
- Has not identified the problems in the patient's living circumstance (recovery environment) and begun to respond to them within 72 hours after admission. It is preposterous to claim on day three that an addicted person's recovery environment will be dealt with during family week of a 28-day program.
- Agrees to elective admissions. If inpatient care is supposed to be for people who require intensive medical monitoring, how necessary can it be if the person is able to schedule an admission date?
- Exhibits a consistent pattern of setting up smoke screens for UR administrators. Specifically, beware of facilities that insist on doctor-to-doctor discussions in every case, are slow to return calls or that instruct their patients (your employees) and/or patients' families to fight with the UR program.

Clearly, inpatient strategies are effective and appropriate for some psychiatric patients. The problem is that the inpatient milieu has been overemphasized by payers and overused by providers. It is certainly possible, and necessary, to change this orientation.

OUTPATIENT TREATMENT

Of the myriad of outpatient treatments available, we want to concentrate on the *psychological* therapies as opposed to the *somatic* or drug therapies. Of course somatic and psychological therapies are often administered simultaneously and in *both* inpatient and outpatient settings, but the vast majority of psychological therapies are individual (one-on-one) therapy, group therapy (usually with eight to 12 patients), couples therapy and family therapy.

Outpatient therapy can also be classified by duration. *Brief* or *time-limited* therapies usually occur on a once-a-week basis for no more than 15 sessions. Emerging research is suggesting that anxiety and mood disorders can be treated in brief therapies of different types, usually in combination with medication. Long-term therapy attempts to change a person's character or way of living rather than to treat a discrete episode of illness. Such therapy can occur one to three times a week over a period of years. Although long-term therapy is costly, its advocates argue that it prevents recurrences of chronic disorders. Unfortunately, these advocates have little scientific evidence to support this claim. Family or couples treatment is usually employed when one of the members of the unit appears for help. Such treatment is almost mandatory for adolescent patients.

Psychodynamic Therapies

Outpatient therapies can be classified loosely by treatment philosophy. *Psychodynamic (or psychoanalytic) therapies* usually occur on a one-to-one basis but can also occur in group settings. They attempt to help patients gain insight into themselves and change maladaptive behaviors by integrating past experience with current issues. Typically, such therapy is not time limited and therefore is costly, taking years to complete on a once- or twice-a-week basis. However, dynamic therapy *can* occur in brief or time-limited interactions as described above.

Psychoanalysis involves a specially trained therapist (an analyst) and a resource-rich patient (analysand) who meet in daily sessions over years, the latter lying on a couch to promote free thinking.

Supportive Therapy

Supportive therapy focuses on immediate feelings, stress reduction and problem solving. It does not emphasize past experience like psychodynamic therapy, focusing on helping the person get through a particular episode or crisis. Depending on the condition, supportive therapy can occur at various frequencies, i.e., once a week to once a month, and for varying durations, i.e., weeks to years.

Behavioral Therapy

Behavioral therapy used principles of reward and punishment that were developed by Pavlov and Skinner to help patients alter unwanted behavior or strengthen necessary ones. Teaching, coaching, field trips, relaxation training, instruction, medication and homework are standard fare in this modality. Behavioral treatments are typically shorter (weeks to months) in duration.

Cognitive Therapy

Cognitive therapy is a specialized form of behavior therapy that employees an information processing approach to psychiatric conditions. An advocate of this approach, Dr. Aaron Beck of the University of Pennsylvania, defines *cognitive therapy* as an "empirically based, results-oriented therapy."[10] The therapy is structured and time limited and has been found to be useful for numerous conditions, including depression and anxiety disorders. The treatment is aimed at teaching coping skills by correct habitual mental distortions, e.g., "I'm inferior," and substituting more adaptive ways of thinking such as, "I'm as good as the next person."

One author[11] gave a vivid example of how cognitive therapy works by describing his work with an Asian patient who believed that Americans scowled at him in public. The patient believed this so strongly that at times he would become enraged and scowl back at people, thus stimulating a surprised and sometimes negative response that reinforced his idea that Americans looked down on him and were unfriendly. The therapists assigned him the task of smiling at people whom he perceived to be scowling at him. When he followed these instructions, he was astounded to experience warm relationships with these strangers.

Patients in cognitive therapy are given "homework" assignments such as reviewing audiotapes of sessions, completing self-assessment tests between sessions, reading and writing assignments. When cognitive therapy helps patients think and act more realistically, they experience improvement in mood and ability to cope with life.

Rehabilitative Therapy

Rehabilitative therapies, often provided by counselors, may utilize music, painting, exercise and other approaches to help patients learn to express inner feelings and ultimately strengthen deficits.

Managed care principles call for the appropriate assignment of outpatient treatment. This is a challenging task, since there is no specificity to outpatient methods and no particular diagnosis is associated with a specific treatment. When the psychiatric condition is prolonged in nature, patients require long-term treatment after they have recovered from acute episodes, or they risk relapse. On the other hand, many psychiatric conditions, such as situational adjustment reactions, are brief or self-limited in nature. In fact, the majority of patients seeking outpatient care decide to leave such treatment after about seven contacts. With utilization management, there is hope that outpatient therapy can be assigned in a fair and effective manner. At this writing, however, utilization management approaches to outpatient treatment are in their infancy.[12]

During this current transition period, when many mental health benefit plan designs still do not include alternative levels of care, there are a number of companies that contract with HMOs, EAPs and self-insured employers to identify inpatient alternatives to treatment for specific patients. One such firm is Positive Alternatives to Hospitalization (PATH) in West Hartford, Connecticut. PATH providers meet with patients and family members prior to psychiatric hospital admission to explore alternatives to hospitalization and then develop a treatment plan that avoids admission when possible.

According to PATH, 65 percent of the patients it sees are ready to be hospitalized without ever having seen a mental health provider and are unaware that there are alternatives to hospitalization. PATH avoids hospitalization for 80 percent of the cases it handles and, in situations where admission is necessary, its services reduce the average length of stay from 12 days to 7.5 days.[13]

Case Example

First Chicago Corporation, with 17,000 employees in three states, claims to have saved money for nearly a decade by covering most mental health alternative treatment costs. In 1983, 15 percent of the company's health care costs were being spent on mental health. As a result, First Chicago made changes in its plan design that included paying 85 percent of outpatient costs for treatment accessed through its EAP. In so doing, the firm reduced inpatient costs by 60 percent over the first four years, and costs have remained at that level ever since.

Though increased utilization has raised outpatient mental health costs because of the generous benefits, overall behavioral health care costs fell by nearly 30 percent over the first four years to about $1 million annually, down from $1.4 million, and they have remained today.[14]

MANAGED PSYCHIATRIC PRACTICE OF THE FUTURE

How will private psychiatric practice change once the above-described principles have been integrated into the culture? The major change that we see will be a significant reduction in psychiatric hospitals. They will be replaced by multidisciplinary group practices, run by psychiatrists, who will oversee all levels of patient care, from acute inpatient (which will rarely last more than 72 hours) to outpatient psychotherapy, which will be divided among the various mental health professionals depending on the needs of the patient. Office-based psychotherapy performed by psychiatrists will be replaced by less expensive treatments provided by nonphysician mental health professionals. Home-based care by these teams will be the norm rather than the exception. These teams will be on 24-hour call to respond to patients' psychiatric needs as soon as possible. They will stay with patients throughout the course of their illness, ensuring that they receive the appropriate support and care over the long term.

Another major change in this delivery system will be in financing. These groups of providers will negotiate risk sharing agreements of various types directly with employers as well as managed care companies rather than working on a fee-for-service basis.

Editor's note: This article is an adaptation of a chapter in *Mental Health Benefits: A Purchaser's Guide* by William M. Glazer and Nancy N. Bell, recently published by the International Foundation of Employee Benefit Plans.

1. Michael Schachner, "Behavioral Care Outside Hospitals Backed to Cut Costs," *Business Insurance,* June 8, 1992, p.18.

2. Ibid.

3. W. Glazer, R. Kramer and J. Montgomery, "Medical Necessity Scales for Inpatient Psychiatric Concurrent Review," *Hospital & Community Psychiatry* 43, no. 9 (1992): 935-937.

4. M.A. Test and L.I. Stein, "The Clinical Rationale for Community Treatment: A Review of the Literature," in L.I. Stein and M.A. Test (eds.), *Alternatives to Mental Hospital Treatment* (New York: Plenum Press, 1976).

5. Ibid, p, 21.

6. Hoge, L. Davidson and W.L. Hill, "The Promise of Partial Hospitalization: A Reassessment," *Hospital & Community Psychiatry* 43 (1992): 345-354.

7. "News and Notes," *Hospital & Community Psychiatry* 43, no. 9 (1992): 347-348.

8. W. Glazer, "Doctors' Response to Managed Care, *Medical Interface* 5, no. 4 (1992): 14-16.

9. "News and Notes," *Hospital & Community Psychiatry* 43, no. 9 (1992): 347-348.

10. A. Beck, "Cognitive Therapy and Psychiatric Practice," *Psychiatric Annals* 22 no. 9 (1992): 449-450.

11. Burns and A.H. Auerbach, "Does Homework Compliance Enhance Recovery From Depression? *Psychiatric Annals* 22, no. 9 (1992): 464-469.

12. D.C. Moore, "Utilization Management and Outpatient Treatment," *Psychiatric Annals* 22 no. 7 (1992): 373-377.

13. Schachner, "Behavioral Care Outside Hospitals," p. 20, note 1.

14. D.J. Conti and W.N. Burton, "Swimming Upstream: How First Chicago Manages Costs While Expanding Behavioral Health Benefits," *Behavioral Healthcare Tomorrow,* premier issue, September 1992, pp. 24-27.

31. Industry Statistics:
Conoco Internal Managed Behavioral Health Program Reports Significant Changes
Martin Z. Sipkoff   Monica E. Oss

More than three years ago, Conoco Inc. restructured its internal employee assistance program (EAP) to manage the behavioral health benefits provided to its 13,000 employees and their dependents, a total of 56,000 covered lives. In 1992, that restructuring resulted in claims savings to the Texas-based petroleum corporation of $2.82 million.

According to the Conoco EAP's 1992 annual report, the EAP's utilization rate (i.e., treatments managed), increased from 1,749 in 1990 to 2,289 in 1992. The behavioral health treatment costs authorized through the EAP during that period decreased, however, from $4.02 million in 1990 to $3.42 million in 1992. The 1992 figure represents a reduction of $665,000 (16.5 percent) from the total claims amount paid through the EAP for 1991, even though the number of cases increased by 11.7 percent.

Total behavioral health claims paid by Conoco in 1989, the year prior to the establishment of managed care through the EAP, were $4.45 million. In 1990 and 1991, the total behavioral health claims paid within and outside the EAP network were $.54 million and $4.52 million, respectively, representing essentially no increase in claims costs over the two years. These figures include $4.02 million within the EAP network and $502,000 outside the EAP network for 1990 and $4.04 million and $480,000 respectively for 1991. An average of only 10.8 percent of the claims went outside the EAP in 1990–91. In 1992, behavioral health

Reprinted with permission from *Open Minds,* 4465 Old Harrisburg Road, Gettysburg, Pennsylvania 17325. October 1993, Volume 7, Issue 7.

claims totalled $3.8 million, including $400,000 in out-of-network payments. This was $2.82 million less than the amount projected if the costs had followed the inflation rate experienced by the rest of Conoco's medical benefits plan during that same period.

Conoco's managed care efforts were focused on all acute inpatient admissions or structured alternatives to inpatient care. There were 10 cases identified as "catastrophic cases" defined as any case with more than $40,000 in annual claims) for special case management in 1992. The cost savings on these 10 cases from contracted prices alone came to $518,000. The payment of total approved claims is $3.4 million for 1992. The use of all-inclusive, managed care contracts negotiated with the EAP's preferred provider network resulted in a savings of $1.60 million in 1992, when compared to the cost of full-rate provider services.

Conoco's behavioral health costs had risen by 30 to 40 percent in both 1987 and 1988. Other petroleum companies had attempted to resolve similar cost problems through reduction or elimination of behavioral health benefits. However, Conoco determined that such a solution was a "short-term, short-sighted solution to a long-term, complex problem involving our entire system," according to Robert Johnson, Conoco's EAP Director. Conoco redesigned its benefit to support the expansion of the EAP to include case management responsibilities. "Rather than restricting benefits and providers, Conoco adopted the radical posture of achieving cost containment by making benefits more 'user friendly,' " Johnson said.

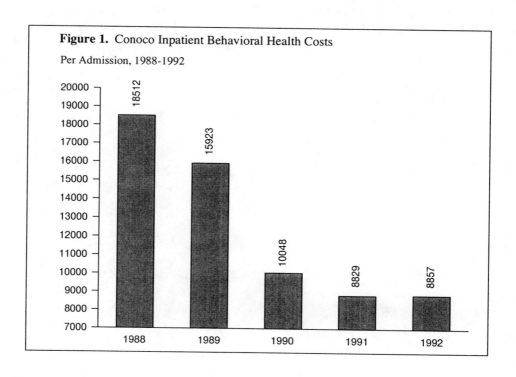

Figure 1. Conoco Inpatient Behavioral Health Costs Per Admission, 1988-1992

Other benefit design changes instituted by Conoco to support the new plan included:

- Incentives to use the EAP by reducing non-EAP managed inpatient coverage to 50 percent.
- Covering outpatient treatment and inpatient alternatives at 80 percent, instead of 50 percent.
- Covering all types of credentialed therapists.
- Extending benefits to include all levels of care, including group therapy, in-home services, intensive short-term outpatient programs, residential, halfway houses, therapeutic wilderness programs, and therapeutic foster care.

"Through Conoco's managed care efforts we have demonstrated a savings of as much as $2.82 million for 1992 alone over what could have been if the mental health and substance abuse claims had been left unmanaged," Dr. Johnson said. "Our experience of the last three years in behavioral health managed care has led us to broader view of risk management in the corporation. As we think more systemically about employee health cost management, we must include in our model not only the costs of behavioral health claims through the company medical plan, but also the effect of these problems on other medical claims and the related issues of workers' compensation, disability wage management, lost time, and lost productivity. Our efforts to save or manage costs in one area may just lead to an expensive shifting of costs to another area, therefore not reducing but potentially expanding our costs and our risks." For more information, contact Robert B. Johnson, Ed.D., EAP Director, Conoco, Inc., 600 North Dairy Ashford, Post Office Box 2197, Houston, Texas 77252, 713-293-5100, fax: 713-293-1361.

32.   EAPs and the Law:
What You Don't Know Can Hurt You

Barbara C. Keaton   Paul M. Bernstein

Not too long ago, finding an EAP in court was almost unheard of. But today the number of EAP lawsuits—and the issues they raise—are increasing. Unfortunately, the evidence suggests few EA professionals recognize the pitfalls, and few, until now, seem to have thought much about liability.

An employee assistance professional contacted a male client a year after treatment ended to check on his current status. It was just a routine follow-up call, but then the client asked for a lunch date. Before long a romance developed. When the EA professional decided to end the relationship, the client claimed she had urged him to divorce his wife during their EAP sessions. He filed a lawsuit.

In the court papers, he said the EAP counselor had harbored a secret intent to pursue a relationship with him, even though she purported to be offering marriage counseling. He claimed negligence.

Defending this case has cost the EAP's insurer more than $10,000 in legal fees alone. Malpractice awards could cost a lot more. Meanwhile, a court is tackling the thorny issue of just how much time should elapse before a social relationship between an EA professional and a client begins.

Richard Lehr, a partner in the law firm of Sirote, Permutt, Friend, Friedman, Held & Apolinsky and a specialist in EA law, urges employers and EA professionals to learn about potential legal disputes and preventive measures they can take.

"EAPs and the Law: What You Don't Know Can Hurt You," Barbara Keaton and Paul Bernstein, *Employee Assistance,* November 1993, pages 28-34.

"The legal issues affecting an EA could range from availability of counseling to job security, based on receiving EAP counseling," Lehr says.

Several years ago, ALMACA, the forerunner of today's Employee Assistance Professionals Association, cited some examples of charges EAPs were already facing in the courts: improper referral to a program and subsequent suicide, counselor negligence and sexual exploitation, slandering a treatment facility as dirty, substandard and unsuitable, unauthorized release of client records, and breach of confidentiality leading to job loss (Carnahan, 1984).

With cases such as these, EAP liability insurers have started to pay closer attention to the profession's application of legal principles. According to a major national carrier, lawsuits against EAPs most often allege breaches of confidentiality and sexual misconduct. Although this firm had only two cases of malpractice awarded against its policyholders in eight years, they fear major upheaval—and significantly more lawsuits—as attorneys enter what has been relatively untouched territory and find out about insurance coverage for EAPs.

COMING OF AGE

Growing fear of litigation partly mirrors growth and change in the profession. In the 1950s, fewer than 50 EAPs were on record. In 1988, the Bureau of Labor Statistics estimated as many as 300,000 programs operated in the United States alone. In addition to numerical growth, EAPs are counseling more. Today, many provide a maximum of six sessions instead of the old norm of two or three. The longer relationships reflect a larger EAP role in aftercare and follow-up as managed care companies limit psychiatric and mental health benefits.

EAPs often have had staffs of recovering alcoholics with little or no formal education and professionals with unrelated educational backgrounds. Now a trend has evolved demanding more clinical EAP treatment and more consideration of the qualifications of the EAP professional.

One insurance carrier said that in the face of these trends, it behooves us to ask whether EAPs also face more litigation because they are denying their legal vulnerability.

Do legal issues not concern EA professionals or do they have a false sense of security, believing that their sponsor company will protect them? In 1988, McClellan and Miller (cited in Holosko, 1988) asked 182 EA professionals to identify the most important skill for employee assistance work.

None identified legal/safety skills as important. This may not seem surprising, given the expectation that assessment and referral skills would be identified most often. But the lack of importance given to legal/safety skills becomes interesting when compared with 2.3 percent of the respondents identifying administrative skills as most important, 0.8 percent identifying benefit management skills and 1.5 percent identifying marketing skills as most important. No additional studies could be found to shed light on this question.

Another interesting question is whether the external EAP trend, "the largest segment of growth in the field over the past 10 years," (Steele, 1989) has been motivated by the concern of businesses over potential liability involving EA programs and professionals.

For example, in *Crivellaro vs. Pennsylvania Power & Light Co.,* an employee of PP&L in Bethlehem, Pa., sued the company, the EAP counselor and a drug detoxification center for $1.2 million. The plaintiff denied any chemical dependency and said she was forced to submit herself to treatment or lose her job. PP&L asserted that the employee's supervisor referred her to the company's EAP and that she voluntarily entered the treatment center (Carnahan, 1984).

A SOCIAL WORK LESSON

EA professionals may be able to take a cue from the experience of their social work colleagues. From 1978 to 1980, claims against professional liability insurance sponsored by the National Association of Social Workers more than tripled, rising from 50 to more than 150 (Imbert, 1980).

In a subsequent study, Jankovic and Green (1981) examined training needs and implications for social work education and identified four problems that impede social workers from acquiring basic legal knowledge pertinent to their practice:

- No academic exposure to basic legal principles that affect either their profession or their clients.
- Rare access to legal references, court decisions or administrative regulations.
- Lack of access to legal counsel.
- Belated training in skills necessary for dealing with legal processes.

The researchers concluded: "While practitioners are not expected to be legal experts, it should be assumed that they have some basic knowledge of clients and their rights, the agency processes in which they are involved and the extent to which their work is shaped by legislative developments, administrative edicts and case law."

In addition, social workers should ". . . be able to identify those legal issues that require legal consultation for the benefit of the client or the protection of the worker."

The researchers recommended that the Council of Social Work Education's accreditation standards and curriculum policy statement incorporate legal issues to better prepare social work practitioners.

In the EA profession also, a legal framework has begun to develop as the field has become more formalized. Common law precedents from related fields of law have begun to define relationships, rights and responsibilities of programs, sponsors and clients when legal problems arise.

General contract law regulates the relationships of the sponsoring company and external EAPs. Labor law affects the rights and responsibilities of the employer or union to form an EAP in the context of a collective-bargaining agreement. Employment law determines the rights of employer and employee when the EAP and the employer's disciplinary system interface.

Knowledge of this legal framework lets the EA professional design stable programs, take reasonable and customary action to meet client needs and identify situations in which the professional should seek the advice of an attorney. Armed with such knowledge, EAPs can avoid existing legal pitfalls and limit their liability.

One prerequisite to a working knowledge of this legal framework is for the EA professional to understand basic legal language and the location of specific codes and acts relevant to the issues in question.

As Lanier and Gray note, "Since the EAP field is a relatively new one, [even] some otherwise competent attorneys might not be knowledgeable about the various codes and acts which apply to this profession. As a guide to locating relevant information on EAP legal issues, an administrator or consultant should refer an attorney to [specific] codes." (Lanier and Gray, 1986).

Most literature on legal issues that affect EA professionals appears in journals associated with the professions of labor relations, health benefits and the law.

Along with understanding basic legal language and knowing where to find guidance on EA-specific issues, the EAP should have a firm grasp of three key principles of law: duty to warn, privilege communication and informed consent.

DUTY TO WARN

To comply with the legal principle of "duty to warn," EA professionals must forecast a client's danger to others. The courts will judge how well a professional applies this principle by comparing his behavior with others in the EAP field who possess and exercise a reasonable degree of skill, knowledge and care.

Public policy has evolved from a time when the therapeutic relationship was sacrosanct. A more current view holds that the welfare and safety of the client and society come before the confidentiality of the therapeutic relationship. Litigation has clearly established the mental health professional's responsibility to disclose information when a serious threat of harm to another exists.

Probably the most recognized case on this issue, *Tarasoff vs. Regents of the University of California,* prompted most states to develop procedures for mental health professionals to follow. Some states require application of this principle when the client threatens to damage property. Other states do not.

In the Tarasoff case (Woody, 1984), a mental outpatient at a University of California (UCD) Hospital, Posenjit Poddar, disclosed his intention to kill one Tatiana Tarasoff because she had spurned his romantic advances. The psychologist who learned of his intention, notified campus police and three staff psychiatrists, but after a cursory investigation, those involved decided confining Poddar was unnecessary. Tatiana was not warned of Poddar's intentions. Two months later, Poddar shot and killed her.

Poddar's trial revealed that he had discontinued his treatment at the UCD hospital after the incident two months earlier. Tatiana's parents thereupon sued UCD, alleging that the hospital's negligent failure to warn Tatiana of Poddar's intention had caused her wrongful death. The Alameda County Superior Court found for the defendant in 1973. An appeal to the California Supreme Court followed, and the case was heard again in 1976.

The case raised the issue of whether doctors have any duty to warn potential victims about known tendencies and intentions of their patients. The answer, in the words of the court: "A doctor or a psychotherapist treating a mentally ill patient. . .bears a duty to use reasonable care to give threatened persons such warnings as are essential to avert foreseeable danger arising from his patient's condition or treatment." The rule requires doctors to take such action to prevent harm from a patient's physical illness as well.

UCD contended that deciding which of the many threats that doctors hear should be taken seriously imposes too great a burden, but the law can properly require a professional to exercise his professional judgment. The university also argued that requiring disclosure of such threats would destroy the confidentiality necessary to effective psychotherapy.

Nonetheless, the court allowed the suit to proceed, finding that the interest of society in protecting itself from physical violence must take precedence. (Woody, 1984.)

DEFINING THE LIMITS

The literature recommends that the parameters of the EAP's confidentiality be stated in the company's policy.

L. Hoffman, EAP administrator at Jersey Central Power and Light, suggests language regarding this issue, "Jeopardy to life or to the welfare of the company releases the EAP from the pledge of confidentiality and invokes the duty to warn the concerned others."

Hoffman further remarks that the counselor's supervisor and the client's therapist (if applicable) need notice of such danger to others. If the EAP counselor believes the employee cannot work in safety, Hoffman suggests the counselor should act on a need-to-know basis and should place in the employee's work file a statement such as "This employee should not be allowed to perform his work at this time on the advice and recommendation of the EAP. Details to be worked out later." (Hoffman, UNK.)

The EAP also faces a duty to warn when the client has threatened damage to property—such as sabotaging the company's premises or harming the property of others.

It should be noted that not all courts have ruled alike on the duty to warn. In *Bellah vs. Greenson,* for example, the therapist need not disclose the contents of a confidential communication where the risk of harm is self-inflicted (e.g., suicide) or where mere property damage is at stake.

In duty-to-warn cases, therefore, EA professionals should obtain legal counsel regarding the laws, regulations and procedures established in their state.

A study conducted in 1991 (Keaton) on a sample of 101 EA professionals in the United States revealed that about 75 percent of the professionals practice in states that have established procedures to follow if they predict clients could endanger themselves of others. However, only half of the professionals work in EAPs that have developed internal procedures for compliance with state procedures.

The absence of internal procedures leaves EA professionals in the position of making critical decisions with little direction in a highly emotional situation. Faced with a dangerous client in such a case, they are extremely vulnerable. To begin to formulate a procedure, consider these questions:

1. What do you do with the client while calling the police?
2. Do you inform the client you are going to call the police?
3. Do you call company security?
4. Do you have a responsibility to notify anyone if the client threatens to damage property?
5. If you act on a need-to-know basis within the company, whom, if anyone, should you contact—the supervisor, medical personnel?
6. How should a dangerous employee be removed from company premises?

EA professionals may find themselves facing difficult conflicts as they weight professional ethics, court-dictated legal requirements, company policy and their own morality, while trying to balance protection of the client with public safety.

MATTERS OF PRIVILEGE

A state statute confers the right of privileged communications, sometimes referred to as testimonial privilege, to an individual when dealing with certain professionals.

This right arises from ". . .society's belief that certain favored relationships should be protected in order to ensure that individuals will seek advice freely without the risk of jeopardizing their legal rights." (Schroeder, 1982.)

Commonly, this privilege applies to an individual's relationship with the clergy, accountants, attorneys, journalists, social workers, psychiatrists, marriage counselors and psychologists. Information shared by the client with the professional is not to be revealed without due process of law.

Although no specific privilege exists in state laws for the EA professional, educational backgrounds protect some. For example, some states grant privilege to professionals holding a social work license. some statutes that cover certified professionals would include Certified Employee Assistance Professionals (CEAPs).

Privilege typically does not apply when a client files for insurance reimbursement for an emotional health problem. Information obtained by the insurance company lacks the sanctity of a protected relationship. Furthermore, employers often review this information—especially diagnosis and provider and treatment cost. EA professionals should make clients aware of any such practice when they refer a client to a provider.

Sandra Nye, JD, MSW, recommends that the EA professional consult with an attorney ". . . to ascertain in detail the state privilege laws governing his or her practice." In addition, she cautions that the state law regarding privileged communication should be understood before staffing an EAP. In established programs, care should be taken in assigning clients to counselors who may not be exempted by law.

In Keaton's study of EAPs mentioned earlier, she also found that nearly half the professionals were unsure whether state laws protecting privileged communication applied to their relationship with clients. Furthermore, only one-third of the respondents said they would offer to transfer a client facing (or likely to face) involvement in the legal arena to a professional whose relationship with the client would be protected.

INFORMED CONSENT

Certainly, since the right to privileged communication belongs to the clients, the EAP should inform clients before they decide to engage in a treatment or assessment relationship. The literature recommends that professionals seek the maximum informed consent allowed by public policy to ensure that the client understands and consents to treatment. Failure to do so, according to Nye, very often puts EAPs at risk for a malpractice action or discipline for unethical conduct.

The ideology of informed consent presupposes a basic human right to "know, when you are sick, what is happening to you, how it is happening, by whom, and under what conditions of risk." (Parry, 1981.)

Informed consent protects this right and subsequently enhances the personal integrity of clients as they maintain their responsibility for treatment.

Informed consent also implies quality treatment should follow—as the landmark *Wyatt vs. Stickney* decision by an Alabama court illustrates. The court issued an order mandating the need for adequate professional staff, patient-staff ratio, space size and program supervision by qualified mental health professionals (Woody, 1984).

Clients may also refuse treatment—and end it at any time (While and White, 1981). "In most states, even involuntary inpatient commitment to a mental health facility will not, in itself, deprive, a patient of the right to accept or refuse mental healthcare or substance abuse treatment." (Nye, 1990.)

Pratt vs. Davis [79 N.E. 562 (1906)] established that a legally competent person cannot be forced to accept clinical services even when such refusal appears symptomatic of the person's illness.

Nye has written that the right to refuse treatment also applies to mandatory EAP referrals—a client should not be terminated from employment because of refusal to participate in the EAP. Professionals must accept the fact that responsibility for treatment rests with the client.

In addition to EA professionals providing clinical care, it appears that professionals involved in EAP research must also be concerned with informed consent. According to a federal position statement dating back to the old Department of Health, Education and Welfare, "Human subjects who are to be used in research projects must be competent to consent, must give voluntary consent and must receive adequate information about what will transpire." (Woody, 1984.)

A FEW TOUCHSTONES

Guidelines have been developed for professionals in the provision of informed consent (G. Margolin, 1982).

The professional should offer: "(a) an explanation of the procedures and their purpose, (b) the role of the person who is providing therapy and his or her professional qualifications, (c) discomforts or risks reasonably to be expected, (d) benefits reasonably to be expected, (e) alternatives to treatment that might be of similar benefit, (f) a statement that any questions about the procedures will be answered at any time, and (g) a statement that the person can withdraw his or her consent and discontinue at any time."

Nye recommends that the client be informed of any risks associated with treatment refusal. Furthermore, when use of a diagnostic label is clinically contraindicated, Nye suggests that the EA professional use phenomenological terminology (i.e., unable to sleep, difficulty concentrating, and so on vs. depressed) when describing the condition to the client.

In addition, Nye writes, "If a recognized treatment exists for the client's condition, he or she should be informed of it, even if it is not available within the context of the EAP or in the client's home community. Clients sometimes have resources unknown to the provider." Professionals working in an EA setting must "clarify the nature and direction of his or her loyalties and responsibilities and keep all parties informed of his or her commitments. Clients must be fully informed of the consequences of accepting or refusing EAP services, as well as their freedom of choice with regard to participation." (Nye, 1990.)

Keaton's 1991 study of EA professionals found that most explain the purpose of the EAP service and offer to answer any questions from clients. However, less than half inform clients of their qualification and only a few explain the risks of treatment or treatment refusal. In addition, only about one-third of the professionals record the action taken regarding informed consent. Alarmingly, the study indicated that as EAP's salaries, educational levels and lengths of time in the field increased, they grew less likely to apply this principle.

Duty to warn, privileged communication and informed consent embody only three of many basic legal principles that EAP professionals must know. As the field develops and becomes more complex, the prospect of litigation grows more likely. We urge EA professionals to raise their awareness of the legal issues so they may better serve their clients, their companies and their profession.

References

Bellah v. Greenson [81 Cal. App. 3d 614, 622(1978)].

Carnahan, W.A. (1984). *Legal Issues Affecting Employee Assistance Programs.* Arlington, VA: The Association of Labor-Management Administrators and Consultants on Alcoholism.

Hoffman, J. (1988). The duty to warn UNK. New York: National Council on Alcoholism.

Jankovic, J. & Green, R. (1981). Teaching legal principles to social workers. *Journal of Education for Social Work,* 17(3), 28-35.

Lanier, D. & Gray, M. (1986). *A Guide for Administrators and Consultants.* Troy, MI: Performance Resource Press.

Lehr, R. & Davis, B. (1982). Employee assitance programs and legal issues. *EAP Digest.* Nov./Dec., 19-21.

Margolin, G. (1982). Ethical and legal considerations in marital and family therapy. *American Psychologist,* 37, 788-801.

Nye, S. (1990). *Employee Assistance Answer Book.* New York: Panel Publishers.

Parry, J.K. (1981). Informed Consent: For whose benefit? *Social Casework,* 62, 537-542.

Pratt v. Davis [79 N.E. 562 (1906)].

Schroeder, L.O. (1982). *The Legal Environment of Social Work.* Englewood Cliffs, NJ: Prentice-Hall.

Tarasoff v. Regents of University of California [17 Cal. 3d 425, 551 p. 2d 334, 131 Cal. Rptr. 14 (1976)].

White, M.B. & White, C.A. (1981). Involuntarily Committed Patient's Constitutional Right to Refuse Treatment: A Challenge to Psychology. *American Psychologist,* 36, 953-962.

Woody, R.H. & Associates. (1984). *The Law and the Practice* of Human Services. San Francisco, CA: Jossey-Bass.

Wyatt v. Stickney [325 F Supp 781 (M.D. Ala. 1971)].

Wylie, P. & Gothe, M. (1981). *Problem Employees: How to Improve Their Performance.* Belmont, California: Piman Learning, Inc.

Part 9

QUALITY AND COST CONTROL

33. Health Care Outcomes Measurement and Management
Michael S. Hendryx, PhD

To achieve the highest possible quality of care, administrators must be able to measure health care outcomes validly and improve outcomes through appropriate management efforts. Once administrators know how to improve outcomes, care can be made more consistent, efficient, and effective, benefiting patients and reducing unnecessary use and cost. This article discusses strategies for conducting outcomes measurement and management.

Through improvements in measuring and managing health care outcomes— taking into account geographic variations in health care services use— treatment choices can be made more appropriate to patient needs, reducing unnecessary variation in treatment delivery and costs.

Health care outcomes, simply defined, are the results of health care services. *Outcomes measurement* refers to methods of consistent and accurate quantification of these results. Examples of outcomes measures include mortality and morbidity rates, costs or other measures of resource use and patient functional status, quality of life, and satisfaction with care.

Outcomes management refers to operational-level efforts to structure the delivery of services to maximize patient health outcomes in the most efficient and appropriate way. Providing the highest quality of care may be seen as providing care of the highest possible effectiveness, efficiency, and appropriateness. Efforts at outcomes management flow logically from the results of outcomes measurement.

SIGNIFICANCE OF GEOGRAPHIC VARIATION IN HEALTH SERVICES USE

From one geographic area to another, there are large differences in the proportion of populations that receive a particular service, such as hospitalization or surgery. This variation has been observed for many surgical procedures and illnesses and across many levels of geographic aggregation. An important level of aggregation is the "small area"—a county, township, market area or metropolitan statistical area varying in size from a few urban neighborhoods to large rural tracts. Each area defines a population that tends to receive care from particular facilities. To cite just a few examples of geographic variation, Wennberg and Gittelsohn noted significant variation across small areas in the rates at which populations underwent many surgical procedures.[1] Chassin et al. studied population rates for 123 medical and surgical procedures and found at least a threefold variation across sites in 67 of them.[2] Griffith et al. analyzed wide geographic variation in hospital discharge rates for many disease groups.[3]

Treatment Decision Inconsistencies

Why should populations that are geographically proximal and similar demographically vary so widely in use of health care services? There may be many contributory factors, including differences in insurance coverage, population needs, patient demand, and supply of physical resources and providers. However, even after taking these factors into account, large differences across areas often remain. One important factor contributing to geographic variation is inconsistencies among physicians and other providers in reaching treatment decisions.

There is still much to be learned regarding the nature of treatment decision inconsistencies. It has sometimes been assumed that wide variation in treatment choices across providers exists because some providers must be admitting patients, or performing surgical procedures, conducting surgeries, at different rates of appropriateness than other providers in ways that systematically relate to area rate variation (that is, areas with high surgery rates have physicians doing proportionately more inappropriate surgeries). This is not necessarily the case. Evidence indicates that treatment decision inconsistences, at least in some instances, are unrelated to appropriateness; areas with high rates have proportionately as many appropriate cases as areas with low rates.[4] This is important because it suggests that individual providers make treatment decisions in highly idiosyncratic ways. The challenge then, is not just to encourage providers to give appropriate care, because in many cases, what constitutes appropriate care is not known and/or agreed upon. The challenge is first to learn about and agree on what is appropriate.

It has been observed that there is less variation across geographic areas for medical conditions or procedures in which the treatment indications are well known and agreed upon. When the profession can reach agreement on what works best to maximize outcomes, then those practices will show less variation. Knowing what works best requires measuring outcomes.

OUTCOMES MEASUREMENT

Although the discussion thus far may seem to argue for large research studies health care outcomes, the need to measure outcomes and relate them to prior care is equally important at the local facility level. It is at this level that knowledge of best outcomes and how to achieve them will have their largest possible impact; it is where the "rubber meets the road" for the ultimate test of the ability to improve outcomes.

Data Gathering

Data to measure outcomes may be obtained by using existing sources, such as medical records, or by collecting new data. Existing administrative and medical data may be used to track outcomes for similar patients—similar in age and medical history—as well as to track morbidity and mortality outcomes and measures of resource use.

Obtaining outcomes information directly from patients is increasingly important and a number of validated instruments have been developed for particular purposes. For example, the health status questionnaire, and corresponding disease- or procedure-specific technology of patient experience (TyPES), may be used to track patient functional ability over time (discussed in a previous edition of *Driving Down Health Care Costs*).[5] Other patient self-report measures that may be used to assess functional status in response to treatment include the functional status questionnaire,[6] and the sickness impact profile.[7] A good, brief self-report measure of mental health functioning is the mental health inventory-18.[8]

Problems and Limitations

There are certainly problems and limitations to conducting outcomes measurement. Limited human resources may require prioritizing outcomes measurement areas: It may be possible, for example, in an orthopedics clinic, to track functional outcomes of all patients over time, but it may not be possible to follow all patients treated in an acute-care hospital. The personnel who conduct outcomes measurement must have the necessary computer skills and equipment as well as facility with spreadsheets, although software is available that may make this task easier.

The issue of case mix and prior health status is a thorny one, with no completely satisfactory solution. How can we know for certain that outcomes are due to care received and not to health status before care? When measuring functional outcomes, it is necessary to get pretreatment data on those functions. Pretreatment data may be obtained most readily in planned situations, such as elective surgical procedures, but it may also be obtained at the start of treatment, during initial history and assessment. Changes in patient outcomes may then be tracked as functions of differences in surgery types or other procedures, providers, clinics, or other variables. When one is measuring medical outcomes such as mortality, data on health status at initiation of treatment may be used, such as an APACHE score (acute physiology and chronic health evaluation score) to measure severity of illness for patients admitted to intensive care units.[9]

Another potential limitation is lack of comparative data. Tracking outcomes in one setting provides no information on comparative performance in other settings. Possible solutions to this problem include setting standards relative to prior internal performance, creating meaningful subgroups within a setting for comparison (e.g., multiple nursing units that treat similar patients), purchasing comparative databases available through vendors for particular purposes, or forming collaborative arrangements with other treatment sites to share information. This last suggestion works best when there are multiple organizations participating and a mechanism is in place to prevent linking identifiable data among participating organizations.

One final risk of outcomes measurement that I will mention is the move toward "report cards" to compare performance among providers. Report card data on outcomes may be used by purchasers or consumers to choose hospitals or physicians. The use of report cards is a very popular idea in current health care reform discussions. The risk is not the report cards themselves, but in how they are constructed and interpreted. They must be based on reliable and valid measures of performance, be collected in a uniform manner from providers, adjust appropriately for case mix, and develop appropriate comparison statistics so that providers are not disadvantaged based on chance differences in scores. If all of these criteria are not met, report cards may damage patients and providers through faulty information.

Measuring outcomes in isolation is not enough. Outcomes must be related to prior care. Do certain patients who receive prostatectomy benefit, in specific ways, versus those who elect to postpone surgery (watchful waiters)? Which patients hospitalized for depression show better outcomes, including symptom levels, job performance, and other measures, versus those treated as outpatients? Based on specific outcomes tied to processes of care for particular patients, we can create patient profiles for making appropriate treatment decisions. Implementing these decisions in health care facilities in ways that reduce unnecessary variation requires outcomes management.

OUTCOMES MANAGEMENT

The basic approach that I take is based on principles of continuous quality improvement (CQI), sometimes used interchangeably with total quality management (TQM). I wish to differentiate the two terms here. TQM refers to a broad management strategy that includes many techniques, some of which may be CQI methods. CQI explicitly focuses on the use of information to monitor and improve quality of care on an ongoing basis—the focus is on the use of information, and key within this is measures of outcomes.

The Goal: Identifying "Best Current Practices"

Under the CQI outcomes management approach, outcome measures are used to identify the process of care and establish a performance pattern. Next, efforts are undertaken by the persons responsible for care in that area to define possible sources of "special variation" in process performance. (*Special variation in performance* refers to variation due to unique, time-limited events.) To the extent possible, sources of special variation are eliminated so that the process of care operates in a reliable and consistent manner across time and patients. The best current practice becomes standardized. Achieving this consistency may be accomplished through implementing guidelines or critical paths that specify how the process is actually conducted when it operates as intended.

The variation that remains is "common variation," consistent and inherent in the process. The next step is to experiment with changes in the process to decrease common variation and improve average performance. Ideas for changes may be generated internally from staff suggestions or physician knowledge, or may come from external sources such as literature reports of best current practices. Experimenting with process changes should be done in collegial, non-threatening ways, with the goal of improving overall performance and not identifying "bad" performers.

Obstacles to Care Process Improvement

There are many practical obstacles to successful outcomes management that other writers on CQI present in more detail. Obstacles include resistance to defining outcomes measures and using them to change care processes. This resistance should be taken seriously, for it may reflect valid concerns on what is an appropriate measure of outcome and how processes should be changed. Persons involved in the process must be able to see how it will improve their ability to do their job and to improve patient care—initial attempts at process improvement should focus on identifying how the process could be improved from the perspective of key players, such as physicians, and implementing changes to achieve quick results to get these players on board. A lack of long-term administrative commitment from upper and middle levels places the outcomes management process at high risk of failure. Guidelines that are vague or self-serving (such as guidelines developed by a specialist group that are designed to protect the specialists rather than serve patients) will not lead to successful outcomes management.

Outcomes Management as a Prospective Tool

The prior discussion of outcomes management assumes that the decision to deliver care has already been made. Outcomes management can also be used when the question under investigation is whether or not to deliver a service. Outcomes may be compared among people who undergo an elective surgical procedure relative to those who are "watchful waiters," e.g., transurethral resection for prostatism.[10] Outcomes may be compared among people who receive different levels of treatment, such as inpatient versus outpatient care for a given condition, or among people who undergo alternative experiences, such as C-section versus vaginal delivery. It is through careful comparisons of these people that we may make the most progress in reducing unnecessary geographic variation.

A Dynamic Cycle

Note, finally, that outcomes measurement and management constitute a dynamic cycle, not a sequence. Results of measurement influence management activities, and results of management efforts may suggest a need to revisit outcomes measures, as the need for new information comes to light.

THE FUTURE OF OUTCOMES MEASUREMENT AND MANAGEMENT

Outcomes measurement and management activities will play an important role in reforming health care delivery. In turn many evolving changes in the way health care services are structured and delivered have implications for outcomes measurement and management. For example, the growth of integrated networks, such as organized delivery systems, may provide a means for tracking patients better over time as they move among parts of the system. Integrated networks may also provide a means to develop large comparative databases.

Similar to organized networks, but much less formal and coordinated, are voluntary consortia.[11] A consortium may consist of a group of providers, such as hospitals and/or clinics, that meet to share ideas and resources to improve quality of patient care. Consortia may engage in a variety of activities, but an important one is the development of shared comparative databases on patient outcomes. By investing in a common data collection repository, group members can split the costs and receive in return comparative data on a range of outcomes. Legal protection from disclosure may be established to prevent any one member from acquiring data specific to any other member.

Regulatory, employer, and payor demand for accountability will make outcomes measurement more important. The major pitfall to avoid is not to operationalize accountability through faulty "report card systems." Demands for accountability, any accountability, should not be made at the expense of meaningful data.

Guidelines of care will continue to evolve as medical knowledge develops, and should be flexible enough to adapt to local conditions. However, in an ideal setting, guidelines will be only a limited part of a measurement and management process designed to improve the appropriateness of care. Also important will be improvement of assessment practices so we know that two physicians following the same treatment guidelines use them in the same ways and will come to the same conclusion regarding appropriate treatment needed for a particular patient. How processes of care will be changed as a result of guidelines must also be built into the outcomes management activities.

Also of growing importance will be critical paths and patient decision models. Critical paths provide the ability to follow processes of care in depth—a significant aid to outcomes management activities. Patient decision models are being developed with the increasing recognition and consideration of how patients value the multiple uncertain risks and benefits of medical intervention. One patient will value the probability of a particular outcome differently than another, and how patients value competing outcomes may determine whether or not a procedure is indicated. When patients are given information on the risks and benefits of treatment options as they relate to various quality of life as well as medical outcomes, they often opt for conservative approaches. Thus, incorporation of patient decision models may serve to decrease some procedure rates.

CONCLUSION

This article presents an overview of some of the issues involved in outcomes measurement and management. When we understand what treatments are necessary and appropriate to achieve desired outcomes, and what treatments do not improve outcomes, we will be in a better position to deliver care in more appropriate and consistent ways across populations.

1. Wennberg JE, Gittelsohn A. Variations in medical care among small areas. Scientific American. 1982;246(4):120-134.

2. Chassin MR, Brook RH, Park RE, et al. Variations in the use of medical and surgical services by the Medicare population. New England Journal of Medicine. 1986;314:285-290.

3. Griffith JR, Wilson PA, Wolfe RA, et al. Clinical profiles of hospital discharge rates in local communities. Health Services Research. 1985;20:131-151.

4. Roos NP. Hospitalization style of physicians in Manitoba: The disturbing lack of logic in medical practice. Health Services Research. 1992;27:361-384.

5. Ball PA. Outcomes management systems: Tools for measuring and managing health care quality. Driving Down Health Care Costs: Strategies and Solutions. New York: Panel Publishers, 1994, pp 353-362.

6. Jette AM, Davies AR, Cleary PD, et al. The functional status questionnaire: reliability and validity when used in primary care. Journal of General Internal Medicine. 1986;1:143-149.

7. Bergner M, Bobbitt RA, Carter WB, et al. The sickness impact profile: development and final revision of a health status measure. Medical Care. 1981;19:787-805.

8. Weinstein MC, Berwick DM, Goldman PA, et al. A comparison of three psychiatric screening tests using receiver operating characteristic (ROC) analysis. Medical Care. 1989;27:593-607.

9. Knaus WA, Wagner DP, Draper EA, et al. The APACHE III prognostic system: Risk prediction of hospital mortality for critically ill hospitalized patients. Chest. 1991;100:1619-1636.

10. Barry MJ, Mulley AG, Fowler FJ, et al. Watchful waiting vs immediate transurethral resection for symptomatic prostatism: the importance of patients' preferences. JAMA. 1988;259:3010-3017.

11. Helms CM, Wakefield DS, Hendryx MS. Hospital quality improvement programs: Meeting the challenges of public expectations, professional responsibility, and survival in a reformed health care system. Clinical Performance and Quality Health Care. 1994;2:92-94.

34. Developing a "Best Practices" Critical Pathway
Matt Schuller, RRA

Under the auspices of a business coalition, four Chicago-based hospitals demonstrated a unique pioneering spirit by cooperatively implementing a health care management tool called a critical pathway. *This article discusses how it was done, and how providers and employers in any community can work together to achieve the same goal—continuous improvement of the quality of care patients receive.*

OVERVIEW

Partnership with Providers and Purchasers

Critical pathway is defined as a planned progression of treatment based on standard physician orders and optimal scheduling of tests and other treatments. The hospitals were brought together through a business-provider partnership (Midwest Business Group on Health) in a forum called the Quality Improvement Council (QIC), and facilitated by Community Care Network, Inc. (CCNI), a health care management company. CCNI developed and operates and the EPIQual Healthcare Program, a PPO network.

The Quality Improvement Council is thus a partnership of medical providers and purchasers. In this covenant, medical providers strive to improve the effectiveness of health care services and to pursue opportunities for refining the processes of care delivery. Purchasers promote individual responsibility for health care as well as effective use of provider-partners. Together, they strive to improve the quality and value of health care services.

349

EPIQUAL HOSPITAL NETWORK
CRITICAL PATH FOR CORONARY BYPASS SURGERY W/O CATH (DRG 107)

DRG: 107
HCFA LOS: 11.2
EXPECTED LOS 9.0
MD:

	PRE-SURGERY	PRE-OP DOS	DAY OF SURGERY	POST-OP DOS	POST-OP DAY 1	POST-OP DAY 2	POST-OP DAY 3	POST-OP DAY 4	POST-OP DAY 5	POST-OP DAY 6	POST-OP DAY 7
CARE UNIT	MED/SURG OR TELEMETRY OR HOME	MED/SURG OR TELEMETRY	SURGICAL INTENSIVE CARE	SURGICAL INTENSIVE CARE	TELEMETRY	TELEMETRY	TELEMETRY	TELEMETRY	TELEMETRY	TELEMETRY	TELEMETRY
TESTS	CBC, UA, PT, PTT, CHEM PROFILE, CXR, EKG, H&P, TYPE & SCREEN OR CROSS MATCH	TEST RESULTS ON CHART	ACT, BASELINE & PRN CBC, LYTES, BUN, CREAT, FBS CXR EKG CPK ABG'S	PULSE OX p ART LINE DC'd	EKG PRN LABS AS ORDERED DC DAILY CXR DC DAILY EKG	PULSE OX					
ACTIVITY	AS TOLERATED		OBR TURN Q 2 HRS p HEMODYNAMICALLY STABLE	DANGLE p EXTUBATION OOB X1 IF TOL DANGLE		EXERCISE BID ELEVATE OP LEG MAY SHOWER ACTIVITY AS TOL CARDIAC REHAB PROTOCOL					
TREATMENTS	INCENTIVE SPIROMETRY BID x 24 HRS PRE OP ANTIMICROBIAL SHOWER OR WASH OBTAIN CONSENT HT (CM) & WT (KG) MEASURE TEDS OBTAIN PERTINENT RECORDS	VS Q 8 HRS/PRN PRE-SURG PREP	PROTOCOLS: VS INSULIN AUTOTRANSFUSION VENTILATOR/WEAN HEMODYNAMIC MONITOR WOUND CARE VASOACTIVE DRUGS K+ REPLACEMENT ULCER PROPHYLAXIS HYPO/HYPERTHERMIA FOLEY INCENTIVE SPIRO Q 1 HR W/A SUPPLEMENTAL O2 p EXTUBATE PACER ON STANDBY	DC DC DC DC DC DC DC	DC DC DC	WEIGHT I & O Q SHIFT ANTIEMBOLIC STOCKINGS IF APPROPRIATE DC DC D/C			TELEMETRY CXR	DC PACER WIRES DC HEP LOCK	D/C SUTURES/STAPLES WHEN APPROPRIATE
MEDICATIONS	AS ORDERED SLEEPER Q HS BETA BLOCKERS IF OK WITH MD	PRE-OP ON CALL OTHER MEDS AS ORDERED	IV FLUIDS AS ORDERED ANTIBIOTICS		PAIN MANAGEMENT	DC IF PO INTAKE OK/HEP LOCK	MD ORDER TO DC O2 IF APP. DC ANTIBIOTICS				
DIET	LOW CHO/LOW SALT CAFFEINE FREE NPO p MIDNOC	NPO	NPO	CLEAR LIQUIDS IF BS POSITIVE		ADV AS TOL LOW SALT CAFFEINE FREE	LOW CHO/ LOW SALT				
DISCHARGE PLANNING	DISCUSS LOS AND FAMILY RESOURCES				PREPARE FOR TRANSFER TO TELEMETRY	DISCUSS EXPECTED LOS	RE-DISCUSS EXPECTED LOS		CONFIRM DC DATE	DISCUSS CARDIAC REHAB PHASE II	DC IF APPROPRIATE
PATIENT EDUCATION	PRE-OP TEACHING RE: PROCEDURE, RISK/ BENEFITS, POST-OP COURSE	PRE-OP TEACHING COMPLETED	DISCUSS WITH FAMILY POST-OP COURSE			DISCUSS ACTIVITY PROGRESSION WITH PT & FAMILY	BEGIN TEACHING ON: DIET, MEDS, WOUND CARE, EXERCISE, AND POST DC ACTIVITY	RE-ENFORCE TEACHING		DEMONSTRATE PROPER WOUND CARE COMPLETE PT TEACHING	CONFIRM DOCUMENTATION OF PATIENT TEACHING & NEED FOR F/U APPT
CONSULTS	SURGEON ANESTHESIA CARDIOLOGY OTHER CONSULTS PRN					CARDIAC REHABILITATION DIETICIAN					
ASSESS NEED FOR	SPIROMETRY FOR COPD DIRECTED DONOR INFO DIDOAN LEVEL OTHER LABS FLEETS ENEMA FINANCIAL INTERVENTION	IV FLUIDS KNOWLEDGE BASE	FBS COVERAGE, IV K+, NA/H2O, NG TUBE, BL TRANSFUSIONS, EXTRACER, BL C/S ACL PROTOCOLS	CHEST X-RAY p CHEST TUBE REMOVAL		RESPIRATORY TREATMENTS ADA DIET SOCIAL SERVICE/DC PLANNER	DUCOLAX HEP/LOCK PULSE OX		DUCOLAX	TELEMETRY CXR	
EXPECTED OUTCOMES	PRE-ADM TSTG COMPLETED PT VERBALIZES UNDER- STANDING OF PROCEDURE PT VERBALIZES UNDER- STANDING OF ADMIT PROTOCOL PT DEMONSTRATES INCENTIVE SPIROMETRY CONSENT SIGNED	PT & FAMILY CONSENT & VERBALIZE UNDERSTANDING OF PRE- & INTRA-OP COURSE CHECKLIST COMPLETED CONSENT SIGNED	PT TOLERATES EXTUBATION PT COMMUNICATES PAIN RELIEF PT DEMONSTRATES HEMODYNAMIC STABILITY	PT DEMONSTRATES INCENTIVE SPIROMETRY PT TOLERATES ORAL INTAKE PT RETURNS TO PRE-OP NEURO STATUS PT TOLERATES DANGLING	PT TOL PROGRESSIVE DIET STANDING CALS UNDER- STANDING OF ACTIVITY PROGRESSION PT TOL INCREASED ACTIVITY		PT HAS BOWEL MOVEMENT PT AMBULATES 50 FT	PT PARTICIPATES IN SELF- CARE ACTIVITIES (WOUND CARE WITH SUPERVISION) PT AMBULATES 75 FT PT VERBALIZES DIETARY RESTRICTIONS	PT AMBULATES 100 FT	PT & FAMILY SATISFIED WITH D/C PLANS PT ABLE TO DO STAIRS & AMBULATE 100 FT BID PT VERBALIZES UNDERSTANDING OF: ACTIVITY, MEDS, WOUND CARE, DIET, EXERCISE LIMITS	F/U PLAN, PHY., MENTAL, EMOTIONAL STATUS, VSS X 24 HRS PRIOR TO DC, DC, NO IV FLUIDS OR IV DRUGS p MIDNOC PRIOR TO DC, LAB VALUES WNL 24 HRS PRIOR
DISCHARGE DOCUMENTATION										CONFIRM/DOCUMENTATION OF ABOVE	
VARIATIONS	PATIENT PROGRESS CORRESPONDS TO CRITICAL PATH: YES___ NO___ IF NO, CODE:___ COMMENTS:	PATIENT PROGRESS CORRESPONDS TO CRITICAL PATH: YES___ NO___ IF NO, CODE:___ COMMENTS:	PATIENT PROGRESS CORRESPONDS TO CRITICAL PATH: YES___ NO___ IF NO, CODE:___ COMMENTS:	PATIENT PROGRESS CORRESPONDS TO CRITICAL PATH: YES___ NO___ IF NO, CODE:___ COMMENTS:	PATIENT PROGRESS CORRESPONDS TO CRITICAL PATH: YES___ NO___ IF NO, CODE:___ COMMENTS:	PATIENT PROGRESS CORRESPONDS TO CRITICAL PATH: YES___ NO___ IF NO, CODE:___ COMMENTS:	PATIENT PROGRESS CORRESPONDS TO CRITICAL PATH: YES___ NO___ IF NO, CODE:___ COMMENTS:	PATIENT PROGRESS CORRESPONDS TO CRITICAL PATH: YES___ NO___ IF NO, CODE:___ COMMENTS:	PATIENT PROGRESS CORRESPONDS TO CRITICAL PATH: YES___ NO___ IF NO, CODE:___ COMMENTS:	PATIENT PROGRESS CORRESPONDS TO CRITICAL PATH: YES___ NO___ IF NO, CODE:___ COMMENTS:	PATIENT PROGRESS CORRESPONDS TO CRITICAL PATH: YES___ NO___ IF NO, CODE:___ COMMENTS:
CAUSE & ACTION TAKEN											

Value-Based Health Care Purchasing

This project, and similar ongoing quality initiatives, stand apart from other employer-sponsored health care programs by virtue of their team approach. Other programs highlight their "Quality Assurance Plans" that retrospectively identify problems in care and then take action. This program allows for systematic analysis of opportunities to improve care. Then, when such an opportunity is identified, the programs allows for logically gathering the personnel closest to the issue to work together, develop, and implement outcome-improving changes in clinical and administrative processes. These initiatives work on the premise of teams and partnerships.

PROJECT HISTORY

Why a Critical Pathway?

In choosing a project where both employers and providers would benefit, the QIC analyzed paid claims data for 1989 and 1990. It was noted that the EPIQual Healthcare Program spent over two million dollars in 1989 and over four million dollars in 1990 for inpatient hospitalization related to diseases and disorders of the circulatory system—most importantly, coronary bypass, both with and without cardiac catheterization: DRGs 106 and 107. In order to work productively with the personnel closest to cardiovascular patient care to form a critical path team, the QIC sponsored a team of clinical nurse specialists from the four participating Chicago area hospitals.

The development and use of critical paths are not new in the health care industry. However, what is exciting about this initiative is that these four hospitals were competitors and yet developed the path prototype as a way of sharing "best practices" among institutions. These specialists achieved consensus on brainstormed solutions to high cost, high-volume cardiac surgical procedures. A critical path was chosen to create a case management tool to allow professionals to reach a defined goal in the most efficient and effective manner. Using the multi-voting technique, the Critical Path Team chose to pursue a pathway for the coronary bypass procedure without the catheterization, DRG 107.

GOALS

The Critical Path Team developed a "generic" critical path to be used as a prototype for the clinical nurse specialists to take to their respective institutions and customize to their unique processes. The Critical Path Team members facilitated internal teams within their organization to customize the pathway,

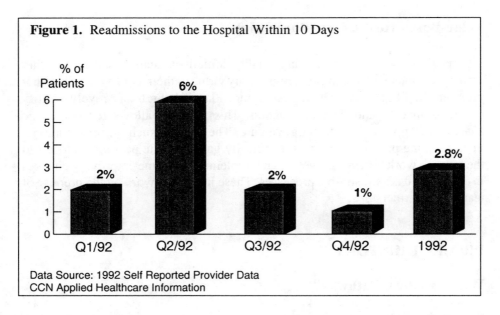

Figure 1. Readmissions to the Hospital Within 10 Days

Data Source: 1992 Self Reported Provider Data
CCN Applied Healthcare Information

establish "buy-in" from all users of the pathway, and oversee implementation. The pathway was implemented for all patients in the hospitals who presented for coronary bypass without cardiac catheterization.

The goals of the Critical Path Team were identified:

- Reduce the average length of stay from 11.5 days to 9 days if the patient stayed on the critical pathway.
- Improve cost-effectiveness.
- Reduce in utilization of resources.
- Improve patient satisfaction.
- Improve and maintain clinical outcomes.

CLINICAL AND FINANCIAL RESULTS

To measure the effectiveness of the critical pathway on patients, a baseline data set was established using 1991 data available through a state hospital inpatient data base from the Illinois Health Care Cost Containment Council. The Critical Pathway Team members agreed to monitor the clinical results of the pathway implementation through six identified indicators. The data gathered from the indicators were shared with all four hospitals, and aggregate results were shared publicly.

The indicators included:

- Readmission to the hospital within 10 days (Figure 1)
- Returns to surgery related to surgical procedure (Figure 2)
- Prolonged intubation—over 48 hours (Figure 3)

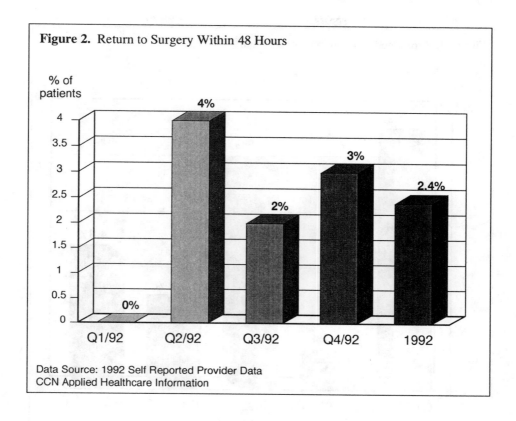

Figure 2. Return to Surgery Within 48 Hours

Data Source: 1992 Self Reported Provider Data
CCN Applied Healthcare Information

- Average length of stay (Figures 4 and 5)
- Changes in average billed charges—1991 compared to 1992 (Figure 6)
- Results of patient satisfaction survey, a tool jointly developed by purchasers and providers (Figures 7 and 8)

The quantifiable results of the critical pathway have demonstrated an average length of stay reduction of 1.7 days and a reduction of average charges by $3,395 for the participating hospitals. The estimated annual saving for 1992 is over $875,000.

As noted, these results are remarkable since all four hospitals shared information to develop the most appropriate pathway for the patients undergoing this surgical procedure. The unique partnership of this Critical Pathway Team demonstrates a willingness to share clinical expertise of "best practices" and develop solutions when opportunities to improve care are identified. The critical pathway was not selectively implemented for specific patient groups. The results of the uniquely developed patient satisfaction survey demonstrate the positive experience of the patient through the care process. The survey notes glowing comments from patients concerning their satisfaction with the care in these institutions.

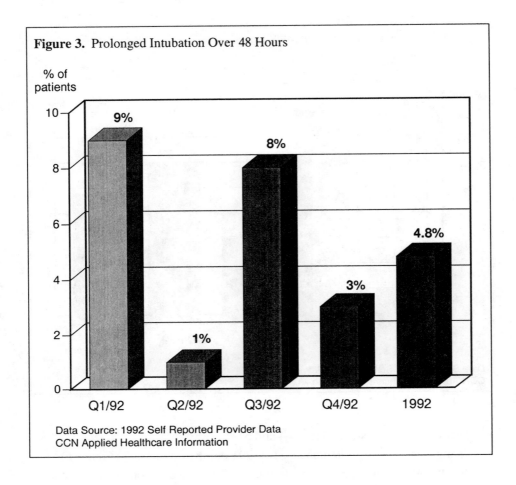

Figure 3. Prolonged Intubation Over 48 Hours

Data Source: 1992 Self Reported Provider Data
CCN Applied Healthcare Information

BENEFITS AND BARRIERS

The providers benefitted from this project by having the opportunity to share information among institutions and the ability to establish a process to effectively utilize resources with consensus input from four leading institutions. The hospitals were in a forum to compare systems and processes in order to effectively coordinate the activities of a multi-disciplinary process of care delivery. Working as a team with purchasers, the clinicians received valuable education on the needs of major health care purchasers in the Chicago area. The clinicians at their respective institutions experienced increased communication and cooperation between clinical nurse specialists and physicians. Physicians from these institutions met to share, compare, and contrast clinical processes. The Critical Pathway Team members noted an increased interaction between internal departments as they collected indicator data and educated others (e.g., business office, medical records, dietary department) about the pathway.

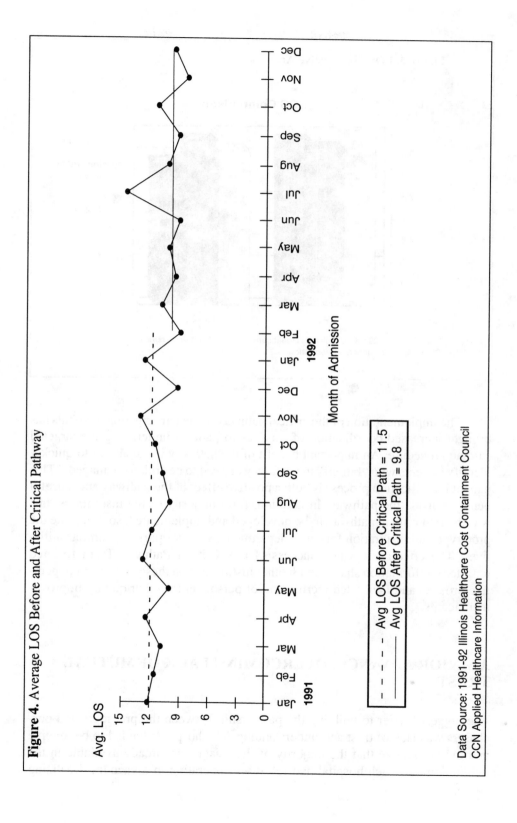

Figure 4. Average LOS Before and After Critical Pathway

Data Source: 1991-92 Illinois Healthcare Cost Containment Council
CCN Applied Healthcare Information

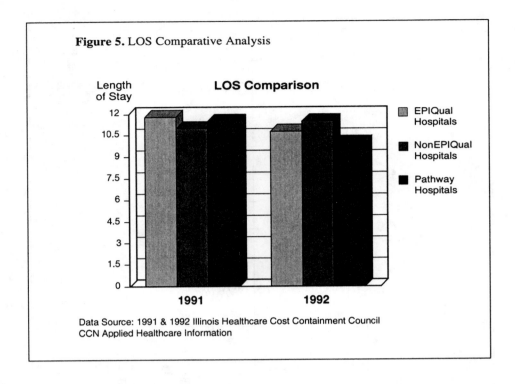

Figure 5. LOS Comparative Analysis

Data Source: 1991 & 1992 Illinois Healthcare Cost Containment Council
CCN Applied Healthcare Information

The implementation of the critical pathway in the participating hospitals has brought increased coordination of services to patients undergoing the targeted cardiac procedure. An important benefit of the pathway is the ability to quickly identify patients who "fall off" the pathway or need to be "micro-managed." This patient identification process is both a positive effect of the pathway and a useful benefit outside the pathway. In addition, for a majority of the institutions, this was the first critical pathway to be developed and implemented, so it became the prototype and inspiration for other departments/services pursuing similar initiatives. The effectiveness and success of this Critical Pathway Team fostered long-term information sharing with other institutions on these and other cooperative projects and facilitated recruitment of personnel for other quality improvement teams.

A MAJOR ADVANCE: OVERCOMING LACK OF MUTUAL TRUST

The biggest barrier to building the partnership between the providers and purchasers was lack of trust and understanding. The hospitals tended to be myopic and did not realize that the majority of their data was already available in the public domain. Each hospital had felt it was operating in a vacuum. Realizing

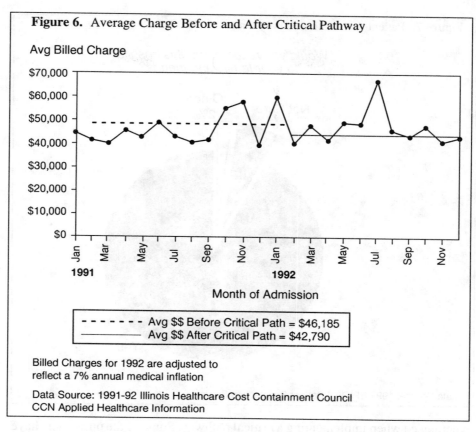

Figure 6. Average Charge Before and After Critical Pathway

Avg Billed Charge

Month of Admission

- - - - - - Avg $$ Before Critical Path = $46,185
———— Avg $$ After Critical Path = $42,790

Billed Charges for 1992 are adjusted to
reflect a 7% annual medical inflation

Data Source: 1991-92 Illinois Healthcare Cost Containment Council
CCN Applied Healthcare Information

that employers were making their purchasing decisions based on this publicly available information, the nurse specialists recognized that the information needed translation. They wanted to help employers understand where it came from, make sure it was correct, and thus help influence cost, charge, and outcome.

When physicians learned that the providers and employers would be working as a team and pooling their data, they understood that their practice patterns would be observed and their outcomes measured and monitored. This awareness helped influence their practice patterns and gave them motivation to become involved. The group recognized that teamwork could prove beneficial. Hospitals learned that their competitors sometimes knew ways of doing things better—the best time to remove chest tubes, for example, or an optimal regimen of pain medication. By drawing from each other, they learned valuable techniques to enhance quality, they also learned that the collective experience of the group can prove advantageous to all patients needing open-heart surgery.

The purchasers benefitted by participating in a project that allowed them to partner with providers in a forum where trust was formed through open communication and information sharing. The data reveal high patient satisfaction and reduced length of stay. Participation in the project allowed purchasers valuable insight into the workings of a hospital organization and the internal hurdles

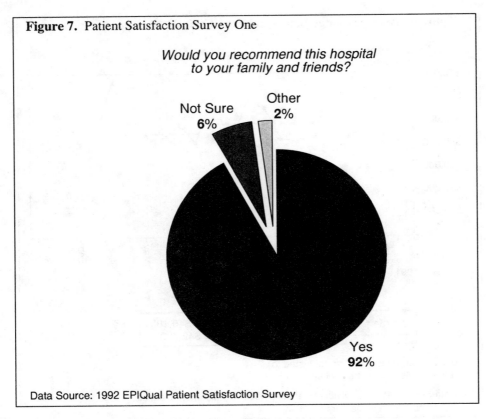

Figure 7. Patient Satisfaction Survey One

*Would you recommend this hospital
to your family and friends?*

Not Sure
6%

Other
2%

Yes
92%

Data Source: 1992 EPIQual Patient Satisfaction Survey

experienced when implementing a critical pathway. Some of the purchasers have compared the experience of the hospitals to the implementation of a new process/policy in their own assembly plant or business.

In addition, the developed critical pathway can be utilized outside of the four hospitals and can be adapted to other hospitals either on a regional or national basis. The pathway has been copyrighted to ensure credit to the developers, not for monetary gain. This critical pathway is distributed at health care conferences nationally and will be sent to any organization requesting a copy. The Critical Pathway Team and the partners feel that for others to "reinvent the wheel" is not productive. Believing that this generic pathway is the first step for other health care organizations, they are distributing it at no cost. With the generic pathway, institutions could form internal teams to develop their own unique pathway.

NEXT STEPS

New Charter for the QIC

As projects like the critical pathway are spotlighted in trade publications and health care seminars, the critical pathway prototype is being distributed to

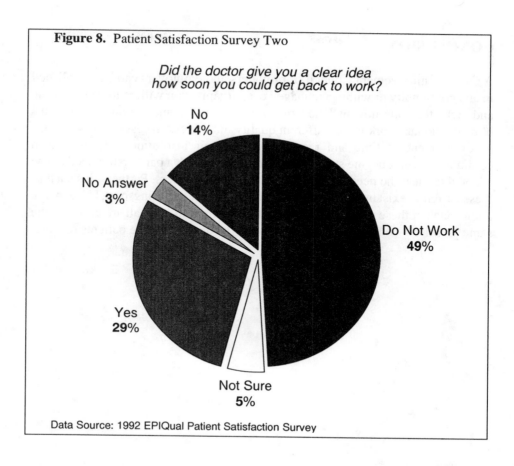

Figure 8. Patient Satisfaction Survey Two

Did the doctor give you a clear idea how soon you could get back to work?

No 14%
No Answer 3%
Do Not Work 49%
Yes 29%
Not Sure 5%

Data Source: 1992 EPIQual Patient Satisfaction Survey

competitors and noncompetitors alike. Providers researching a similar path could use the progress made by this team to avoid duplication of effort; eventually, the whole health care industry can benefit from the team's work, which can be adapted to changes in hospital structure, new technologies, and any other need to fine-tune the pathway.

This partnership and other quality improvement projects were established with long-range plans in mind. For the Critical Pathway Team members, there are plans already underway to look at the preventive and wellness side of coronary bypass surgery, which is the next logical step. In addition to preventive care, appropriateness of care is also being considered.

The Critical Pathway Team is a group of highly motivated and committed individuals who work cohesively. Annually, the team assesses their work to identify any opportunities to improve the team process and to ensure that the team is meeting the needs of all participants. The QIC is updated on the status of the team and others on a bimonthly basis to ensure support and long-term commitment. The Council is committed to clearing roadblocks and reducing hurdles whenever possible.

CONCLUSION

A Quality Improvement Council of providers and employers can be established in any community or within a managed care organization willing to take the time and make the commitment. The Council acts as a steering committee for teams of professionals working on different quality initiatives, professionals who need a commitment of time and resources from their institutions. Because each community is unique, the start-up and structure of such a partnership needs to be adapted to meet the needs and expectations of the partners. Partnerships such as these currently exist in Milwaukee, WI, Rockford, IL, and Kingsport,TN, to name a few. Each of these partnerships is structured differently, but all are based on the same premise—continuous improvement of the quality of care patients receive.

35. Measuring and Enhancing the Quality of Health Care

Margaret E. O'Kane   Martin W. G. King

The central concerns of health plans, employers, and plan participants alike are improving the quality and increasing the value of health care. The lack of a viable system for measuring these two factors, however, has long been an obstacle to enhancing the overall quality of health benefits. The National Committee for Quality Assurance addresses this issue, developing important new standards and systems for measuring quality and value in health care so that health care providers can be held accountable for the services they provide.

In the 1980s, as public and private purchasers struggled to contain escalating health care costs by using new payment systems with incentives to manage resources, there was increasing concern about the impact of these financial incentives on the quality of care. As a result, public policy makers and private purchasers sought ways to make health care providers accountable for the quality of care and service that they or their organizations delivered.

That desire for accountability resulted in the founding of the National Committee for Quality Assurance (NCQA). Originally established by the Group Health Association of America and the American Managed Care and Review Association, then more formally launched as an independent non-profit organization with the financial backing of the Robert Wood Johnson Foundation and many members of the HMO industry, NCQA has begun to play an important role in the evolution of the nation's health care system.

NCQA is a partnership of purchasers, experts on quality, consumers, and managed care providers. It exists to hold health plans accountable for the care they provide, and to make sure they provide a responsible and appropriate level of service to consumers at a reasonable and predictable price. NCQA's original staff of three has grown to more than 50, with more than 200 physicians and other health care professionals on call to perform well over 100 on-site health plan accreditation reviews each year. In addition, its large planning and development staff is working to develop "report cards" and other systems for measuring the quality of care provided by the nation's health plans. Frequently, these projects reflect the concerns of the most demanding corporate purchasers of health care.

NCQA also works hard to ensure that employers who purchase health care for their employees and the consumers of that care become knowledgeable in learning how to use the information that results from accreditation reviews and from study of NCQA's performance measures.

NCQA's board of directors reflects its commitment and the scope of its responsibilities. Among its board members are six members from health plans; three independent quality experts; four corporate purchasers; one union representative; one consumer representative; one physician-consultant; and NCQA's president. NCQA is neutral and non-partisan, and frequently serves as an expert witness in testimony before Congress and state legislatures.

NCQA accomplishes its goals—to improve quality and hold health plans accountable—through two major processes that are interrelated, but distinct in operation: the Accreditation Program, which methodically evaluates the care provided by many of the nation's managed care health plans, especially as represented by their own internal quality management systems; and the Performance Measures Program, which includes one major project and another that is still being developed. These have evolved from the need to provide consumers, providers, and purchasers with comparative data on a variety of aspects of health plan performance. The HEDIS program (Health Plan Employer Data and Information Set) is a system of measurement that allows employers to make comparisons of the quality and efficiency of health plans. The report card project, its ultimate outcome, will implement the HEDIS program by providing the same audience with standardized measures that they can use to evaluate the host of managed care plans that have entered the marketplace.

ACCREDITATION PROGRAM

NCQA evaluates the quality of care provided by individual health plans at their request. Although only the health plan itself can contract with NCQA for a review, the plans frequently do so in response to a state government or purchaser mandate. USAir, Pepsico, and Xerox are among the large purchasers that require NCQA accreditation. NCQA also has relationships with varying degrees of scope and responsibility with the states of Kansas, Florida, Oklahoma, and Pennsylvania. Minnesota has mandated NCQA's review of plans that provide health services to people covered by Medicaid.

In all cases, NCQA strives to achieve three goals:

1.   To be balanced and fair to both the health plan and to its consumers;
2.   To be comprehensive, examining all aspects of the plan's delivery system; and
3.   To be positive, providing incentives for continuous improvement through the provision of specific recommendations for enhancing the quality of care.

Subsequent reviews (re-reviews) of plans that fail to garner fulltime accreditation provide plans that are developing quality management programs with an opportunity to improve the care they are delivering based on NCQA's recommendations.

NCQA's review standards are rigorous and explicit, and they are published and available to the public. The NCQA review teams that conduct site visits to plans as part of the review process examine the plans on the basis of more than 50 standards and substandards. They are experts in health care, whether by administrative or medical background, and all are trained by NCQA, which contracts for their services. They are expected to use their expert judgment in evaluating plans against NCQA's standards. NCQA's Review Oversight Committee, itself composed of health care experts, provides a final level of review and makes the process as impartial as possible.

NCQA examines the quality of care that a health plan provides through evaluations against six groups of standards, each of which is discussed below.

Quality Management and Improvement

Managing for quality means that a health plan must continuously assess and improve its care and services. This area is the most comprehensive of the six groups of NCQA standards. There are three elements to this standard:

1.   *The guideline structure must be in place.* NCQA requires the plan to set practice guidelines for physicians in key areas, and to set standards for member access. NCQA requires plans to show that boards of directors, management, and practicing physicians actively participate in the quality management effort.
2.   *The process of quality management must be working.* The plan must monitor whether its standards for care and access are being met and determine how to address members' key health problems. The plan must use data from all parts of the delivery system, including hospital care, doctor visits, and mental health care services, to monitor care. All departments of the health plan should be involved.
3.   *There must be evidence of actual improvement.* This is a difficult standard to meet fully, and the plan can do so only by showing that it has enhanced its care or service to members in significant areas, such as lowering the incidence

of, or complications from, surgery, or improving children's rates of immunization.

Credentialing

Physicians are the health plan's partners in delivering health care. NCQA standards require "due diligence" to ensure that the plan's physicians have the required credentials and offer care that meets the plan's standards. Specifically, the credentialing process affords members ongoing protection against fraud and misrepresentation by doctors. This requires meticulous research and recordkeeping by the plan and the active participation of its medical staff. The plan must also verify that each affiliated physician carries malpractice insurance, and it must check for any claims against that insurance. In addition, the plan must find out if either the state or the federal government has sanctioned the physician. The physician must attest that he or she is not impaired by substance abuse, is in good mental and physical health, and has no history of loss or limitation with respect to licensure or hospital privileges.

Furthermore, the plan must recertify each physician according to NCQA standards, and examine member complaints and member satisfaction related to the physician's performance, and his or her record in utilization management. The plan must also make an on-site inspection of each primary care physician's office, and those of other high-volume specialists, such as obstetricians and gynecologists, before the initial credentialing and every two years after.

Finally, the organization must have policies that prescribe how to suspend or terminate a physician for quality-related problems.

Members' Rights and Responsibilities

NCQA requires health plans to maintain active relationships with their members that promote two-way communication and contribute to the quality of care and service plans provide. The plan must have a policy of recognizing members' rights and responsibilities, and a functioning complaint and grievance system that effectively responds to member concerns. The plan also must have a detailed statement about these complaint and grievance procedures that is widely disseminated to members and physicians. That statement must outline the following member rights:

1. The right to voice complaints and grievances;
2. The right to participate in decision making about their health care;

3. The right to be provided with all pertinent information about the plan, its policies, and its participating physicians; and
4. The right to be treated with respect.

Also, there must be a formal grievance procedure. The NCQA review team looks at a sample of complaint and grievance files to make sure the plan is addressing its members concerns.

There is also a requirement that the written information that the plan provides to members about access to care, the kind of care provided, and other like matters must be written in easily understood language and be available in the languages of the major population groups served.

Finally, the health plan must conduct periodic surveys of its members' satisfaction, and systematically address any identified sources of dissatisfaction.

Utilization Management

Utilization management is a key characteristic of managed care. The term refers to the requirement that a member, or his or her physician, must obtain permission in advance for surgery or hospitalizations, or to stay longer in the hospital than the plan had originally agreed. NCQA requires the use of written protocols that are based on reasonable medical evidence in making utilization decisions. NCQA also requires the plan to document all cases when permission is denied for one or more of these services. The plan must have an effective appeals process for members and their physicians.

Medical Records

NCQA's survey includes a physician's review of medical records in which the physician considers a 21-item questionnaire related to medical recordkeeping and the quality of care. Physician members of the NCQA assessment team review a sample of medical records on-site to see how consistently the plan meets those standards. This review allows NCQA to determine whether the care documented in the record is appropriate for the diagnosis, and whether the primary care physician coordinates any care by specialists. NCQA also requires plans to develop their own performance goals for keeping medical records and actively monitoring their care. These goals and monitoring systems are unique to each plan and grow out of the plan's own health care delivery culture and systems.

Delegation

How a plan handles delegation of some of its health care services to other organizations is a matter of significant concern. This is especially true when plans delegate quality-monitoring functions, to, for example, mental health care providers or physician groups. Under NCQA's standards, however, the health plan is still responsible for ensuring that each function is performed appropriately.

Full accreditation means that a health plan has an infrastructure that performs effective medical management and quality improvement. It ensures the integrity of the systems upon which patients depend, guaranteeing that they provide a safety net for patients.

PERFORMANCE MEASURES PROGRAM

HEDIS 2.0, the most recent version of the HEDIS measuring system, was developed to help standardize the ways health plans measure and report performance data. This second version was built on the success of an earlier effort, HEDIS 1.0, which was developed and introduced in September 1991 by a group of health plans and employer-purchasers (the members of this group were The HMO Group, Kaiser Permanente, Towers Perrin, BULL HN, DEC, GTE and Xerox).

NCQA assembled a Performance Assessment Committee, made up of experts from a similar group, when it decided to proceed with HEDIS 2.0, which it introduced in October 1993. Its members included the original four employers plus representatives from Aetna Health Plans, Harvard Community Health Plan, Kaiser Permanente, The Prudential Insurance Company, United HealthCare Corporation and US Healthcare.

HEDIS 2.0 provides a tool for purchasers to glean information and assess value. It also provides a way for health plans to simplify measurement and reporting. Both uses are essential components of any quality improvement process. The Performance Assessment Committee chose six principles to serve as the foundation for its work in developing HEDIS 2.0. These principles were:

1. The need to integrate performance measures;
2. The need for measures to address the needs of both health plans and purchasers;
3. The need for measures to facilitate future benchmarking and comparability;
4. The need to rely on existing data sources wherever possible;
5. The need for measures to be dynamic so that they can keep on evolving; and
6. The need to respect patient confidentiality.

Further, when the committee selected individual measures, it made sure that each measure's content was relevant and that the data it was requesting were feasible to obtain. But, above all, the developers of HEDIS 2.0 made certain that there was room in the system for growth, since they saw HEDIS 2.0 not as a final end result, but as a step in a process that would continue to evolve over time. The committee stated its belief that HEDIS 2.0 is important, but, nevertheless, only the first step toward developing a system of comparable performance measures.

Like NCQA's accreditation standards, HEDIS 2.0 presents a large number of measurement standards. The major areas of measurement include quality of care; member access and satisfaction; membership and utilization (the largest set of measures); finance; and health plan management and activities. These measures respond to the needs of employers and other payers to demonstrate the value of health plans and to document accountability for performance. In line with this goal and the concept of the necessary evolution of HEDIS, a team will soon begin developing HEDIS 3.0. That team's goal is to refine HEDIS 2.0 to produce an enhanced measuring system that:

1. Includes a comprehensive, well-balanced set of performance measures;
2. Offers more refined specifications and methodological approaches;
3. Improves our ability to measure the relationship between process and outcomes;
4. Creates incentives for health plans to improve their internal data management capabilities;
5. Provides access to comparative data;
6. Improves the utility of the data by addressing issues such as severity and risk adjustment; and
7. Provides effective communication and reporting mechanisms.

In addition, to make sure that the people who will use HEDIS 2.0 and its successors have a say in the development process, NCQA has developed a HEDIS users group. This group provides for two-way communication between NCQA and all types of users; issues technical notes, updates, and clarifications; responds to questions from users; and records suggestions for improvement for use in the development of HEDIS 3.0.

NCQA's Report Card Pilot Project will implement the HEDIS system, and, in this way, represents an evolutionary process. It will establish an ongoing mechanism to make reliable, comparative data on health plan performance available to the public. While purchasers will glean the most benefits from HEDIS, insofar as improving the quality of health care is concerned, the one-year report card project is decidedly consumer-oriented. It involves 21 participating health plans, and the substantial involvement of consumers, purchasers, and the public sector. The goal of the report card project is to develop a reporting mechanism that will:

1. Provide an auditing process to be performed by a credible external entity;
2. Provide comparative reports on different managed care plans to the general public; and
3. Provide a central database for performance measurement data from health plans.

NCQA is committed to enhancing the quality of care provided by the nation's health plans and to helping the plans improve the quality of the services they provide. It is also committed to making certain that the information needs of purchasers and consumers are met in a manner that is practical and fair.

New pressures to be accountable for the quality and value of health services are reshaping traditional relationships within the health care system. This is especially true with the rapid emergence of managed care organizations as an essential and increasingly large provider of care. Health plans, employers, and purchasers are all experiencing some degree of discomfort as this realignment of the health care delivery system unfolds, especially in the context of the debate over health care reform. All parts of this system, and all parties to the debate, will have to be flexible and creative not just to survive, but to deliver the best possible quality of care.

Part 10

WELLNESS

36. Wellness Programs: Complying with the Americans With Disabilities Act (ADA)

Sibyl C. Bogardus

Employers that offer wellness programs must be careful to comply with the guidelines of ADA. As the dollar amounts involved in these programs and the number of participants increase, so does the risk of lawsuits.

As health care costs have skyrocketed, employers have embraced wellness programs in an effort to hold down short- and long-term health care costs. These programs are often tied to group health plans through the use of incentives such as lower premium rates or increased flex plan credits and through penalties such as increased premiums or relatively lower flex credits. By placing increased costs on those who are less healthy, the health care plan and the wellness program may decrease current costs, while promising long-term savings resulting from a healthier participant population and lower claims experience.

Despite their potential advantages, some commentators have attacked the legality of wellness programs under various discrimination laws.[1] These programs are currently being criticized within the context of the Americans with Disabilities Act (ADA), which became effective for employers with 25 or more employees on July 26, 1992.[2] ADA generally provides that an employer may not discriminate against the disabled. Despite this seemingly brightline rule, many gray areas exist. One such gray area is wellness programs. Those persons who are targeted by wellness programs—people with high blood pressure, obesity,

"Wellness Programs: Complying with the Americans With Disabilities Act," by Sibyl Bogardus, which appeared in the First Quarter 1993 issue, was reprinted with permission from the *Benefits Quarterly,* published by the International Society of Certified Employee Benefit Specialists, Brookfield, WI. Statements or opinions expressed in this article are those of the author and do not necessarily represent the views or positions of the International Foundation, its officers, directors, or staff.

high cholesterol and mobility impairments, to name only a few—could well assert they should be classified as *disabled* and protected from discrimination by ADA.

Although ADA affects wellness programs, the law does not prohibit them. Employers may still offer wellness programs that distinguish among employees based on certain factors. Employers that are subject to ADA should reconsider and redesign their wellness programs to conform to the specific guidelines and applicable rules of ADA.

This article describes the four main types of wellness programs and discusses the legal concerns raised by ADA. In addition, this article describes how to design a wellness program that is most likely to save a plan sponsor's money while satisfying ADA.

TYPES OF WELLNESS PROGRAMS

Employers adopt a wide variety of wellness strategies with different emphases on education, prevention and screening. These strategies are typically embodied in four main types of wellness programs: behavior modification, disease prevention, lifestyle change and safety promotion.

Behavior Modification

Behavior modification programs attempt to contain health care costs by encouraging employees to modify an off-the-job behavior that affects their safety. These plans may operate by waiving or paying insurance deductibles if a participant can show he or she took the required precautions. A common example is a health plan provision that pays a participant's deductible under an automobile insurance policy if he or she is wearing a seat belt during an accident. Conversely, a plan may drop an employee's life or health coverage or refuse to pay benefit if he or she is not wearing a seat belt during an accident.

Disease Prevention

Disease prevention programs encourage good health through early detection and prevention of medical problems. An employer offering this type of wellness program might offer 100 percent coverage for specific diagnostic tests or procedures by waiving deductibles and copayments under the group health plan. Some of the popular screenings and preventive procedures offered include annual physical examinations, mammograms, blood pressure tests, cholesterol tests and childhood immunizations.

Lifestyle Change

Lifestyle change programs are the most controversial wellness programs under ADA (as well as under other state and federal laws on disabilities, privacy and discrimination). A lifestyle wellness program is a rating system that determines an employee's cost for health care based on personal lifestyle choices. An employer may identify unhealthy lifestyles, such as smoking, drinking, overeating and not exercising. Based on the assumption that such activities cause higher health plan claims, the employer will use rewards or penalties, or a combination of both, to discourage these behaviors. By rating employees based on an assessment of their risks and by varying costs or benefits under their group health plans, employers that offer these programs are classifying and underwriting risks just as insurance companies do when writing policies on an individual basis.

Employers offering these programs may monitor initial and continuing health status through medical questionnaires and physical examinations. The use of incentives or penalties may encourage employees to be dishonest, so employers often prefer medical examinations over medical questionnaires.

The behaviors that lifestyle change programs target are linked to an employee's health due to their long-term effects, such as the link between smoking and lung cancer. This distinguishes lifestyle change programs from behavior modification programs that focus on risks associated with one-time events such as automobile accidents. Employers typically consider the following factors in an employee's lifestyle health profile:

- Smoking and tobacco use
- Alcohol and drug use
- Exercise habits
- Obesity
- Blood pressure
- Cholesterol level
- Heart rate

These factors are easily detected in an initial screening and are easily monitored to evaluate problems or progress. Moreover, employers believe that employees can be educated and encouraged or penalized to modify controllable behaviors that are linked to these health problems. Some personal behaviors targeted by lifestyle change programs are probably not disabilities under ADA, such as smoking, but the *effects* of these habits may rise to level of a disability.

Safety Promotion

Wellness programs based on safety promotion attempt to reduce health care costs through lower insurance premiums or lower costs for self-insured benefits and through lower workers' compensation costs. These programs encourage a safe workplace and safe work habits to reduce on-the-job accidents and injuries. For example, an employer may establish peer review programs that reward accident-free service. These safety promotion programs generally will not raise ADA concerns.

DESIGN FEATURES: REWARDS AND PENALTIES

Employers typically design their wellness programs so that as many employees as possible participate. Many employers simply require all employees to participate, while others rely on rewards and penalties to attract participants. Rewards and penalties are most commonly associated with lifestyle change wellness programs, which generally cause greater ADA concerns than other wellness programs.

Rewards

Employees who successfully complete their wellness programs—as shown by lower blood pressure, for example—may receive rewards, also called "carrots." Examples of such rewards are:

- Benefit enhancements (e.g., greater life insurance coverage for nonsmokers)
- Lower deductibles
- Premium reductions
- Extra cafeteria plan credits
- Cash incentives to improve health factors
- Cash incentives to attend health education programs

Penalties

Employees who do not participate, or who do not participate successfully, as shown by unchanged or worsened health factors, may be penalized. Examples of such penalties, also called "sticks," are:

- Limited or no access to coverage
- Reduced coverage
- Reduced benefits
- Surcharges for lifestyles related to poor health

To illustrate, assume an employee is more than 50 pounds overweight, as shown by his health questionnaire. The employer's wellness program may offer the employee coverage only for illnesses or accidents not related to obesity. The program also could offer the employee the same coverage as other participants, but impose a $50 a month surcharge if the employee fails to decrease his weight by a certain amount after a specified period of time, such as three months.

Analysis of Rewards and Penalties

The effectiveness of incentives and penalties is questionable. Employees may lie on health questionnaires or may not seek necessary medical care in order to maintain their preferred health plan status. The fairness and ethics of penalizing employees who fail to meet a health profile is suspect, given that group health insurance is designed to spread the cost of such risks across a group. In addition, courts may hold that other laws, such as § 510 of ERISA, require fair treatment of plan participants.[3]

All employers offering wellness programs or adopting them for the first time must evaluate whether their designs meet their goals and are valid under ADA. The main issue raised by wellness programs, especially lifestyle change programs, is whether nondiscriminatory treatment of disabled or potentially disabled employees protected by ADA may involve penalties and rewards tied to employee health plans.

ADA GENERAL RULES

"Disabled" Persons Protected by ADA

The disabled persons protected by ADA are:

- People who have a mental or physical condition that substantially limits one or more of their everyday activities, such as walking or working;
- People who have a history of a disability; and
- People who are regarded as disabled.[4]

The Equal Employment Opportunity Commission (EEOC) has avoided reliance on a laundry list of conditions that are disabling.[5] The EEOC has stated that even obesity *may* be a disability in certain circumstances.[6] In addition, former illegal drug abusers who are not currently using illegal drugs and alcoholics are "disabled" under ADA, representing a large percentage of the U.S. disabled. While the definition of a disability is broader than the meaning many people commonly understand, it is important to remember that a person with a medical condition is not necessarily disabled if he or she is not substantially limited by it.[7]

Prohibited Discrimination

Under ADA, an employer must not discriminate against disabled employees and job applicants on the basis of disability.[8] ADA also prohibits discrimination with regard to fringe benefits offered to employees (whether or not administered by the employer).[9] In addition, employers subject to ADA cannot discriminate against the disabled with regard to any other term, condition or privilege of employment.[10]

An employer cannot refuse to hire a qualified disabled applicant due to increased insurance costs or a lack of coverage.[11] An employer also may not discriminate against a person because that person is associated with disabled persons.[12] For example, an employer cannot discriminate against a person who volunteers at an AIDS clinic or against a person with a disabled dependent who may increase insurance costs.

An employer's group health plan may apply uniform limits on benefits, but only if it does not target the disabled in order to evade ADA.[13] The general ADA rules against discrimination thus encompass group health plans and may particularly affect those that coordinate their cost-containment strategies with wellness programs.

WELLNESS PROGRAMS UNDER ADA

ADA affects how wellness programs and employee fringe benefit plans intertwine through the use of incentives and penalties. The EEOC has stated that ADA requires employers to afford disabled employees "equal access to whatever health insurance coverage the employer provides to other employees."[14] These rules apply to insured *and* self-insured plans.[15] The EEOC stresses that any limits on coverage for certain procedures or treatments or limits on reimbursements must be applied equally to individuals with and without disabilities.[16] Employers must not offer a wellness program that violates this equal access rule or other ADA rules, but several provisions in ADA support the concept that employers may continue to offer wellness programs tied to employee health insurance plans.

The EEOC stresses that while equal access is required, an employer is not expected to ensure that the disabled receive the same *results* of benefits or "*precisely* the same benefits and privileges."[17] One can interpret the EEOC's position to indicate that an employer may distinguish between low-risk and high-risk employees in employee benefits through wellness programs without violating ADA. The argument supporting this conclusion is that everyone has an equal opportunity to receive the health benefits and that any differences in benefits and privileges are permissible because they need not be precisely the same as those received by nondisabled employees. As penalties under wellness programs become greater (or incentives unattainable), this argument becomes weaker.

The general ADA rule on equal access does not affect preexisting condition clauses in employer-sponsored health plans.[18] An employer may use a preexisting condition clause to exclude a disabled employee from a health plan, provided it is applied evenly to the disabled and the nondisabled.[19]

ADA also states that permissible underwriting practices do not violate ADA.[20] This underwriting exception, perhaps more than any other ADA rule, supports the position that employers may continue to offer wellness programs with rewards and penalties that are designed to shift or contain health care costs in connection with their insured or self-insured group health plans. Some employers hope to rely on this underwriting rule to exclude certain high-risk people entirely from coverage, just as some insurers do. This ability to exclude the disabled from plan coverage is particularly important to those small employers whose insurers refuse to cover some employees.

SPECIFIC ADA ISSUES IN WELLNESS PROGRAMS

An employer subject to ADA that offers a wellness program should be familiar with reasonable accommodation within the wellness program, confidentiality of medical information, and proper gathering of medical histories and examinations of applicants and employees.

Reasonable Accommodations

Employers subject to ADA generally must provide reasonable accommodations for disabled employees to enable them to perform their jobs, and this requirement extends to all employee benefits.[21] An employer is required to provide modifications or adjustments that enable disabled employees to enjoy equal benefits and privileges of employment as provided to similarly situated nondisabled employees.[22] In the context of wellness programs, the reasonable accommodation obligation means that an employer offering a wellness incentive for a lifestyle change, such as reduced premiums for walking during lunch, should modify the program for someone with a disability who is not able to participate.[23] For example, a disabled person in a wheelchair could be required to do arm exercises or read about nutrition instead of walking for exercise. The reasonable accommodation requirement as it relates to employee benefits should not be as difficult and as expensive to satisfy in a wellness program as it will be in other aspects of employment. Nonetheless, an employer should understand what *reasonable accommodation* means and should follow specific guidelines to assure that its wellness program is firm, yet flexible.

The reasonable accommodation process begins with the disabled employee, who is obligated to ask for a reasonable accommodation.[24] Although ADA does not require employers to distribute a disclosure, the employer should state before the fact that an accommodation in employee benefits may be available for a disabled person who submits acceptable evidence of disability. The employer may disclose the wellness program to all participants in a company policy or an SPD (if the wellness program is tied to the employer-sponsored group health plan). If the wellness program is coordinated with the employer's health plan through incentives or penalties, the employee group health plan document also should describe the program and mention the availability of the reasonable accommodation. If the plan sponsor omits this information, the plan arguably is not administered according to the terms of the written plan document, as required by ERISA.[25] The ADA permits employers to request employees to submit medical proof of their disability when needed or desired for the reasonable accommodation process.[26] The ADA regulations envision an employer and employee working together to consider accommodations that will be effective,[27] but the employer makes the final decision on what adjustments will be made.[28]

In an extreme case, an employer may offer a wellness program that a person with a disability cannot satisfy, and alternatives may not be available. This could occur, for example, where an employee has genetic high cholesterol and the employer's wellness program requires such an employee to lower the cholesterol level or pay $50 a month in additional health care plan contributions. After the employee initiates the process by requesting a reasonable accommodation, the employer requests medical proof of a disability. The employee then proves the existence of the hereditary condition through medical opinions stating that he has a condition that substantially limits the employee in a life function considered by ADA. A stalemate is reached. The sponsor of the wellness program should then rely on the flexibility it has built into its wellness program. Written policy or plan provisions should state that changes in the program are available for the disabled. Pursuant to that policy, the employer either should not penalize this disabled person or should offer him the same benefits.

An employer may not wish to make an exception to its wellness program for a disabled person in any circumstances. However, this position is likely to be indefensible. The employer could argue that the accommodation creates an undue hardship by bypassing the purpose of the wellness program (cost containment) and by burdening employee morale. Nonetheless, an EEOC charge or a lawsuit by a disabled person affected by the program is likely to be more costly than the price of making an exception to the wellness program (this will probably be the difference in the employee's contributions). In addition, the employer would likely lose this argument in court. An employer's finances and normal business operations are relevant when deciding if an accommodation is reasonable, not the employer's strategies for health care cost containment or the morale of other employees.[29]

CONFIDENTIALITY AND USE OF MEDICAL INFORMATION

Confidentiality Rules

Under ADA, all medical information relating to applicants and employees must be written on separate forms, kept in separate medical files and treated as confidential medical records.[30] This rule applies to *all* medical information, regardless of how it is obtained, including all information relating to drug tests, pre-employment physicals, postemployment physicals, employee health plans and wellness programs.[31] The only four exceptions to this confidentiality are disclosure to:

- Workers' compensation officials as required by law;
- Supervisors and managers of information regarding necessary restrictions on work and duties of the employee and necessary accommodations;
- First-aid and safety personnel, when appropriate, if the disability might require emergency treatment; and
- Government officials investigating ADA compliance.[32]

The EEOC's ADA regulations generally provide that medical information "shall not be used for any purpose inconsistent with" ADA.[33] These disclosure rules raise the question of whether an employer violates ADA when it uses medical information obtained in a wellness program to determine whether certain employees should be charged a different rate for group health coverage. As discussed below, different rules for use of applicant's records and a specific exception in ADA for voluntary wellness plans imply that it may be improper to use medical information *not* gathered under such circumstances for purposes of monitoring wellness.

Use of Applicant's Medical Records

The EEOC's appendix to the ADA regulations provides that information obtained in the course of a "permitted entrance examination or inquiry" may be used for insurance purposes described in § 1630.16(f) of the ADA regulations.[34] The meaning of this exception is somewhat unclear, but its context indicates that use of an applicant's medical records is very limited. The ADA regulations permit medical inquiries under certain conditions, but this exception for applicants' information is the only one permitting use of the information for insurance purposes.

The EEOC refers to permitted entrance examinations or inquiries without defining them, but since the section described in the appendix deals only with post-offer medical examinations or inquiries, the medical information that may be used for insurance underwriting appears to be limited to the information obtained in such post-offer examinations. Therefore, an employer cannot use other types of medical examinations to underwrite risks in a lifestyle change wellness program, including fitness-for-duty examinations, annual physical examinations, physical examinations of late entrants for coverage by group health plans or voluntary wellness examinations, described below. Any differences in coverage or contribution levels would have to based on post-offer medical information only.

The application of the exception for post-offer testing is unclear in the area of drug testing. An applicant who tests positive for use of illegal drugs presumably would not be hired and would not be protected by ADA. However, assume that an employer learns that an applicant (who does not test positive for illegal drug use) has high levels of a drug used to treat high blood pressure. Under a literal reading of ADA, the results of drug tests could not be used for underwriting purposes because they are not post-offer medical examinations. On the other hand, the ADA rules permit use of medical information for insurance purposes if it is from "permitted entrance examinations or inquiries." Therefore, the results of post-offer drug tests, which ADA specifically permits, arguably may be used for insurance purposes and to adjust contribution levels in a lifestyle change wellness program. Nonetheless, an applicant or employee with a disability could bring suit under many different laws for violation of privacy in connection with a drug test, in addition to ADA discrimination charges, based on the argument that the employer knew of the disability and acted upon that knowledge by discriminating against him or her. Therefore, the most conservative course of action is to use drug tests that only reveal the presence of illegal drugs. In addition, an employer should not use the results of any drug tests done *during* employment to adjust contributions under a wellness program, since these tests definitely fall outside the boundaries of employment entrance examinations.

Voluntary Wellness Programs

Under a specific ADA rule, an employer may conduct a voluntary medical inquiry or voluntary examination as part of a voluntary employee health program available to employees at the worksite.[35] Voluntary wellness programs are an exception to ADA's general rule prohibiting an employer from making medical inquiries.[36] The general rules on confidentiality of medical information still apply, and the information gathered for the wellness program may not be used for any purpose inconsistent with ADA.[37]

This rule on voluntary employee health programs raises two key questions:

- Does the term *voluntary employee health program* include a wellness program tied to employee health coverage?
- May employers use the medical information obtained from the voluntary wellness program to charge employees different insurance rates through penalties or incentives, or is this a "purpose inconsistent with ADA"?

The EEOC's guidance on voluntary health programs is sketchy. The EEOC states:

> [Employee health] programs often include, for example, medical screening for high blood pressure, weight control counseling, and cancer detection. Voluntary activities, such as blood pressure monitoring and the administering

of prescription drugs, such as insulin, are also permitted. It should be noted, however, that the medical records developed in the course of such activities must be maintained in the confidential manner required by this part and *must not be used for any purpose in violation of this part, such as limiting health insurance eligibility.*[38] (Emphasis added.)

The EEOC's position on wellness programs indicates that voluntary wellness programs are more similar to disease prevention programs rather than to lifestyle change programs. The EEOC may interpret the exception narrowly to prohibit many lifestyle change programs, particularly those that use rewards and incentives. The medical information given by employees would be used for an improper purpose—*limiting* health insurance eligibility, as prohibited by the EEOC. These lifestyle change programs do not appear to be "voluntary" because an employee's health coverage is at stake, and the purpose of the screenings is cost containment rather than disease detection. Although an employer may argue that all employees are *eligible* for health insurance, and some individuals simply pay different rates based on their individual risks, the EEOC could strictly interpret the rules against improper use of medical information. Nonetheless, an employer clearly may offer three types of wellness programs: behavior and safety programs that do not rely on medical information and disease prevention programs, such as those described by the EEOC, which do not limit health insurance eligibility.

The use of medical information in a wellness program appears to be forbidden, unless the employer gathers the information under a post-offer examination or a voluntary wellness program. Any information *not* gathered this way probably cannot be used as part of a wellness program without violating ADA. That information would include medical information gathered through an involuntary wellness program or through other means, such as from medical claims records. For example, if an employee is required to have an annual physical that reveals diabetes, the employer could not use the information to charge the employee higher premiums for group health coverage.

BONA FIDE EMPLOYEES BENEFIT PLAN EXCEPTION

Despite the EEOC's position and assertions that lifestyle-based programs violate ADA, an employer may continue to offer a lifestyle wellness program by restructuring it to fit within ADA guidelines. ADA provides that employers, insured and self-insured, may establish, sponsor, observe or administer the terms of a bona fide benefit plan that are based on underwriting risks, classifying risks or administering such risks that are based on (or not inconsistent with) state law.[39]

The plan must not be used as a "subterfuge" to evade the purposes of ADA.[40] The EEOC comments in the appendix accompanying this portion of the ADA regulations state that an employer cannot use the plan to deny a disabled employee equal access to insurance or "subject [him or her] to different terms or conditions of insurance based on disability alone, if the disability does not pose increased risks."[41] Therefore, if a disability *does* pose increased risks, the employer may, based solely on the disability, subject an employee with that disability to different terms or conditions of insurance. Provided an employer has sufficient data, empirical evidence and actuarial support, the employer may charge a disabled employee a different rate so long as it does not do so in order to evade ADA's purposes. Nonetheless, until further guidance is available on the meaning of ADA, the validity of this position is questionable and subject to challenge regardless of an employer's supporting data.

According to Naomi Levin, a senior attorney adviser at the EEOC specializing in ADA, the Commission is unlikely to issue advice soon on the issue of employee benefit plan compliance with ADA. According to Levin, the agency is actively working but has resolved no hard and fast rules. The EEOC cites two hurdles: The EEOC must address many very serious employment discrimination charges, and Congress gave the Commission very little guidance regarding ADA's effect on employee benefit plans. For example, the EEOC is currently wrestling with when a plan is a subterfuge to evade the purposes of ADA, a standard set by Congress with no definition or advice on what constitutes a *subterfuge*. Given the lack of congressional guidance, the agency may allow the courts to decide.

The EEOC has described the existence of a subterfuge for ADA purposes in two ways but has not yet defined the term. According to the EEOC, singling out one high-cost illness for exclusion, while continuing to cover other high-cost illnesses, might be evidence of a subterfuge (regardless of the overwhelming cost of an illness such as AIDS).[42] The EEOC also emphasizes that any decision to limit certain treatments "should be based on cost or medical efficiency or some other appropriate, objective factor applied across the board," but that these limitations could *still* be a subterfuge in violation of ADA.[43]

Nonetheless, commentators have confused the issue of how the EEOC will interpret this provision. According to one commentator, the EEOC stated informally that where an insurer refuses to cover a disabled person, and the employer does not otherwise provide the plan's benefits to the disabled, the EEOC will pursue the employer, the plan and the insurance carrier.[44] This position casts doubt not only on exclusionary underwriting, but also on all underwriting practices, including individualized risk rating under lifestyle wellness programs that penalize the disabled group health plan participants or that do not reward them due to their disability. However, the EEOC apparently has not established such rules yet. Meanwhile, however, EEOC personnel have had intensive training in insurance underwriting principles, so the EEOC hopefully will be ready shortly to address welfare benefit plan underwriting issues.

Levin, the EEOC attorney, acknowledges that not all underwriting issues have been resolved. While excluding a disabled person from coverage based on a preexisting condition or placing a separate cap on coverage for a disabling condition like AIDS or epilepsy is probably discriminatory, the EEOC has not determined whether it is discriminatory in all situations to exclude completely someone from health coverage based on risk underwriting. Nonetheless, the agency is leaning toward the conclusion that if an insurer is discriminating by refusing to cover an employee or an employee's dependent based on a risk associated with a disability, an employer who entered into an insurance contract covering the rest of its group would be committing an illegal act. This position seems harsh, since small employers may be unable to purchase coverage for persons with disabilities and may be required to self-insure the risk. The EEOC may anticipate that the result of this hard-line approach will be greater availability of insurance for small groups. As small employers refuse to enter into insurance contracts excluding the disabled, the insurers ideally would have to change their policies or forgo the business. Unfortunately, many employers fear insurers simply will not pursue the small group market under conditions.

ACTION PLAN

Selecting the Wellness Program

- Analyze the employer's aggregate costs related to employee health, including insurance premiums or self-insured benefits, workers' compensation costs, lost work time and wellness programs.
- Analyze patterns of benefit utilization under the employer's health and disability programs. Determine which health problems or conditions generate most of this employer's health costs. Many employers' wellness programs have targeted certain conditions and have missed the mark. For example, targeting a condition such as high blood pressure is not very effective if preventable childhood illnesses typically cost a particular employer more money.
- Based on this study of the costs of employee health care, choose the type of wellness program that will reduce those costs. Develop clear and realistic objectives for the wellness program. Apply a focused rather than "scattershot" approach. For example, if an employer's most costly health claims result from on-the-job accidents and preventable childhood diseases, the employer should select a safety program and a disease prevention program.

Deciding Whether the Program Is Mandatory or Voluntary

- Determine whether the wellness program should be mandatory or voluntary. Under ADA, as well as other applicable laws, behavior modification and safety wellness programs may be mandatory. On the other hand, employers implementing disease prevention and lifestyle change wellness programs may decide to take the most conservative position under ADA and other applicable laws and implement completely voluntary programs.

- Employers that decide to offer mandatory programs can develop programs that withstand challenge under ADA. To do so, the employer should either avoid using incentives and penalties or should not tie the incentives or penalties to specific employee benefits. An employer could require an employee to participate in the program as a condition of employment, but the employer should design ways to enforce the programs that do not affect benefits, such as making participation one factor (of many) in job evaluations. Promoting wellness by giving away mugs and T-shirts would also satisfy the condition that participation be voluntary. (If the wellness program does not involve incentives or penalties of *any* kind, the program *may* be mandatory without violating ADA.)
- The employer needs to weigh the risks involved with nonvoluntary programs with consideration for the program's design, as well as other factors, including the need for the program and whether its employees have filed EEOC complaints in the past under other discrimination laws.

Equal Access to Wellness Programs

- In any case, the employer needs to be aware of its responsibility to provide all employees with equal access to the wellness programs (for example, equal access to a health education training program). Nonetheless, it is unlikely that any court would require an employer to restructure programs such as exercise or health training programs to address and benefit the specific needs of a disabled individual.

Physical Examinations and Medical Questionnaires

- Under the most conservative approach, a wellness program should not *require* employees to take physical examinations or to complete a medical question-naire as a condition of receiving medical coverage or as a means to screen whether employees are meeting required standards. In addition, no penalties or incentives under these types of programs should be related to the employee's health care plan.
- A less conservative (but feasible) approach is to require employee physicals and to offer incentives related to the employee's health care plan, but the employer should meet certain conditions. First, the employer should notify all employees that a reasonable accommodation will be made for any

employee who shows he or she is *disabled* as defined by ADA. Second, the employer should keep all employee medical information confidential under the ADA guidelines. The safest way to accomplish true confidentiality is to have a third party monitor the wellness program.

Effect of Wellness Programs on Employment Decisions

- An employer should not make a decision about a wellness program without considering the impact of the program on other aspects of its relationship with disabled applicants and employees. If an employer gathers medical information for use in a voluntary wellness program, for example, the employer's decisions regarding a disabled employee may be challenged based on the employer's knowledge regarding the disability. Although ADA sets rules for confidentiality of medical records, the burden shifts to the employer to demonstrate that the proper procedures were actually followed, which may be difficult to prove. A discharged employee would argue that the employer discriminated against him or her based on a disability known to the employer, pitting the employee's word against the employer's.
- An employer should consider who within the organization can have access to wellness information. An employer can screen the medical information from people making employment decisions and could take a very conservative position by having an independent third party administer the wellness program without any employer involvement and knowledge.

CONCLUSION

While ADA's rules indicate that an employer *may* be able to offer all types of wellness programs, employers that offer such programs must be careful to comply with the guidelines of ADA. Future guidance on the meaning of ADA as it applies to wellness programs is not expected for some time. The EEOC has many serious issues to resolve regarding the protection of the disabled, and guidance and enforcement efforts are likely to focus on discrimination in hiring and complete exclusion from employee benefits rather than wellness programs that have a less drastic immediate effect on the disabled. In addition, the focus of these enforcement efforts is likely to delay court decisions on this issue.

Nonetheless, employers that currently offer wellness programs tied to employee health plans and employers that want to implement wellness programs cannot take the "wait and see" approach. As the dollar amounts involved in a wellness program increase and as the number of affected participants increases, so does the risk of a lawsuit. In addition, given the value placed on health benefits by the disabled and the assistance of the EEOC in enforcement efforts, a lawsuit is a realistic possibility. By following the guidelines described in this article and modifying their programs as the law develops employers may offer these programs while remaining appropriately cautious.

1. Wellness programs have come under fire on several fronts. State laws on disability discrimination, medical confidentiality and privacy; federal civil rights laws; and § 510 of ERISA prohibit illegal discrimination in wellness programs. In addition, wellness programs are based on the premise that unhealthy participants deserve to bear the responsibility for rising health care costs. Commentators have questioned whether certain "at risk" participants cause rising health care costs and whether wellness programs actually save employers money. While some surveys indicate cost savings, other employers have been disappointed with their wellness programs as health care costs continue to rise. Even the "healthiest" participants will eventually become old, frail and sick. Some argue that the healthier persons who live longer due to improved health care may actually increase health care costs because they may be more likely to eventually die of more costly debilitating diseases.

2. 42 U.S.C. §§ 12101-12213 (1990).

3. In *McGann v. H&H Music* (CA 5, No. 90-2672, November 4, 1991), a U.S. court of appeals held that a medical plan sponsor could place a cap on benefits for AIDS without violating § 510 of ERISA (29 U.S.C. § 1140). In *McGann,* the court found that the employee failed to prove intentional discrimination against him. Nonetheless, if a disabled plan participant could demonstrate this discrimination, the participant might be able to sue based on an employer's discriminatory wellness program under § 510 of ERISA, as well as under ADA.

4. 42 U.S.C. § 12102(2) (1992); 29 CFR § 1630.2(g) (1992).

5. 29 CFR § 1630.2(j)(Appendix) (1992).

6. *Id.*

7. 29 CFR § 1630.2(g) (1992).

8. 42 U.S.C. § 12112(a) (1992); 29 CFR § 1630.4 (1992).

9. 29 CFR § 1630.4(f) (1992).

10. 29 CFR § 1630.4(i) (1992).

11. 29 CFR § 1630.5(Appendix) (1992).

12. 29 CFR § 1630.8 (1992).

13. 29 CFR § 1630.5(Appendix) (1992).

14. *Id.*

15. 29 CFR § 1630.16(f) (1992).

16. 29 CFR § 1630.5 (1992).

17. 56 *Fed. Reg.* 35726 (7/26/91) and 29 CFR § 1630.2(o) (1992).

18. 29 CFR § 1630.5 (1992).

19. 29 CFR § 1630.5(Appendix) (1992).

20. 29 CFR § 1630.16(f)(1) (1992).

21. 29 CFR § 1630.2(o) (1992).

22. *Id.*

23. 29 CFR § 1630.2(o)(Appendix) (1992).

24. 56 *Fed. Reg.* 35726, (7/26/91) and 29 CFR § 1630.2(o) (1992).

25. ERISA § 402(a)(1).

26. 56 *Fed. Reg.* 35726 (7/26/91) and 29 CFR § 1630.9(o)(Appendix) (1992).

27. 29 CFR § 1630.2(o)(3); 29 CFR § 1630.2(o)(Appendix) (1992).

28. 29 CFR § 1630.9(Appendix) (1992).

29. 42 U.S.C. § 12111(10)(B)(1992); 29 CFR §§ 1630.2(p)(1992).

30. 42 U.S.C. § 12111(10)(B)(1992); 29 CFR §§ 1630.14(b) and (c) and 1630.16(f).

31. *Id.*

32. *Id.* and 29 CFR § 1630.14(b)(Appendix) (1992).

33. See footnote 30, *supra.*

34. 29 CFR § 1630.14(b)(Appendix) (1992) and 29 CFR § 1630.16(f0 (1992).

35. 42 U.S.C. § 12112(d)(4)(B) (1992); 29 CFR § 1630.14(d) (1992).

36. 42 U.S.C. § 12112(d)(4)(B) (1992); 29 CFR § 1630.13 (1992).

37. 29 CFR § 1630.14(d)(1) (1992).

38. 29 CFR § 1630.14(d)(1)(Appendix) (1992).

39. 29 CFR § 1630.16(f)(2) and (3) (1992).

40. 42 U.S.C. § 12201(c) (1992); 29 CFR § 1630.16(f)(1) (1992).

41. 29 CFR § 1630.16(f)(Appendix) (1992).

42. 1991 Joint Committee on Employee Benefits Questions and Answers, Reports of Technical Session with the Equal Employment Opportunity Commission, the Department of Labor, the Pension Benefit Guaranty Corporation and the Securities and Exchange Commission held in May 1991 and questions responded to by the Internal Revenue Service and the Department of Treasury at the May 17, 1991 meeting of the Employee Benefits Committee of the Tax Section (ABA), Q&A 17.

43. *Id.* at Q&A 20.

44. Address by D. Ward Kallstrom, Lillick & Charles, American Bar Association's Section of Labor and Employment Law Meeting (August 12, 1992), cited in Bureau of National Affairs *Pension Reporter,* August 17, 1992, at 1485.

37. Health Promotion and Disease Prevention: Can Corporate Programs Really Lower Health Care Costs?
Susan Murray Young

Given the current climate surrounding the U.S. health care system, it is the rare individual who does not know that health care costs in this country have been increasing rapidly for many years. Most of the cost burden is borne by employers, both public and private, who have been aggressively searching for effective cost-containment strategies. Although few if any employers rely on health promotion programs as a major cost-saving strategy, there is evidence, as discussed in this article, that those who offer such programs can expect some cost savings.

A major benefits consulting firm recently released the results of its survey of 179 companies about the current state of worksite health promotion. Fifty-two percent of the companies surveyed reported that they provide worksite health promotion programs for their employees. Moreover, 80 percent of those companies indicated that their primary reason for offering such programs is to save on health benefit costs. However, only 12 percent of companies surveyed with plans that have been in effect for more than one year can clearly attribute cost-savings to them (William M. Mercer, 1993).

Does this mean that worksite health promotion does not save health care dollars, or does so, for only a few companies? Or saves money only in the long term? Is there something health promotion programs can do to save money in the short term? This article presents some answers to these timely questions.

SAVING MONEY BY IMPROVING HEALTH: AN INTEGRATED APPROACH

Along with their concern about ensuring that the health care they purchase is both high quality and cost effective, most employers are becoming more sophisticated in the practice of health promotion. Fortunately, a steadily growing knowledge base is available to assist their efforts.

During the early growth of worksite wellness programs, there were no examples or guidelines to follow. Programs were typically sporadic attempts to raise awareness and encourage behavior change. A company might conduct a screening for high blood pressure without also providing education about how to lower blood pressure, or might initiate an intervention for only one employee group, such as executive physicals. Yet, even though the programs were not always well planned or carefully designed, eventually the successes outnumbered the failures, and some principles of sound health promotion in the workplace began to emerge.

Realizing that fragmented programs can fail to reach those most at risk, employers are designing comprehensive programs targeting high-risk employees *and* high-risk dependents, and retirees who together may account for 40 percent to 60 percent of employer health care costs (Behrens, 1990). Progressive employers are also pooling the resources of all corporation areas charged with addressing employees' health needs, integrating everyone's efforts, and holding everyone accountable for health and financial outcomes.

Needed: Specific Goals

What is involved in such a program? First, a well-designed program has specific program goals. These are determined by a careful needs assessment involving examination of health and other data for employees, dependents, and retirees (particularly crucial if cost-containment is a goal). Health claims (including mental health, disability claims, employee assistance program (EAP) utilization), workers' compensation claims, safety records, and health risk appraisal results (if available) provide detailed information about employee health needs. Integrating these databases yields a still more complete picture of workforce health care needs (Yenney, 1992). This is particularly important for meeting another cost-containment goal: Identifying high-cost health problems in the system.

Once high-cost health problems have been identified, a concerted effort can be launched to address employee health needs in these areas. Ideally, such an effort will be integrated across departments and at all corporate levels including any and all organizational units involved in overseeing employee health and well-being.

For example, if analysis of employee health data determines that cardiovascular disease is a significant contributor to a company's high health care costs, and a large percentage of the workforce are smokers, perhaps an effort to reduce the number of smokers would be appropriate. An integrated effort would address corporate policies, programs, environment, and incentives, and might go something like this:

- The health promotion staff offers a smoking cessation class to those who want to quit.
- Class participants are encouraged to join the corporate walking program to reinforce a healthy lifestyle and combat the potential weight gain that often discourages those who quit smoking.
- The benefits staff ensures that the company's health plans cover the cost of nicotine replacement therapy or other pharmacologic aids to smoking cessation and offer a financial incentive to nonsmokers in the form of reduced health insurance premiums.
- The human resources department spearheads an effort to institute a smoking ban in the workplace and to remove cigarette vending machines from the worksite.
- Finally, the company EAP arranges support groups or short-term counseling to assist smokers in dealing with life stresses that may interfere with their attempts to quit smoking now and over the long term.

TWO MODEL PREVENTION STRATEGIES

Two examples from the real world of corporate experience illustrate the principles involved in a comprehensive integrated approach to improving employee health status by targeting prevalent high-cost health problems. The first example, maternal and child health at First National Bank of Chicago, represents a primary prevention approach to improving employee health—that is, preventing a health problem from developing (in this case, low birthweight and other poor birth outcomes). By contrast, the experience of several employers in managing existing mental health problems (depression) represents both secondary prevention (early recognition and intervention) and tertiary prevention (appropriate care to minimize the effects of the disorder).

Promoting Maternal and Child Health at First National Bank of Chicago

Information gathered as part of the National Business Partnership to Improve Family Health, a cooperative initiative of the Washington Business Group on Health and the U.S. Maternal and Child Health Bureau, provides strong evidence that employers, employees, and dependents have much to gain from efforts to promote maternal and child health (American Academy of Pediatrics et al., 1993). One of the best corporate examples is the experience of the First National Bank of Chicago.

In the early 1980s, First National Bank of Chicago examined its employee health data and found that pregnancy represented the single largest component of health care and short-term disability costs. This progressive employer already had an on-site gynecologist who provided free services during working hours.

However, after paying the costs for care of several low-birthweight infants (about $100,000 each), the company—recognizing that the pregnancy complications that lead to such high costs and poor birth outcomes are largely preventable—decided it needed to do more for its pregnant employees and dependents. So First National teamed up with the March of Dimes to bring the "Babies and You" prenatal program to the bank's employees and spouses.

Seminars on healthy childbearing, nutrition, and general prenatal care are open to both employees and spouses. Employees who enter the program by the fourth month of pregnancy have their $300 health plan deductible waived for the first year of the new baby's life—an incentive for both prenatal education and well-baby care. First National communicates the program through posters, newsletters, cafeteria announcements, and an informative videotape for spouses and off-site employees (Burton, Erickson & Briones, 1991)

Results have been impressive. For example, 50 percent of eligible Chicago-area employees who delivered in 1989 or 1990 attended the prenatal classes. Delivery costs for these women averaged $6,581; for the women who did not participate, $9,815. Also, 12 percent of class participants had cesarean births, compared with 25 percent of nonparticipants. Class participants also returned to work earlier than nonparticipants. (Zicklin, 1992). In 1991, the average cost for an uncomplicated cesarean delivery was $7,826, compared with $4,720 for a vaginal delivery (Health Insurance Association of America, 1992). So any reduction in the incidence of cesarean sections represents substantial savings to the employer.

Managing Depression in the Workplace

Clinical depression is a costly medical problem affecting nearly 10 percent of American adults each year (Regier et al. 1993). A recent study estimated that the economic burden of depression in 1990 was $44 billion, of which 55 percent represented "workplace costs," including absenteeism and decreased productivity (Greenberg, Stiglin, Finkelstein, and Berndt, 1993). It is estimated that 60 percent of suicides are attributable to some form of depression.

The good news: 80 percent of those suffering from depression can be effectively treated with psychotherapy, medication, or both. Most depressed people can be treated on an outpatient basis, often improving within a matter of weeks (Elkin, Shea, Watkins et al., 1989; Regier, Hirschfeld, and Goodwin, 1988; Stroudemire, Frank, Hedemark et al., 1986). Depression often goes unrecognized, however, and two out of three people with depression do receive appropriate care (Wells, Stewart, Hays et al., 1989; Regier, Hirschfeld, and Goodwin, 1988).

Employers who examine their employee health care data are finding that depression is indeed a significant and costly problem in the workforce. Information gathered as part of the Depression Awareness, Recognition and Treatment National Worksite Program (Vaccaro, 1991), a collaborative project of the Washington Business Group on Health and the National Institute of Mental Health, revealed that:

- At Westinghouse, one-year prevalence rates for major depression were 17 percent for women and 9 percent for men (Bromet, Parkinson, Curtis et al., 1990).

- Depression accounted for 11 percent of all days lost from work during one year and for half the total time lost due to mental health problems at Pacific Bell.

- An employee survey at Wells Fargo Bank revealed that 30 to 35 percent of respondents were experiencing depressive symptoms. The incidence of clinical depression could be as high as 12 percent to 15 percent.

In response, employers are addressing the need for early recognition of depression, access to appropriate treatment, and on-the-job support. Again, an integrated approach in most likely to be successful. For example:

- After learning that 32 percent of employees would turn to their supervisors first with a personal problem,Wells Fargo Bank addressed the problem of depression in its workforce by educating employees and supervisors about it, training EAP staff, and collaborating with its managed mental health vendor and health insurance carrier to ensure appropriate, cost-effective treatment.

- Champion International and the State of Virginia educated employees about the types and signs and symptoms of depression through brochures, seminars, and videotapes.

- Pacific Bell integrated its health promotion, employee assistance, health benefits, disability management, workers' compensation, and safety programs within one department. This single-team approach to meeting mental and other health care needs provides a continuum of care from prevention, through early and appropriate treatment, to rehabilitation.

- After initiating a comprehensive mental health program (including prevention and early intervention programs) and redesigning mental health benefits, the First National Bank of Chicago realized a 32 percent reduction in inpatient psychiatric charges (Burton, Hoy, Bonin and Gladstone, 1989).

COST CONTAINMENT THROUGH HEALTH CARE CONSUMER EDUCATION

There is one problem with reliance upon improved employee health as a cost-containment strategy. Health care costs are crucially influenced as well by how individuals use the health care system and by how providers make choices within that system.

The health care system is now being reformed to change the way health care is both delivered and financed. For example, in *Organized Systems of Care* (Cronin and Milgate, 1993), providers are held accountable for the cost, quality, and outcomes of care. So how can health promotion programs impact the health care system? By focusing on the other part of the equation: individual behavior.

Reducing Demand for Health Care

Strategies for influencing employees' behavior regarding health care include the following. In a recent article in The New England Journal of Medicine, Fries, Koop, Beadle et al. (1993) spoke of the differences between reducing the need for health care by promoting health and preventing disease and reducing the demand for health care by teaching people to use the health care system wisely.

Although both strategies offer the potential for cost savings, the authors argued that the health and financial benefits of the former strategy are generally realized in the long term. The latter strategy, reducing the demand for health care, they concluded, is more likely to yield short-term cost savings.

How can employers reduce demand for health care services among their workforce? First, by helping employees understand when and what type of health care is needed. Fries et al. (1993) offer evidence that inappropriate use of the health care system can often be avoided if individuals have guidelines to help them decide if they need professional care or some form of basic self-care. For instruction in basic self-care, a useful and time-tested resource is *Take Care of Yourself* (Vickery and Fries, 1993), used by many employers for health care consumer education.

Second, employers can empower employees to participate actively in medical decision making about their care. Regional variability in the rates for certain procedures, such as cesarean sections, hysterectomies, and prostatectomies, indicates that many such procedures may be unnecessary. Moreover, when patients are involved in the decision-making process, they generally choose less invasive and less expensive alternatives, with little or no adverse effect on outcomes (Fries et al., 1993).

Finally, employers can encourage the use of "advance directives"—written instructions that reflect an individual's preferences regarding life-sustaining care in the event of a terminal illness or injury. Fries et al. (1993) cite numerous studies in support of their argument that a disproportionate amount of health care dollars are spent in the last year of life. So far, however, although many people prefer that extraordinary measures not be taken to prolong their lives, very few have made this preference known officially through an advance directive.

THE HEALTH PROJECT CONSORTIUM: AN EXAMPLE FROM THE REAL WORLD

Fries and his coauthors are not simply theorists regarding the value of health promotion and health care consumer education. They are all members of The Health Project Consortium, made up of business leaders, health insurers, policy scholars, and members of government who believe that, "reducing demand and need can have a substantial positive effect on health care costs."

The Health Project Consortium is devoted to identifying and replicating worksite and community programs with demonstrated ability to reduce health care costs through need reduction (i.e., health promotion) and demand reduction (i.e., consumer education) strategies. To that end, in 1992, they awarded the C. Everett Koop National Health Award to eight corporations. In 1993, they gave awards to two corporate programs and four community programs.

As Fries et al. point out,

> Collectively, these programs had developed many of the features that in-fluence costs directly over the short term. Two had a heavy emphasis on self-management, two used cost incentives, one emphasized advance direc-tives for terminal care, several contained elements directed at enhancing self-confidence with regard to health-related decisions, and several had defined approaches to people at high [health] risk. (p. 323).

To illustrate the principles discussed in this article, a case study from one of The Health Project Consortium's corporate award recipients follows.

Blue Shield of California

Blue Shield of California provide a low-cost health promotion and disease prevention program designed to lower employee health risks and to educate employees to become conscientious health care consumers. Using the building blocks of behavioral change—action, awareness, and reinforcement—the pro-gram has been successful in helping individuals achieve better health and a higher level of involvement in the health care decision-making process.

The program, called Healthtrac, uses health-risk data acquired through carefully validated health-risk appraisal questionnaires that employees fill out every six months. Computer files are serially linked, enabling the program to provide each participant with regular progress reinforcement and recognition of behavioral changes. Information on individual participants is strictly confidential.

Employees receive a variety of materials that target their specific health needs. These include self-care materials such as the well-proven *Take Care of Yourself* sourcebook (Vickery and Fries, 1993), "personal vitality reports" that provide graphic documentation of progress over time, personalized letters suggesting plans of action for improving health, and additional information specific to the needs of each individual.

Blue Shield of California also offers a prenatal/preparenting program. Designed to guide women toward healthy pregnancy and delivery, the program is particularly effective in targeting women at high risk for preterm or complicated deliveries. Through a risk assessment component and case management features, high-risk participants are provided immediate access to specialized guidance, education, and support.

Healthtrac has resulted in significant risk reductions for Blue Shield employees: a 60.7 percent reduction in high dietary fat consumption, a 17.5 percent reduction in reported back pain, a 54.9 percent reduction in dietary salt intake, a 43.4 percent reduction in the number of smokers, and a 29.4 percent deduction in the average employee health-risk profile.

Healthtrac's self-care component, the book *Take Care of Yourself,* has been demonstrated in several studies to reduce overall health care costs, to decrease physician visits by 15 percent, and to decrease visits for minor illness up to 34 percent (Vickery, Golaszewski, Wright, Kalmer, 1988; Vickery, Kalmer, Lowrey, Constantine, Wright, Loren, 1983).

The Healthtrac program at Blue Shield of California serves the dual purpose of improving individual health and of lowering health care costs by reducing the consumer's need and demand for care. In addition, Blue Shield of California and its employees realize many less tangible benefits from the program, including increased productivity, reduced absenteeism, increased self-efficacy, and an overall improvement in quality of life.

CONCLUSION

To the question, "Can worksite health promotion save money on health care costs?"—the answer is clearly, "yes." Furthermore, if has been shown that although programs such as cardiovascular or cancer risk reduction programs tend to save money mainly over the long term, some interventions can save money in the short term, such as, programs that target prenatal health.

Employers can also help reduce their health care costs in the short term by adopting comprehensive, integrated approaches to reducing both the need and the demand for health care. Strategies include employee education in appropriate use of the health care system through improved self-care; active patient participation in medical decisionmaking; and use of advance directives.

The Health Project Consortium program descriptions provided herein were excerpted with permission from The Health Project Consortium information kit. For details and references on these programs contact The Health Project Consortium at 212/345-7336.

REFERENCES

American Academy of Pediatrics, National Commission to Prevent Infant Mortality, Washington Business Group on Health. (1993). *An action blueprint for business: Forging partnerships to make a difference in maternal and child health.* Washington, D.C.: National Commission to Prevent Infant Mortality

Behrens, R. (1990). *Reaching families through worksite and community health promotion programs* (Monograph). Washington, D.C.: Washington Business Group on Health.

Bromet, E.J., Parkinson, D.K., Curtis, E.C., Schulberg, H.C., Blane, H., Dunn, L.O., Phelan, J., Dew, M.A., and Schwartz, J.E. (1990). Epidemiology of depression and alcohol abuse/dependence in a managerial and professional work force. *Journal of Occupational Medicine, 32*(10), 989-995.

Burton, W.N., Hoy, D.A., Bonin, R.L., and Gladstone, L. (1989). Quality and cost-effective management of mental health care. *Journal of Occupational Medicine, 31*(4), 363-366.

Burton, W.N., Erickson, D., and Briones, J.. (1991). Women's health programs at the workplace. *Journal of Occupational Medicine, 33,* 349-50.

Cronin, C. and Milgate, K. (1993). *A vision of the future health care delivery system: Organized systems of care* (Monograph). Washington, D.C.: Washington Business Group on Health.

Elkin, I., Shea, M.T., Watkins, J.T., Imber, S.D., Sotsky, S.M., Collins, J.F., Glass, D.R., Pilkonis, P.A., Leber, W.R., Docherty, J.P., Fiester, S.J., and Parloff, M.B. (1989). National Institute of Mental Health Treatment of Depression Collaborative Research Program. *Archives of General Psychiatry, 46,* 971-982.

Fries, J.F., Koop, C.E., Beadle, C.E., Cooper, P.P., England, M.J., Greaves, R.F., Sokolov, J.J., Wright, D., and The Health Project Consortium. (1993). Reducing health care costs by reducing the need and demand for medical services. *The New England Journal of Medicine, 329*(5), 321-325.

Greenberg, P.E., Stiglin, L.E., Finkelstein, S.N., and Berndt, E.R. (1993). The economic burden of depression in 1990. *Journal of Clinical Psychiatry, 54,* 1-14.

Health Insurance Association of America. (1992). Cost of maternity care, physician's fees, and hospital charges, by census region, based on the Consumer Price Index, 1991. *1992 Source Book on Health Insurance Data.* Washington, D.C.: Author.

Regier, D.A., Hirschfeld, R.M.A., and Goodwin, F.K. The NIMH Depression Awareness, Recognition, and Treatment Program: Structure, aims, and scientific basis. *American Journal of Psychiatry, 145*(11), 1351-1357.

Regier, D.A., Narrow, W.E., Rae, D.S., Manderscheid, R.W., Locke, B.Z. and Goodwin, F.K. (1993). The de facto U.S. mental and addictive disorders service system: Epidemiological catchment area prospective 1-year prevalence rates of disorders and services. *Archives of General Psychiatry, 50,* 85-95.

Stroudemire, A., Frank, R., Hedemark, N., Kamlet, M., and Blazer, B. (1986). The economic burden of depression. *General Hospital Psychiatry. 8,* 387-394.

Vaccaro, V.A. (1991). *Depression: Corporate experiences and innovations* (Monograph). Washington, D.C.: Washington Business Group on Health.

Vickery, D.M., and Fries, J.F. (1993). *Take Care of Yourself,* 5th edition. Reading, MA: Addison-Wesley.

William M. Mercer, Inc. (1993, October). In shadow of health reform, employers continue to stress wellness programs. [Press release from offices of William M. Mercer, New York, NY].

Wells, K.B., Stewart, A., Hays, R.D., Burnam, M.A., Rogers, W., Daniels, M., Berry, S., Greenfield, S., and Ware, J. (1989). Detection of depressive disorder for patients receiving pre-paid or fee-for-service care. *JAMA, 262*(23), 3298-3302.

Yenney, S.L. (1992). *Putting the pieces together: A guide to the implementation of integrated health data management systems* (Monograph). Washington, D.C.: Washington Business Group on Health

Zicklin, E. (1992). Prenatal teamwork fosters an employer/employee partnership. *Business and Health.* Mid-March, 36-40.

Vickery, D.M., Golaszewski, T.J., Wright, E.C., Kalmer, H. (1988) The effect of self-care interventions on the use of medical sercies within a Medicare population. *Medical Care,* 26, 580-588.

Vickery, D.M., Kalmer, H., Lowrey, D., Constantine, M., Wright, E., Loren, W. (1983). Effect of a self-care education program on medical visits. *JAMA,* 250, 2952-2956.

Part 11

ADMINISTRATION AND COMMUNICATION

38. Communicating Changes in Health Care Benefits to Union Employees

Richard D. Quinn

Like most large companies, Public Service Electric and Gas Company of Newark, NJ was concerned about its health care costs. But how to tell employees—especially union employees—about the Company's idea of abandoning the traditional first-dollar health benefits plan and introducing a comprehensive plan along with flex choices required a communications strategy. This article discusses the evolution and outcome of that strategy.

The Company's idea was first discussed with the unions in 1989. Needless to say the idea of leaving the Blue Cross plan of the last 50 years for something unknown met with less than enthusiastic support. The result was implementation of the proposed strategy for non-union employees and three more years of discussion with the unions. Between 1989 and 1992 the Company's benefits staff and industrial relations staff met monthly with all union leaders via the Company's Health Cost Containment Committee.

This Committee proved to be one of the most valuable steps the Company had ever taken to enhance relations with its unions. During the three-year period a mutual exchange of ideas, concerns, and issues enabled both sides to better understand the problems each was facing. In an environment removed from the heat of labor negotiations, both sides discussed the facts and details of what steps needed to be taken to control health care costs. It was also during this period that represented employees could see how the proposed program was working for nonrepresented employees of the Company. The transition was not easy because the program designed by the Company was radically different from the benefits previously provided. Indeed, this work force had grown up with Blue Cross as its health benefits provider and looked to the Blues as the security for health benefits rather than the

401

employer. The idea of self-insurance was alien to employees, not to mention the idea of applying deductibles to hospital, medical-surgical as well as other health care expenses.

Today, all 12,000 employees of PSE&G have the same health benefits program—three comprehensive fee-for-service options, a point-of-service option, and choice among three HMOs. Prescription drugs are provided through a managed care program combining a card and mail order alternative. Unreimbursed medical bills can be paid through flexible spending accounts. During the 1993 transition year the Company added $100 to each employee's flexible spending account. Fifty-seven percent of PSE&G employees have elected a managed care alternative. For 1993 the Company's health care costs increased by slightly more than 3 percent while the percentage of costs paid by employees decreased from 20 percent of premium to 12 percent. Like other companies, PSE&G is still not happy with its health care bill or its rate of increase, but to date its strategy has put the Company on the road to regaining some control while also preserving the concepts of choice and reasonable cost-sharing among employees. Looking in 1994 at some of the strategies being proposed in Congress, the PSE&G approach is virtually a model of the systems under consideration.

No discussion of health care costs would be complete without mention of retirees. PSE&G, as has been traditional in the utility business, provides a generous health benefits package to all its retired employees. Beginning in 1994, new retirees will also have a comprehensive program with the point-of-service and HMO options (depending on where the retiree resides). Retirees contribute to the cost of their benefits based on a scale reflecting their pay before retirement and their years of service. This may appear to be a minor change, but, in fact, was very dramatic for a company that had provided "free" health benefits for retirees and their dependents through a first-dollar medical plan for over 50 years.

If all the above sounds complex in its reading, imagine trying to explain and implement this new program to 7,700 union workers and their families. To make the task that much more difficult, employees saw the new program as nothing more than a take-away and were apprehensive about which choices were the right decisions.

In addition, as part of the process of redesigning the health benefits program, the Company studied the effectiveness and viability of the seven HMOs it offered. As a result of this study, four plans were dropped. This meant that many employees previously enrolled in the HMOs that were eliminated had to decide whether to join one of the remaining HMOs or dive into uncharted waters and select the point-of-service plan or a comprehensive option.

A FORMAL COMMUNICATION STRATEGY REFLECTING COMPANY PHILOSOPHY

PSE&G believes that effectively communicating employee benefit programs is an important part of an overall benefits strategy. At PSE&G there is a formal benefit communications budget. The communication strategy is designed to support the benefits strategy and long-term Company objectives. Benefit communications is viewed as an ongoing process, not something to be rolled out when an event occurs and then relegated to little more than summary plan descriptions between major events. The communications process is designed to educate employees (and their families), to explain Company philosophy, to explain the details of plan changes, to listen to employees and to integrate employee benefits into the changing corporate culture.

This strategy is helping PSE&G and its affiliate companies change from an old line, paternalistic utility into an organization positioned to compete at home and abroad. The key is a productive, participatory work force educated to assume a greater share of responsibility for their benefit decisions and with the ability to maximize the value of benefit programs. At PSE&G benefits are no longer viewed as individual plans such as health insurance, life insurance, pensions, and the like, which may be perceived as little more than a necessary evil and expense. Instead, benefits at PSE&G provide real life solutions which, when used effectively, result in a more productive work force aligned with company goals. The benefits staff administers a comprehensive financial planning program, tuition aid services, eldercare and childcare programs and retirement planning in addition to all the traditional benefit functions. All of these programs are aligned to provide employees with a wide variety of tools they can use to meet their real life concerns and problems, whether it's buying their first home, finding day care for a child, a nursing home for a parent, or financing their child's college education.

Consistent with this strategy, the flexible benefits program for represented employees includes employee-pay-all long-term care insurance. Employees, their spouse, their parents and in-laws may purchase long-term care insurance in any of three levels of coverage providing a $50, $100, or $150 daily nursing home benefit.

COMMUNICATING HEALTH BENEFIT CHANGE

The new benefit program was effective January 1, 1993, but preparation for its introduction began in July 1992. A strategy was designed to communicate with employees and their family. The objective was not only to tell people about the new program, but also to explain the larger objective of the program—in other words, the why and what of what was going to occur.

Some represented employees previously had minimal choice among medical plans, and all had HMO alternatives since 1977. The idea of choice was not entirely new, but still caused many people to be apprehensive. In addition, there was still a great deal of misinformation about the program. The biggest problem was overcoming the rumor that the covered benefits were vastly different under the new plan. In fact, there were no reductions in benefits. Rather, some routine child care and preventive services for women were added.

Another critical issue was the notion that employees would have a substantially higher out-of-pocket cost with the comprehensive approach to fee-for-service options. The employee perception was that every employee was going to meet their deductible and that every employee was going to have a hospital admission and thus be faced with an immediate payment of $750 or more to meet the deductible and out-of-pocket limit.

INDEMNITY OPTIONS AVAILABLE			
	Option 1	*Option 2*	*Option 3*
Deductible	$150	$ 250	$ 500
Out-of-Pocket Limit	$600	$1,000	$1,000

Another popular myth surrounded the flexible spending accounts. People were convinced they would lose their money because of the *use it or lose it* provisions of the IRS Code. It was difficult to get employees to understand their new-found ability to manage out-of-pocket medical expenses. Interestingly, on one hand employees were certain the new medical plan would greatly increase their out-of-pocket expenses, yet when told they could prefund these expenses through a flexible spending account, they were just as certain they would lose the money as a result of not incurring eligible medical expenses. This dichotomy simply reinforces the unique way most people view health care costs and their responsibility for health care expenses, a point which Washington policy makers should note carefully.

THE COMMUNICATION PROCESS

Given that most employees were comfortable with their current health benefits, the first task of the communication process was to establish the need for change. Although the union leaders had participated in this education process over a three-year period, the union employees had a different perspective. The initial task was as much a union goal as a Company goal—make sure people knew why changes were being made. This was accomplished through a special issue of the Company employee benefits newsletter, "Spectrum." Spectrum is not released on a regular basis, but instead is used as needed to address specific issues, problems, or plan changes. For example, the most recent issue of this publication explains health care reform to employees, its possible implication for them, and the Company position on some of the proposals being considered by Congress.

Spectrum provided employees with facts and figures about health benefits at PSE&G. It attempted to educate employees about the Company's concerns and why a new look at health benefits was necessary. The theme was "the changing world of health care." This initial communication piece was released in late June 1992.

In early August a second Spectrum was released to affected employees. In this issue the focus was on "what's happening," what's going on with your benefits. Employees were told exactly what changes were going to take place and when. They were alerted to the decisions they would have to make and the timing of those decisions. Employees made their decision during October with new coverage effective the following January 1. (Each year the same enrollment process is followed.)

Following the special Spectrum issues the communication strategy focused on specifics. A series of four payroll stuffers were used to highlight specific benefits within the new package. These stuffers explained in brief detail the flexible spending accounts (medical and dependent care), medical plan choices including introduction of the point-of-service option, dental benefits, and the new long-term care plan. Because of the scope of changes employees were asked to absorb, it was important to make this information available in small pieces.

PSE&G believes that involving the employee's spouse in the benefit decision process is critical. This is especially true when it comes to health benefits where research has shown that the spouse frequently makes health benefit decisions and generally is the partner who files claims and resolves related problems. Because of this, benefit communication vehicles are frequently mailed to the employee's home. The process of introducing a flexible benefit program and new medical benefits was no exception. The open enrollment kit was mailed to every represented employee's home and included several important pieces of information:

- A medical choice calculation slide rule
- A flexible savings account worksheet
- A long term care enrollment kit
- An enrollment booklet and form
- A special video
- A benefit option comparison chart

A serious attempt was made to keep this kit as simple to use as possible. Even its look was designed so as not to be overly slick or formal. The kit was mailed in a plain brown box and the enrollment booklet was presented as a plain spiral binder with a look similar to a note book frequently used by employees in their work. Despite these efforts, in retrospect, the kit may have been overpowering, containing too much information at one time. At times, companies become absorbed with the communications process and the attractive look of the communications instead of focusing on the message and the ability of the audience to absorb the material. More important is understanding the interest level of the employees and their need or desire to focus on the material and to make decisions. In PSE&G's case, the need to make decisions would appear obvious. However, there were still a large number of employees who failed to take even the relatively few minutes necessary to understand their new benefits. This is a critical and ongoing communications challenge, especially in seeking to promote greater individual responsibility on the job when managing employee benefits.

The **medical choice calculation slide rule** allowed individuals to estimate the dollar and cents impact of their benefit choice. Based on the employee's estimate of health care costs for the following year, he or she could find out which benefit option offered the lowest total out-of-pocket cost. This estimate included the employee's cost for payroll deductions for the choice selected. Also, by estimating out-of-pocket costs the employee could better determine the amount to be placed in the flexible savings account (FSA).

The **choice account worksheet** focused the employee on the potential value of the FSA and encouraged the individual to evaluate health benefit options in light of the availability of the FSA. Specifically, the employee was encouraged to evaluate how much of the financial risk he or she was willing to absorb in exchange for lower premiums. The worksheet encouraged people with dual coverage to consider this extra source of benefits in their decisions. The primary objective was getting people to opt for a high-deductible plan and use coordination of benefits to offset the possible additional cost to them.

The **long-term care enrollment kit** was a kit within a kit. Information about long-term care included enrollment material and a separate booklet explaining the program, along with an enrollment form designed for optical scanning.

The **enrollment booklet** provided plan details, including the rules governing the initial enrollment and subsequent changes that could be made. The new point-of-service option was explained in detail in this piece.

The **video** explained in concept the new program employees were being asked to learn about. Little was said about specific plan provisions. Instead, the video explained the concepts of choice, the value of an FSA, and how the employee could make selections to best meet their individual needs.

PSE&G relies heavily on the use of videos. A survey of employees found that nearly 80 percent had a VCR. In addition to the new-plan video discussed here, PSE&G has produced a long-range financial planning video to compliment its financial planning program. The newest production is a retirement planning video. This video is mailed to each employee who submits retirement papers. All decisions associated with retirement are covered in the video, and employees are encouraged to share this information with their spouse. The financial planning and retirement videos come with written pamphlets. The idea is education with practical objectives. For example, the retirement video has enhanced the information given to employees, assured a consistent message, and reduced the time necessary to process people for retirement. Since 1991, PSE&G has reduced the size of its benefits staff from 32 to 17 while expanding services to employees and adding new benefit programs. Communications and the use of new technology such as voice response systems and interactive PC-based video systems designed by the Company have had a great deal to do with this accomplishment.

The final tool in this enrollment kit was a **benefit option comparison chart**. This chart, in table format, allowed the employee to quickly see the different way specific health care services would be handled by the medical options available to them. The comparison included the indemnity options, the point-of-service option, and the HMOs.

During the enrollment period all employees had an opportunity to attend a meeting on company time to learn more about the new program. In addition, a telephone hotline was set up for any employee or spouse to call. The hotline received a great deal of activity, but not from employees. The spouses of employees were the biggest user of the hotline. This revelation lead the Company to quickly organize family meetings on Saturdays. Employees were encouraged to bring their spouse or other interested family members to the meeting to ask questions about their new program. In addition to benefit department staff, representatives from the indemnity option administrator, the point-of-service plan, and the HMOs were on hand to answer general and specific questions and to distribute supplemental literature.

These meetings provided an excellent opportunity to clear up misconceptions about the new benefits and to deal with real life situations. Many people under medical care were concerned about continuity and whether their doctor would "accept" anything other than Blue Cross. The Company had the opportunity to explain self-insurance and the fact that health benefit security was not found with the insurance company but with their employer. Pregnant spouses expressed concern over the need to change doctors. Families with catastrophic health care situations were shown how the new plan provided greater coverage for them when their perception had been one of potential financial ruin. In short, an important dialog took place. The Company and employees and their families learned a great deal about what employee benefit programs mean when real life solutions are needed.

The meetings were very successful, but the overall attendance represented a fraction of the people affected by the new plan. The reluctance of people to invest even a few hours of their own time in something as important to them as their benefits and related family security is still a source of amazement. This lack of involvement is one of the most important communication and education challenges companies face. The idea that, "the company decides my benefits," and the "one size fits all" mentality still prevails.

Beginning in 1994, PSE&G will use family meetings on an ongoing basis. One Saturday each month employees and their families will have the opportunity to spend a few hours in the morning or afternoon learning about their benefit programs and how these programs can assist them if properly understood and used.

PRESCRIPTION DRUGS

Coping with the cost of prescription drugs is a unique problem for PSE&G. Employees have had a card program for many years and changing that was not an option. On the other hand, costs had to be controlled. The solution was a managed care program accompanied by a mail order pharmacy. The card program and the mail order option are linked within a common data base that is used to monitor utilization and potential abuse of drugs. In conjunction with PCS, PSE&G developed a network of pharmacies in New Jersey that was willing to provide a discount to the Company. The Company also built in a strong generic drug incentive. At the same time the co-payment was increased from $2.00 to $5.00.

The new program works this way. If an employee uses a brand name drug when a generic exists, the employee pays the $5.00 copayment plus the full difference between the cost of the brand and generic drug, an amount which can be considerable. If a non-network pharmacy is used the employee pays the lost discount in addition to the above cost. A generic drug from a retail pharmacy has a $1.00 copayment.

As an alternative, a 90-day supply of either a brand or generic drug is available for $1.00 from the mail order service. At first employees perceived this program as business as usual, but with a higher copayment. However, employees quickly realized that using a brand drug when a generic was available was costly. Frequently, this choice left the employee with a bill of $45.00 or more. The communication challenge was to explain why there were no exceptions to the rule. The immediate employee reaction was "Why do I have to use a generic if my doctor orders a brand name?' or " I'm allergic to the generic drug." There are no exceptions under even these circumstances, but the mail order is always available to allow the employee to obtain a brand name drug for $1.00.

This dual approach to providing prescription drugs has proved effective in helping to control costs. Costs in 1993 were less than originally budgeted, and the use of generic drugs and the mail order pharmacy have increased considerably.

CONCLUSION

Employee benefit communication plays an important role in cost containment and other specific benefit strategies. However, communication and a broader role for the employee benefits program have a much larger mission. PSE&G sees a direct relationship between the employee's ability to cope with life situations, many of which detract from the ability of the employee to concentrate on the job, and the organizations desire to maximize customer satisfaction, employee productivity, and generally to be a world class, competitive organization. Employee benefit programs are no longer fringes, but have a vital role to play in supporting the human resources and corporate strategy. No organization can be successful without a committed, focused work force. Such a work force will not be there if it is distracted by the many life situations facing today's workers and their families. A well designed benefit program and related communications can relieve many of the distracting situations. This is not an issue of spending more money on employee benefits, but of designing benefits to provide real value for the company and its employees.

39. Communicating Health Benefits Changes: A Case Study

Stanley Friedman

Over the last decade, IBM, like most large companies, was forced to make a series of cost-cutting changes in its employee health benefits programs, and managed to do so without any serious employee backlash or negative response. IBM's efforts at communicating benefit changes to employees played a crucial role in their ultimate success at evolving their organization's benefits philosophy from one of entitlement to one based on competitiveness.

Communicating health care benefits changes to employees—specifically, that the cost of benefits will be more or the level of benefits less—is becoming commonplace in American industry today. But that does not diminish the communications challenge of convincing employees of the need for such changes or in motivating them to help control costs by choosing cost-effective, sound medical care.

Starting in 1984, IBM faced this challenge on a number of occasions as the company moved its health care benefits philosophy along a continuum—from entitlement, to shared responsibility, to cost control, to competitiveness. This paper briefly examines some of the communications approaches and messages used by IBM in each phase of this evolution.

THE PRE-1984 ERA

Prior to 1984, IBM's health care philosophy could be characterized as one of "entitlement." Except for a modest $150 deductible for major medical expenses, first-dollar coverage was standard for surgery and hospitalization; non-contributory, full-family coverage was the norm; and managed care options (HMOs),

410

while available, were hardly acknowledged. IBM employees enjoyed one of the most highly rated benefits programs in American industry, and communications related to rising health care costs and the need for controls were basically confined to memoranda within the human resources and financial communities.

But in late 1984, IBM employees awoke to find that the company's health care philosophy and benefits plans had changed.

NOVEMBER 1984

IBM's new approach to health care benefits—shared responsibility—was explained in a letter to employees by then IBM Chairman John Opel. After indicating that IBM's medical costs, on average, had more than doubled between 1978 and 1984, he went on to introduce two of four central themes that would be used in the company's benefits communications during the next decade:

- **Balance and flexibility.** "With [medical costs] in mind, we recently examined our medical and dental plans. Where increased reimbursements were appropriate, they were added. Where broader coverage was indicated, it was included. And where reasonable steps were necessary to help control spiraling medical costs, they were taken." For example, the November announcement introduced a new plan feature, the personal health account. This provided benefits for preventive care, immunizations, eye exams, and glasses—a plus for all. At the same time, the annual major medical deductible was changed to make it a salary-based amount—a minus for some.
- **Employee responsibility.** ". . .[Y]ou share—with IBM—a responsibility for controlling rising medical costs. You can help by choosing medical care that is both medically sound and cost effective." To encourage employees—with their doctor's advice—to consider more cost-effective medical care alternatives, the level of benefits was increased for a wide range of outpatient care alternatives.

Using these themes, IBM sought to assure employees that, despite any change it would make to its benefits plans, the company remained committed to helping employees and their families receive a wide range of medical services and maintain their health at a high level.

Along with the letter, a boxed set of simply designed booklets explained and rationalized the changes, providing applicable examples illustrating the financial consequences of each change to both IBM and the employee. But the need to control health care costs, while mentioned, was articulated more as a way of ensuring IBM's leadership in the years to come than as a near-term concern. It was not until 1990 that a greater sense of urgency was reflected in both IBM's plan changes and communications material.

JULY 1990

The shift in July 1990 from a philosophy of shared responsibility to one of cost control was marked by a significant set of benefits changes and the introduction of the third communications theme: *affordability*. "The cost of providing medical benefits has soared in recent years," said John Akers, IBM chairman at the time, in his letter to employees. "This year, IBM's medical benefits costs will approach $1 billion."

As part of its cost control efforts, IBM introduced a preferred provider network for psychiatric and substance abuse treatment, with lower benefits coverage for out-of-network care; brought its coordination of benefits provisions more in line with industry practices; extended its annual family deductible to surgical charges; and announced retiree medical caps.

To provide balance and flexibility, a number of new programs and plan improvements were announced at the same time. For example, reimbursement levels under the IBM dental plan and personal health account were increased, and new long-term care insurance and catastrophic care assistance programs were introduced. But there was still concern that employees—most of whom had grown up in an era of entitlement—would not be able to put these changes in proper perspective.

As a result, the communications material distributed in July had the threefold objective of convincing employees that:

1. Cost controls had become a necessary and immediate objective;
2. IBM had addressed the issue in a responsible way; and
3. IBM employee benefits continued to be among the best in industry.

A six-page "white paper" on IBM's benefits program was developed, which acted as the announcement overview in the printed material. Complete with graphs, the overview (1) compared the IBM plans with those of 18 other major national companies to show that the plans were outstanding across the medical benefits spectrum; (2) displayed employee satisfaction data on IBM benefits gained through surveys and focus groups; and (3) provided charts showing the dramatic escalation in national health care and IBM medical plan costs.

The theme of employee responsibility was emphasized as well. The material urged employees to become more effective consumers of health care by understanding the coverage the company's medical plans provided and asking questions about the treatment programs doctors prescribed. "You can also maintain a healthy life style. . .use pre-admission testing. . .ask your doctor about generic drugs. . .look into alternative approaches to surgery or hospitalization."

Managers were given the overview in presentation format and asked to hold department meetings with their employees. A videotape also was produced, which employees could borrow to take home and view with their spouses. The videotape explained each of the changes IBM was making and the reasons why. While the amount of communications material developed was significant, a follow-up survey indicated that the material was read and the need for changes generally understood and accepted by the employee population.

APRIL 1992

In April 1992, IBM made several more changes to its medical and dental plans, explaining that, while the medical plan changes announced in 1990 resulted in savings, IBM's health care costs had continued to rise at a more rapid rate than revenue.

An annual deductible was introduced for the IBM dental plan; the use of utilization reviews was expanded; and non-duplication of benefits was adopted under IBM's coordination of benefits rules. Balance and flexibility were achieved by announcing a managed dental care program as an alternative to the regular IBM dental plan. The "Dental Maintenance Alternative" had no deductibles, no annual or lifetime maximums, and no copayments for most preventive services. IBM also fully covered the premiums for the first year.

Affordability was still an issue, but there was a new, more externally based perspective that now emerged: *competitiveness*. At a time when IBM had begun to transform its structure and approach to the marketplace, the April 30th bulletin board notice signaled the shift in philosophy: "[These changes are] part of an overall strategy to assist IBM business units in improving their competitiveness through appropriate benefits offerings." In essence, IBM's benefits programs would change to bring employee costs and plan design more in line with that of the competition.

To avoid possible criticism that money was being wasted on communications that otherwise might have gone to maintain employee benefits, the announcement material was disseminated electronically to employees over IBM's internal network and provided as typed pages to individuals without terminal access.

OCTOBER 1993

On October 28, 1993, IBM took the final step in its benefits evolution and restructured its delivery system under a flexible benefits framework, called the IBM Personal Benefits Program.

To effectively communicate the need to move from decades of non-contributory health care benefits to a program with monthly contributions, IBM brought together the four communications themes described above to rationalize and gain support for the change.

Here are the opening paragraphs of the announcement brochure:

IBM has long been recognized as having one of the most generous benefits plans in U.S. industry. Today, as the company strives to become profitable and preserve future opportunities for employees, this rating is a source of both pride and concern.

IBM wants to continue offering benefits that provide security and protection for you and your family. At the same time, IBM must manage its costs to remain competitive.

In 1992, IBM spent over $1 billion on health care for U.S. employees and retirees—a year in which the company reported net earnings of negative $5 billion. Although benefits changes over the past three years have helped keep IBM's rate of cost growth below the national average, the amount of money IBM is spending in this area threatens the health of the company and its ability to compete.

For this reason, IBM is introducing a new way to continue providing quality health care benefits, while having you share in these costs through reasonable monthly contributions. It's called the IBM Personal Benefits Program.

This new "flexible benefits" type of program offers you and IBM the best alternative for preserving excellent benefits while helping control the company's overall costs.

Using the results of recent surveys and benchmarking studies, the brochure compared IBM's total benefits package with that of other companies—ranking it in the top 25 percent. The "news," while still positive, reflected a more candid, sobering approach in IBM's communications. Monthly contributions and copayment levels also were compared to those of other major companies.

The announcement brochure was followed by an enrollment workbook and employee videotape that described, in more detail, how the IBM Personal Benefits Program worked and what options were available to employees. In addition, a special booklet was produced to assist employees in making informed medical care decisions. The opening prologue underscored the theme of employee responsibility:

> With health care in the news every day and national health care reform on the horizon, it's more important than ever to become informed about the health care choices you make. Your own and your family's health depends on it. But it isn't easy. With choice comes responsibility. There's more to consider— about quality of care and service, cost, choice of doctors and medical philosophy. . . . It's up to you to decide what's best for you and your family.

The *IBM Personal Benefits Program Decision Guide* not only compared the indemnity plans being offered to employees, but, for the first time in IBM, proactively examined the alternative of managed care. The guide showed examples of typical family medical expenses and compared out-of-pocket costs for employees under each medical option. It discussed coordination of benefits issues, the potential tax advantages of flexible spending accounts, and the philosophical and practical differences between "fee-for-service" and managed care.

Were the messages heard? The answer was a resounding yes. There was little, if any, negative feedback from employees concerning the introduction of monthly contributions, and approximately 30 percent of the employee population enrolled in HMOs—tripling 1993's enrollment numbers!

The evolution was complete.

MORE TO DO

During the last decade, IBM has been able to maintain a high level of employee satisfaction with its benefits plans, while evolving its benefits philosophy from one of entitlement to competitiveness. But while communications has been key to achieving that success, the work is far from over. Having employees recognize the need for change is only part of the battle. Better ways must be found to enhance employees' understanding and appreciation for their benefits plans, through both innovative print material and computer technology, such as multimedia. In addition, the likely impact of national health care legislation on employee benefits will pose its own set of unique and formidable challenges on communications.

IBM has started to pursue a number of ideas in these areas, but work is still in the formative stages.

40. High Tech Benefit Solutions
Donald G. Jones, CEBS

Any company that has been involved in the internal administration of a cafeteria plan for its employees soon becomes aware of the burden that paper creates. Enrollment forms, change forms, underwriting, and coverage continuation forms are just a few examples of documents that must be managed in a cafeteria plan. Florida Hospital was determined to develop a solution through technology.

T he prevalence of forms is burdensome not only for employers but for employees as well. While in the employer's mind the use of paper-based systems creates additional labor, storage, and other inefficiency-type costs, in the mind of an employee the typical form-based benefit plan often creates confusion, misunderstanding, frustration, and ultimately a diminished appreciation of the benefits offered. These problems are obviously compounded in larger employer environments.

Florida Hospital, a part of the Adventist Health System, is a 1,462-bed tertiary care facility located in Orlando, Florida. With 7,600 employees functioning at five hospital sites plus 30 other locations, the administrative complexities involved in the administration of our cafeteria plan were significant.

The Florida Hospital cafeteria plan contained health, life, disability, dental, specified disease, and medical and dependant care flexible spending accounts. As is the case in most similar plans, employees make benefit elections at the time of hire and must maintain those elections throughout the course of the plan year unless certain qualifying events occur. Employees are permitted to make changes annually during an open enrollment period.

PROBLEM AND GOALS

We were dissatisfied with the paper-based open enrollment process because it was extremely labor intensive, paper intensive, and required a great deal of processing time on our part. It was also clear that the process did not provide enough quality information to employees and, therefore, required too much of their time to effect changes to their benefits. This, in turn, resulted in a fairly high error rate. Open enrollments had required employees to physically report to certain centralized locations during specific hours if they wished to make benefits changes. Because of the manual nature of the system, long lines resulted and the entire exercise was frustrating for employees and the benefits staff. All required application and other forms were completed by employees during this process; should underwriting be required by a particular company, health questionnaires would be mailed for review. Following the four-week open enrollment period, the necessary data entry would be done to set up the proper deductions in the human resources payroll system.

We approached the task of creating a new system with a number of goals in mind. It was our desire to provide better information to our employees, a much quicker process, easier access for employees, and much less paper. We further wished to reduce the significant labor requirements of the manual system and, at the same time, greatly increase the accuracy of our data. We proposed to achieve these goals by first making ourselves aware of new technologies and by then matching our needs with the appropriate technologies.

SOLUTION

The approach that was ultimately selected involved a combination of technologies: telephone voice response, relatively inexpensive personal computers, high speed laser printing, and electronic mail. Our home grown system ultimately consisted of six personal computers, four voice response add-in boards, a number of laser printers, a modem, and eight telephone lines. Generally speaking, telephone voice response describes an interaction between an individual and a computer in which a computer uses a digitized human voice to initiate or respond to the touch tone telephone entries of the individual. Properly applied, this technology permits a meaningful "conversation" to occur between a computer and a person.

Under the new open enrollment approach, each eligible employee receives a comprehensive open enrollment kit in the mail about one week before the open enrollment period. Each kit, in addition to containing complete information on each of the benefits options, provides the employee with an individual benefits statement. The statement clearly identifies the specific benefits that the employee is currently receiving and provides, in work-sheet format, an area for the employee to mark the specific benefits that they desire for the new year. Those employees wishing to make changes for the new year are instructed to complete the work sheet and, using the telephone voice response system, record their choices over the telephone. Since many individuals are intimidated by the use of automated telephone systems, the open enrollment kit contains the actual script of a simulated employee call in the printed form. This provides an opportunity for the employee to actually become familiar with the system before making the call.

When the employee calls the voice response system, they are requested to punch in their Social Security number followed by a previously issued personal identification number. After confirming the status of the caller, the voice response system talks the caller through the process of punching in their benefit choices for the new year. Each call generally takes about three minutes, with each entry being confirmed as valid by previously programmed logic. To assure that the system has recorded the employee's desired selections, a written confirmation is produced by the computer and mailed directly to the employee for their review. Each call to the system produces a confirmation notice as well as a computerized record of each transaction.

As employees enroll for benefits that require insurance company underwriting, our system prepares a special file of data to be transmitted electronically to the insurance company. The data transmitted includes much of the demographic or other information that is required by the company, thereby expediting the underwriting process. The company then corresponds directly with the employee about its underwriting criteria, and ultimately decides whether coverage will be provided. Decisions are communicated back to our system by a computer. Our system then sets up the appropriate employee deductions. This process has saved considerable time and effort on the part of the hospital, insurance company, and employees.

During the open enrollment, our system functions 24 hours a day. As previously mentioned, each entry made by a caller is evaluated to ensure that it is valid for that individual caller. The system permits multiple calls by the same employee to accommodate those who sometimes change their minds during the open enrollment process. In addition, Spanish-speaking employees are invited to call a special Spanish language line to record their changes.

USER FRIENDLINESS

We went into this process with a great deal of concern about the user friendliness of the system. We most certainly did not want to trade our old, inefficient system for a new one that would be ineffective due to its complexity. We addressed this concern by building into the system the capability to sense a series of three invalid entries on the part of a caller. Should such a situation occur, the system will scan across our network to determine which benefits representatives are logged onto their computers. It then announces to the caller that their call is being transferred to an operator and that they should remain on the line. A special telephone line then rings on the desk of the appropriate benefits representative and, when the receiver is picked up, the system announces that it is transferring a call from the voice response system. The benefits representative's computer screen then changes to a special format that provides the complete benefits profile on the individual whose call is being transferred. The representative is then able to answer the transferred call by greeting the employee by name. The benefits representative will then see a complete listing of the employee's current benefit structure as well as the selections that they made on the voice response system before being transferred. The representative then answers any questions that the employee may have and records the remainder of the employee's choices. Employees who call the system and hang up before completing the process are identified on a special report, so that a member of the benefits staff can contact them to complete their selections.

RESULTS

The new system through the open enrollment process has been outstanding. The system handles in excess of 2,000 encounters over a period of about four weeks. Statistics maintained by the system indicated that 98 percent of all employee callers successfully recorded their benefit choices without intervention. The remaining 2 percent had their calls transferred to a benefits representative who assisted them with their selections. As expected, there were a number of employees who were intimidated at the very thought of using an automated voice response system. These individuals typically brought their enrollment kits to the human resources department and asked to complete the process on a manual basis. Each employee was provided one-on-one assistance and was instructed on the proper use of the system. A speaker phone was used, so that the employee and the human resource department representative could hear the automated voice response system. Invariably these employees commented on how easy the process actually was.

The design and development of our system was a challenging experience, and I would certainly not suggest that our approach is appropriate for every employer. Our organization possesses a significant number of internal resources that were available to us. We have a rather large information systems department that was able to provide all hardware and software support. An alternative to our approach would be to use the services of any of the major employee benefits consulting firms, who can offer turn-key systems designed to fit the unique circumstances of your organization. Either way, you will be amazed at the improvements that this technology can bring to the administration of your benefits program.

THE FUTURE

So, now that we have resolved our open enrollment problems, where do we go from here? Our most immediate plans are to expand the use of the voice response system to handle new employee benefit elections and mid-year benefits changes. It is also our goal to more fully integrate the insurance company underwriting functions within our system. For example, in the future the employee will be able to respond to required health history questions at the time coverage is selected on the voice response system. This approach will eliminate more paper and delays from the process.

We are also developing a multifunction computerized multimedia kiosk that will be deployed at sites where we have concentrations of employees. This system will provide for interactive multimedia presentations on benefits and other human resources topics and will permit a number of real-time transactions to occur.

We have become convinced that there are a wide variety of benefits-related areas that can benefit from new technologies. Whether you create your own solutions in-house or use the services of consultants, you too can reap the benefits of applying new technology.

Part 12

WORKERS'
COMPENSATION

41. Cutting Your Workers' Compensation Costs This Year
Brent A. Winans, CPCU, CIC, ARM

The fastest ways to cut your workers' compensation costs is to negotiate the lowest possible premium cost. Doing this, however, requires an understanding of how the workers' comp market works, and how to use it to your best advantage. The author of this article has been on both sides of workers' compensation insurance negotiations and offers advice and insights that can result in immediate savings for your company.

While there has been a great deal written recently on various loss control techniques, there has been little meaningful discussion of how to be a savvy buyer of workers' compensation insurance. Yet, knowing how to play the game can greatly affect the outcome and reduce your workers' compensation costs immeadiately.

UNDERSTAND THE MARKETPLACE

The sales pitch of many independent agents and brokers, especially large ones, often centers on the theme, "We are the biggest and the best. We represent many different insurers, and they will do things for us that they will not do for anyone else. Put your insurance in our hands. If we can't do it, no one can."

This pitch is usually not true, however. Even the largest insurance brokers do not represent all of the "independent agency" insurance companies. In fact, several such insurers generally refuse to do business with large brokers, and many others refuse to do business with small independent agents. No agent or broker does business with all the insurers who may be interested in your account. Beyond that, just because an agency represents an insurer does not mean that the insurer will respond favorably to the agency's business.

Furthermore, some of the country's largest workers' compensation insurers are almost never represented by any independent agent, large or small. For example, Liberty Mutual has been the country's largest workers' compensation insurer for decades, which sells through its own salespeople. They will often write workers' compensation coverage for a company even when they do not write the rest of that company's insurance. An insurer presently writing a lot of workers' compensation insurance for companies that are not in high risk businesses is Farmers Insurance Group, which may also write workers' compensation insurance without the rest of the client's business. They are rarely accessed by independent agents. State Farm, the largest writer of insurance in the United States, insures workers' compensation for many of the country's small businesses. They are represented only by their own agents. In addition to these private insurers, 18 states have established state run workers' compensation insurance companies that often offer very attractive rates in order to compete with the private insurers. Few of the state funds are represented by any insurance agent and usually must be contacted directly by the insurance buyer.

To ensure that you are getting the best buy on your workers' compensation insurance, you need to make sure that you are going to all of the people who might like to write your coverage. But how do you do this without creating havoc in the marketplace? And how do you make sure that everyone is quoting on the same basis? Following are some specific suggestions.

Prepare Specifications

Preparing specifications is a useful step in pricing any kind of insurance, but is especially important for workers' compensation. Many an insurance buyer has been duped into placing an order with the agent who offered the lowest bid, only to find out later (when the buyer's premium was audited and he received a large additional bill) that the winning agent was not quoting on an apples-to-apples basis.

An essential step in a well-managed competitive bidding process is to provide each of the competitors with exactly the same set of specifications. This will require that you either learn enough about how workers' compensation insurance is written and rated to be able to prepare the specification or hire an independent risk management consultant to do so. These consultants do not sell insurance but provide insurance advice to buyers on an hourly fee basis. You can obtain the name of someone in your area by calling the offices of the Society of Risk Management Consultants at 1-800-765-7762. Fees may range from $85 to over $150 an hour, but if you have a large workers' compensation premium and you do not want to spend the time to become an expert yourself, the fee is usually worth it.

If you decide to prepare the submission yourself, your present agent should be willing to help you. Once you have the first draft of the specifications completed, ask the other agents you are considering to review it and make suggestions. When you have heard everyone's point of view, finalize the specifications and send them out to all participants with a letter that explicitly states that their quotations are to be based on the specifications you have prepared and that you will assume that their proposal will be 100 percent in compliance unless they specify otherwise in writing.

Your specifications should include:

1. A fully completed workers' compensation application. (Your agent will be able to provide you with the form.)
2. Information on your firm and your products.
3. A summary of your audited workers' compensation premiums and your incurred (paid plus reserved) losses for the last three to five years. This summary should also show your loss ratio by year and for the total period.
4. Copies of the insurance company's computerized loss runs for the same period.
5. A copy of your formal safety policy and a description of your ongoing efforts to reduce losses. If you do not already have a meaningful safety program, now is the time to start one.
6. An explanation of any large or unusual losses and what you are doing to prevent similar accidents in the future.

Assigning Markets

The next step is to make sure that the independent agents involved are not going to the same insurers for quotes. You should not involve more than two or three independent agents even on a very large account. While using a larger number of agents might ensure that your risk will be presented to all of the available markets, agents will lose enthusiasm for your account if they think there is too much competition.

If an insurance company receives an application on your account from more than one agent, they will only quote for one, usually the one who submits the account first. Unfortunately, the first agent through the door may not be the agent most likely to obtain the best quote from that insurer. In fact, some agents, seeking their own best interest rather than that of their clients, will rush applications to every company they represent in an attempt to prevent other agents from competing. Another problem with having two agents approach the same insurer is the psychological effect it has on the insurer. Insurance companies also are discouraged by too much competition. If they think there are a lot of agents involved in the bidding and that no agent has "control" of the business, they may refuse to quote or may not give it their best effort.

For these reasons you want to ensure that only one agent goes to each company and that that agent is the one with the best chance of obtaining a favorable quotation from that company. Making market assignments will accomplish both goals. Tell each independent agent what you are doing and how you will make the assignments. Ask each to give you a list of the insurers they want to quote ranked in order of preference. This tells you what companies each agent sincerely believes will be the most competitive for them. I have never seen agents submit identical lists. If the incumbent agent is quoting, give that agent the incumbent market and do not count this as that agent's first selection. Then, give each agent the companies they rank highest. In the event of a tie, talk to each agent about how much business they have with that insurer and why they feel they should be the one to approach that market. Keep in mind that markets will sometimes work hardest for the incumbent broker because they believe the incumbent has the best chance of success. Then make a judgment call, and do not worry too much if the losing agent is upset about your decision.

Once you have decided which agents are to approach which markets, give each agent a written list of the insurers they will be permitted to approach on your behalf. Also, instruct them in writing that they will be the only agent permitted to approach their markets and that they are not to approach any other markets without your written permission. Reserve the right to reassign an insurer in the event the assigned agent is not making a good-faith effort to market your account. For insurers like Liberty Mutual and Farmers Group, market assignments are not necessary since generally only their own agents approach them.

Allow Enough Time

One of the most frequent mistakes made by insurance buyers is not giving themselves, their agents, and their prospective insurers enough time. Following is a suggested timetable that will work for most businesses; very large companies may need to allow more time.

Five months before renewal. Request that your agent provide you with computer generated claim histories from your insurer for the last five years. Agents and companies are sometimes less than helpful here because they know that this request means that you are planning to bid the account. Why should they help you take the business someplace else? Be pleasant but firm. Follow up every two weeks until you receive the loss runs. If you are still not getting what you need on a timely basis, a letter sent directly to the insurance company is often effective.

Four months before renewal. Begin preparation of your specifications. Also, interview agents that you may want to involve. Giving them an opportunity to critique your specifications may be a good way to see how much they really know about workers' compensation insurance. There is an enormous range of expertise in the area. Some agents are specialists in the field, while others do not completely understand even the basics. You will end up paying the same commission to both, so try to find an expert who can really help you.

Three and a half months before renewal. Select your agents and ask them to have their market assignment requests to you within a week. Give the agents a draft of your specifications and ask them for their suggestions, instructing them not to submit the specifications to any insurers yet.

Three months before renewal. Provide the agents with the finalized specifications and their market assignments. Tell them that the due date for their quotations is two weeks before the renewal date and that any quotations submitted later than that may not be considered. Also specify that all quotations must be submitted in writing. Stick to this—a verbal quotation is not worth the paper it is written on.

Three months to two weeks before renewal. Follow up with your agents every two to three weeks. If an agent is not coming back to you for more information, this is not a good sign. It usually means that the underwriter has stuck your application in a stack somewhere and probably will not look at it until he or she no longer has the time left to give it the attention it deserves. Ask your agent to follow up with any insurers that has not yet responded, and remind the agent that the quotations must be received two weeks before the renewal date. During this period, loss control representatives from the insurance companies may want to inspect your facilities. Do everything you honestly can to showcase a proactive loss control program. If your top management people provide strong support for loss control, do not allow the insurance inspector to leave your facility until he or she hears that from the president's own mouth. It could translate into premium savings very quickly.

Two weeks before renewal. Most of your quotes will probably come in by the due date, but some may be delayed. Use your own judgment about whether or not to accept them. You do not want to refuse to look at what may be the best quotation you will receive. On the other hand, you must maintain your credibility. If the quotations are at all complex you will want two weeks to make sure you understand them. Complex plans—such as retrospectively rated policies or high deductible plans—involve lengthy supplemental documents in addition to the insurance policy; insist on seeing and reading actual copies of these. Agents sometimes do not read these documents themselves, and they often contain hidden premium loopholes.

At least a day before the renewal date. All of your efforts can be wasted if you do not follow through at the end. Remember that insurance policies expire at 12:01 A.M. on the date listed on the policy. In other words, your policy actually expires at midnight on the day before the day shown as the expiration date. Do not get caught short. Also, write a letter to the agent summarizing your understanding of the final negotiated terms. This is an essential step in minimizing misunderstanding in the future. Insist that you receive a binder before the new policy goes into force.

A FEW OTHER THOUGHTS

Should you put your insurance out to open bid every year? Should you allow your present agent to have her most competitive markets bid every year? No. Both of these approaches are usually counterproductive. Both agents and companies are looking for clients who will show them some loyalty. Quoting your insurance more than every three years will give you the reputation of being a perpetual shopper who is not worth spending time on. As an alternative, find out from your agent and other agents what has been happening in the workers' compensation market in your state since the last renewal. What terms are the most competitive carriers offering on your type of risk? Then go to your present insurer well before the expiration date and tell them that you do not want to go out to quote but that you do believe that a competitive renewal would meet the terms you have outlined. Ask for their commitment to a quotation that meets these guidelines, and only go out to bid if they refuse to come close.

Keep in mind that many insurance companies will not write your workers' compensation coverage unless they also write your other insurance. For this reason, it may be necessary to bid your entire insurance program just to obtain a better quotation on your workers' compensation coverage. If this is the case, the same marketing procedures outlined here apply to other coverages as well.

CONCLUSION

Just like any sport, the workers' compensation insurance game is usually won by those who have a better-than-average understanding of how it is played. In the workers' compensation game, the insurance buyer must:

1. Know how to access the insurance companies that may be interested in writing the coverage.
2. Prepare insurance specifications that will assure that everyone is quoting on the same basis.
3. Assign markets so that only the agent with the greatest likelihood of success approaches each company.
4. Work on a timetable that allows the agents adequate time to obtain a quotation and you with adequate time to analyze and finalize it.

5. Seek to work out future renewals through direct negotiations rather than through annual competitive biddings.

Following the suggestions given here can help you quickly lower your workers' compensation costs by obtaining the very best insurance quotation available.

42.   Workers' Compensation Case Management

Judith Greenwood, PhD   Patricia Posey, RN, LPC

Managed care, having emerged as the standard for group health care delivery in recent years, is now being adopted by workers' compensation programs. To be adopted, however, it must be adapted to the special needs of workers' compensation. Those needs and strategies for meeting them are discussed in this article.

Because musculoskeletal injuries and fractures predominate in workers' compensation claims, a managed care organization must ensure a provider mix with a predominance of orthopedic surgeons, neurosurgeons, plastic surgeons, outpatient treatment centers, physical therapists, and chiropractors, compared with the predominance of primary care physicians found in general health practice.

Furthermore, managed care is a process, and managing medical care delivery in a workers' compensation claim is quite different from the process of managing an episode of care under group health insurance or within a general health maintenance organization (HMO). In workers' compensation, work-relatedness must be determined before treatment, and then treatment must be directed toward return to work. To ensure this, a managed care provider must understand the workers' compensation law within their jurisdiction and in bordering jurisdictions. Providers also need to communicate treatment progress and outcomes to the insurer, the employer, and the administrative agency, in language free of medical jargon.

The need for directing treatment toward return to work cannot be overstated. To this end, state workers' compensation jurisdictions are moving away from a laissez-faire approach to medical treatment and are adopting guidelines for providers to use in treating work-related injuries. Thus, managed care in workers' compensation will increasingly involve various review activities directed not only at controlling costs of care but also at facilitating return to work. Because treatment is so highly discretionary in soft-tissue injuries (the most commonly compensated work-related injuries), well-structured concurrent and retrospective managed care review or utilization management, using treatment guidelines, can identify ineffective or inappropriate treatment patterns over time and help treating physicians redirect treatment to more productive outcomes.

Absolutely essential to optimal managed care outcomes in workers' compensation cases is a *case management approach* to all claims and hands-on case management in claims where there is a risk for extended disability.

CASE MANAGEMENT AS A MANAGED CARE TOOL IN WORKERS' COMPENSATION

Case management in the general health insurance industry has evolved from an expensive necessity in catastrophic illnesses and injuries to an active intervention for all whose medical problems keep them from enjoying health and autonomy.

People who lack problem-solving skills tend to become overly dependent on the health care system when they are ill. The inefficiency and unnecessary cost of this situation can be avoided using the case management approach. The case manager becomes the facilitator for ensuring quality services and resolving problems through patient advocacy, patient education, and coordination of services. Thus, over the long term, case management should help contain health care costs.

In addition to ensuring quality care and cost containment, workers' compensation case management helps limit indemnity costs, because the injured maintains return to work as a primary goal along with recovery from an occupational injury or illness.

In the traditional case management approach, the patient is considered within the context of a family or social support system of significant others. In workers' compensation case management, the employer becomes a significant other as well, and the workers' compensation case manager keeps the lines of communication open between employee and employer. In addition, the workers' compensation case manager acts as a liaison between the employer and the physician to maintain focus on an early return to work. This role, and the process of case management itself, require a specialized body of knowledge not required of the general health insurance case manager.

THE PHILOSOPHY OF WORKERS' COMPENSATION CASE MANAGEMENT

Workers' compensation case management must ensure promotion of the tenet, "What's best for the injured worker is best for all." Promotion of this tenet requires that the case manager treat both the employer and the injured employee as clients of services where the goal is return to work. To realize this goal, the workers' compensation case manager must constantly examine interventions to be sure they will result in fairness to both the employer and employee as well as in restoration of the employee's productivity, either through return to preinjury employment or through referral for vocational rehabilitation.

Consider what questions the case workers' compensation manager may have to ask when deciding what's "best" in a particular case. Is it best for the employee to return to a setting where reinjury is highly probable? Is it best for the employee to take a modified work assignment that will place him or her in a situation where fellow workers resent the additional workload placed on them, because the injured worker cannot do his or her fair share? Will placing an injured worker in a modified work assignment significantly reduce the employer's output? In such difficult decision-making circumstances, a philosophy of fairness must be based on openness and negotiation. The workers' compensation case manager must emphasize the benefits of open communication to both employee and employer, including the benefit of negotiation where the workers' compensation case manager assumes an active liaison advocacy role.

WHAT MUST THE WORKERS' COMPENSATION CASE MANAGER KNOW?

Legal Issues

In a general health benefits setting, the case manager must know the medical condition of the patient, available service resources, and techniques for using those resources to promote quality care. In workers' compensation case management, the case manager must also know the legal issues that can affect the employee's recovery. Since workers' compensation is an insurance program limited to coverage of work-related injuries and illnesses, there may be questions of coverage of other conditions that affect the recovery process. Consider the following example:

> Mr. H., a 54-year-old construction supervisor, sustained a lost-time back injury on the job. One of his complaints was that after a period of sitting, his left leg would go numb. One day when he attempted to get up after being seated for a prolonged period, he said his left leg gave out, causing him to fall. The fall resulted in a complicated wrist fracture. He did not have any health insurance in effect. He must have treatment for the wrist fracture. He gets the surgical fixation, but now, he says, he cannot pay for the required physical therapy. The back injury treatment requires him to have full use of his wrist to carry out the recommended exercises.

Is workers' compensation responsible for the wrist fracture and its treatment? If the disability period will be prolonged because the wrist fracture is not managed properly, is payment for the physical rehabilitation program for the wrist appropriate?

To sort out answers to such problems, the workers' compensation case manager must be familiar with the state's workers' compensation law as well as with the laws of bordering states. One important issue is how a state's law directs choice of physician. Restrictions on an employee's choice vary considerably from state to state, but they generally take one of four forms: (1) the employee's initial choice is unrestricted, (2) the employer or insurer makes the initial choice, (3) the employee is restricted in changing physicians, or (4) the employer or insurer can initiate physician changes. Finally, the workers' compensation case manager must know the potential legal ramifications of any action taken in a claim. How does one maintain an advocacy role when the employee retains an attorney to assure his or her rights? What is the appropriate position to take when an employer challenges the work relatedness of an injury or the degree of residual disability following recovery? In most instances, the case manager shuld focus on the primary task of helping return to work and avoid giving opinions that may affect legal issues.

The Worksite Environment

The workers' compensation case manager must also know the world of work and be aware of the issues that can facilitate or hamper early return to work. Knowledge of the employer's policies and procedures about work-related injuries and absence from work is essential: Does the employer require the employee to take a leave of absence until fully recovered? Does the employer have a formula for how long the employee can remain off the job before the job is no longer available? Does the employer provide modified work assignments? Does the employer have a contract with a union? If so, what are the prohibitions for returning a worker to modified duty?

The workers' compensation case manager must also determine how the injury could affect the employee's duties on the job. Is there a job description? If not, the case manager must write one or get an appropriate professional to observe the worksite and get the information for writing one. In addition, the workers' compensation case manager must know how to use the *Dictionary of Occupational Titles* to categorized jobs and identify transferable skills.

Compensation Issues

The workers' compensation case manager must know that indemnity benefits are non-taxable and additional income may be derived from insurance payments for home, automobile, and other loans during the period of disability. If the combined indemnity benefits and insurance payments exceed the pre-injury take home pay, there is a disincentive to recover and return to work.

Vocational Rehabilitation Concerns

The workers' compensation case manager must know when to make referrals for vocational rehabilitation and what it will be able to do for the disabled employee in terms of both functional restoration and vocational training and placement. In particular, the case manager must be careful to avoid recommendations that contradict the employer's policies and procedures (e.g., suggesting retraining when it is last on the employer's list of available options.)

THE PROCESS OF CASE MANAGEMENT IN WORKERS' COMPENSATION

When the case manager tries to apply the principles of quality service and cost containment to the management of a workers' compensation claim, the issue of indemnity may take precedence. For instance:

> Dr. J. manages all back injury cases alike. Before he institutes treatment, he likes to include the use of an magnetic reorance imaging (MRI) scan in making a diagnosis, whether the MRI is considered medically necessary or not. In a general health insurance claim under utilization review, Dr. J. would probably be denied certification for an MRI when the diagnosis is a simple back strain. However, in a workers' compensation claim, even with utilization review, Dr. J. says, "No imaging study, no treatment, *and* no release to work." This means indemnity costs continue. In addition, in the states where employees have the right to choose their own physicians, redirection of care to avoid such a situation is difficult if not impossible.

In this instance, standards of care and cost containment cannot be the primary focus. Instead, getting the employee what the chosen physician says is necessary for treatment, in a timely manner, must be recognized as positively affecting the return to work goal. Once the diagnosis of back strain/sprain is confirmed by a negative MRI for disc involvement, the worker will probably get needed treatment. An unnecessary diagnostic study has been done, with its attendant costs, but necessary treatment has been provided, which allows an earlier return to work. The fact that extended disability compounds the problems of returning an employee to pre-injury work enhances the cost-effectiveness of this case management decision. (Of course this does not preclude attempting to change the physician's method of diagnosis by another means such as peer-to-peer discussion about treatment practice which the case manager can arrange.)

The question the workers' compensation case manager must always ask is, "What can I do to facilitate an early, appropriate, and productive return to work?" In order to answer this question, the case manger must know how to apply the problem-solving process. (In the nursing profession, this is called the nursing process.)

The problem-solving process requires data gathering. The workers' compensation case manager gathers data that will identify both assets and problem areas in achieving the goal of timely return to work. Such data includes what the employee thinks about his or her work and about his or her employer; what the employer thinks about the employee and his or her performance, and what the physician understands about what both the employee and the employer think. Data will also include a job description and will compare that description to the functional effects of the work-related injury or illness. Exploring the data allows the workers' compensation case manager to identify problems in returning to work and help the employee set goals for problem resolution. Appropriate interventions should be considered in light of quality care, cost containment, the legal extent of coverage, and the issue of continued indemnity.

As the facilitator in problem solving, the workers' compensation case manager must collaborate with employee and employer to set realistic goals. Inherent in the problem-solving process is the evaluation of effectiveness of interventions and decisions about whether goals have been met. The workers' compensation case manager must therefore monitor the effectiveness of the selected interventions and recommend changes in the problem-solving process if the goals are not met. The case manager also plays the role of coordinator in the medical care process when an independent medical evaluator recommends a change in treatment. This is because the case manager is ideally positioned for negotiating the change with employee and physician.

Facilitating Employer-Employee Relationships

In assisting an employee back to preinjury work, the workers' compensation case manager must also understand and respond to a variety of critical factors having little to do with medical issues. For example, a study done at Boeing Aircraft shows that nonmedical factors such as job dissatisfaction and poor performance appraisals can be critical factors in achieving the return-to-work goal.[1] When these factors are present in a workers' compensation case, the case manager may need to help employee and employer to improve their relationship.

Family situations (e.g. a terminally ill family member or a wife with a complicated pregnancy) can also cause discord and impair treatment effectiveness. In this situation, the workers' compensation case manager may need to become a counselor, helping to keep the employee's return to work in primary focus and possibly offering the employee guidance in managing stressful situations.

WHO SHOULD TAKE THE ROLE OF WORKERS' COMPENSATION CASE MANAGER?

Insurance claims adjustors sometimes begin to function as case managers in claims, but typically their case load is too large to permit them to do anything more than monitor medical treatment and progress and make decisions about the extent of work disability. Employers often can provide more effective case managers who interact face to face with employees, their treating physicians, and their attorneys (if there is a dispute). Insurance companies and/or administrative agencies may also employ or contract with case managers, who most often are specially trained nurses. Overall, the case manager who is employed by the state workers' compensation agency is less likely to be biased and can act in the advocate role of communicating with all other interested parties in the system.

Registered professional nurses are frequently considered most knowledgeable in fulfilling the role of case manager. The preparation of the registered professional nurse (R.N.) ensures that the problem-solving approach (the nursing process) will be used, and the R.N. is usually able to communicate the concerns of both the employee and the employer to the attending physician. Furthermore, the attending physician is more likely to interact with the R.N. on a collaborative level than with an insurance claims adjustor.

A tiered approach to case management may also eventually develop, with state agencies, health plans, or insurers providing the basic framework for claims in the aggregate, and case managers in the field providing the one-on-one contacts as they work with individual claimants, providers, and employers.

THE FUTURE OF WORKERS' COMPENSATION CASE MANAGEMENT

As with any other facet of health care delivery, the future of workers' compensation case management is largely dependent on what results from national and state health care reforms.

As of this writing, there are major health care reform proposals before Congress. Only one, the Clinton Administration's Health Security Act (H.R. 3600/S.1757), includes workers' compensation and automobile insurance (Title 10) within the proposed new delivery system. With coordination, insurers (private carriers and state funds) would continue to maintain financial control of an entire workers' compensation claim with reference to medical and wage-replacement benefits. The insurers, then, will offer to employers various health plans purchased from health alliances, and employers, in turn, will offer these health plans to their employees.

In general, health plans will provide services for injured workers, or arrange for them to be provided although a state may also designate specialized workers' compensation providers for one or more types of work-related injuries or illnesses. In any case, the Clinton proposal states that each health plan must "employ or contract with one or more individuals, such as occupational health nurses, with experience in the treatment of occupational illness and injury to provide case management services." This section of the proposal further specifies the functions of the case manager: to ensure that there is an appropriate treatment plan that facilitates return to work, that the plan is coordinated with the workers' compensation carrier, and that the plan complies with legal duties and requirements of the state workers' compensation law.

While such direct recognition of case management is positive, there could be problems if the administration's proposal, including Title 10, passes. For example, the health plans' case managers have no direct accountability to insurers or employers about the outcome of medical treatment. Thus, there is potential for conflict between a health plan's case manager and an insurer's or employer's case manager (and even the state administrative agency) about the best course of treatment for achieving an employee's early return to work.

Some states are not waiting for federal legislation that may affect workers' compensation, however, but are instead undertaking various demonstration projects in managed care. Oregon, California, Florida, and Maine have legislation supporting 24-hour coverage pilot programs that presumably would approximate the coordinated approach described in Title 10. A number of states (e.g., Minnesota, Florida, New Hampshire, and Oregon) are also supporting other approaches to managed care, and still others are considering projects or supportive legislation.

All in all, it would appear that the era of managed care has arrived for workers' compensation—which until recently, has been described as "the last bastion of the open medical checkbook." Case management, the key component of workers' compensation managed care, will develop over the coming years as various public and private entities involved in the delivery of workers' compensation medical services adopt a managed care approach.

1.   Michele C. Battie and Stanley J. Bigus, M.D., "Industrial Back Pain Complaints," *Orthopeace Clinics of North America,* 22(2) April, 1991.

43. Walking a Fine Line:
Managing the Conflicting Obligations
of the Americans with Disabilities Act
and Workers' Compensation Laws
Carla R. Walworth   Lisa J. Damon   Carole F. Wilder

As lawsuits are beginning to be filed under the ADA, one thing is clear—the majority of suits are being filed against employers by current employees rather than by job applicants with claims regarding the hiring process. Among the areas upon which the ADA may have the greatest impact are company medical examination and reporting procedures, return-to-work policies, and stipulations and agreements in workers' compensation proceedings. This article offers some practical suggestions to assist employers in complying with the ADA as they seek to reduce workers' compensation claims.

For employers attempting to wind their way through the thicket of the Americans with Disabilities Act (ADA), there are innumerable questions, very few absolute answers, and plenty of room for judgment calls. Employers that were taught that consistent treatment of employees avoided discrimination problems have had the tables turned. Now, the ADA counsels just the opposite—each case must be evaluated on its own facts. Inconsistent treatment must be considered and may even be required. The age of fact-specific judgment calls is here and with it the increased potential for litigation.

Because the ADA provides protection to employees who are "disabled" under the ADA, including workers' compensation claimants in states where workers' compensation laws are "the exclusive remedy" for on-the-job injuries, one of the many problems faced by employers under the ADA is the tension between the obligations of disability law and workers' compensation requirements. Many company policies and procedures that relate to workers' compensation claimants may violate the ADA. For example, some company medical examination and reporting procedures that have been instituted to reduce workers' compensation claims may violate the ADA. Additionally, employers may unwittingly provide a workers' compensation claimant with the protections of the ADA merely by virtue of the labels used in internal documentation or the provisions of settlements.

Such problems are compounded by the extensive damages available to successful plaintiffs. As a result of the Civil Rights Act of 1991, employers accustomed to the back pay damage limitation under Title VII are facing an abrupt awakening with the potential of a successful plaintiff receiving punitive and compensatory damages for a violation of the ADA.

In this rapidly changing climate, companies should review their workers' compensation policies and procedures with an understanding of how these policies may be affected by the ADA. This review must be accompanied by a new awareness that the employee relations or employment law component of a company can no longer operate in isolation from those that process and monitor workers' compensation claims. Now, every workers' compensation claimant is a potential ADA plaintiff. Companies need to approach these problems cohesively and with full knowledge of employer rights and obligations under the ADA.

ARE WORKERS' COMPENSATION CLAIMANTS "DISABLED" UNDER THE ADA?

The definition of "disability" under the ADA may sometimes—but not always—coincide with the concept of disability under workers' compensation laws. Thus, some, but not all, workers' compensation claimants may also be covered under the ADA.

Employees Covered Under the ADA

Title I of the Americans with Disabilities Act applies to any employer with twenty-five or more employees as of July 26, 1992. Its coverage will be extended to employers with fifteen or more employees on July 26, 1994. Generally, the ADA prohibits covered employers from discriminating against an otherwise "qualified individual with disability" and requires such employers to make "reasonable accommodation" to employees and applicants with disabilities to allow them to perform the essential functions of the job.

An employee may be covered by the ADA if he or she has a physical or mental impairment that substantially limits one or more major life activities, has a record of a substantially limiting impairment, or is "regarded as having a substantially limiting impairment." "Major life activities" include walking, speaking, breathing, performing manual tasks, hearing, learning, caring for oneself, and working. Among the physical or mental conditions that may be considered disabilities as defined by the ADA are a heart condition, a back condition that prevents a person from working in any heavy labor job, arthritis that significantly restricts an individual from performing manual tasks, or a stress disorder diagnosed by a psychiatrist.

Temporary conditions that have little or no long-term impact are not considered disabilities under the ADA. For example, a broken leg that heals normally within a few months would not be a disability under the ADA.

Employees Covered Under Workers' Compensation Acts

State workers' compensation statutes generally provide benefits to employees for job-related injuries, whether or not the injury is permanently disabling. In addition to reimbursement for medical care and treatment for job-related injuries, workers' compensation statutes typically also provide benefits for temporary incapacity, scarring, and permanent impairment of specific parts of the body.

Workers' Compensation Claimants Who May Be Covered Under the ADA

Although not all workers' compensation claimants will be covered under the ADA, many will. For example, a construction worker who falls from a ladder and breaks a leg that heals normally within a few months would not be considered a person with a disability under the ADA because the injury is "temporary," even if the worker is awarded workers' compensation benefits for the injury. Unfortunately, for an employer attempting to assess its legal obligations, when an employee has a workers' compensation injury it is often impossible to determine if the employee is or will be disabled for ADA purposes. For instance, if the broken leg results in a permanent limp that substantially limits the workers' ability to walk, the worker might eventually be considered disabled under the ADA.

Some state workers' compensation statutes can also, by their terms, define someone as disabled. In Massachusetts, for instance, if an employee who has been out on workers' compensation is returned to the job with accommodations and is, thereafter, terminated within one year of returning to work, the employee is *presumed* to have been disabled.

THE INTERACTION BETWEEN THE ADA AND WORKERS' COMPENSATION LAWS

The following are some of the areas in which the ADA is most likely to affect a company's workers' compensation policies and programs.

Preemption of State Workers' Compensation Statutes by the ADA

The ADA does not invalidate any state law that affords greater protection to the disabled. More specifically, the EEOC's Technical Assistance Manual states that the requirements of the ADA supersede any conflicting state workers' compensation laws. One of the principal areas of conflict concerns medical examinations and inquiries.

Medical Examinations and Inquiries Under the ADA and Workers' Compensation Laws

The ADA regulates medical examinations and inquiries and may affect a company's workers' compensation policy at the application stage, the conditional job offer/preemployment stage, and during employment.

Application Stage

As part of its prohibition of discrimination against disabled individuals, the ADA generally prohibits employers from requiring medical examinations or inquiring into an applicant's or employee's medical background or condition, except in very narrow circumstances. At the preemployment stage, an employer cannot require an applicant to submit to a medical examination or inquire whether the applicant has a disability, or the nature or severity of the disability. This provision of the ADA prohibits employers from inquiring about an applicant's workers' compensation history on an employment application, or in any other way, before a conditional offer of employment is made. It supersedes and, in effect, nullifies provisions in workers' compensation statutes, such as Rhode Island's, that penalize employees for failure to disclose their workers' compensation history on employment applications requesting such information.

> Although employers can no longer make a preoffer inquiry into an applicant's workers' compensation history, employers can continue to insist on honesty and full disclosure of material facts in the hiring process. One possible method of protection is to provide an applicant with a job description. Then during the interview, the essential functions of the position can be reviewed, and the applicant can be asked whether he or she can perform them. The applicant should provide the answer in writing and acknowledge by signing that the job

description has been reviewed and that he or she can or cannot perform the essential functions of the job.

The statement should also indicate that the applicant understands that any false statements, omissions, or misrepresentations by the applicant may result in the termination of the hiring process, the termination of employment, if the applicant has been hired, or the termination or restriction of benefits, whenever the false statement, omission, or misrepresentation is discovered. Employers should discuss the possibility of reasonable accommodation with applicants who indicate an inability to perform the essential functions of the job.

With these protections in place, employers may be able to limit or terminate workers' compensation benefits or damages for discrimination in situations in which an employee made a false statement or misrepresentation on the employment application. For example, an employer may not be required to pay workers' compensation benefits to an employee in a job requiring heavy lifting if the employee deliberately failed to disclose a severe back condition that would have barred the employee from being hired in the first place.

Conditional Job Offer/Preemployment Stage

After making a conditional job offer, an employer *may* require a medical examination or conduct a medical inquiry, including questions about a person's workers' compensation history, if the examination and inquiry are required of all entering employees in the same job category.

The employer cannot revoke a job offer because of a history of previous disabling on-the-job injuries without violating the ADA unless the employer can demonstrate that the applicant is unable to perform the essential functions of the job, even with reasonable accommodation, because of the previous injury. The employer may also use the information obtained in employment entrance medical examinations, inquiries, and workers' compensation history to (1) screen out applicants with a history of fraudulent workers' compensation claims or (2) screen out individuals who would pose a "direct threat" to their own health or safety or that of others, if that threat could not be reduced to an acceptable level or eliminated by a reasonable accommodation.

Employers seeking to rely on the direct-threat exception to exclude applicants who are at risk of an on-the-job injury should be aware that the EEOC interprets the term "direct threat" very stringently and narrowly. The risk must be a current, specific, significant risk of substantial harm based on objective medical or other factual evidence regarding a particular individual that cannot be eliminated or reduced by reasonable accommodation. A determination that a worker will be unable to perform a job in the future or that a worker may cause increased health insurance or worker' compensation costs or will have excessive absenteeism is not sufficient to establish a current risk. For example, an employer may not refuse to hire an applicant for a heavy labor job with a disk condition that a physician has indicated might become worse in eight or ten years, or cause the worker to be absent form work.

And, even where there is a significant risk of substantial harm to health or safety, an employer cannot deny employment to a disabled worker if a reasonable accommodation, such as the provision of modified equipment or a modified work schedule, would eliminate or reduce the risk. Thus, for example, an employer could not revoke a job offer to a hearing impaired bus driver if the driver could perform his job with a hearing aid without a safety risk.

During Employment

For current employees, employers can only require medical examinations or make medical inquiries of employees if the examination or inquiry is "job related and consistent with business necessity." If an employee has an on-the-job injury that appears to affect the employee's ability to perform essential job functions, a medical examination or inquiry is job related and consistent with business necessity. A medical examination or inquiry may also be necessary to assist in determining whether a reasonable accommodation can be provided. An employer may also require, as a condition of returning to work, that an injured employee have a job-related medical examination—not a full physical exam—to determine whether the employee can perform job-related functions without posing a direct threat to health or safety.

Even when a job-related injury does not affect an employee's ability to perform essential job functions, an employer should still be able to require a workers' compensation claimant to undergo a medical examination and provide the employer with medical records and information to verify (1) the compensability of the claim and (2) that the medical treatment for which the employer is paying is medically necessary to treat the job-related injury.

Although neither the ADA, the regulations interpreting it, nor the EEOC guidelines address the issue, medical examinations and inquiries under these circumstances are necessary to protect employers from fraudulent claims, and therefore should not violate the ADA, if the information obtained is used only for this job-related purpose.

Thus, the ADA does not appear to conflict with state workers' compensation statutes that require workers' compensation claimants to have medical examinations and submit records of such examinations to their employers. For example, in Connecticut, employees claiming or receiving workers' compensation benefits must submit to a medical examination and have reports of the examination submitted to the employer. Similarly, Maine's workers' compensation statute requires employees receiving workers' compensation to provide employers with copies of all medical reports. Likewise, in Rhode Island, employees receiving workers' compensation benefits must file a copy of the initial medical treatment report with the employer. And, in Alabama, employers are not liable for costs of medical or surgical treatment obtained by an employee without "justification or notice" to the employer.[1]

Compliance with the ADA may require, however, that the examinations and reports obtained are limited to provide only the information necessary to verify the compensability for the claim, the appropriateness of the treatment for the job-related injury, and the ability of the claimant to perform the essential functions of the job, with or without a reasonable accommodation. The mere fact that the employer did not request broad-based information is not sufficient; employers must take affirmative steps to *limit* the information received and reviewed.

Employers should work with their medical providers to establish criteria for the disclosure of medical information. For instance, employers generally should not receive specific test results, detailed diagnoses, medical advice to the employee, or information regarding the employee's family or medical history. Thus, for example, an employer may require a warehouse laborer with a back injury that impairs the ability to lift to have a back examination by an orthopedist and may receive information regarding that examination, but may not require or obtain the results of an HIV or cardiac test done on the employee.

The ADA also does not appear to conflict with state workers' compensation statutes that require workers' compensation claimants to give notice to their employers of the "nature" of their injuries. Like medical examinations and reports, a description of the nature of an employee's injury is necessary to enable an employer to assess the compensability of a claim, the effect of an injury on the employee's ability to perform essential job functions, and the need for reasonable accommodation. Again, this disclosure as to the nature of the injury should be limited to job-related information only.

Protecting the Confidentiality of Medical Records

Information obtained in permitted medical examinations and inquiries is a "confidential medical record," and must be collected and maintained in a separate medical file in a locked cabinet, apart from personnel files. Access to the file and the information contained in it must be strictly limited and disclosed only under the following circumstances:

> (i) supervisors and managers may be informed regarding necessary restrictions on the work or duties of the employee and necessary accommodations;
>
> (ii) first aid safety personnel may be informed, when appropriate, if the disability might require emergency treatment; and
>
> (iii) government officials investigating compliance with this chapter shall be provided relevant information on request.[2]

Thus, employers must be careful not to discuss or disclose medical information about an employee with an employee's coworkers or supervisors when investigating a workers' compensation claim. Self-insured employers need to be particularly vigilant in this area because the very nature of this arrangement involves obtaining medical records that may contain non-job-related information. Self-insured employers should take whatever precautions are necessary to limit the disclosure of medical information. Generally, supervisors and managers should be given no more medical information than they need to know to make accommodations for a disabled employee. Supervisors and managers should not have access to the medical file and should not be provided with medical reports.

Information obtained in permitted medical examinations or inquiries may be submitted to state workers' compensation offices and second injury funds without violating the confidentiality requirements of the ADA.

Returning to Work: Reasonable Accommodation and Light Duty

The ADA requires employers to make reasonable accommodations, if requested by the employee, to enable a disabled employee to perform essential functions of the job and to enjoy equal benefits and privileges as other similarly situated employees who are not disabled. Reasonable accommodations may include a leave of absence; job restructuring; part-time or modified work schedule; reassignment to a vacant position; acquisition or modification of equipment; appropriate adjustments or modifications of examinations; training materials, or policies; and the provision of qualified readers or interpreters.

> Employers should be aware that an employee who is disabled as result of an on-the-job injury will trigger the reasonable accommodation provisions of the ADA when he or she returns to work. Under the ADA, an employer cannot refuse to allow an employee with a disability to return to work because the worker is not fully recovered from an injury if the worker can perform the essential functions of the job, with or without an accommodation. There is a very limited exception for employees who would pose a significant risk of substantial harm that could not be reduced to an acceptable level with reasonable accommodation. The ADA does permit employers to make inquiries or medical examinations to determine whether the employee can perform essential job functions without posing a risk of harm and what, if any, accommodations are necessary.

Although some state workers' compensation statutes require an employer to transfer a claimant to work that is suited to the employee's incapacity, if such work is available, the penalties for noncompliance are generally limited. Under Connecticut's workers' compensation statute, for example, an employer that fails to transfer a claimant to an available suitable job may be subject to a penalty of not more than $500. In contrast, under the ADA, failure to make reasonable accommodations to enable otherwise qualified disabled employees to return to work may subject employers to heavy compensatory and punitive damages.

However, employers that can convince a jury that a good-faith effort was made to reasonably accommodate an employee may avoid the imposition of monetary damages. The Civil Rights Act of 1991 provides that employers found to have failed to reasonably accommodate an employee or applicant may avoid monetary damages and, instead, be subject solely to injunctive relief if the jury finds a good-faith effort.

Prior to the ADA, many employers created "light-duty" positions as a means to reemploy returning workers' compensation claimants with physical restrictions. Although these positions may be viewed as reasonable accommodations under the ADA, the ADA does not mandate that employers create light-duty positions to accommodate disabled employees. However, when nonessential job functions can be transferred to coworkers, the ADA requires employers to restructure jobs by transferring that work to others as a reasonable accommodation to disabled employees. Also, if an employer has a vacant light-duty position available, reassigning a disabled worker to that position may be a reasonable accommodation. These light-duty positions must be open to employees disabled either on or off the job. If the light-duty position is only a temporary job, the reassignment only needs to be for a temporary period. Any limits on duration should be clearly specified, however, prior to the job assignment.

An employer may also be required to provide additional reasonable accommodation to enable an injured employee to perform the essential functions of a light-duty job, even if it is only temporary. Similarly, employers offering light-duty positions may not be absolved from further ADA-mandated reasonable accommodation. For instance, an employer may not be able to require a returning employee to take a light-duty position if other reasonable accommodations could be made to allow the employee to continue in his or her regular position. Additionally, if all of the light-duty positions are filled, an employer may not be able to take the position that it need make no other reasonable accommodations to a returning disabled employee.

The extent of reasonable accommodations that may be required for a returning worker is reflected in the example of a telephone line repair worker who seeks to return to work after breaking both legs as a result of an on-the-job fall. If the worker is unable to walk, even with crutches, for nine months, for example, she may meet the ADA's definition of "disabled." Because the employee is in a wheelchair and cannot do her previous job, as a reasonable accommodation her employer may be required to place her in a light-duty position for which she is qualified, such as a clerical position relating to line repair, if such a position is available. If the office to which she is assigned is not wheelchair-accessible, it may be a further reasonable accommodation to place her in an office that is accessible or to modify the office to make it accessible, if it would not be an undue hardship to do so. The employer might also have to modify the employee's work schedule so that she could attend physical therapy sessions.

Thus, although an injured employee's certification for light-duty work may signal the end of workers' compensation payments, it may also trigger obligations under the ADA. For employers with proactive return-to-work and light-duty programs, the accommodation requirements of the ADA will be entirely consistent with these goals. For employers that take the position that they have no light-duty work and cannot modify work requirements for worker's compensation claimants, the ADA mandates reevaluation of these policies.

Internal Documentation, Stipulations, and Agreements in Workers' Compensation Proceedings May Trigger ADA Coverage

An employer can unwittingly trigger its ADA obligations in the workers' compensation arena. For example, a letter stating that an employee is "out with a disability" may subsequently bar the employer from arguing that the employee has a temporary condition and not a disability. Thus, the employer should review all internal documentation to avoid the unintentional use of the term "disabled" when referring to a workers' compensation claimant. Instead, documentation should refer to the individual's "injury" or "medical condition." Employees who supervise the workers' compensation claim process should also be trained to avoid the label of "disability" in internal notes and records, which may be discoverable if litigation is brought, and in their discussions with employees, as any such statements may be considered admissions by an employer.

> Employers can also trigger ADA obligations when settling a workers' compensation claim. If, for example, an employer stipulates in a workers' compensation proceeding that the injured employee has a permanent partial impairment of the leg, the employer subsequently may be unable to dispute the disability, and the employee would then be entitled to all of the protections of the ADA, including reasonable accommodation in the workplace. Thus, employers may unintentionally establish ADA coverage for workers who might not otherwise be entitled to such protections by entering into stipulations or agreements in workers' compensation proceedings intended for another purpose. Employers should, therefore, review all such stipulations and agreements with an understanding of their implications under the ADA.

Employers may also wish to consider having an employee release any ADA claims as part of a workers' compensation settlement. Before requiring such a release, however, state law should be reviewed. Some states, like Massachusetts, prohibit a workers' compensation settlement that includes the release of other specified claims. In such states, employers that want the protection of a full release need to ensure that separate consideration is provided for the release of non-workers'-compensation claims and that the language of the release reflects the statutory restrictions.

CONCLUSION

The broad scope of the ADA affects all disabled employees, including those injured on the job who also are receiving workers' compensation benefits. Despite state workers' compensation statutes that may allow employers access to a claimant's complete medical record, employers will now be required to limit the scope of medical examinations and inquiries regarding employees injured on the job. To avoid the risk of liability under the ADA, employers will also have to take care to protect the confidentiality of the medical records they are permitted to receive. Employers should also be aware that workers injured on the job who either have a substantially limiting impairment or are regarded as having such an impairment may trigger an employer's obligation to make a reasonable accommodation so that the injured employee can return to work.

1. *United States v. Bear Bros., Inc.* 355 So. 2d 1133 (Ala. Civ. App. 1978).

2. 42 USC § 12221(d)(3)(B).

Part 13

INSURANCE ISSUES

44.   Hedging Health Care Financial Risks with Health Care Futures

James A. Hayes

There is nothing wrong with being big or a bully, but it is no longer necessary to be just big or just a bully to be efficient and imaginative in health care financial management. Many markets such as energy, interest rates (including mortgages and government securities), agriculture, precious metals, and others have found new, efficient ways to reduce financial risk in recent years by hedging with "derivatives." To simplify and to emphasize key ideas about hedging, this article focuses on hedging with futures contracts.

Financial management of risk in health care markets is unnecessarily primitive and expensive. The two most common, antiquated methods of managing risk are being big or being a bully. For example, a managed care company can be so big that it cross-subsidizes current unexpected losses for one group by future larger-than-expected premiums for other groups or lines of business.

Large purchasers of health care such as Medicare and some self-funded companies can bully providers into assuming all financial risk and lower prices than would otherwise prevail because, since they have more market power than local providers, they can cost shift to weaker buyers. Single payers and purchasing alliances reduce expenditures because they are bullies.

Derivatives include futures, options, and swaps. When properly used, they protect companies from unexpected financial risk. Whether "big or small" or "bully or victim," hedging not only levels the economic playing field but also promotes innovation in risk sharing.

WHAT IS A FUTURES CONTRACT?

A futures contract is an agreement between two parties to buy and sell a specified commodity at a mutually agreeable price and time in the future. For example, a gold futures contract specifies that a 100 ounce bar from specific gold refiners with a given purity and weight tolerance, among other technical matters, is to be traded. It will be sold by party A and purchased by party B today for, say, $400 per ounce for delivery 6 months from now. Although the price is $400 per ounce for 100 ounces for a total of $40,000, the buyer does not pay the entire amount today nor does the seller receive the amount today. Only if the buyer takes delivery of the gold bar, will he pay the seller $40,000.

Any time between now and six months from now either party may find some other buyer or seller to take their place. The first buyer may change his or her mind two months from now but before the six months have passed for some legitimate business reason and sell his or her contract at the then current market price to another buyer. In effect buyers (or sellers) can substitute themselves unilaterally at the current market price.

In actively traded markets the ability to move in and out of hedges to protect against sudden, abrupt changes in financial risk is a competitive advantage compared to the sometimes protracted negotiations that are required to modify contracts between 2 companies in private markets. As a result, one of the hallmarks of hedging at futures exchanges is flexibility and speed to meet the challenges of rapidly changing financial risk in local markets.

A limitation of hedging at futures exchanges is that your financial risk must be highly correlated with futures prices over time. As your risk changes, the futures price must change for a hedge to work. If not highly correlated, do not hedge. Exaggerated, futures markets protect everyone or no one. For example, if most or many indemnity insurers have higher-than-expected claims costs for flu-related illnesses, they can hedge against those costs to some extent. On the other hand, if just one insurer has one more heart-lung transplant than expected, it cannot hedge against that unexpected expense in the futures market. It should use stop-loss reinsurance as an alternative.

A futures exchange provides a trading floor where brokers, usually acting on behalf of their clients, execute these agreements. It also provides certain regulatory compliance, credit guarantees, and other administrative support services for buyers and sellers. All U.S. futures exchanges are regulated by an agency of the federal government, the Commodities Futures Trading Commission (CFTC).

WHAT IS HEDGING?

Hedging is the art and science of buying or selling a futures contract at the same time usual business is being conducted, with the result that financial risk is reduced or eliminated. Futures contracts can be designed for many parts of financial risks in complicated health insurance and health services markets.

For example, futures contracts could be designed for indemnity insurance premiums and claims, as well as managed care premiums. In addition, futures contracts could be designed to hedge prices of health services, for example, capitation rates for hospital and physician services—either in combination or separately. They can also be designed for insurance premiums for different parts of the country, retiree benefits, and long-term care.

To appreciate the different hedging possibilities of futures contracts for health care broadly defined, consider the existing futures markets for government securities. Currently, in the United States between the Chicago Board of Trade (CBOT) and the Chicago Mercantile Exchange (CME) there are four futures contracts to hedge interest rates for U.S. government securities.

A treasury bills futures contract trades at the CME, and two treasury note and one treasury bond futures contracts trade at the CBOT. Virtually the entire yield curve can be hedged or cross-hedged in these contracts. A cross-hedge is when one interest rate does not have its own futures contract but is highly correlated with another interest rate that has its own futures contract. Many residential mortgages are hedged while they are bought, sold, or held in the secondary mortgage markets by investors. Many mortgage lenders will cross-hedge anticipated interest rates that they expect to offer prospective home buyers in the near future.

By analogy, virtually any financial risk in health care can be hedged or cross-hedged in one or more health care futures contracts. This article describes just a few possibilities.

HOW AN INDEMNITY INSURER HEDGES CLAIMS

Suppose an indemnity insurance company is paid a $100 premium by an employer for health insurance for the upcoming benefit period. The insurer expects $80 in claims, $15 in administrative expense, and $5 in profit. If paid claims turn out to be $85 or more, then the profit margin is wiped out or there is a net loss. How can the insurer protect itself? In the absence of hedging with futures, the insurer could protect itself by buying reinsurance, cross-subsidizing any losses from other lines or groups, or simply taking its chances that paid claims will be less than or equal to expected claims.

An indemnity claims futures contract could (one has already been designed by the Chicago Board of Trade) hedge the expected $80 in claims. This futures contract would be designed so that, as claims begin to rise (fall) unexpectedly, the futures price rises (falls). At any given time the futures contract price will equal the expected claims. If expected claims are $80, then the futures price is about $80. If expected claims rise to $85 (fall to $75), then the futures price rises to about $85 (falls to $75). Therefore, the insurer "hedges" higher-than-expected claims by buying a futures contract when the agreement to insure is made between the insurer and insured and $80 in claims are expected.

Here's the way it works in greater detail. The insurer is able to hedge $80 in claims because when claims unexpectedly rise to $85, the futures price rises to $85. The insurer pays $85 in claims to providers, and owns a futures contract that appreciated in price from $80 to $85. The insurer now sells that contract for $85, netting a $5 profit before any transaction expenses. The $5 hedging profit offsets the $85 claims payout for a net payout of $80.

Conversely, the hedged claims could have come in at $75. The insurer pays $75 in claims, about which it is delighted, but the futures contract it bought at $80, fearing higher-than-expected claims also fell to $75. The futures contract is sold by the buyer at $75 for a $5 hedging loss. The sum of the $75 claims payout plus $5 hedging loss is $80. *Regardless* of the direction of change of claims, $80 net is paid out.

HOW A PROVIDER HEDGES INDEMNITY CLAIMS PAYMENTS

A provider has an expected claims payment gross cash flow of $80 from the insurer described above. Of the $80, the provider expects $75 in expenses with a residual $5 profit. However, it fears claims payments could unexpectedly be $75 or less rather than $80. In that case its profits are gone, perhaps even resulting in a loss.

How does it hedge with a futures contract? Since futures prices fall when claims fall unexpectedly, it should sell a futures contract at $80 at the beginning of the benefit period when it fears the possible, but not yet realized, lower gross cash flow. If claims are $75, then the provider receives $75 from the insurer. But since it hedged at $80, the futures price also fell to $75. The provider buys back a futures contract at $75 for a $5 hedging profit. The $5 hedging profit plus the $75 claims payments is a net cash flow of $80, which is the objective. Had the claims payments increased to $85, the provider receives the $85 from the insurer but sold a futures contract that later rose from $80 to $85. Buying back a futures contract at $85 that it sold for $80 produces a $5 hedging loss. A $5 hedging loss plus the $85 claims payments is $80. *Regardless* of the direction of change of claims, $80 net is received.

HOW AN EMPLOYER HEDGES INDEMNITY PREMIUMS

An employer could hedge indemnity premiums in an indemnity premium futures contract or cross-hedge in an indemnity claims contract. Moreover, if managed care premiums were highly correlated with either futures contract, they could be cross-hedged in either contract.

Assume an indemnity premium futures contract is trading. The time is six months before scheduled contract negotiations with the local Blue Cross & Blue Shield Plan for the next yearly benefit period. Six-months claims experience from the first half of the current benefit period has been reported and shows a 10 percent trend factor. That means the $100 premium last year will increase by at least 10 percent, or $10, for the next benefit year, if current trends continue. The futures price for indemity premiums for six months from now is $110, confirming general expectations.

How should the employer hedge against a higher-than-expected trend factor in the second half of the year? Since the indemity premium futures contract goes up when premiums go up, the employer should buy the contract now for $110 to protect itself against higher-than-expected premiums due to higher-than-expected trends in the second half of the year.

Sure enough, the second half trend is 20 percent rather than 10 percent, and the yearly average is a 15 percent trend factor. The indemnity premium is $115. By buying a premium futures contract for $110 before the second-half trend factor was known, the employer locked in a $110 *net* premium, even though every other employer that did not hedge will pay $115. The employer pays $115 to the insurer but receives a $5 hedging profit from the sale of the futures contract, which appreciated from $110 to $115 for a net $110 premium.

Had the second half trend been unexpectedly lower, say, a 5 percent annual trend, the premium would have been $105. In that case the employer pays the insurer $105 and has a $5 hedging loss for a *net* premium of $110. Regardless of the direction of change of the trend factor, the employer locked in the premium for the next benefit period six months in advance of negotiations and documented claims experience.

HOW AN INSURER HEDGES MULTIYEAR CAPITATION RATES

A futures contract for capitation rates for hospital and physician services for a given set of benefits is designed with a three-year horizon and quarterly contract months. At any given time 12 capitation futures contracts for the next 12 quarters are trading, and futures prices for each quarter are available to the public.

An insurer wants to negotiate annual capitation rates for three successive years with local providers all at once, at the beginning of the three-year period. To simplify the arithmetic, assume the capitation market expects a $2 increase from one quarter to the next, for all 12 quarters. The first quarter is $100; the second is $102; the third is $104; and the 12th quarter is $122. The following table summarizes these data:

Capitation Futures Price Data for Three Years

Year/Quarter	Quarter	Amount	Yearly Total
1/1	1	$100	
1/2	2	102	
1/3	3	104	
1/4	4	106	$ 412
2/1	5	108	
2/2	6	110	
2/3	7	112	
2/4	8	114	$ 444
3/1	9	116	
3/2	10	118	
3/3	11	120	
3/4	12	122	$ 476
Total			$1,332

Here is an annotated list of the steps the insurer will take to negotiate the three-year fixed rate capitation rate:

1. Buy 12 separate futures contract at each price now; and
2. Simultaneously close the deal for a three-year fixed capitation rate of $412 for the first year, $444 for the second year, and $476 for the third year, for a total of $1,332.

Regardless of what happens to capitation rates over the next 12 quarters or three years, the insurer has locked in a total cost of $1,332. The insurer locked in an implied inflation rate of 3 percent for the first year, 2.78 percent for the second year, and 2.59 percent for the third year, at the beginning of the first year.

That local prices might be lower or higher than the futures prices is immaterial as long as the difference is constant. For example, if California rates are always $3 above futures prices, then the insurers in California will still buy the 12 futures contracts at the start of the three-year benefit period, but the capitation rate that is offered to local providers is $3 higher for each quarter. The first year rate is $424; the second year is $456; and the third year rate is $488. The total three-year price is $1,366, or $36 higher than otherwise would have happened. Even though local California rates are always $3 higher, they are perfectly hedgeable. When they increase unexpectedly from $105 to $106 in the second quarter of the first year, the futures price rises from $102 to $103. Since the insurer bought that contract at $102 and sells it for $103 for a $1 hedging profit, the $1 hedging profit offsets the $106 capitation rate, for a $105 net capitation rate.

HOW A PROVIDER HEDGES MULTIYEAR CAPITATION RATES

The reverse of the previous example has a provider offering a self-funded employer, insurer, or Medicare multiyear fixed capitation rates. Assume a multistate provider alliance bids for a three-year capitation agreement with Medicare to supply medical services at facilities in five different states where the expected capitation rates are all different but the Medicare populations are all equal. How does the provider alliance hedge?

Since the provider alliance is worse off when capitation rates fall, holding constant their own costs of providing services, it should sell five contracts (one for each state) for each of the 12 quarters, for a total of 60 contracts. The reason future expected capitation rates may fall is that competition intensifies, and some competitors will undercut current expected rates to get new, or keep old, business at the expense of reduced profitability, which may already be razor thin.

Since the local capitation rates in each of the five states are all different, but always at a fixed premium or discount to the futures price, the provider alliance quotes five different sets of capitation rates to Medicare for the five different states. All five states for three years are hedged. Medicare gets fixed expenditures for three years, and the provider alliance gets locked-in gross cash flow from the capitation payments from Medicare. In addition, since financial risk is reduced, the provider alliance may reduce capitation rates without reducing profits by some amount to reflect lower costs of uncertainty. Since risks are reduced by hedging, the "risk premium" component of prices can be reduced or eliminated.

BUSINESS AND PUBLIC POLICY BENEFITS OF FUTURES HEDGING

Some of the business and public policy benefits of futures hedging include:

- A well defined, homogeneous commodity is thoroughly understood by all parties, which reduces the costs of uncertainty.
- Prices are immediately available to the public through open outcry, which reduces greatly the cost of "price discovery." The little company can hedge as effectively as the large company.
- Futures exchanges guarantee the financial performance of all traders, which reduces the costs of credit risk.
- Multiyear fixed price contracts are easily and inexpensively hedgeable in actively traded futures markets, which promotes product innovation in contracting and risk sharing.

Successful hedging requires as much common sense, prudence, and sound management controls as any other business activity. The benefits of innovation in risk sharing and flexibility to meet changing market conditions are spectacular and are proven in other markets such as interest rates. Now is the time for health care markets to learn about, and then use, these proven tools to manage financial risks.

Primary and secondary government securities markets hedge to reduce the interest cost of the federal debt. Primary and secondary residential mortgage markets hedge to increase the capital available for home mortgages through the secondary mortgage markets. In my opinion, ten years from now, a full range of health care futures, other derivatives, and secondary markets for health insurance and health services cash flows will be trading, and health care costs will be lower and more capital will be made available to these markets.

45.   Managing The Transition To Reform Is Crucial
Bruce Barlow

Pat Riley understands that NBA championships are won or lost in that part of basketball called transition, in which a team shifts from defense to offense after a basket or after getting a rebound. Insurance and managed care companies should understand the transition to a different health care system that is happening right now. It's not that President Clinton's health care reforms are irrelevant; their importance is in their effect on transition. Applying Pat's lessons, knowing where to go and getting there fast, will make the difference between winners and losers when national reform changes the rules of the game.

Providers, insurers, managed care organizations, employers, state legislators, and regulators are changing the health care system today. These players, rather than national reforms, will shape the delivery and financing of health care during at least the next three years; the national debate serves only as a catalyst.

More than 30 states have enacted small group reform laws. Vermont, Washington, Minnesota, and Florida have addressed universal access. Hawaii addressed it years ago. President Clinton has wisely allowed state exemptions from the national reforms: the governors sent him a clear message to keep out of state efforts, and he needs their support. The market is responding to the same affordability problems as national and state reforms, and players are changing the system today.

Regardless of the reform scenario (except for single payer, which is for now unlikely) five constants and strategic responses define how to play transition:

Reprinted with permission from *National Underwriter*, © 1993, The National Underwriter Company; *National Underwriter, Life & Health/Financial Services Edition*, November 1, 1993.

- "Low cost producers" can't lose. Players who drive down medical and administrative costs fastest will win.
- Gatekeeper-model, network-based managed care wins. Those who establish strong, well-managed provider networks right now will win.
- Those with a strong local presence will prosper. Those who increase share in their local markets fast will win.
- Employers will fund it, but employees will buy it. Players will win who understand "retail" buyer behavior and implement good direct marketing fast.
- Quality is in the eyes of the buyer. Those who understand what quality means to the retail buyer, and sell it, will win.

"LOW COST PRODUCERS" OF MEDICAL CARE

The market buys low cost today, and any new rules favor it. Big carriers, like Aetna, Cigna, Travelers, Met and Prudential are driving down their costs now—through administrative cost reduction and managing medical claim costs more aggressively—to improve their present competitiveness and prepare for the future. During transition, they plan to get there first.

Employer contribution strategies in various reform proposals are pegged to a baseline plan that has the lowest cost (or sometimes average cost) available. Other options for employees exaggerate the cost-sharing, with two predictable outcomes: many younger, healthier employees will immediately move to the lowest-cost plan. Over time, the high-cost plans will enter an adverse selection spiral, and the Clinton proposal allows exclusion of the most expensive plans. The low-cost producer wins immediately, and continues to win. This reform scenario also precisely describes the situation in many larger employers today, where higher-cost carriers are losing accounts.

For insurers, lowering costs is a survival issue. Most reform scenarios recognize that full freedom-of-choice indemnity plans cost more than those that limit selection of providers. Some reforms, including the Clinton proposal, give accounts and Health Alliances the option of limiting choice of indemnity options to a single plan. While indemnity may not be dead yet, the field of players will significantly thin out as they compete with each other and with network-based managed care on a playing field where risk selection is prohibited.

GATEKEEPER-MODEL—NETWORK-BASED MANAGED CARE

Providers and big insurers are figuring out today how to do it better than their competition; employers want it; and employees get used to it. Most state and national reforms give favor to it, and reform economics suggest it will win.

Four large commercial insurers have submitted a proposal in New York to reshape the health care system of that state. Their proposal is based on network-based managed care and pooling small employer buying power through cooperatives. These insurers have invested heavily in building network-based, gatekeeper-model managed care products in New York and nationwide. Also, their principal market has been large employers, with less penetration in small groups. They are well-positioned in transition, and are advocating changes to the rules in their favor.

The employer market is in transition to this model right now. Our market research for one client showed that, of large employers that had put out their health insurance benefits for bid, 80 percent specified gatekeeper-model network-based managed care as a starting point. Our research in this case did not capture those employers who changed to, or added managed care plans with their same carrier without going to bid. Therefore, the business for which carriers can compete and gain share is nearly always specifying a gatekeeper model.

HMOs are learning the insurance business as a transition tool. Our competitor research for one client showed that HMOs are offering an "opt-out" insurance-type benefit that allows patients to see providers outside of the closed HMO panel, similar to POS, as a transition to a closed-panel HMO. Pure, closed-panel, gatekeeper-model HMOs had some difficulty gaining acceptance from employees at first, but experience indicated that out-of-network utilization follows a pattern in many accounts, starting at about 40 percent in the first year, and dropping to only about 10 percent after four years, at which time the employer and the HMO can close the panel with minimal patient disruption.

"Opt-out" for HMOs is understood to be a transition product to gain enrollments now, and later move to the closed-panel, gatekeeper model they know best.

STRONG LOCAL PRESENCE

A strong local presence requires getting market share today, recruiting the best providers, and establishing a brand image with the consumer. These are mutually reinforcing and position companies well to weather reform.

Network volume is an important component of effective network-based managed care: the more patients that are driven through a network, the greater economies of scale, the more providers become familiar with and follow protocols, the less inadvertent, costly out-of-network utilization occurs, and the better the deals that can be cut with providers.

Our competitor research indicates that large insurers and formidable HMOs are "buying business" in certain markets, i.e., investing in network volume through aggressive pricing that they believe would give cost control a kick-start and pay off fairly quickly.

Smart carriers know they're competing for the best providers today, and that enhances local presence and wins patients. It's not good enough to have the second-best pediatricians or the hospital that's almost as good as the one across town. Harvard Community Health Plan in Massachusetts and Oxford Health Plans in New York have done this successfully, creating a local presence and enrollment growth through an image of having a high-quality provider network. Smart carriers recruit the best (as best they can determine them), offering good reimbursement arrangements combined with high patient volume for attractive revenue streams for the providers, but lower per-patient costs for the carrier. Then the carriers sell their network quality. Patient volume and having the carriers to do their marketing for them under an advertising theme of quality keeps providers happy, which helps keep them in the network.

Blue Cross and Blue Shield plans have an advantage when it comes to brand image. A woman in one of our focus groups told us that she "had her Blue Cross with Travelers." For many of the Blues, the trademark is a formidable competitive advantage.

Alliances of hospitals and their medical staffs represent significant patient volume and so are emerging competitors: they can trade on the reputation of the hospitals, and on their recognized "brand names." The immediate reason for these alliances is cost: balancing resources; sharing expensive technology; expanding the availability of specialized, expensive services. They may be well-positioned in transition.

EMPLOYER FUNDED, EMPLOYEE PURCHASED

Health care reforms will continue to use employers as a primary funding source, but buyer decision-making will shift to the "retail" buyer (employee) as it already has with most larger employers offering multiple choices of plans and carriers. Aetna and Cigna have publicly announced plans for major investments in direct marketing capabilities nationwide. Many HMOs are already good at local direct marketing. Other carriers are also investing in it, but not talking. They recognize that the buyer is the patient, and the patient is buying a doctor. Selling their quality only to the account won't sell the patient.

In some zip codes around Boston, HMOs "carpet bomb" every house with direct mail advertising during open enrollment, supplementing it with extensive advertising aimed at consumers. Land's End and L.L. Bean perform careful analyses to determine target audiences defined precisely enough to yield profitable results; mailing too widely can be disastrously expensive. These HMOs hire direct mail consultants who perform similar targeting analyses. Their mailings appear to be precise enough to be profitable, or else they wouldn't keep sending them out.

Employee choices can be "sticky" decisions in that they are hard to undo. The rhetoric of "freedom of choice" has as much to do with keeping the doctor one has chosen as with having total freedom to choose. Once the choice has been made, even in a limited network, the resistance to changing physicians can represent a formidably competitive advantage. Those that market directly to employees and win enrollments now, during transition, will win over the long term.

QUALITY IS IN THE EYES OF THE BUYER

This is particularly provocative in light of the shifting buying decision. The market research by insurers and managed care plans we have seen focuses on quality of service provided primarily to the employer. Performance indicators that track claim and customer service are used as a report card for measuring administrative performance by collecting computer statistics from the administrative systems. These indicators are internally focused, mechanical, and purely objective.

Relatively little market research we have seen at insurers has stressed quality as perceived by the patients, as it affects their buying behavior. This kind of quality is much more subjective and may include such factors as ease of getting appointments, office hours, on-call arrangements, courtesy of the administrative staff, and availability of female OB/GYNs.

Huge, expensive medical quality initiatives seek to measure outcomes and quality of care as defined by medical professionals. This if fine, but once it is measured it must be communicated simply and meaningfully. But it cannot end there. Carriers that can most quickly understand buyer perceptions of quality and incorporate them into tomorrow's direct marketing and advertising are those most likely to get there first during transition.

It would be too provocative to say that health care reform is irrelevant, but at the moment its importance is in shaping what players do in anticipation of reforms at both state and national levels. The good players know where to go, and they're getting there as fast as they can. Waiting to see what reforms may happen or, worse, waiting for the rules to change, defers crucial decisions and actions until it's too late. It's the same as waiting to see if the other team misses the slam dunk at the end of its fast break. Survivors and winners are acting now.

Index